HARUKAZE BITTER★BOP

Volume 1
Created by Court Betten

HAMBURG // LONDON // LOS ANGELES // TOKYO

Harukaze Bitter Bop Volume 1
Created by Court Betten

Translation - Christine Schilling
English Adaptation - Kereth Cowe-Spigai
Retouch and Lettering - Star Print Brokers
Production Artist - Michael Paolilli
Graphic Designer - James Lee

Editor - Alexis Kirsch
Digital Imaging Manager - Chris Buford
Pre-Production Supervisor - Erika Terriquez
Production Manager - Elisabeth Brizzi
Managing Editor - Vy Nguyen
Creative Director - Anne Marie Horne
Editor-in-Chief - Rob Tokar
Publisher - Mike Kiley
President and C.O.O. - John Parker
C.E.O. and Chief Creative Officer - Stuart Levy

A **TOKYOPOP** Manga

TOKYOPOP and 🐸 are trademarks or registered trademarks of TOKYOPOP Inc.

TOKYOPOP Inc.
5900 Wilshire Blvd. Suite 2000
Los Angeles, CA 90036

E-mail: info@TOKYOPOP.com
Come visit us online at www.TOKYOPOP.com

ISBN: 978-1-4278-0328-3

First TOKYOPOP printing: January 2008
10 9 8 7 6 5 4 3 2 1
Printed in the USA

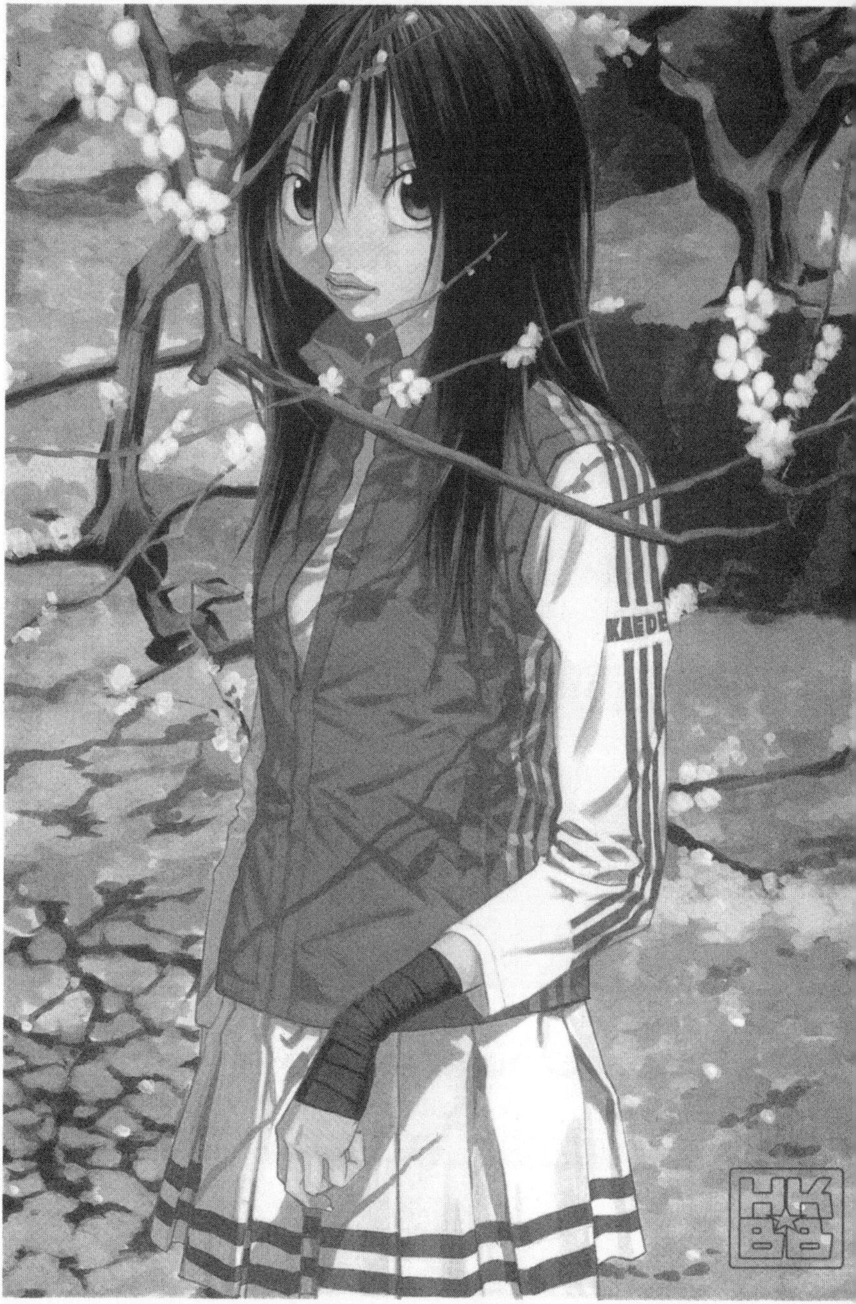
KAEDE

ARU-KAZE BITTER BOP

★

Court
Betten

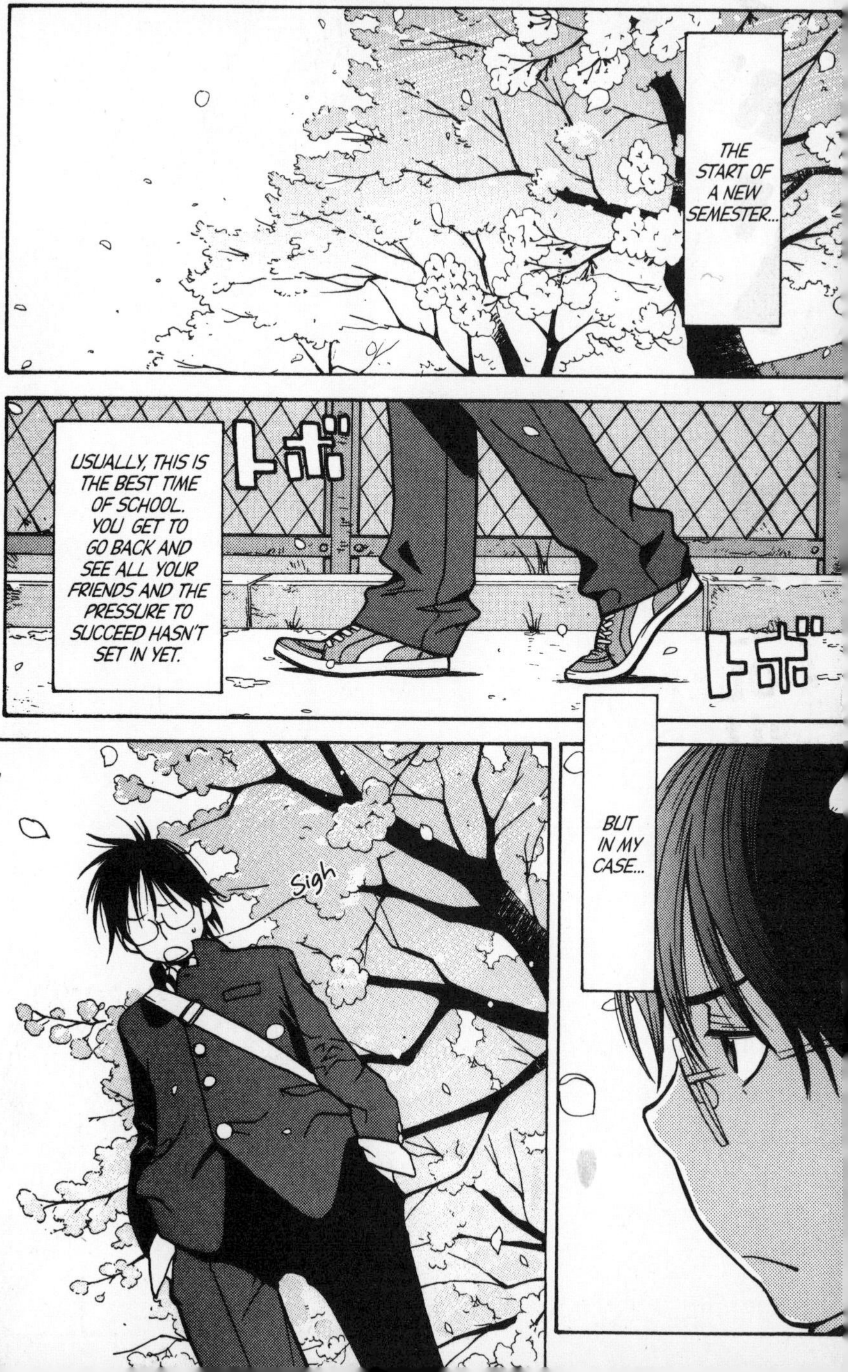
THE START OF A NEW SEMESTER...
トボ
トボ
USUALLY, THIS IS THE BEST TIME OF SCHOOL. YOU GET TO GO BACK AND SEE ALL YOUR FRIENDS AND THE PRESSURE TO SUCCEED HASN'T SET IN YET.
BUT IN MY CASE...
Sigh

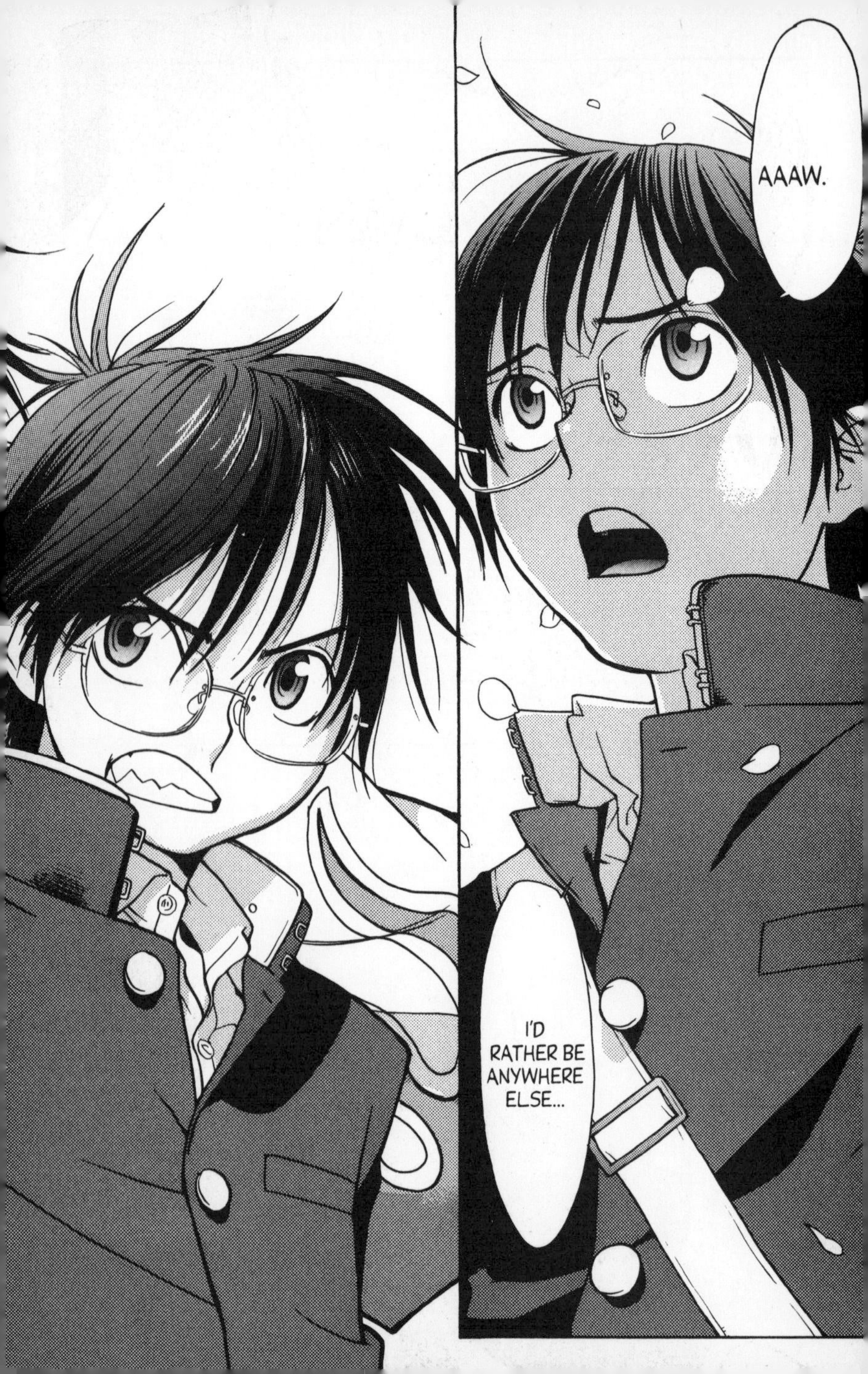
AAAW.
I'D RATHER BE ANYWHERE ELSE...

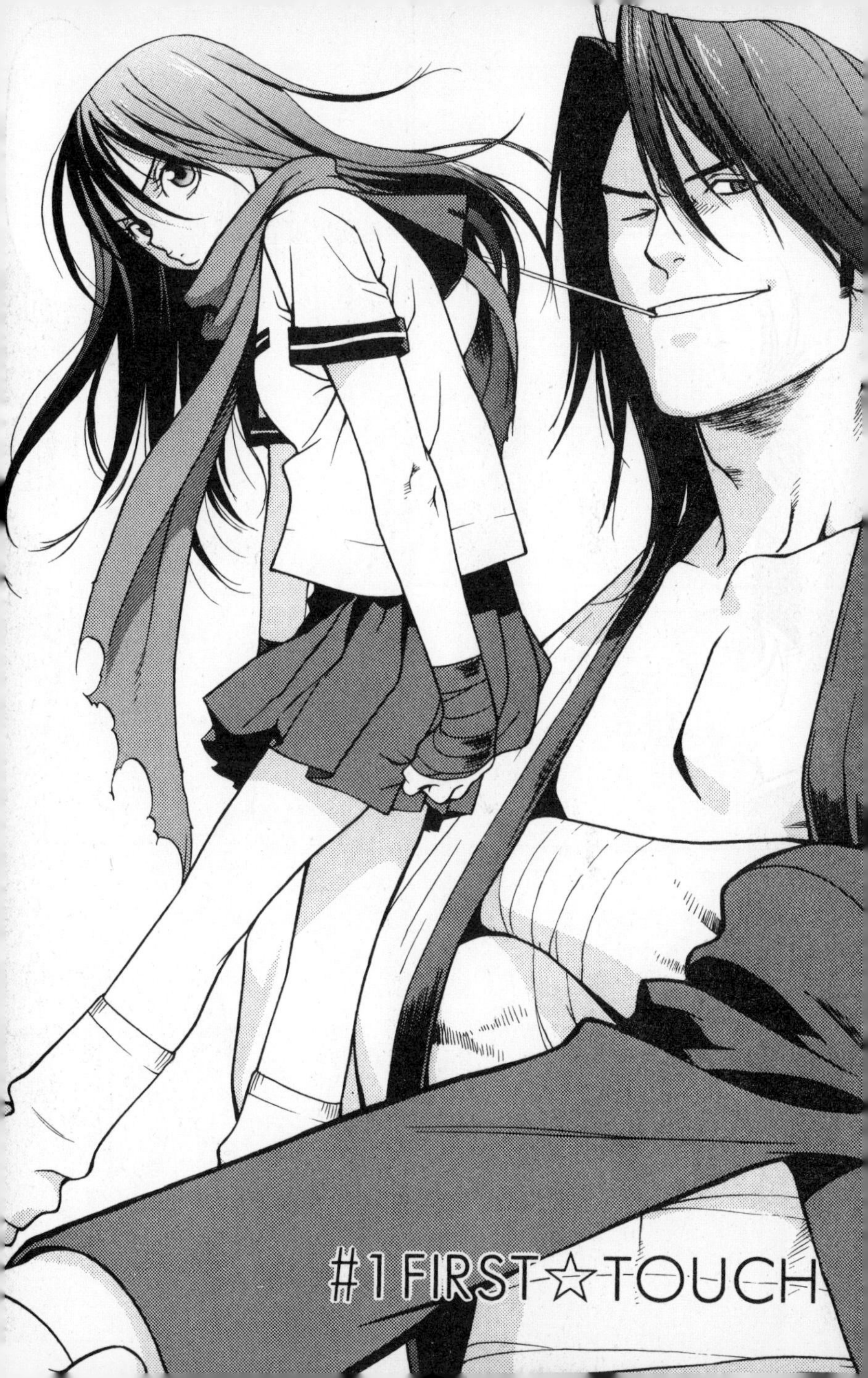
#1 FIRST☆TOUCH

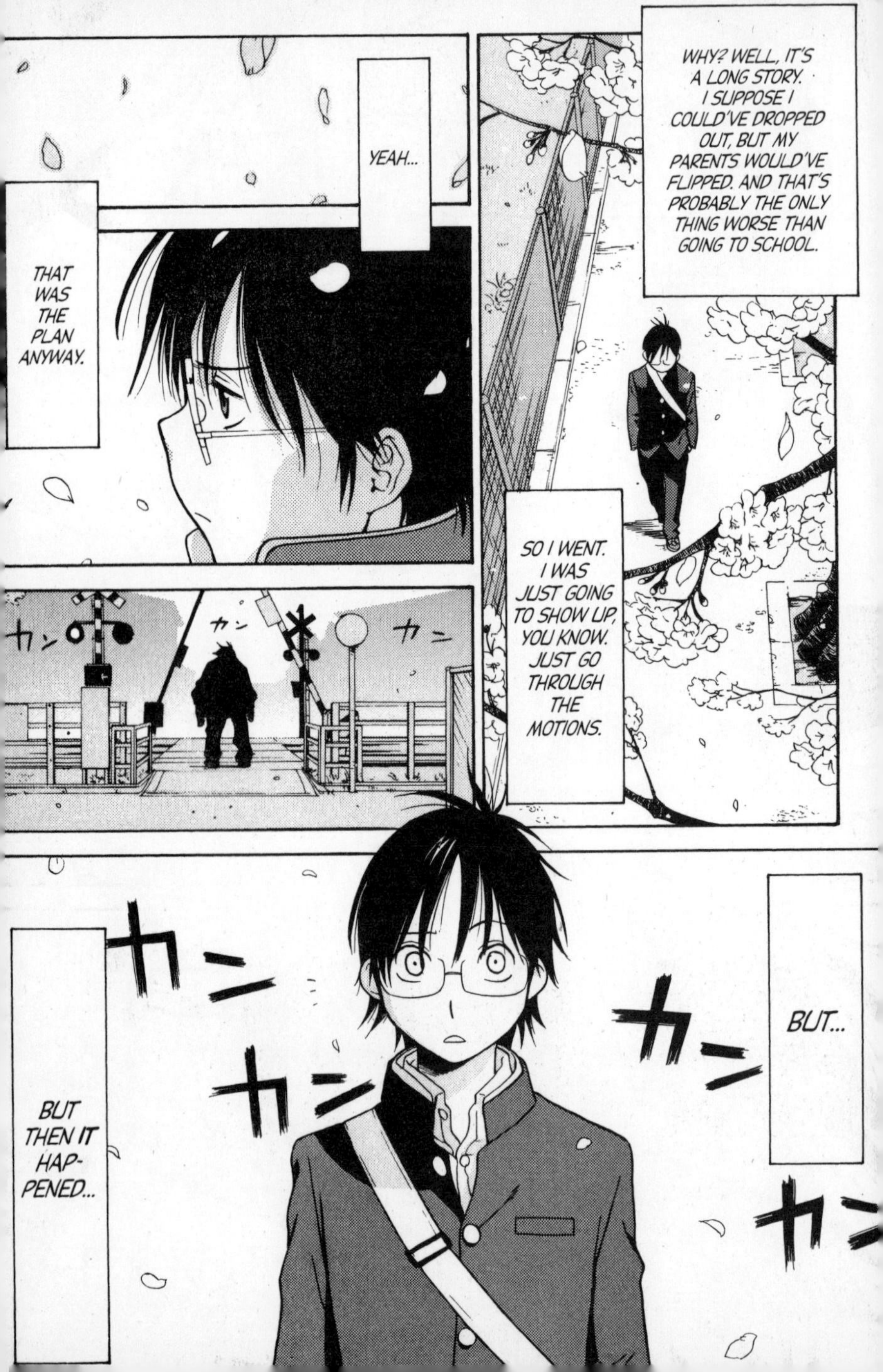
WHY? WELL, IT'S A LONG STORY. I SUPPOSE I COULD'VE DROPPED OUT, BUT MY PARENTS WOULD'VE FLIPPED. AND THAT'S PROBABLY THE ONLY THING WORSE THAN GOING TO SCHOOL.
SO I WENT. I WAS JUST GOING TO SHOW UP, YOU KNOW. JUST GO THROUGH THE MOTIONS.
YEAH...
THAT WAS THE PLAN ANYWAY.
カン
カン
カン
BUT...
カン
カン
カン
カン
BUT THEN IT HAP-PENED...

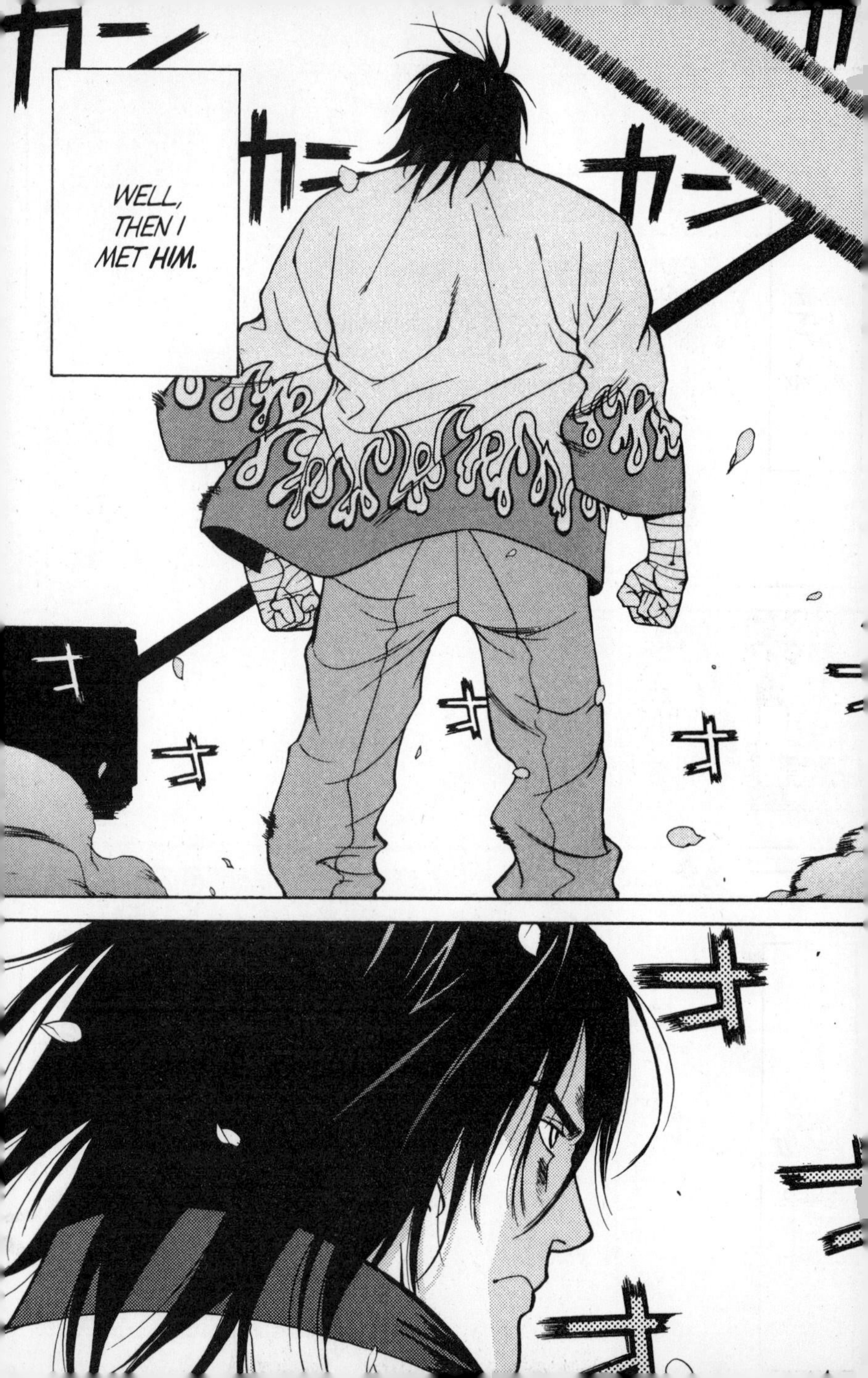
WELL, THEN I MET HIM.

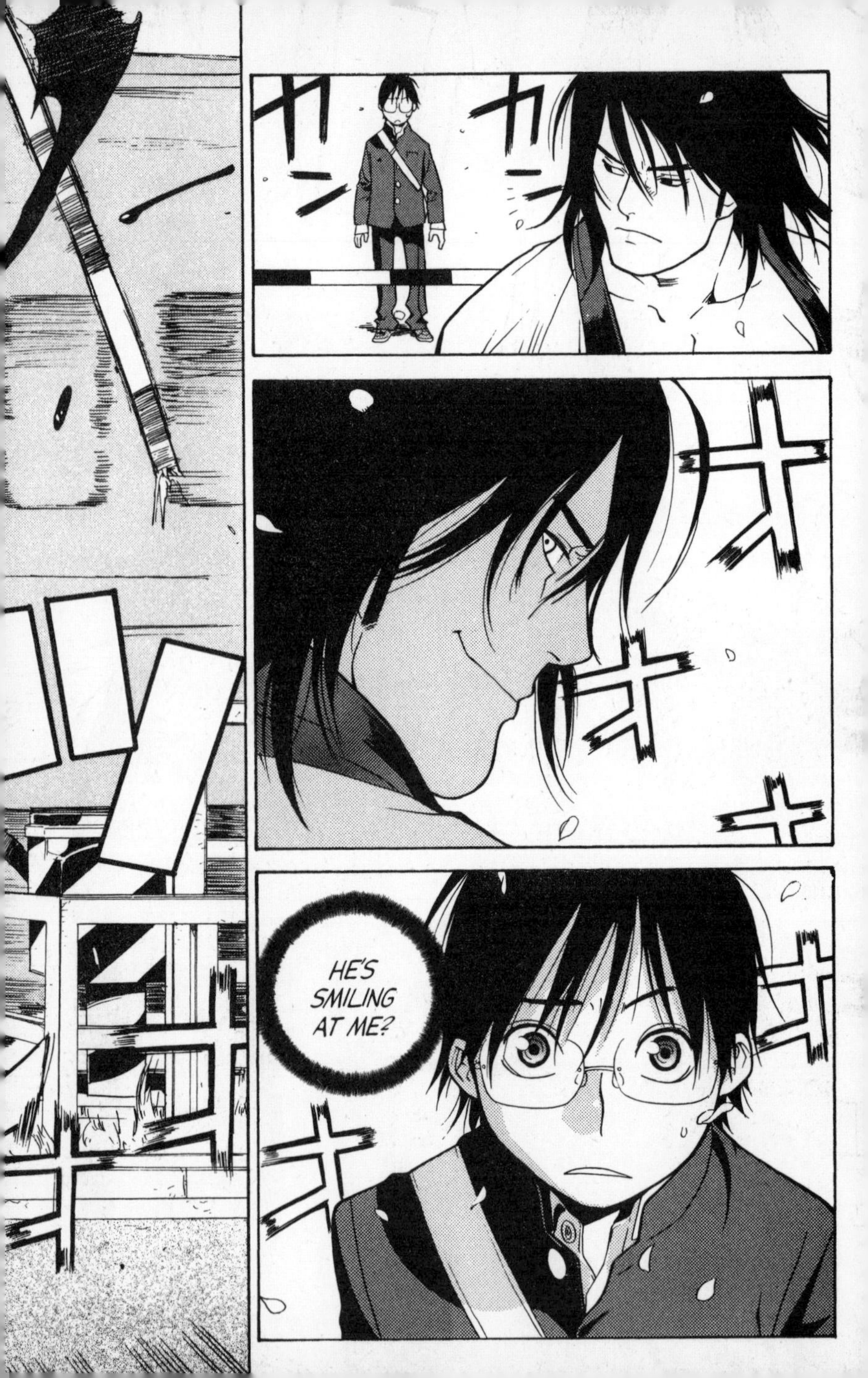
HE'S SMILING AT ME?

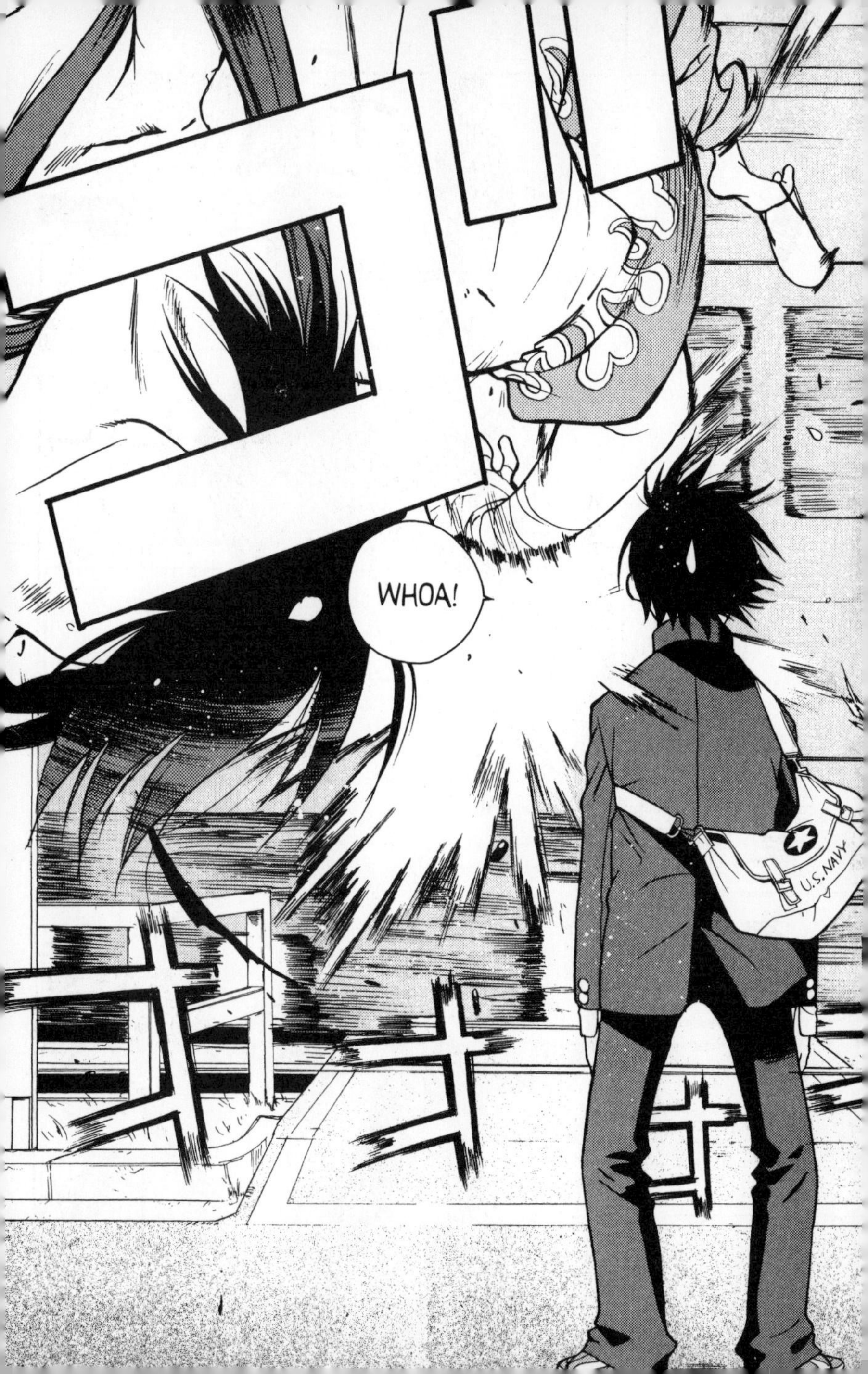
WHOA!

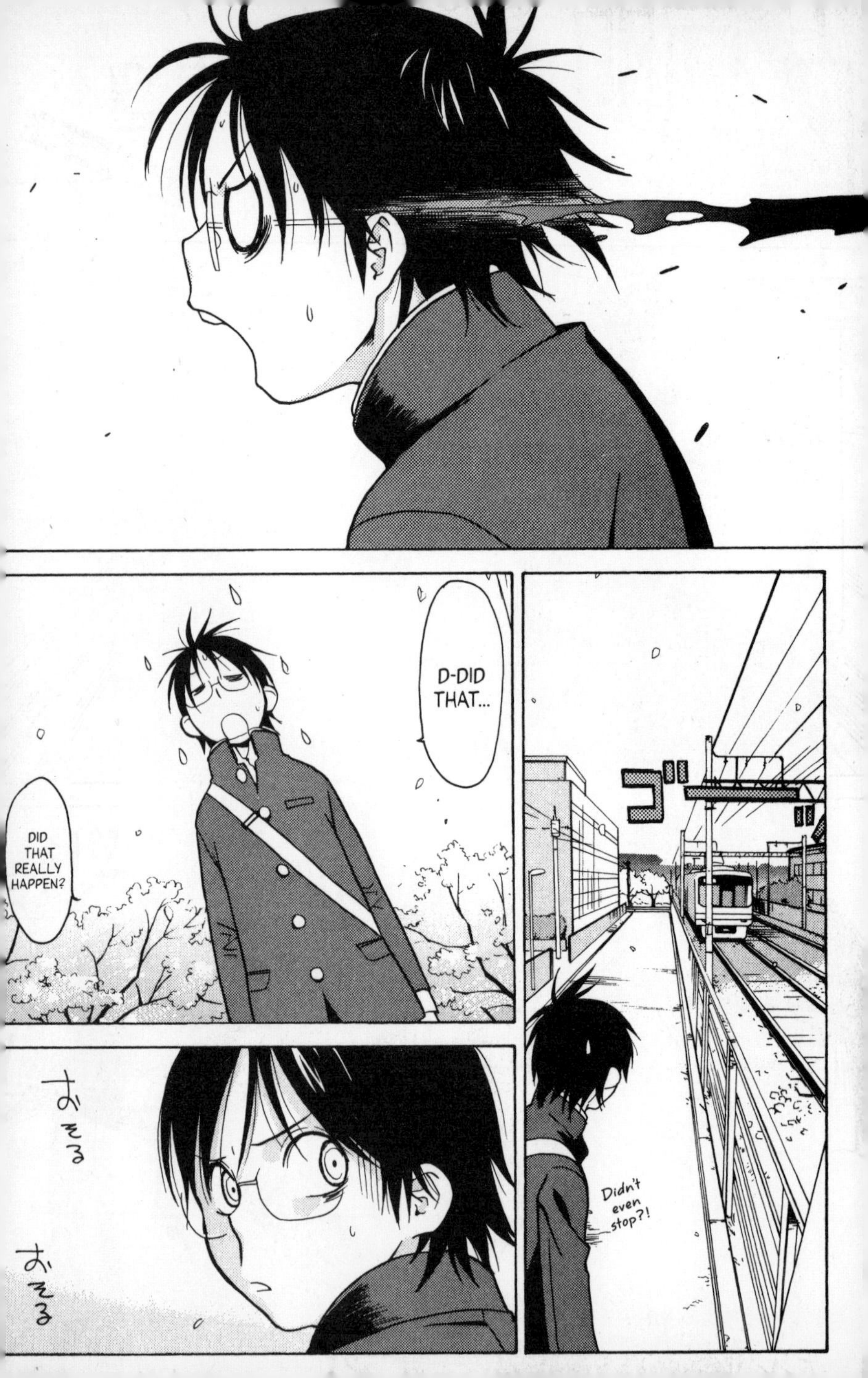
ゴ
Didn't even stop?!
D-DID THAT...
DID THAT REALLY HAPPEN?
おそる
おそる

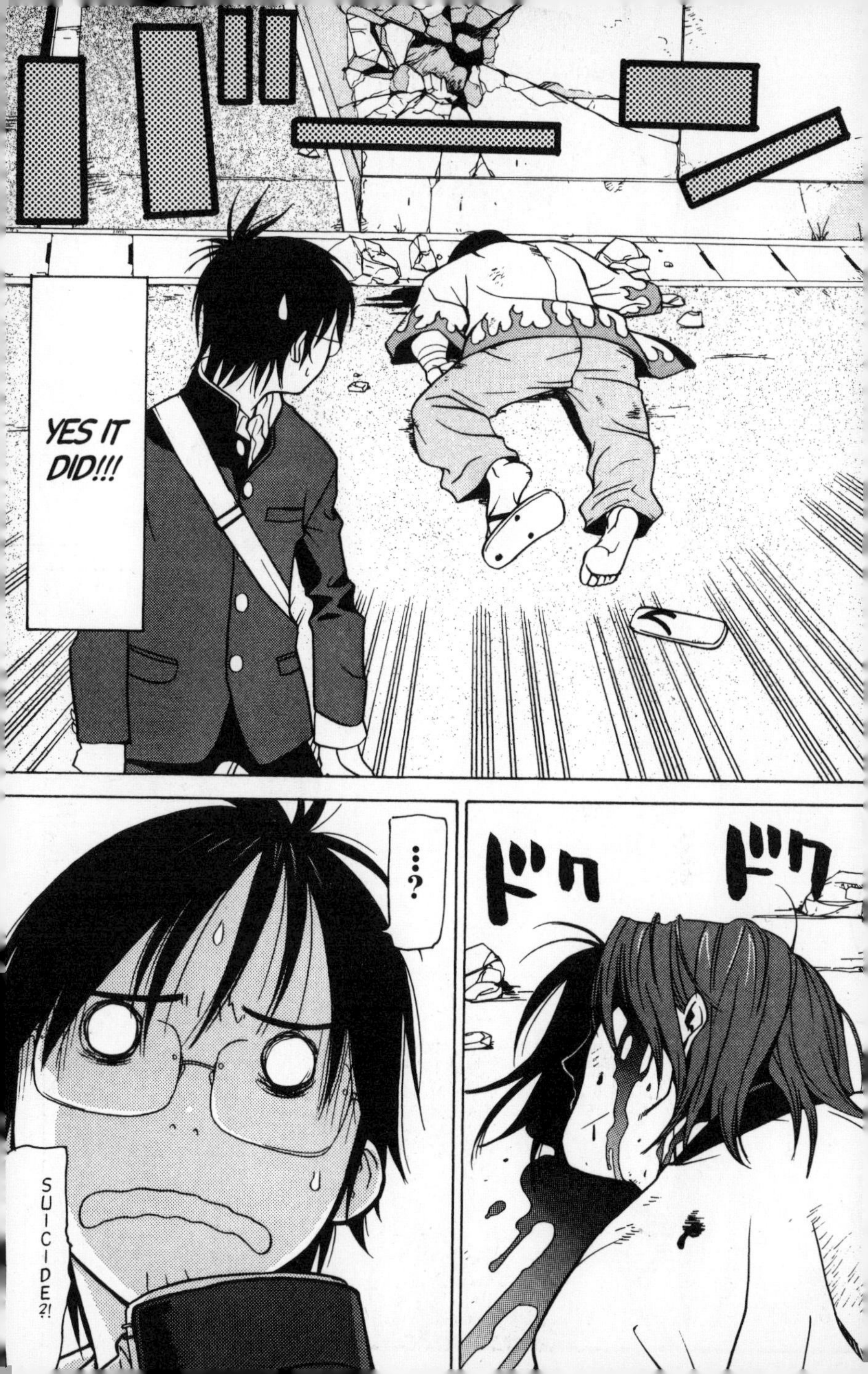
YES IT DID!!!
ドク ドク
...?
SUICIDE?!

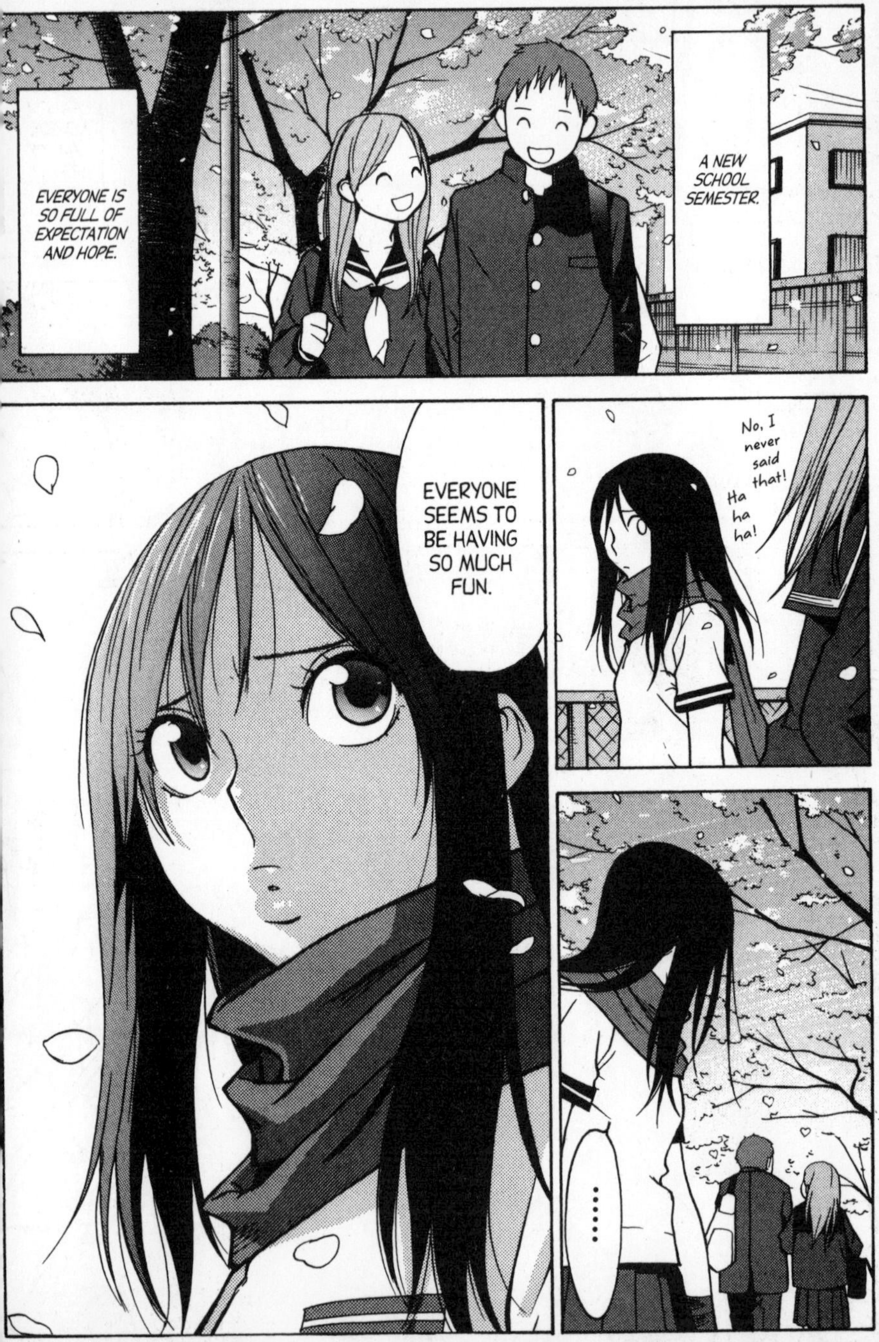
A NEW SCHOOL SEMESTER.
EVERYONE IS SO FULL OF EXPECTATION AND HOPE.
No, I never said that!
Ha ha ha!
......
EVERYONE SEEMS TO BE HAVING SO MUCH FUN.

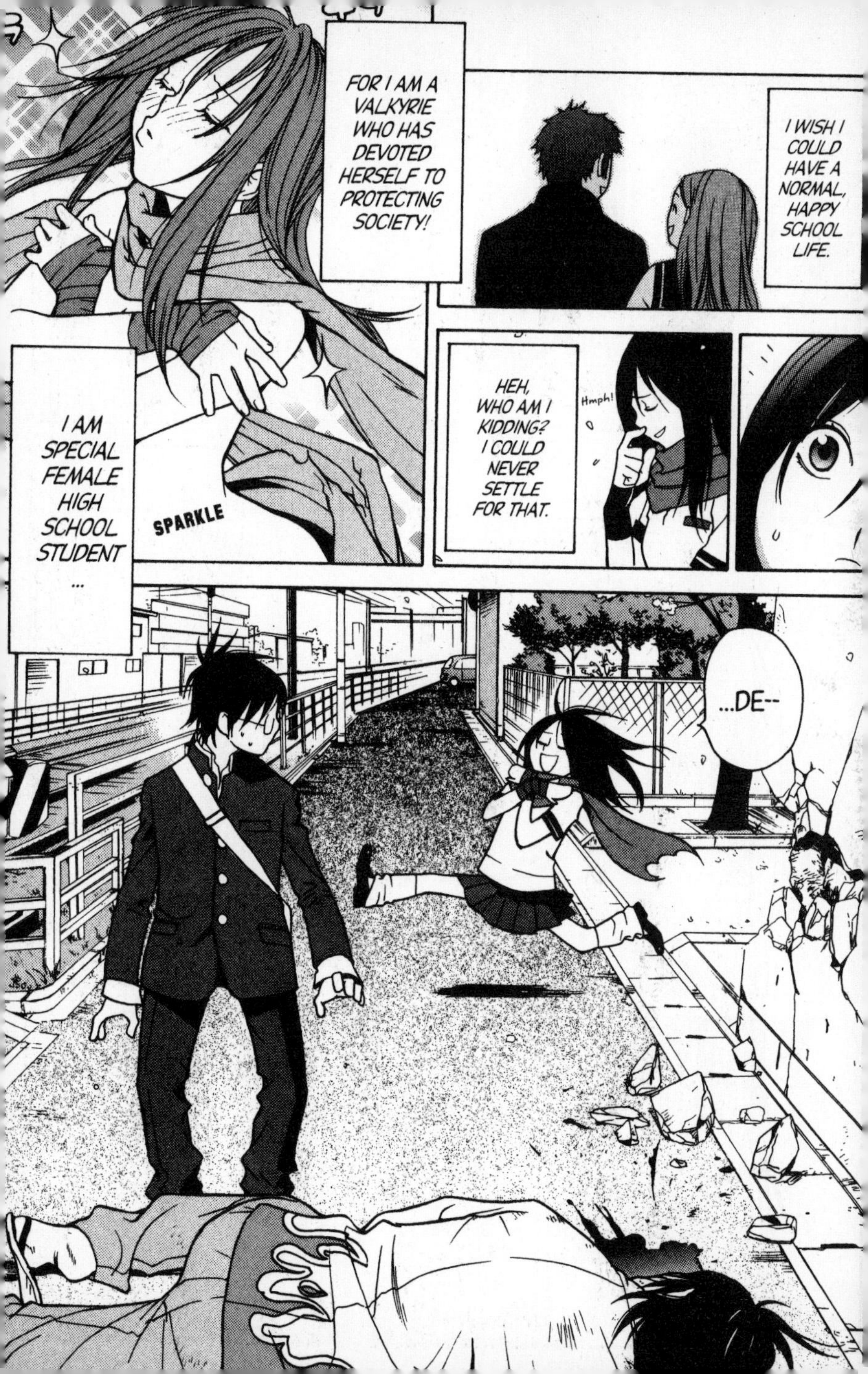
I WISH I COULD HAVE A NORMAL, HAPPY SCHOOL LIFE.
Hmph!
HEH, WHO AM I KIDDING? I COULD NEVER SETTLE FOR THAT.
FOR I AM A VALKYRIE WHO HAS DEVOTED HERSELF TO PROTECTING SOCIETY!
I AM SPECIAL FEMALE HIGH SCHOOL STUDENT ...
SPARKLE
...DE--

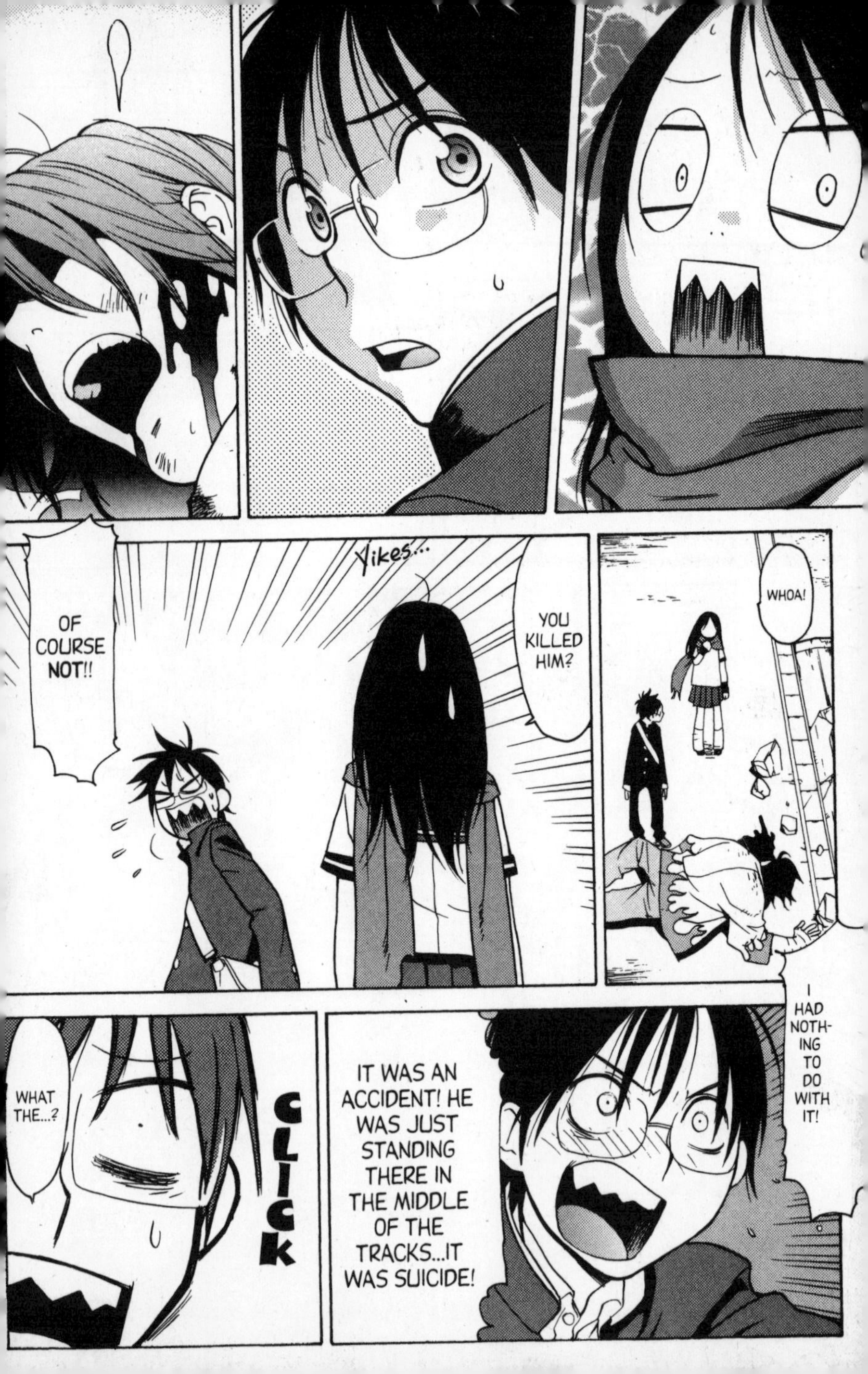
WHOA!
YOU KILLED HIM?
Yikes...
OF COURSE NOT!!
I HAD NOTH-ING TO DO WITH IT!
IT WAS AN ACCIDENT! HE WAS JUST STANDING THERE IN THE MIDDLE OF THE TRACKS...IT WAS SUICIDE!
CLICK
WHAT THE...?

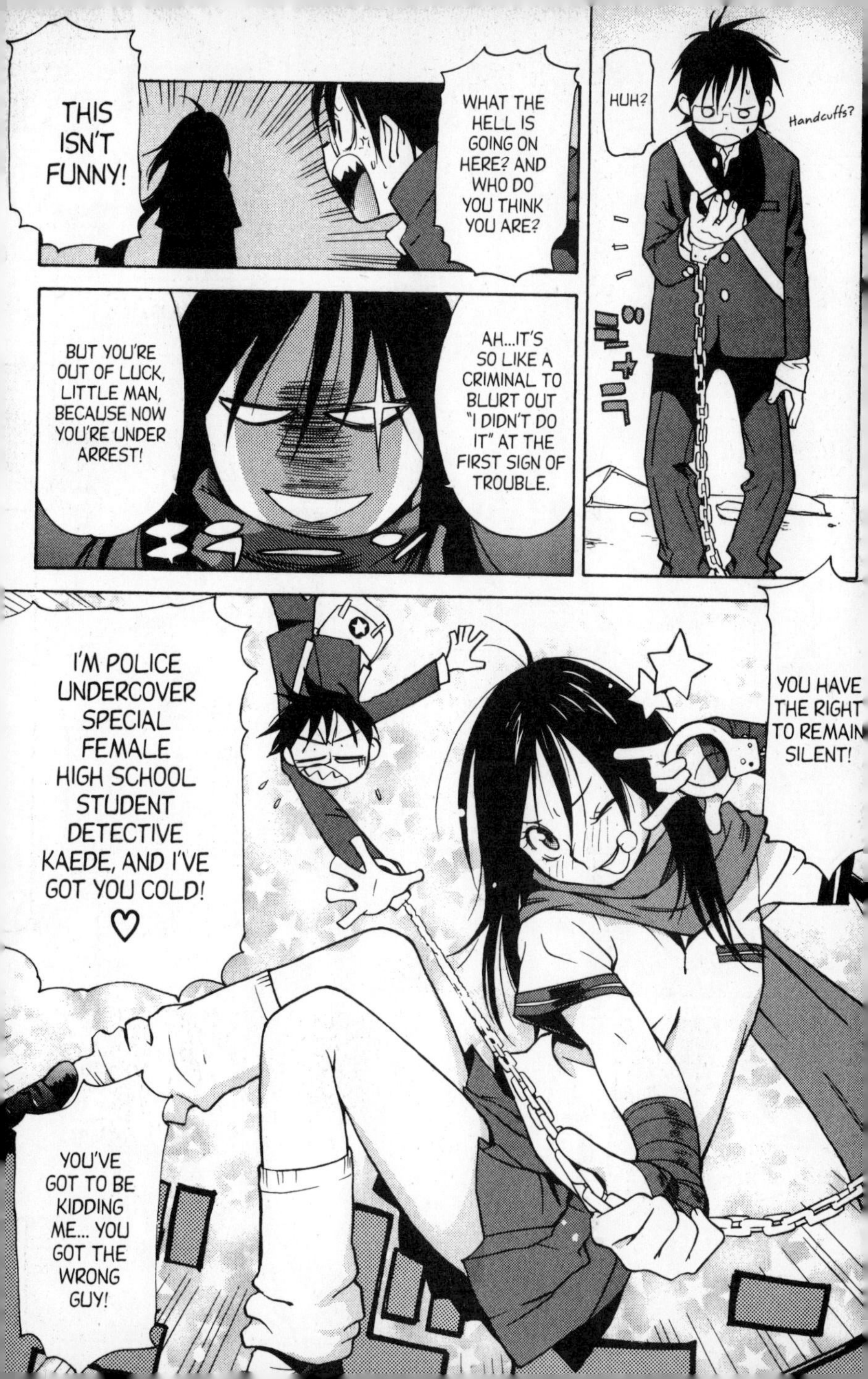
HUH?
Handcuffs?
WHAT THE HELL IS GOING ON HERE? AND WHO DO YOU THINK YOU ARE?
THIS ISN'T FUNNY!
AH...IT'S SO LIKE A CRIMINAL TO BLURT OUT "I DIDN'T DO IT" AT THE FIRST SIGN OF TROUBLE.
BUT YOU'RE OUT OF LUCK, LITTLE MAN, BECAUSE NOW YOU'RE UNDER ARREST!
YOU HAVE THE RIGHT TO REMAIN SILENT!
I'M POLICE UNDERCOVER SPECIAL FEMALE HIGH SCHOOL STUDENT DETECTIVE KAEDE, AND I'VE GOT YOU COLD! ♡
YOU'VE GOT TO BE KIDDING ME... YOU GOT THE WRONG GUY!

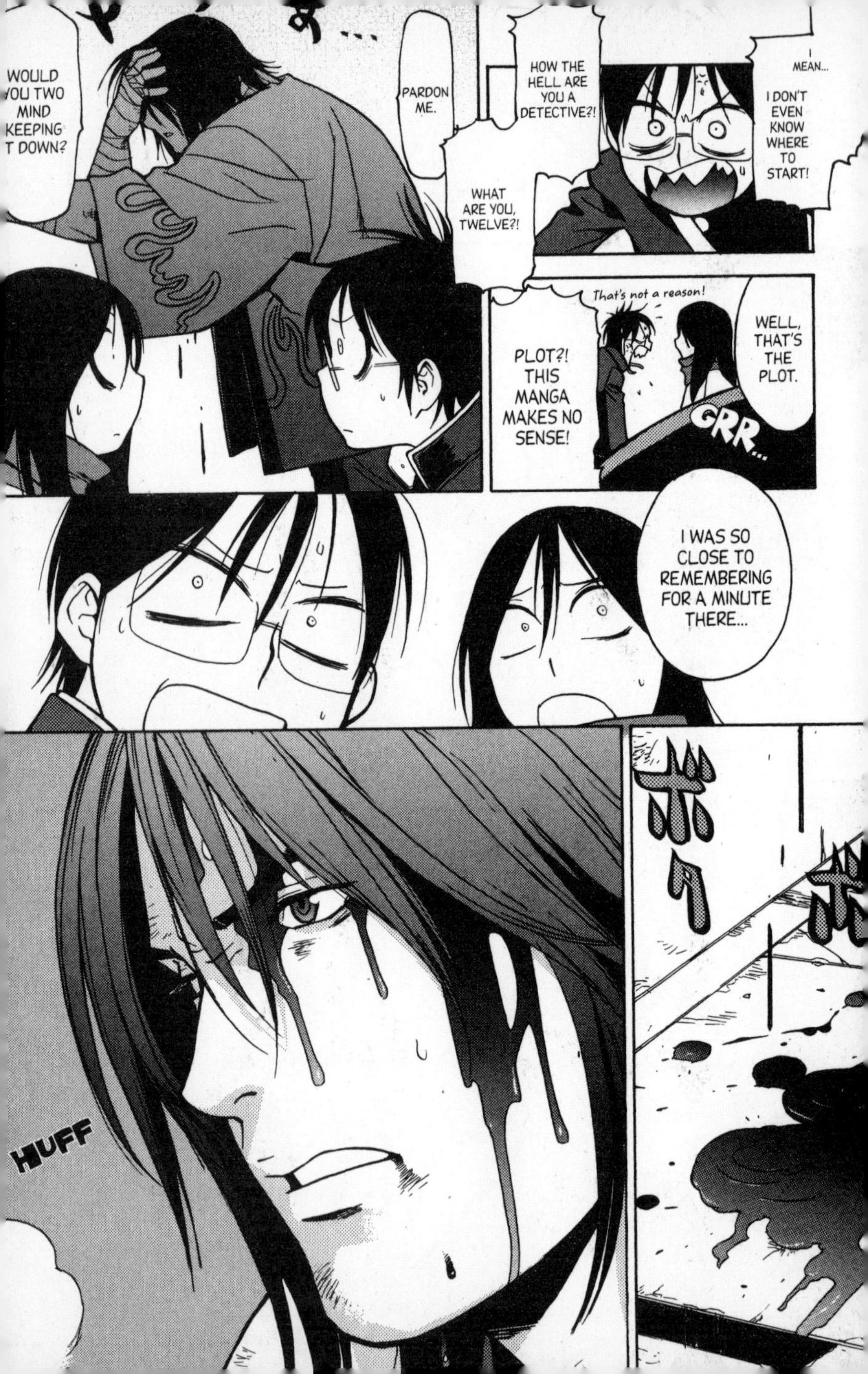
I MEAN...
I DON'T EVEN KNOW WHERE TO START!
HOW THE HELL ARE YOU A DETECTIVE?!
WHAT ARE YOU, TWELVE?!
WELL, THAT'S THE PLOT.
GRR...
PLOT?! THIS MANGA MAKES NO SENSE!
That's not a reason!
PARDON ME.
WOULD YOU TWO MIND KEEPING IT DOWN?
I WAS SO CLOSE TO REMEMBERING FOR A MINUTE THERE...
ポタ
HUFF

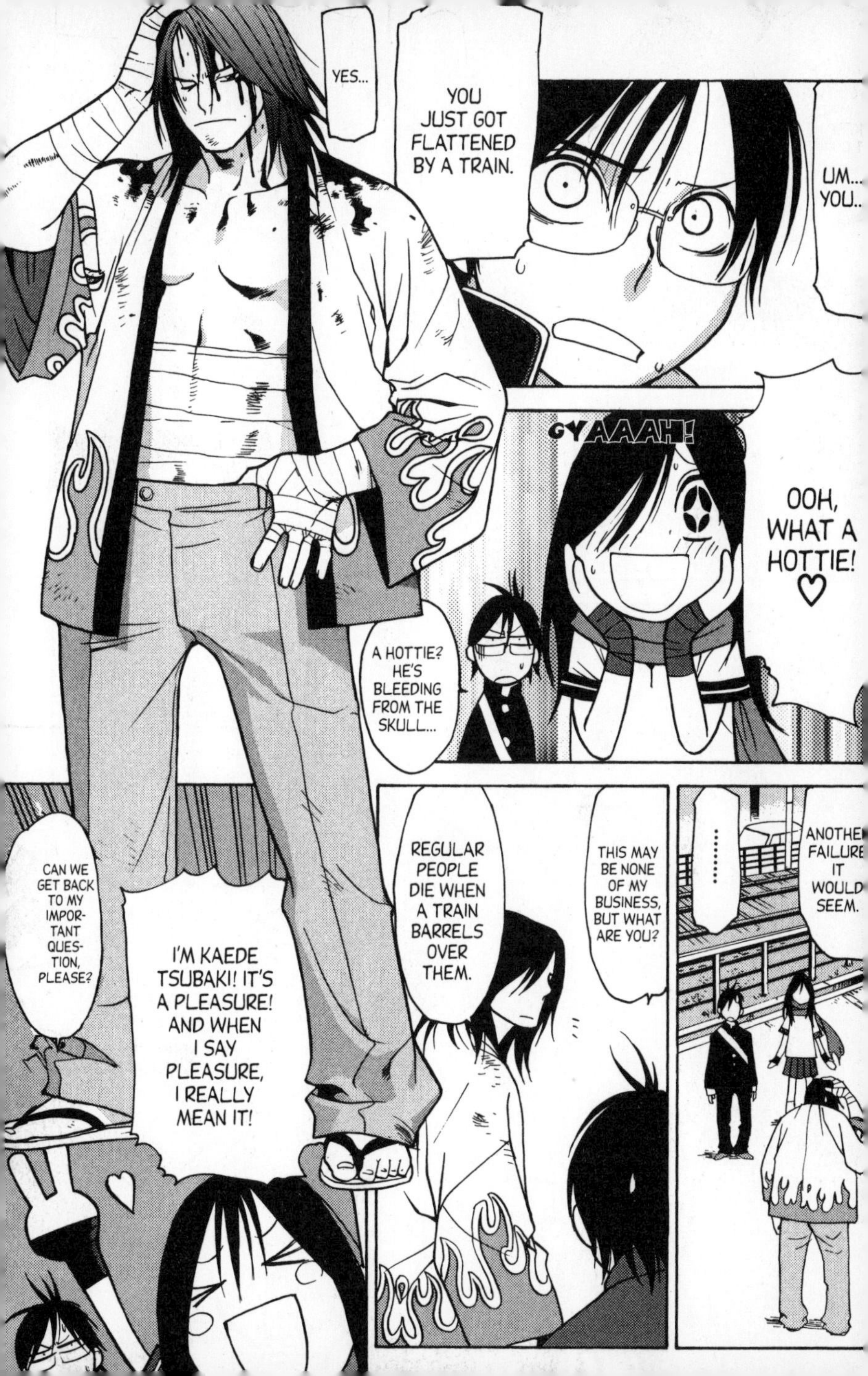

UM... YOU..
YOU JUST GOT FLATTENED BY A TRAIN.
YES...
GYAAAH!
OOH, WHAT A HOTTIE! ♡
A HOTTIE? HE'S BLEEDING FROM THE SKULL...
ANOTHER FAILURE IT WOULD SEEM.
......
THIS MAY BE NONE OF MY BUSINESS, BUT WHAT ARE YOU?
REGULAR PEOPLE DIE WHEN A TRAIN BARRELS OVER THEM.
I'M KAEDE TSUBAKI! IT'S A PLEASURE! AND WHEN I SAY PLEASURE, I REALLY MEAN IT!
CAN WE GET BACK TO MY IMPORTANT QUESTION, PLEASE?

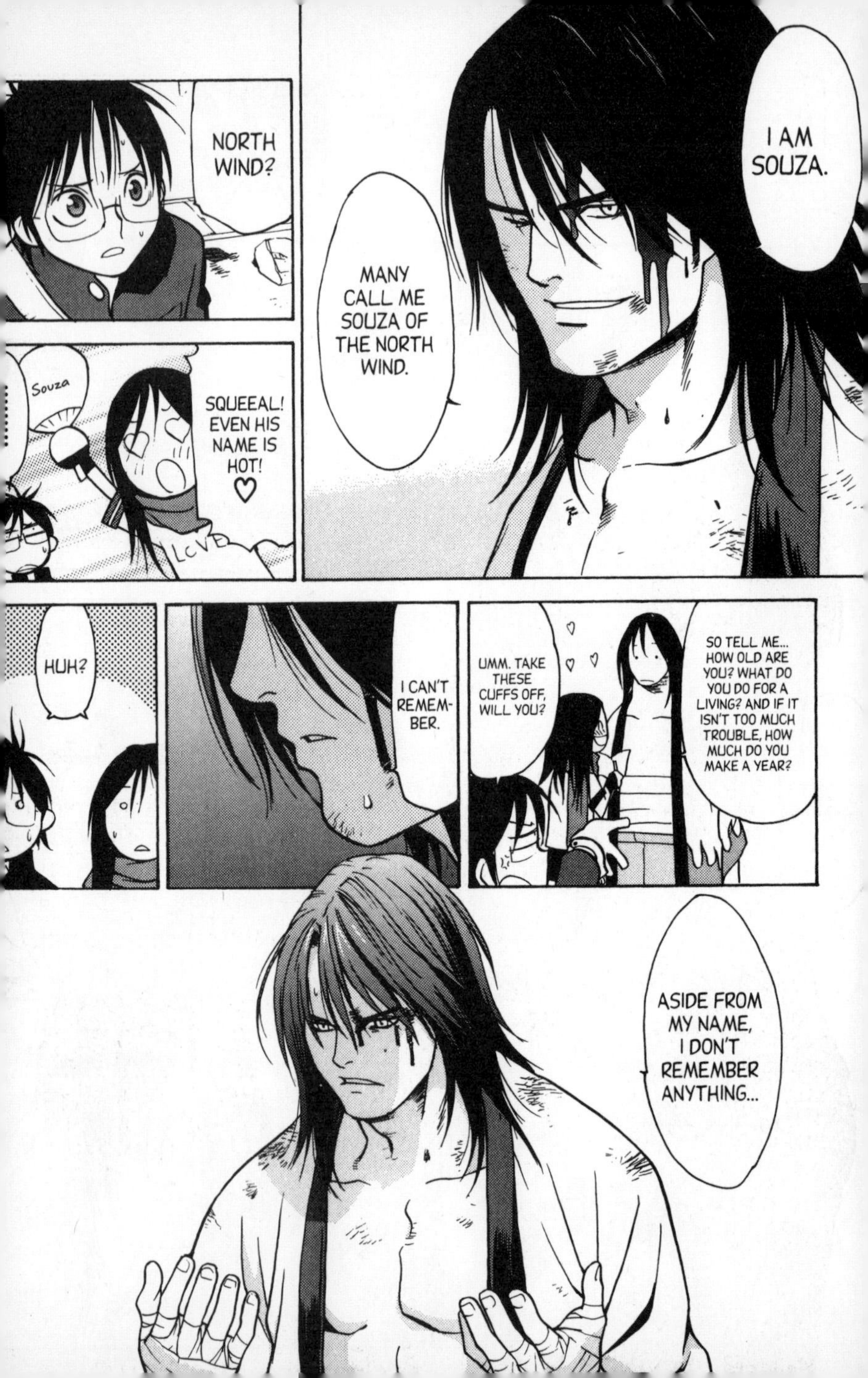
I AM SOUZA.
MANY CALL ME SOUZA OF THE NORTH WIND.
NORTH WIND?
Souza
SQUEEAL! EVEN HIS NAME IS HOT! ♡
LOVE
SO TELL ME... HOW OLD ARE YOU? WHAT DO YOU DO FOR A LIVING? AND IF IT ISN'T TOO MUCH TROUBLE, HOW MUCH DO YOU MAKE A YEAR?
UMM. TAKE THESE CUFFS OFF, WILL YOU?
I CAN'T REMEMBER.
HUH?
ASIDE FROM MY NAME, I DON'T REMEMBER ANYTHING...

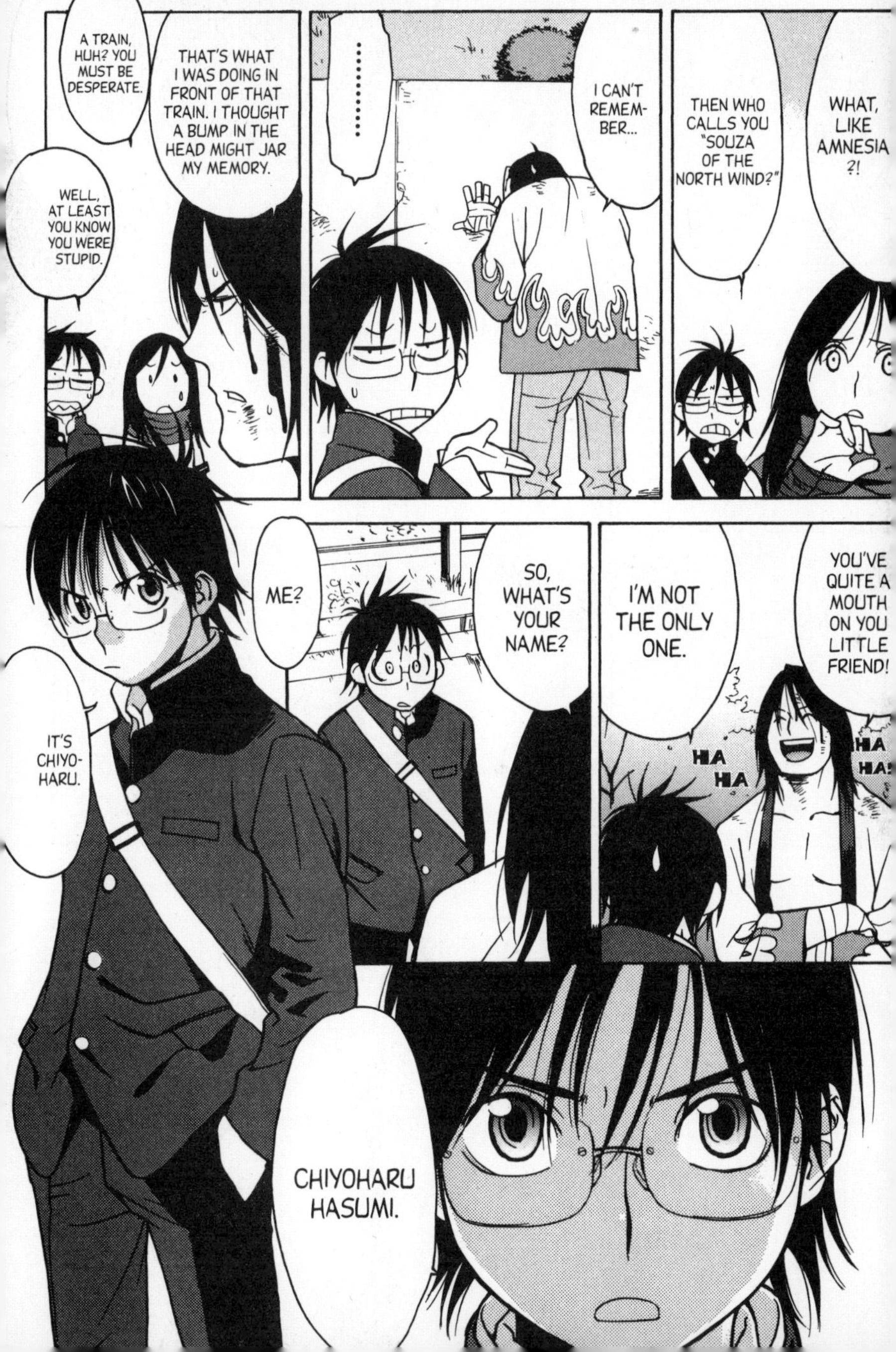
WHAT, LIKE AMNESIA?!
THEN WHO CALLS YOU "SOUZA OF THE NORTH WIND?"
I CAN'T REMEM-BER...
....
THAT'S WHAT I WAS DOING IN FRONT OF THAT TRAIN. I THOUGHT A BUMP IN THE HEAD MIGHT JAR MY MEMORY.
A TRAIN, HUH? YOU MUST BE DESPERATE.
WELL, AT LEAST YOU KNOW YOU WERE STUPID.
YOU'VE QUITE A MOUTH ON YOU LITTLE FRIEND!
HA HA
HA HA
I'M NOT THE ONLY ONE.
SO, WHAT'S YOUR NAME?
ME?
CHIYOHARU HASUMI.
IT'S CHIYO-HARU.

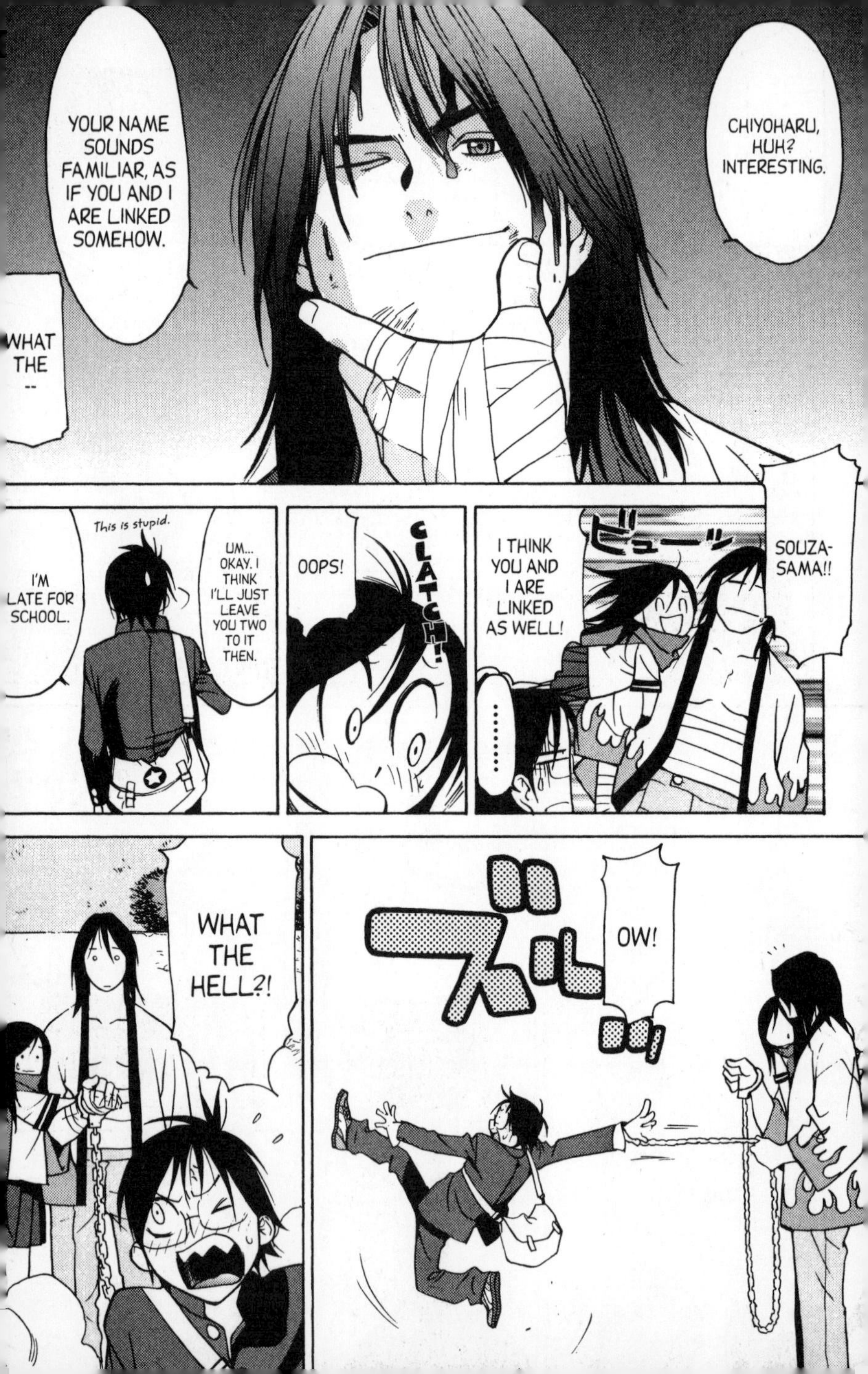
CHIYOHARU, HUH? INTERESTING.
YOUR NAME SOUNDS FAMILIAR, AS IF YOU AND I ARE LINKED SOMEHOW.
WHAT THE --
SOUZA-SAMA!!
ビューッ
I THINK YOU AND I ARE LINKED AS WELL!
......
GLATCH!
OOPS!
UM... OKAY. I THINK I'LL JUST LEAVE YOU TWO TO IT THEN.
This is stupid.
I'M LATE FOR SCHOOL.
OW!
ズル
WHAT THE HELL?!

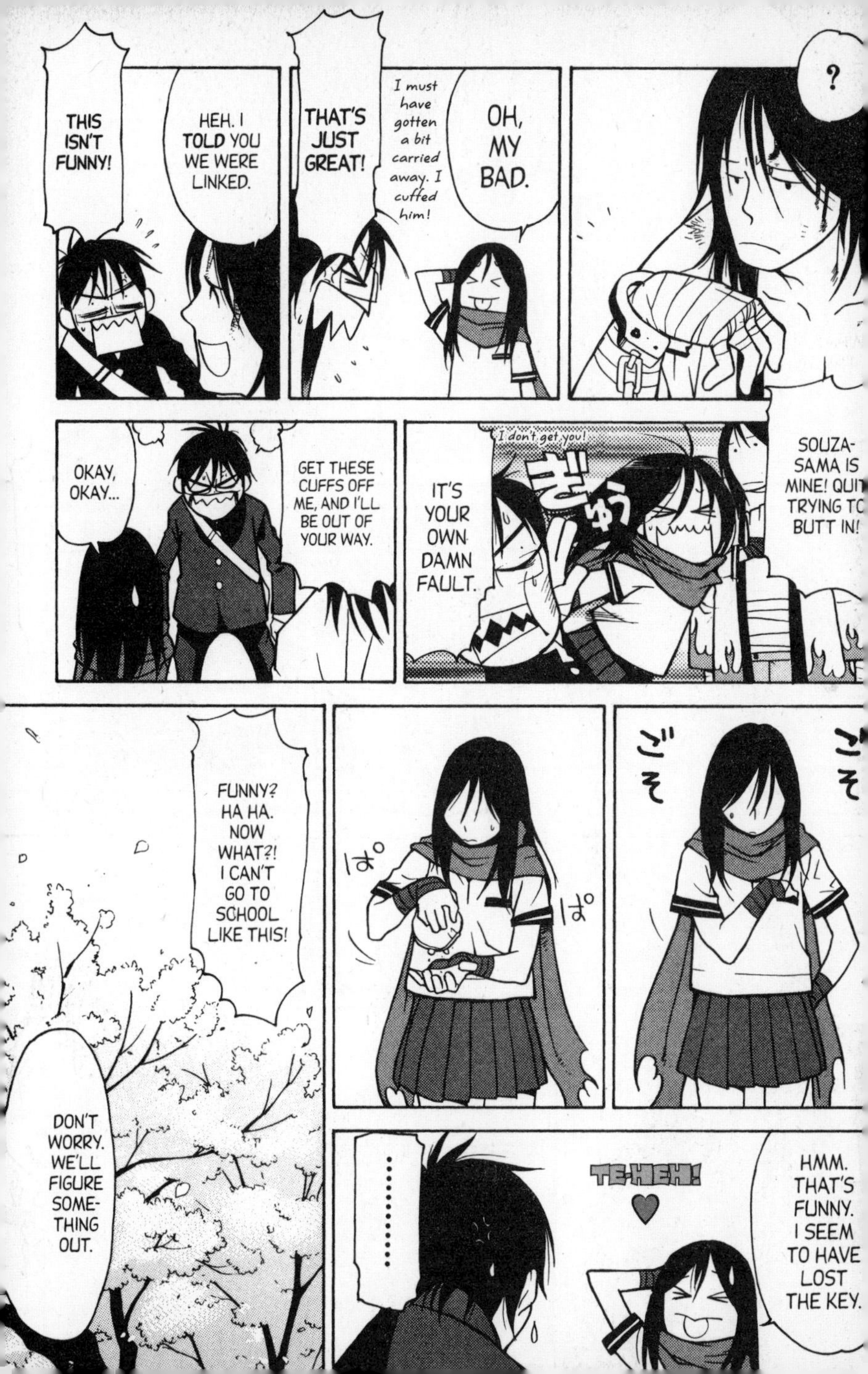
?
OH, MY BAD.
I must have gotten a bit carried away. I cuffed him!
THAT'S JUST GREAT!
HEH. I TOLD YOU WE WERE LINKED.
THIS ISN'T FUNNY!
SOUZA-SAMA IS MINE! QUIT TRYING TO BUTT IN!
ぎゅう
I don't get you!
IT'S YOUR OWN DAMN FAULT.
GET THESE CUFFS OFF ME, AND I'LL BE OUT OF YOUR WAY.
OKAY, OKAY...
ごそ
ごそ
ぱ
ぱ
HMM. THAT'S FUNNY. I SEEM TO HAVE LOST THE KEY.
TE-HEH! ♥
....
FUNNY? HA HA. NOW WHAT?! I CAN'T GO TO SCHOOL LIKE THIS!
DON'T WORRY. WE'LL FIGURE SOMETHING OUT.

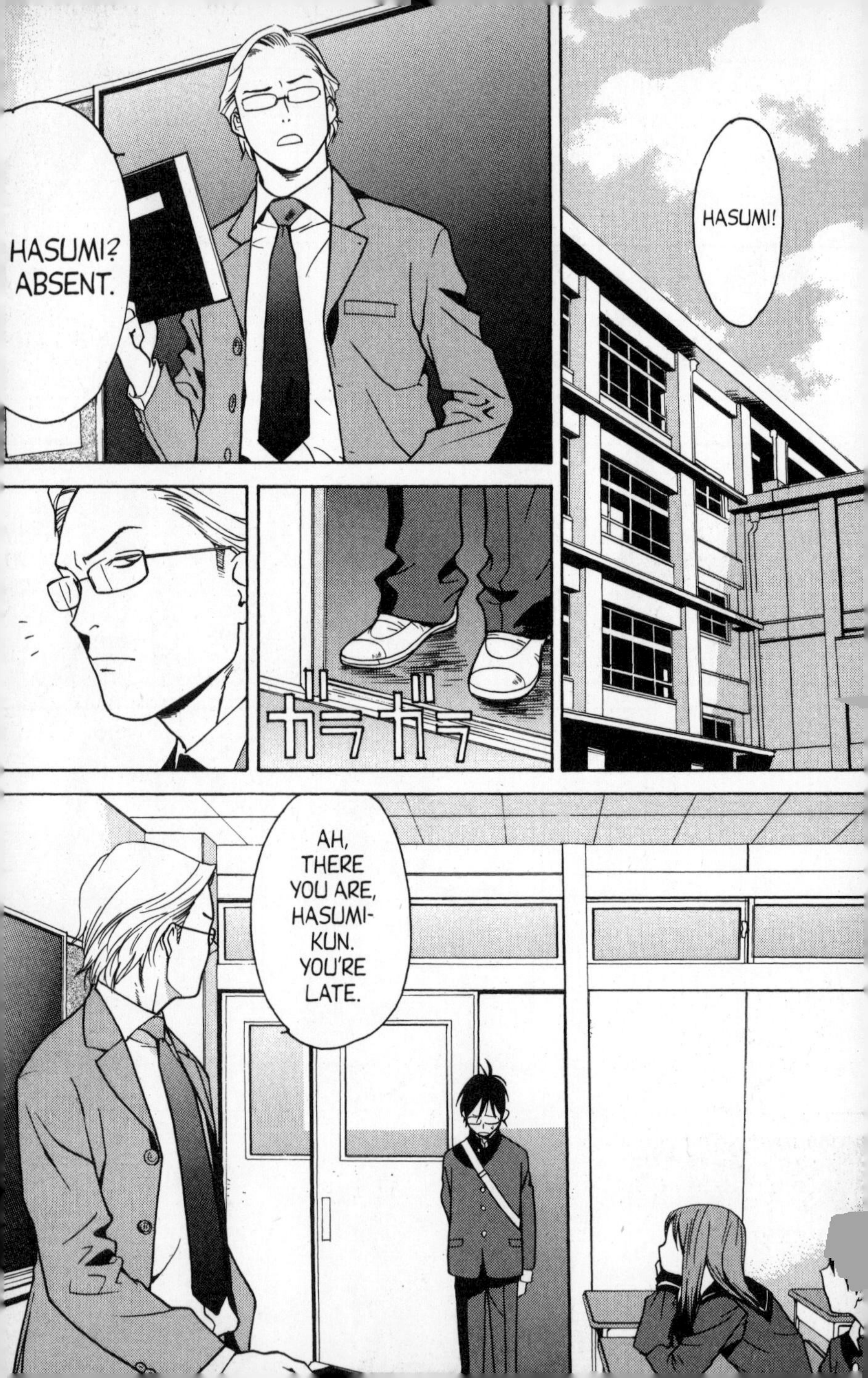
HASUMI!
HASUMI? ABSENT.
ガラ ガラ
AH, THERE YOU ARE, HASUMI-KUN. YOU'RE LATE.

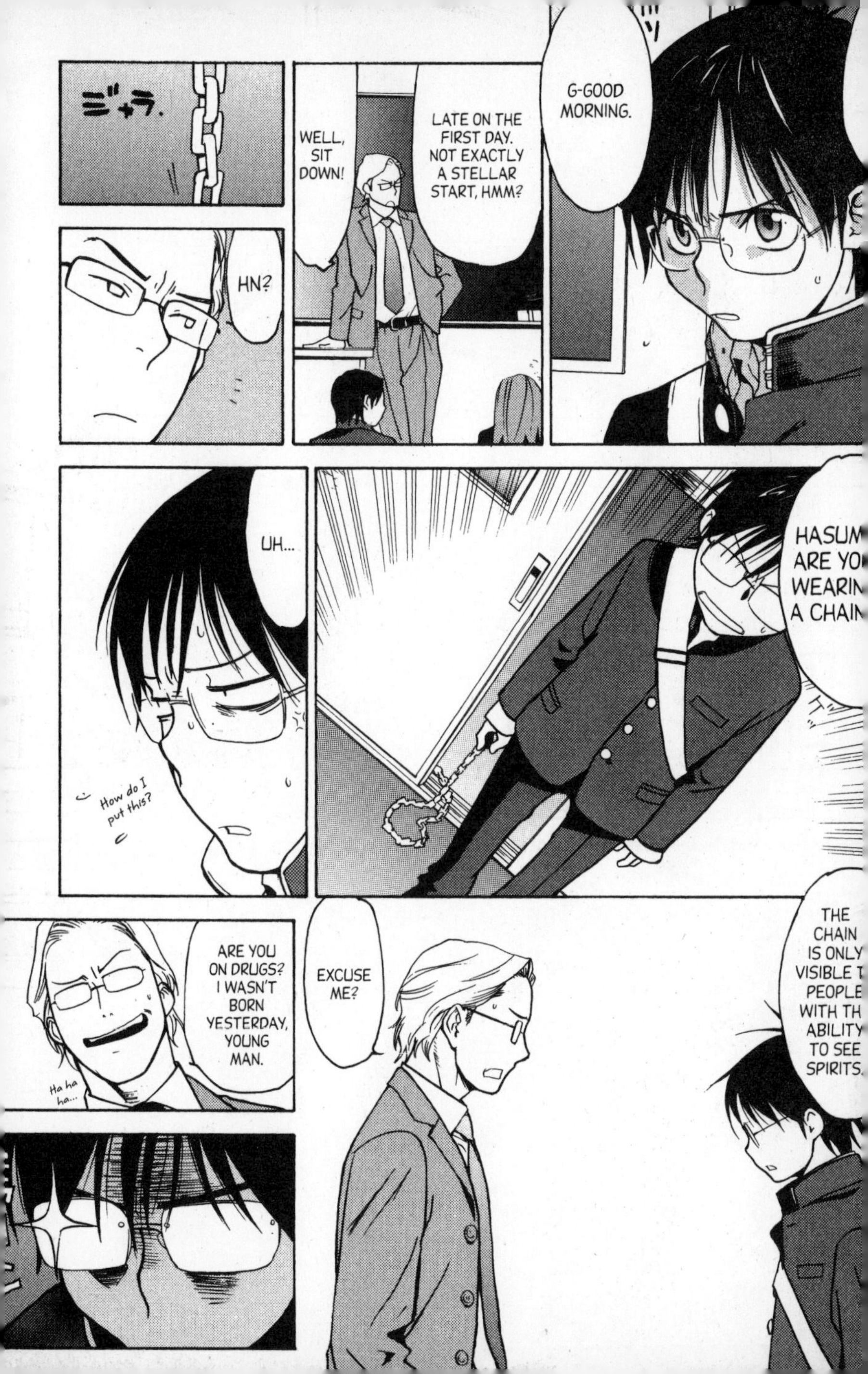

G-GOOD MORNING.
LATE ON THE FIRST DAY. NOT EXACTLY A STELLAR START, HMM?
WELL, SIT DOWN!
ジャラ.
HN?
HASUM ARE YO WEARIN A CHAIN
UH...
How do I put this?
THE CHAIN IS ONLY VISIBLE T PEOPLE WITH TH ABILITY TO SEE SPIRITS.
EXCUSE ME?
ARE YOU ON DRUGS? I WASN'T BORN YESTERDAY, YOUNG MAN.
Ha ha ha...

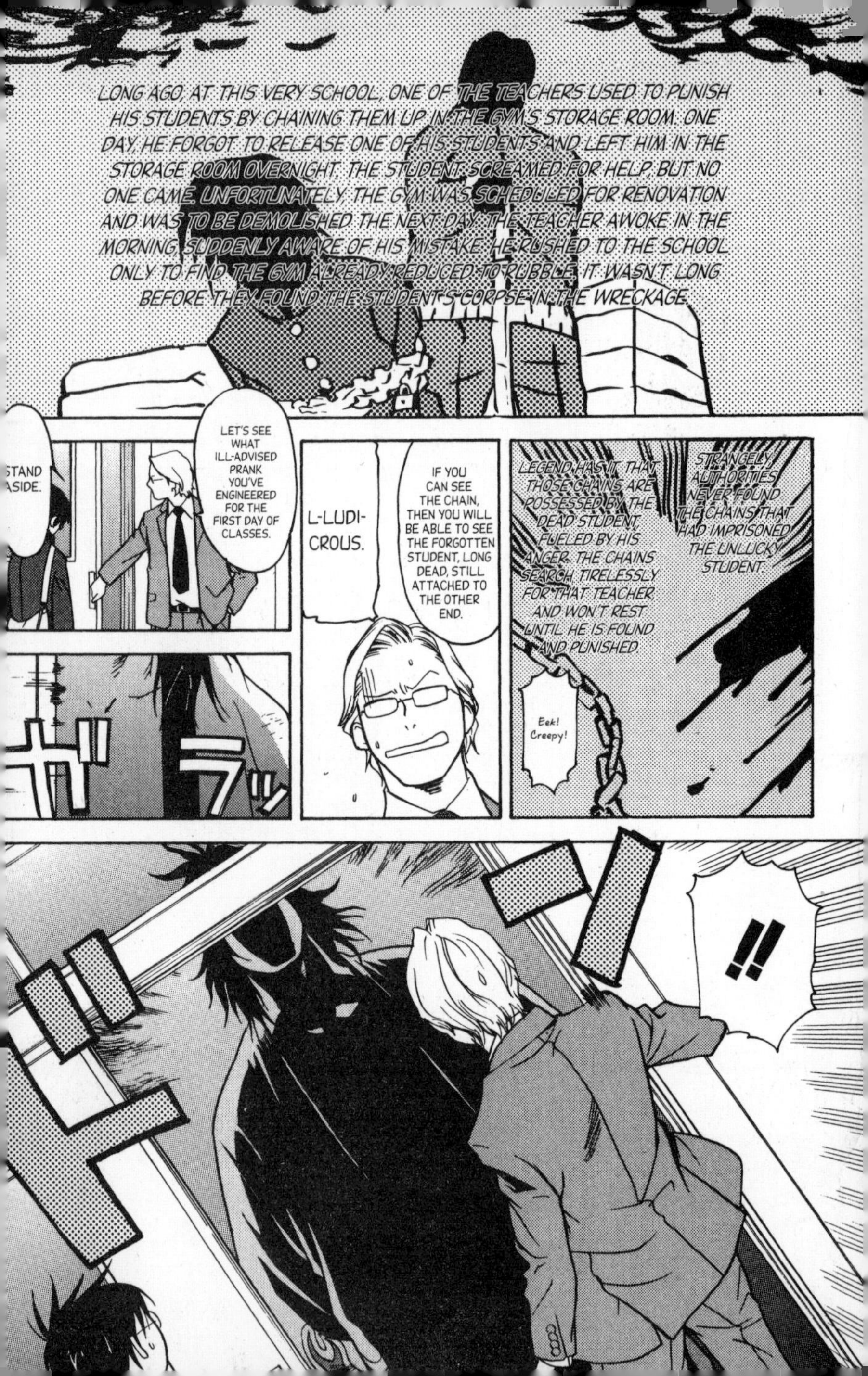
LONG AGO, AT THIS VERY SCHOOL, ONE OF THE TEACHERS USED TO PUNISH HIS STUDENTS BY CHAINING THEM UP IN THE GYM'S STORAGE ROOM. ONE DAY, HE FORGOT TO RELEASE ONE OF HIS STUDENTS AND LEFT HIM IN THE STORAGE ROOM OVERNIGHT. THE STUDENT SCREAMED FOR HELP, BUT NO ONE CAME. UNFORTUNATELY, THE GYM WAS SCHEDULED FOR RENOVATION AND WAS TO BE DEMOLISHED THE NEXT DAY. THE TEACHER AWOKE IN THE MORNING, SUDDENLY AWARE OF HIS MISTAKE. HE RUSHED TO THE SCHOOL ONLY TO FIND THE GYM ALREADY REDUCED TO RUBBLE. IT WASN'T LONG BEFORE THEY FOUND THE STUDENT'S CORPSE IN THE WRECKAGE.
STRANGELY, AUTHORITIES NEVER FOUND THE CHAINS THAT HAD IMPRISONED THE UNLUCKY STUDENT.
LEGEND HAS IT THAT THOSE CHAINS ARE POSSESSED BY THE DEAD STUDENT. FUELED BY HIS ANGER, THE CHAINS SEARCH TIRELESSLY FOR THAT TEACHER AND WON'T REST UNTIL HE IS FOUND AND PUNISHED.
Eek! Creepy!
IF YOU CAN SEE THE CHAIN, THEN YOU WILL BE ABLE TO SEE THE FORGOTTEN STUDENT, LONG DEAD, STILL ATTACHED TO THE OTHER END.
L-LUDICROUS.
LET'S SEE WHAT ILL-ADVISED PRANK YOU'VE ENGINEERED FOR THE FIRST DAY OF CLASSES.
STAND ASIDE.
ガラッ
!!

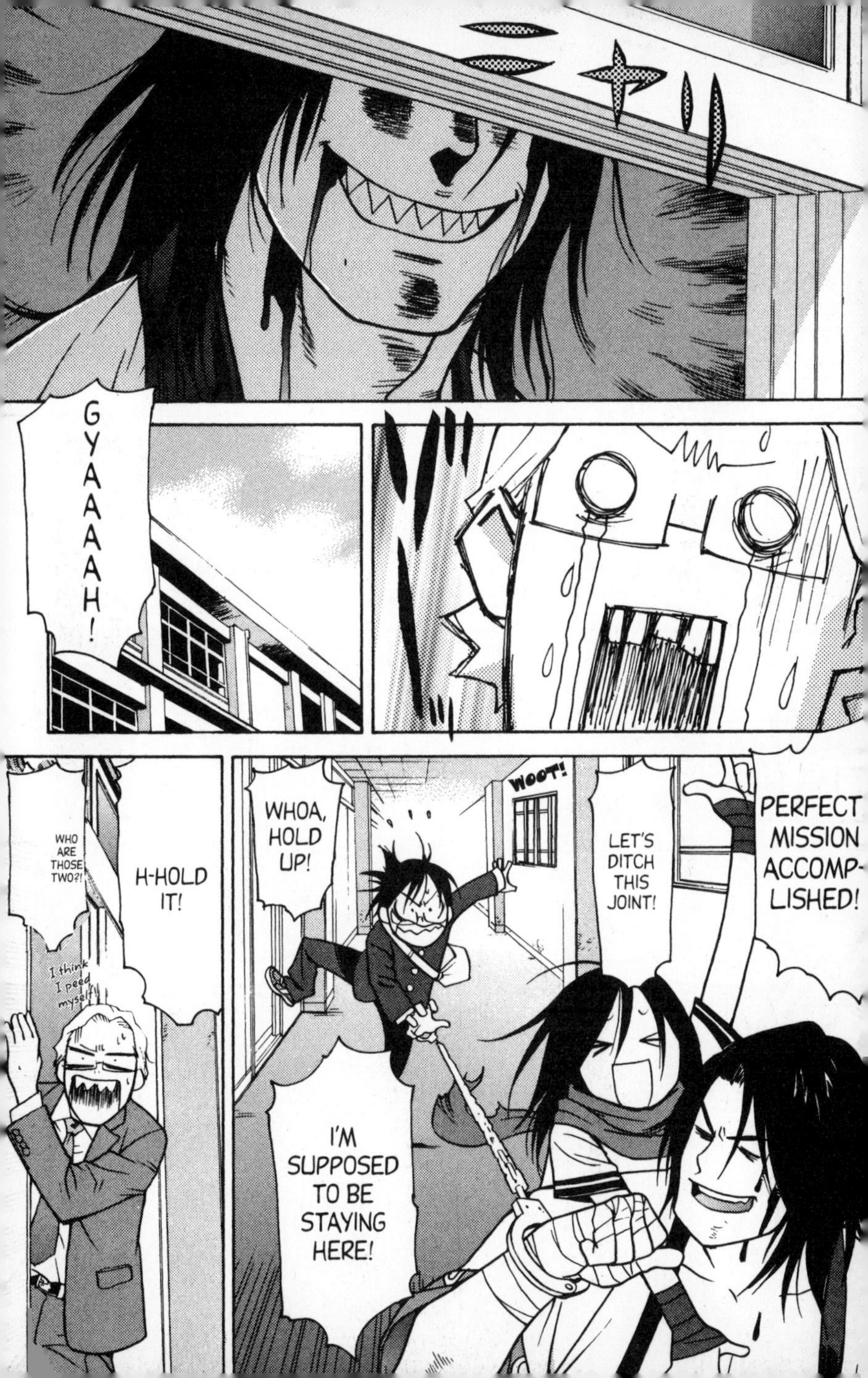
GYAAAAAH!
PERFECT MISSION ACCOMP-LISHED!
LET'S DITCH THIS JOINT!
WOOT!
WHOA, HOLD UP!
I'M SUPPOSED TO BE STAYING HERE!
H-HOLD IT!
WHO ARE THOSE TWO?!
I think I peed myself!

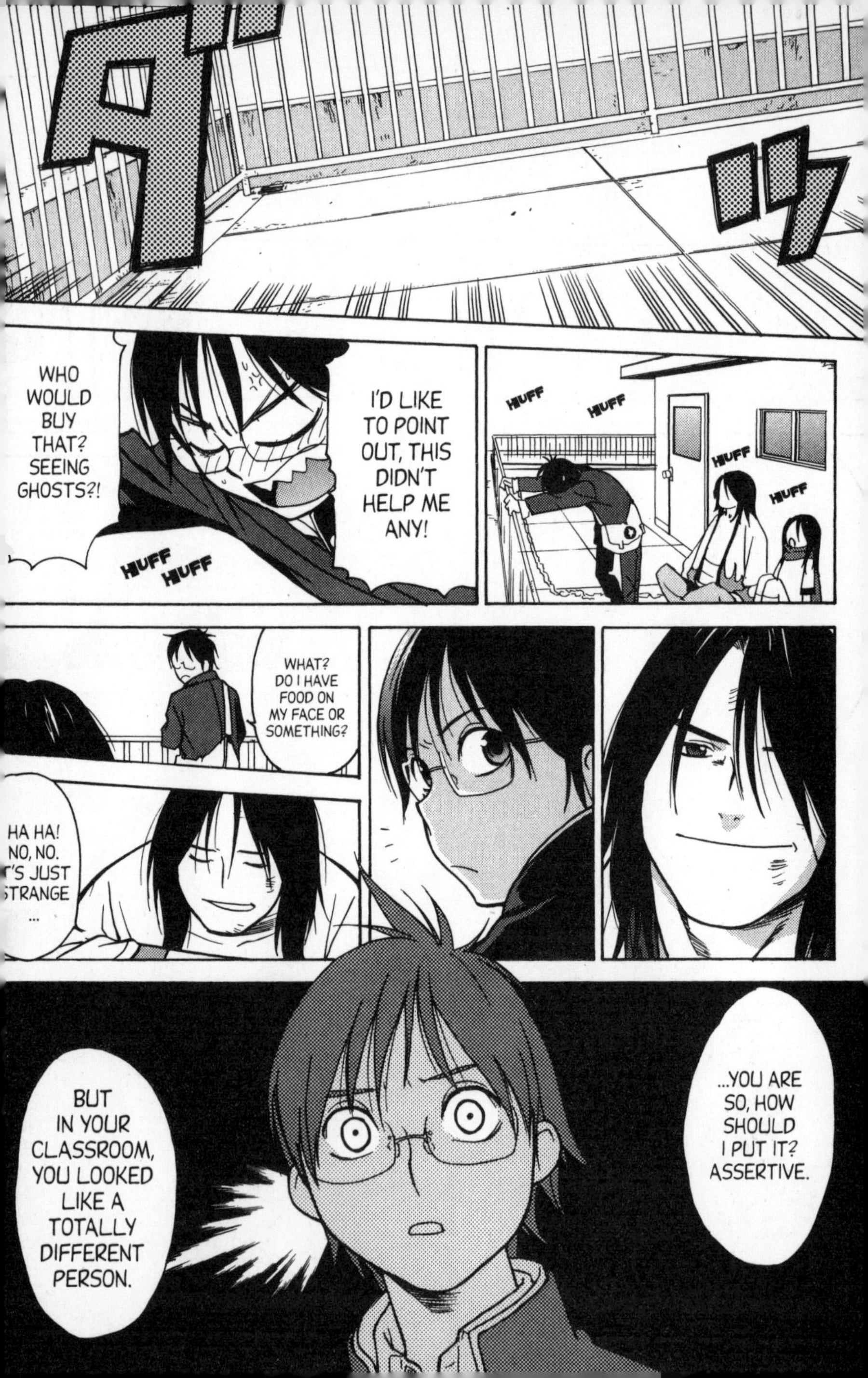
ダッ
HUFF
HUFF
HUFF
HUFF
I'D LIKE TO POINT OUT, THIS DIDN'T HELP ME ANY!
WHO WOULD BUY THAT? SEEING GHOSTS?!
HUFF HUFF
WHAT? DO I HAVE FOOD ON MY FACE OR SOMETHING?
HA HA! NO, NO. T'S JUST STRANGE ...
...YOU ARE SO, HOW SHOULD I PUT IT? ASSERTIVE.
BUT IN YOUR CLASSROOM, YOU LOOKED LIKE A TOTALLY DIFFERENT PERSON.

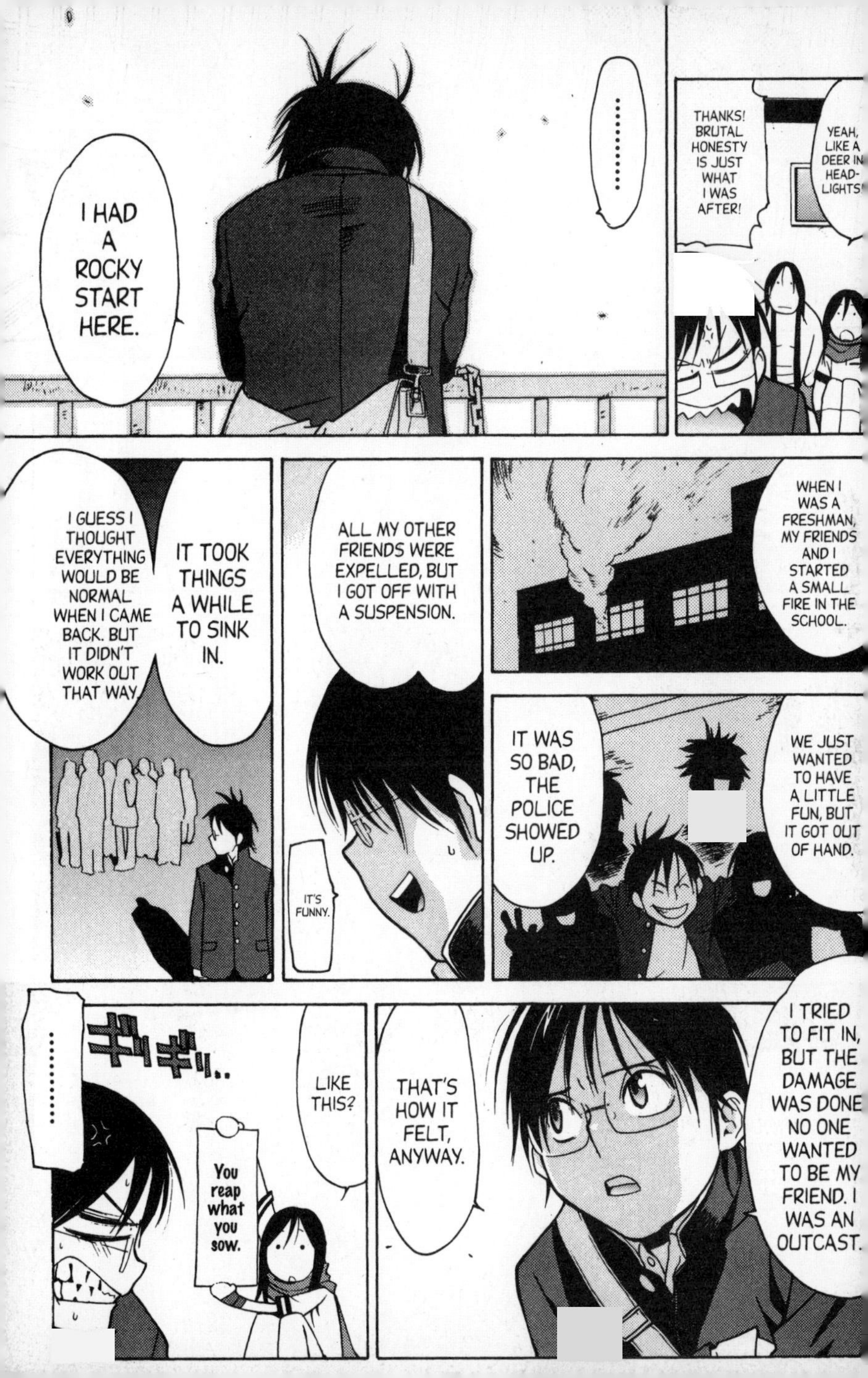
YEAH, LIKE A DEER IN HEADLIGHTS!
THANKS! BRUTAL HONESTY IS JUST WHAT I WAS AFTER!
......
I HAD A ROCKY START HERE.
WHEN I WAS A FRESHMAN, MY FRIENDS AND I STARTED A SMALL FIRE IN THE SCHOOL.
WE JUST WANTED TO HAVE A LITTLE FUN, BUT IT GOT OUT OF HAND.
IT WAS SO BAD, THE POLICE SHOWED UP.
ALL MY OTHER FRIENDS WERE EXPELLED, BUT I GOT OFF WITH A SUSPENSION.
IT'S FUNNY.
IT TOOK THINGS A WHILE TO SINK IN.
I GUESS I THOUGHT EVERYTHING WOULD BE NORMAL WHEN I CAME BACK. BUT IT DIDN'T WORK OUT THAT WAY.
I TRIED TO FIT IN, BUT THE DAMAGE WAS DONE NO ONE WANTED TO BE MY FRIEND. I WAS AN OUTCAST.
THAT'S HOW IT FELT, ANYWAY.
LIKE THIS?
You reap what you sow.
ギリギリ..
......

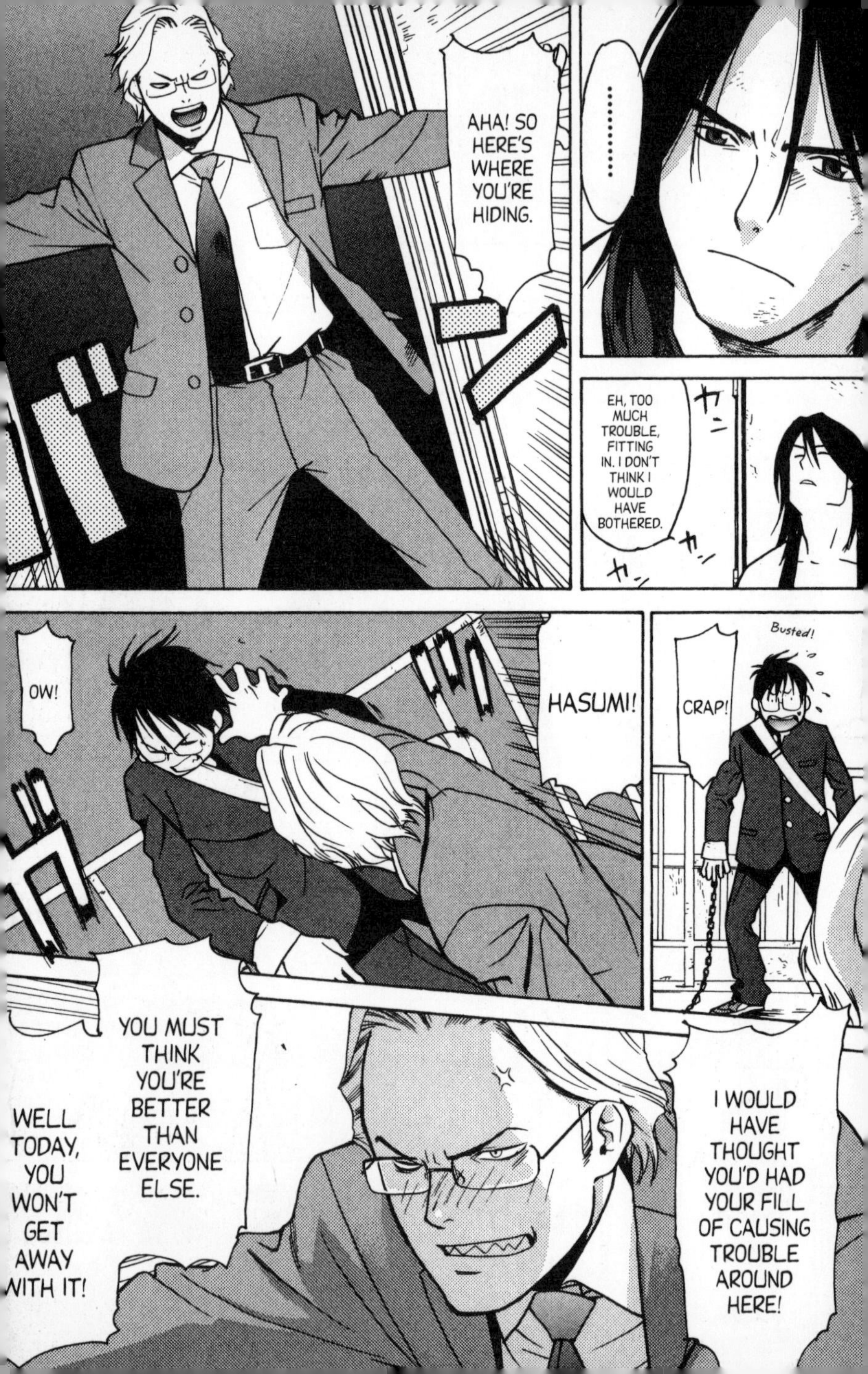

....
EH, TOO MUCH TROUBLE, FITTING IN. I DON'T THINK I WOULD HAVE BOTHERED.
AHA! SO HERE'S WHERE YOU'RE HIDING.
Busted!
CRAP!
HASUMI!
OW!
I WOULD HAVE THOUGHT YOU'D HAD YOUR FILL OF CAUSING TROUBLE AROUND HERE!
YOU MUST THINK YOU'RE BETTER THAN EVERYONE ELSE.
WELL TODAY, YOU WON'T GET AWAY WITH IT!

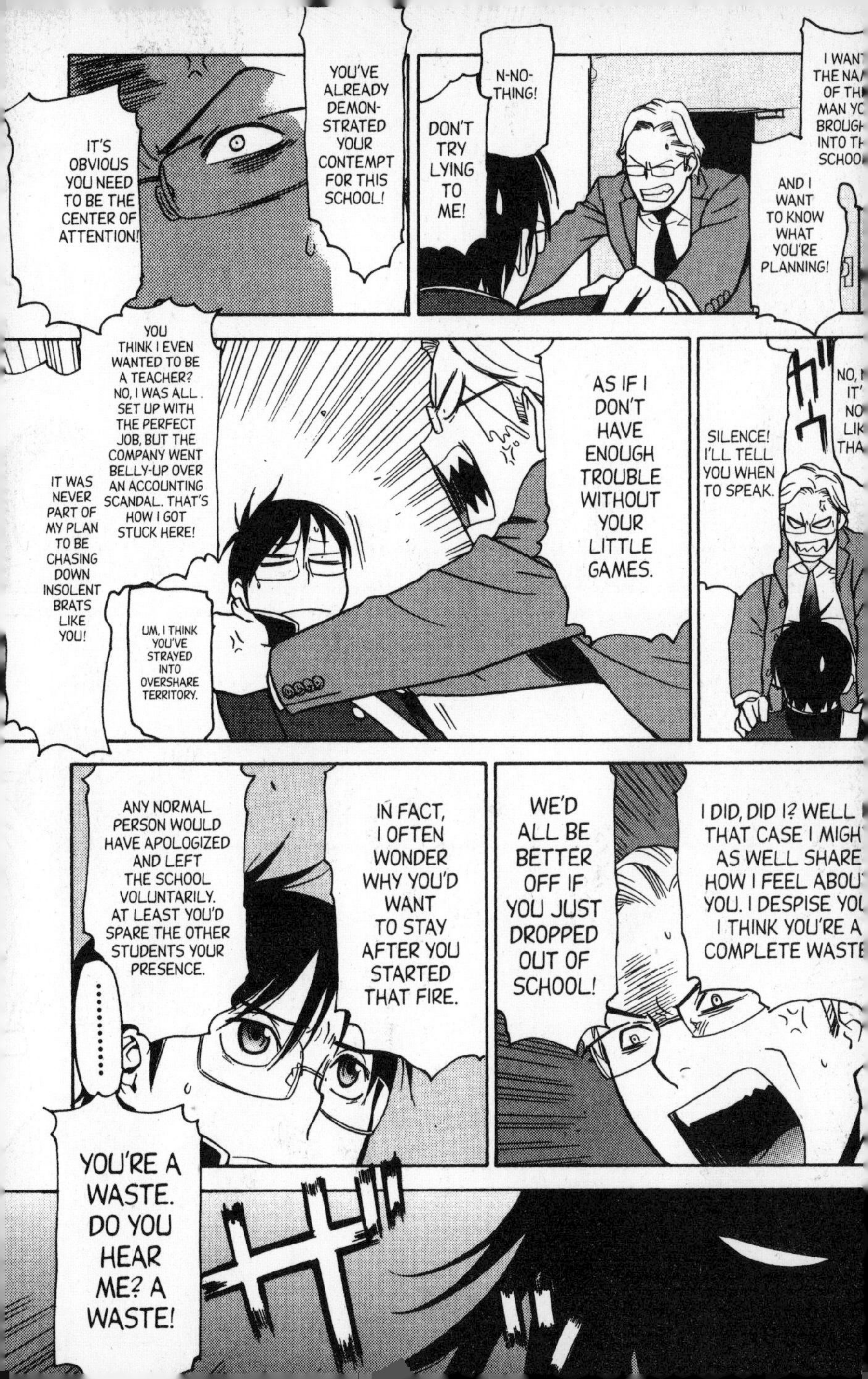
I WANT THE NA OF TH MAN YO BROUGH INTO TH SCHOO
AND I WANT TO KNOW WHAT YOU'RE PLANNING!
N-NO-THING!
DON'T TRY LYING TO ME!
YOU'VE ALREADY DEMON-STRATED YOUR CONTEMPT FOR THIS SCHOOL!
IT'S OBVIOUS YOU NEED TO BE THE CENTER OF ATTENTION!
NO, I IT' NO LIK THA
SILENCE! I'LL TELL YOU WHEN TO SPEAK.
AS IF I DON'T HAVE ENOUGH TROUBLE WITHOUT YOUR LITTLE GAMES.
YOU THINK I EVEN WANTED TO BE A TEACHER? NO, I WAS ALL SET UP WITH THE PERFECT JOB, BUT THE COMPANY WENT BELLY-UP OVER AN ACCOUNTING SCANDAL. THAT'S HOW I GOT STUCK HERE!
IT WAS NEVER PART OF MY PLAN TO BE CHASING DOWN INSOLENT BRATS LIKE YOU!
UM, I THINK YOU'VE STRAYED INTO OVERSHARE TERRITORY.
I DID, DID I? WELL THAT CASE I MIGH AS WELL SHARE HOW I FEEL ABOU YOU. I DESPISE YO I THINK YOU'RE A COMPLETE WAST
WE'D ALL BE BETTER OFF IF YOU JUST DROPPED OUT OF SCHOOL!
IN FACT, I OFTEN WONDER WHY YOU'D WANT TO STAY AFTER YOU STARTED THAT FIRE.
ANY NORMAL PERSON WOULD HAVE APOLOGIZED AND LEFT THE SCHOOL VOLUNTARILY. AT LEAST YOU'D SPARE THE OTHER STUDENTS YOUR PRESENCE.
....
YOU'RE A WASTE. DO YOU HEAR ME? A WASTE!

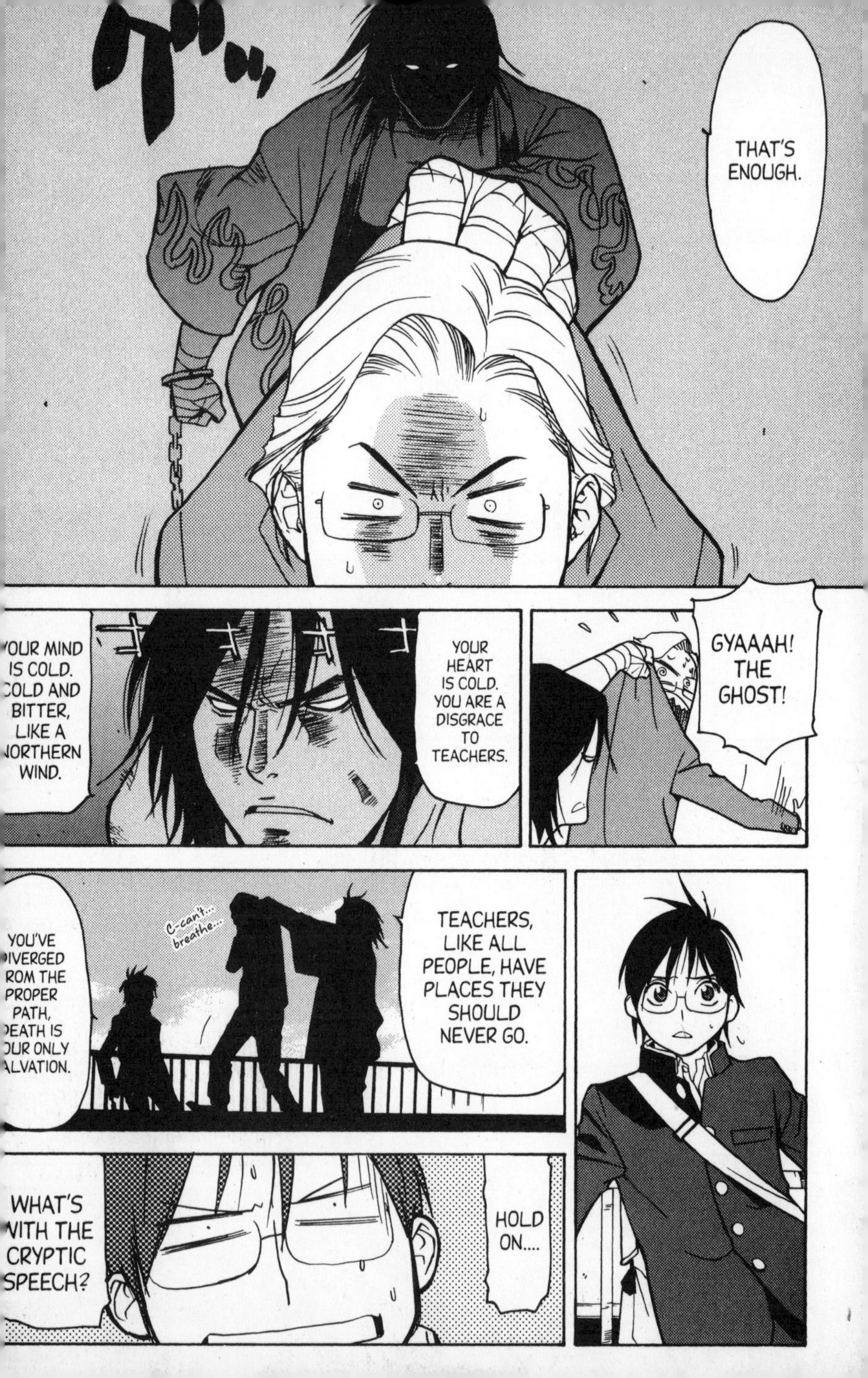
THAT'S ENOUGH.
GYAAAH! THE GHOST!
YOUR HEART IS COLD. YOU ARE A DISGRACE TO TEACHERS.
OUR MIND IS COLD. COLD AND BITTER, LIKE A NORTHERN WIND.
TEACHERS, LIKE ALL PEOPLE, HAVE PLACES THEY SHOULD NEVER GO.
C-can't... breathe...
YOU'VE IVERGED ROM THE PROPER PATH, EATH IS OUR ONLY ALVATION.
HOLD ON....
WHAT'S ITH THE CRYPTIC SPEECH?

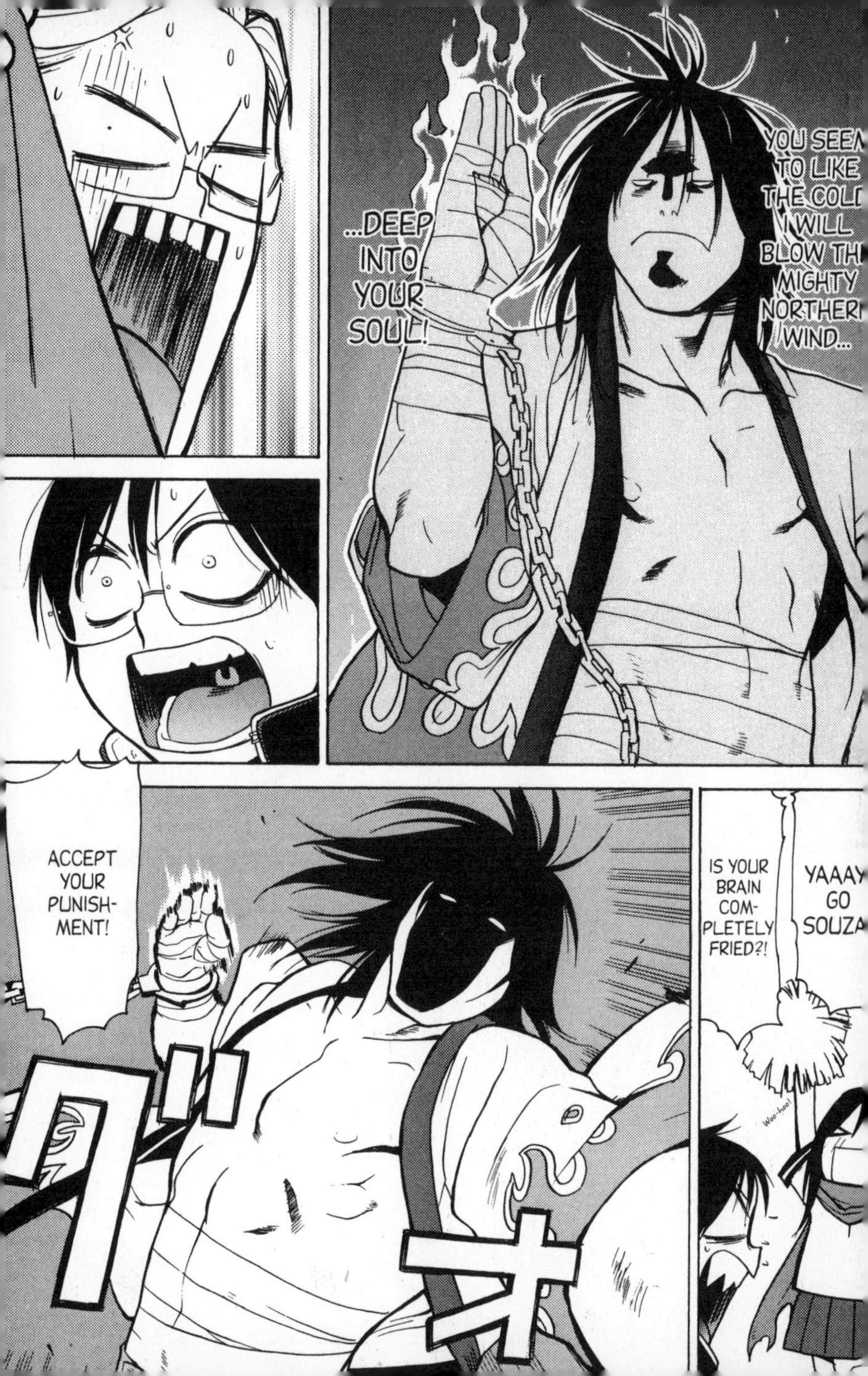
YOU SEEM TO LIKE THE COLD I WILL BLOW THE MIGHTY NORTHERN WIND...
...DEEP INTO YOUR SOUL!
YAAAY GO SOUZA
IS YOUR BRAIN COM-PLETELY FRIED?!
Woo-hoo!
ACCEPT YOUR PUNISH-MENT!

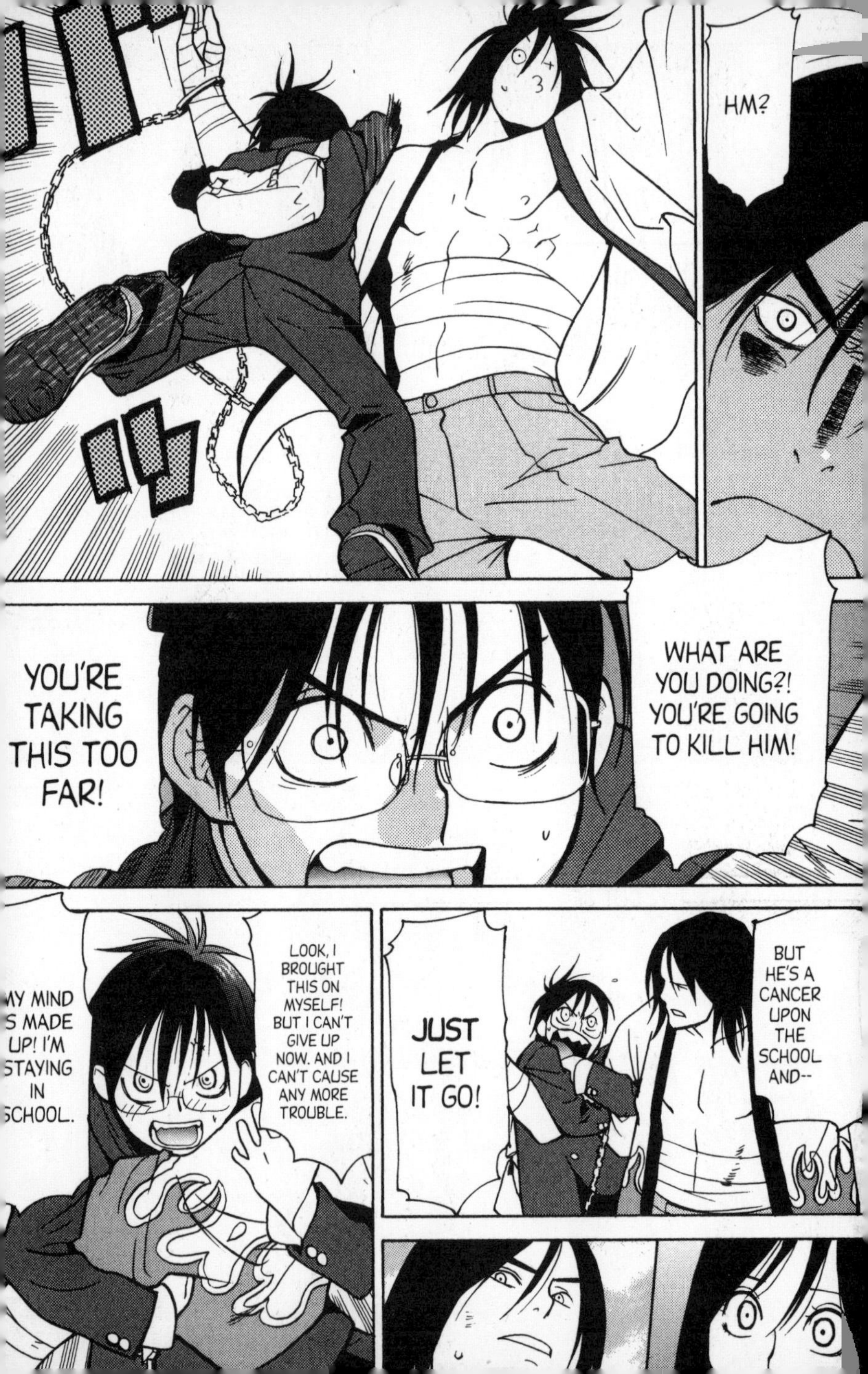
HM?
WHAT ARE YOU DOING?! YOU'RE GOING TO KILL HIM!
YOU'RE TAKING THIS TOO FAR!
BUT HE'S A CANCER UPON THE SCHOOL AND--
JUST LET IT GO!
LOOK, I BROUGHT THIS ON MYSELF! BUT I CAN'T GIVE UP NOW. AND I CAN'T CAUSE ANY MORE TROUBLE.
MY MIND S MADE UP! I'M STAYING IN SCHOOL.

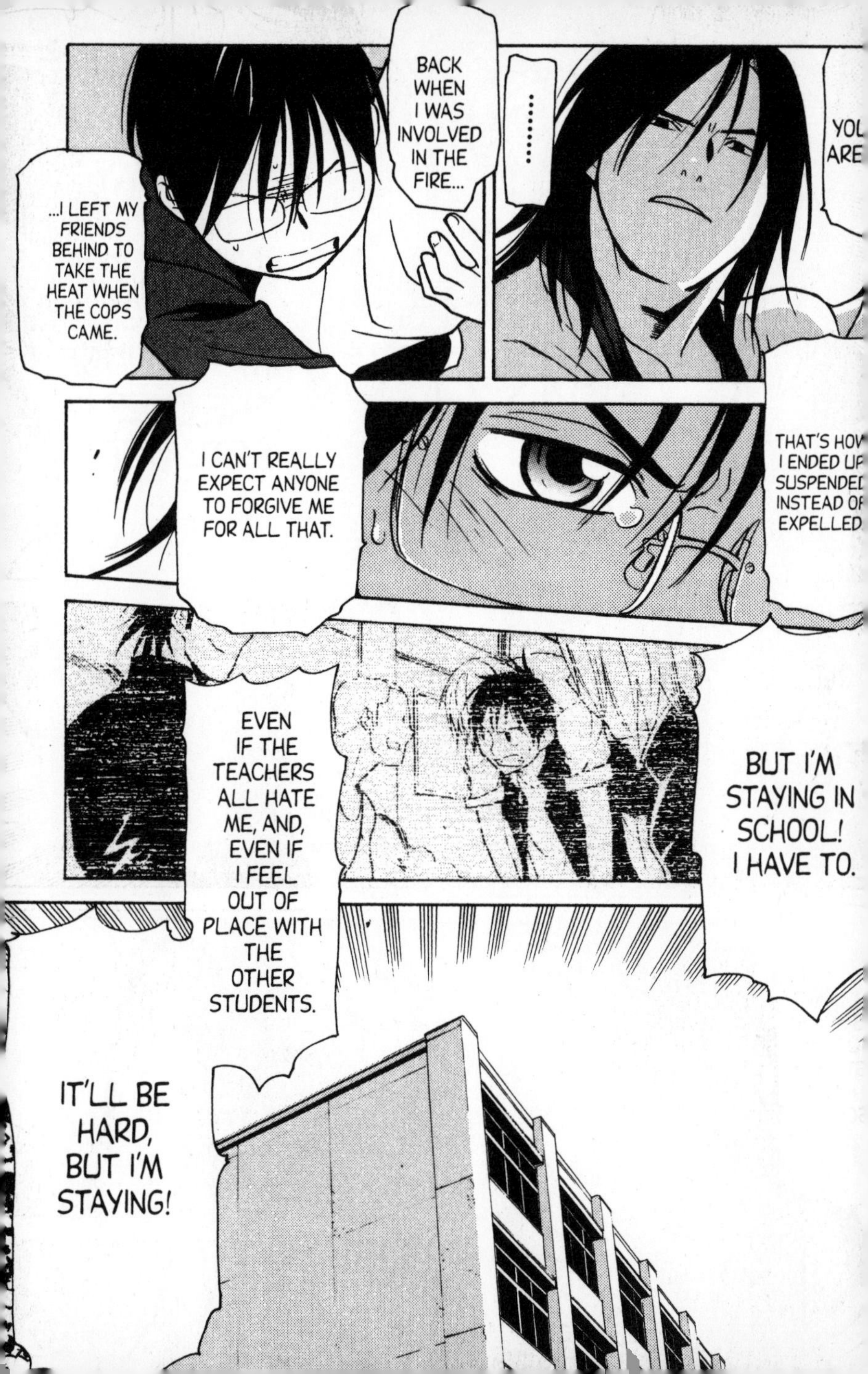
YOU ARE
......
BACK WHEN I WAS INVOLVED IN THE FIRE...
...I LEFT MY FRIENDS BEHIND TO TAKE THE HEAT WHEN THE COPS CAME.
THAT'S HOW I ENDED UP SUSPENDED INSTEAD OF EXPELLED.
I CAN'T REALLY EXPECT ANYONE TO FORGIVE ME FOR ALL THAT.
BUT I'M STAYING IN SCHOOL! I HAVE TO.
EVEN IF THE TEACHERS ALL HATE ME, AND, EVEN IF I FEEL OUT OF PLACE WITH THE OTHER STUDENTS.
IT'LL BE HARD, BUT I'M STAYING!

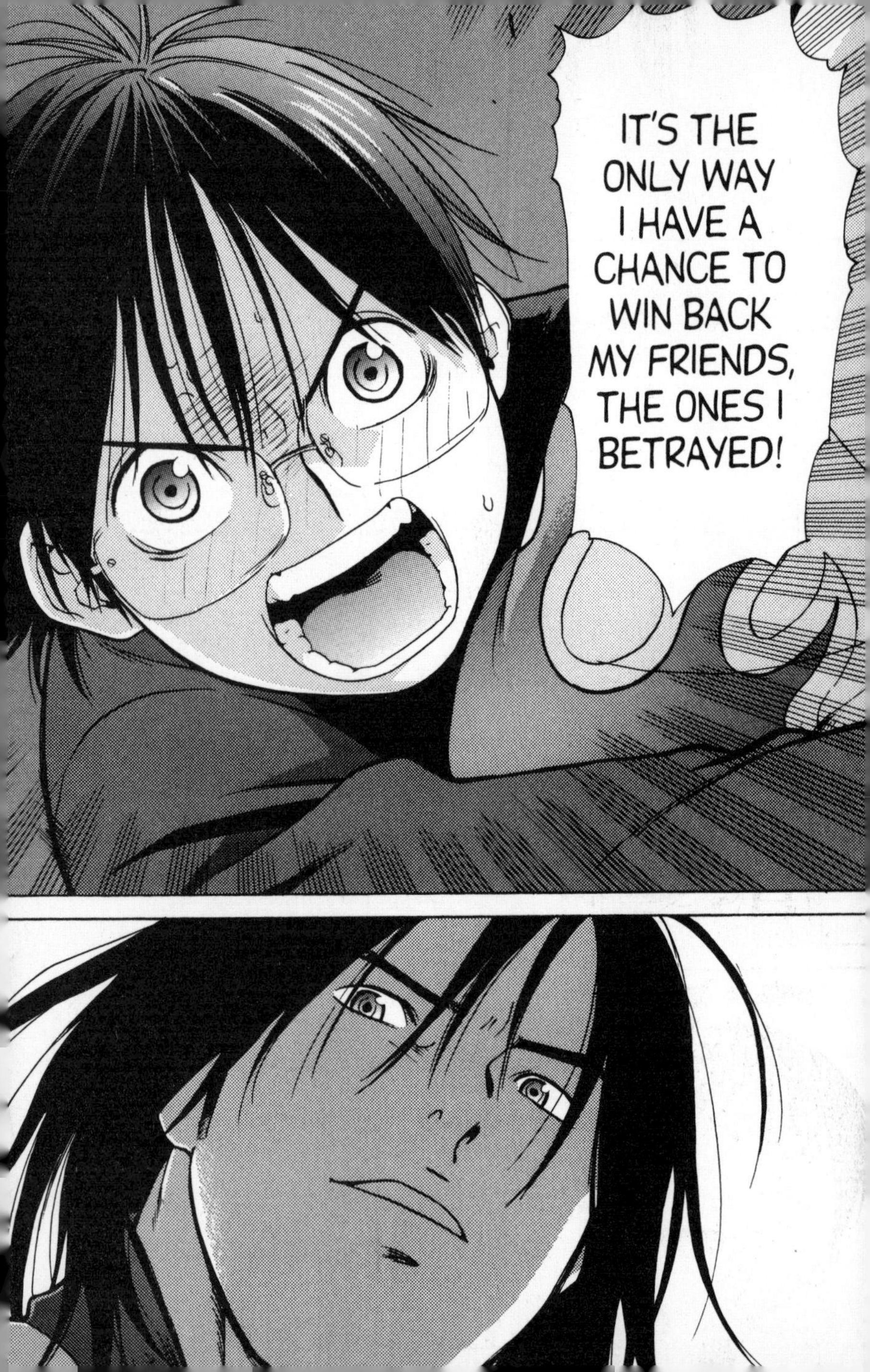
IT'S THE ONLY WAY I HAVE A CHANCE TO WIN BACK MY FRIENDS, THE ONES I BETRAYED!

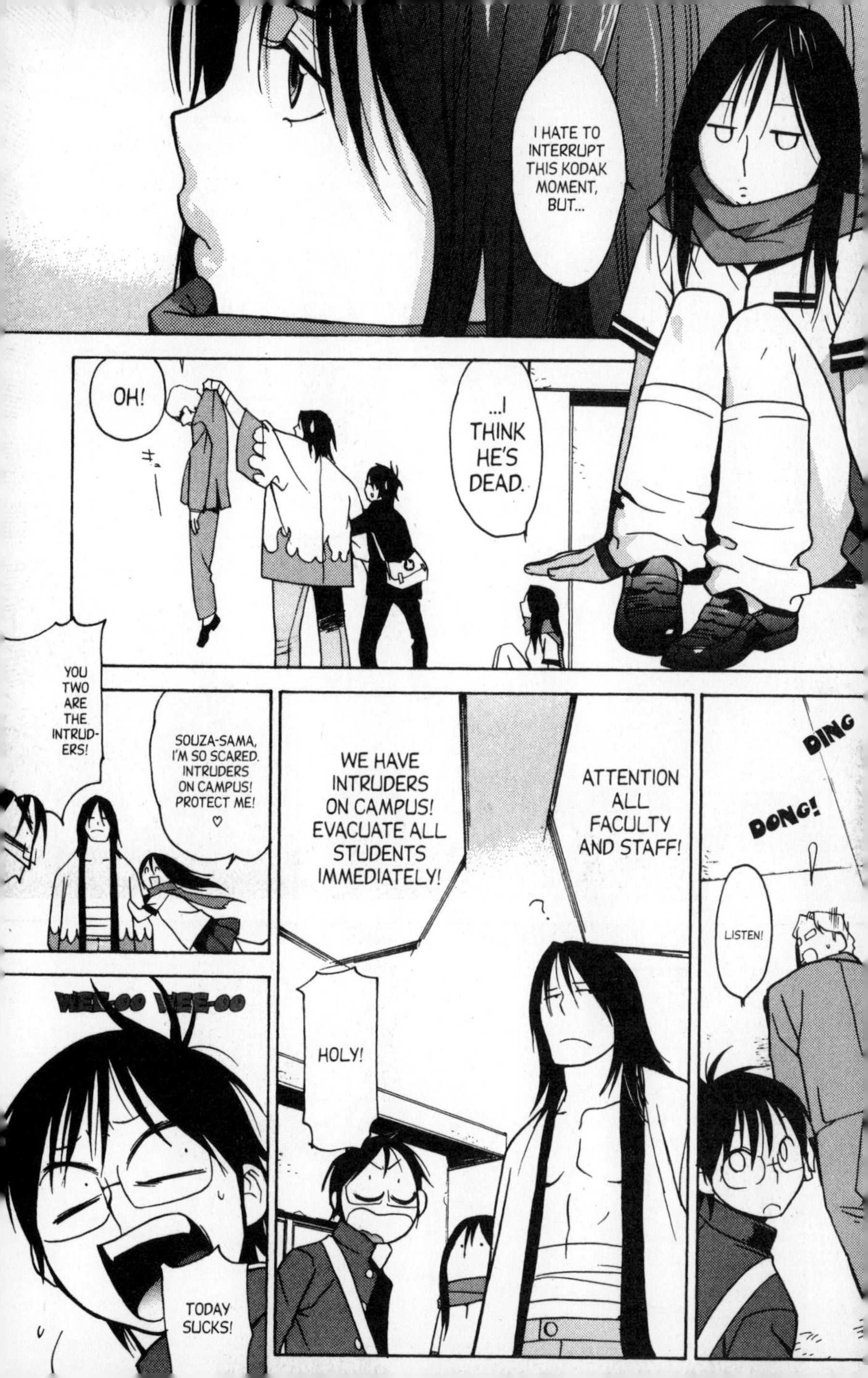
I HATE TO INTERRUPT THIS KODAK MOMENT, BUT...
...I THINK HE'S DEAD.
OH!
DING
DONG!
LISTEN!
ATTENTION ALL FACULTY AND STAFF!
WE HAVE INTRUDERS ON CAMPUS! EVACUATE ALL STUDENTS IMMEDIATELY!
YOU TWO ARE THE INTRUDERS!
SOUZA-SAMA, I'M SO SCARED. INTRUDERS ON CAMPUS! PROTECT ME! ♡
?
HOLY!
WEE-OO WEE-OO
TODAY SUCKS!

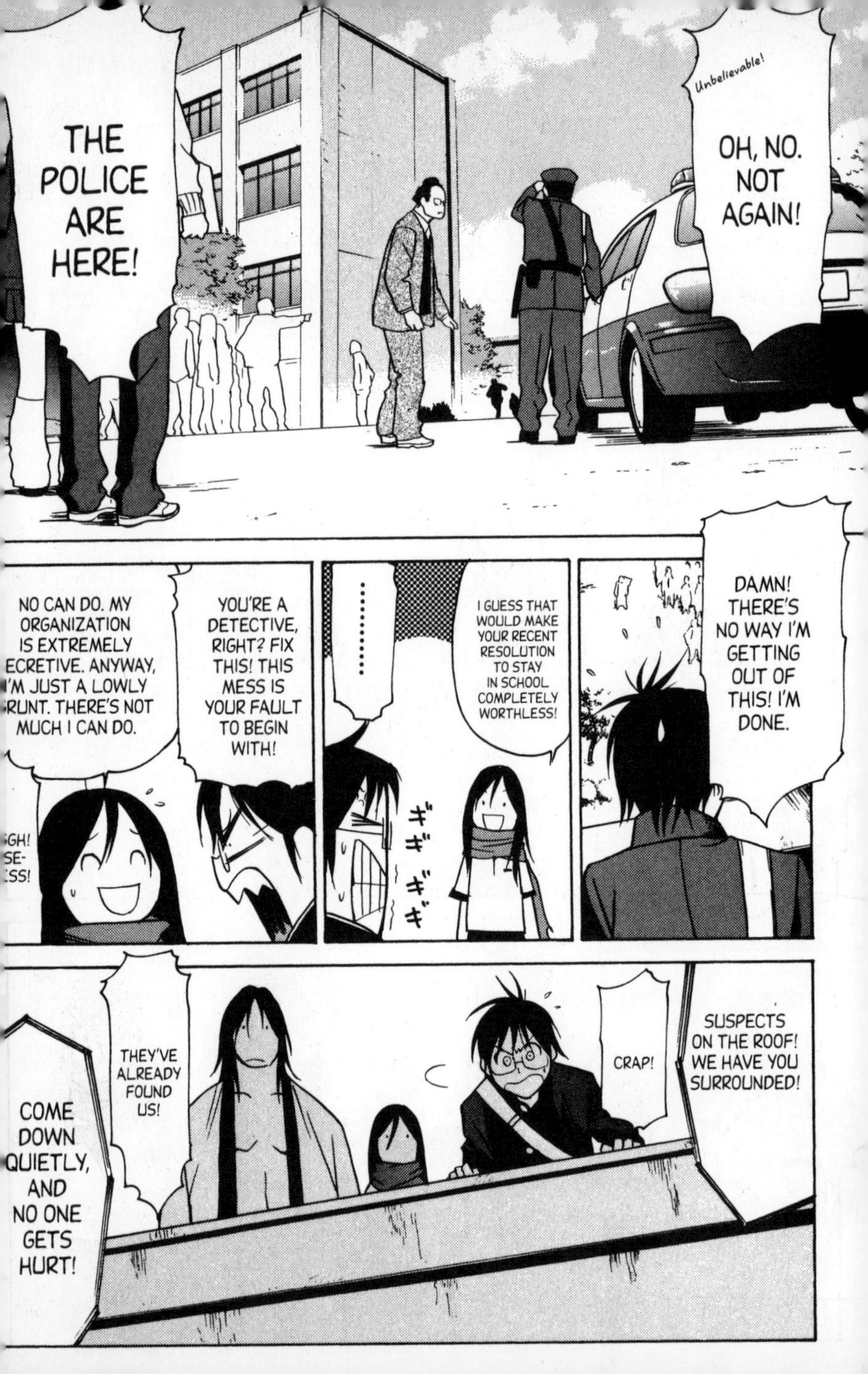
Unbelievable!
OH, NO. NOT AGAIN!
THE POLICE ARE HERE!
DAMN! THERE'S NO WAY I'M GETTING OUT OF THIS! I'M DONE.
I GUESS THAT WOULD MAKE YOUR RECENT RESOLUTION TO STAY IN SCHOOL COMPLETELY WORTHLESS!
....
ギギギギ
YOU'RE A DETECTIVE, RIGHT? FIX THIS! THIS MESS IS YOUR FAULT TO BEGIN WITH!
NO CAN DO. MY ORGANIZATION IS EXTREMELY ECRETIVE. ANYWAY, 'M JUST A LOWLY RUNT. THERE'S NOT MUCH I CAN DO.
SUSPECTS ON THE ROOF! WE HAVE YOU SURROUNDED!
CRAP!
THEY'VE ALREADY FOUND US!
COME DOWN QUIETLY, AND NO ONE GETS HURT!

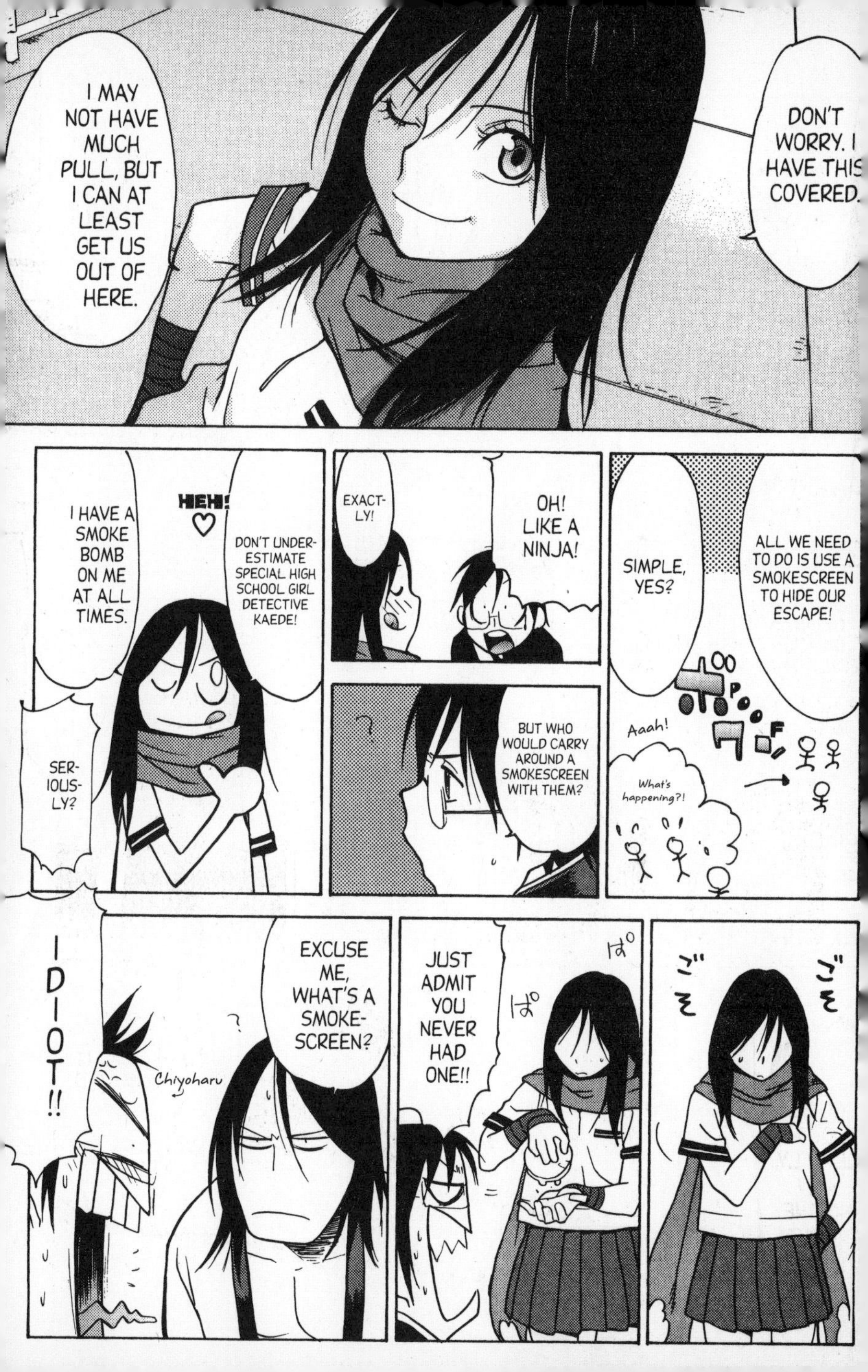
DON'T WORRY. I HAVE THIS COVERED.
I MAY NOT HAVE MUCH PULL, BUT I CAN AT LEAST GET US OUT OF HERE.
ALL WE NEED TO DO IS USE A SMOKESCREEN TO HIDE OUR ESCAPE!
SIMPLE, YES?
POOF
Aaah!
What's happening?!
OH! LIKE A NINJA!
EXACT-LY!
BUT WHO WOULD CARRY AROUND A SMOKESCREEN WITH THEM?
DON'T UNDER-ESTIMATE SPECIAL HIGH SCHOOL GIRL DETECTIVE KAEDE!
HEH!
I HAVE A SMOKE BOMB ON ME AT ALL TIMES.
SER-IOUS-LY?
ごそ
ごそ
ぱ
ぱ
JUST ADMIT YOU NEVER HAD ONE!!
EXCUSE ME, WHAT'S A SMOKE-SCREEN?
Chiyoharu
IDIOT!!

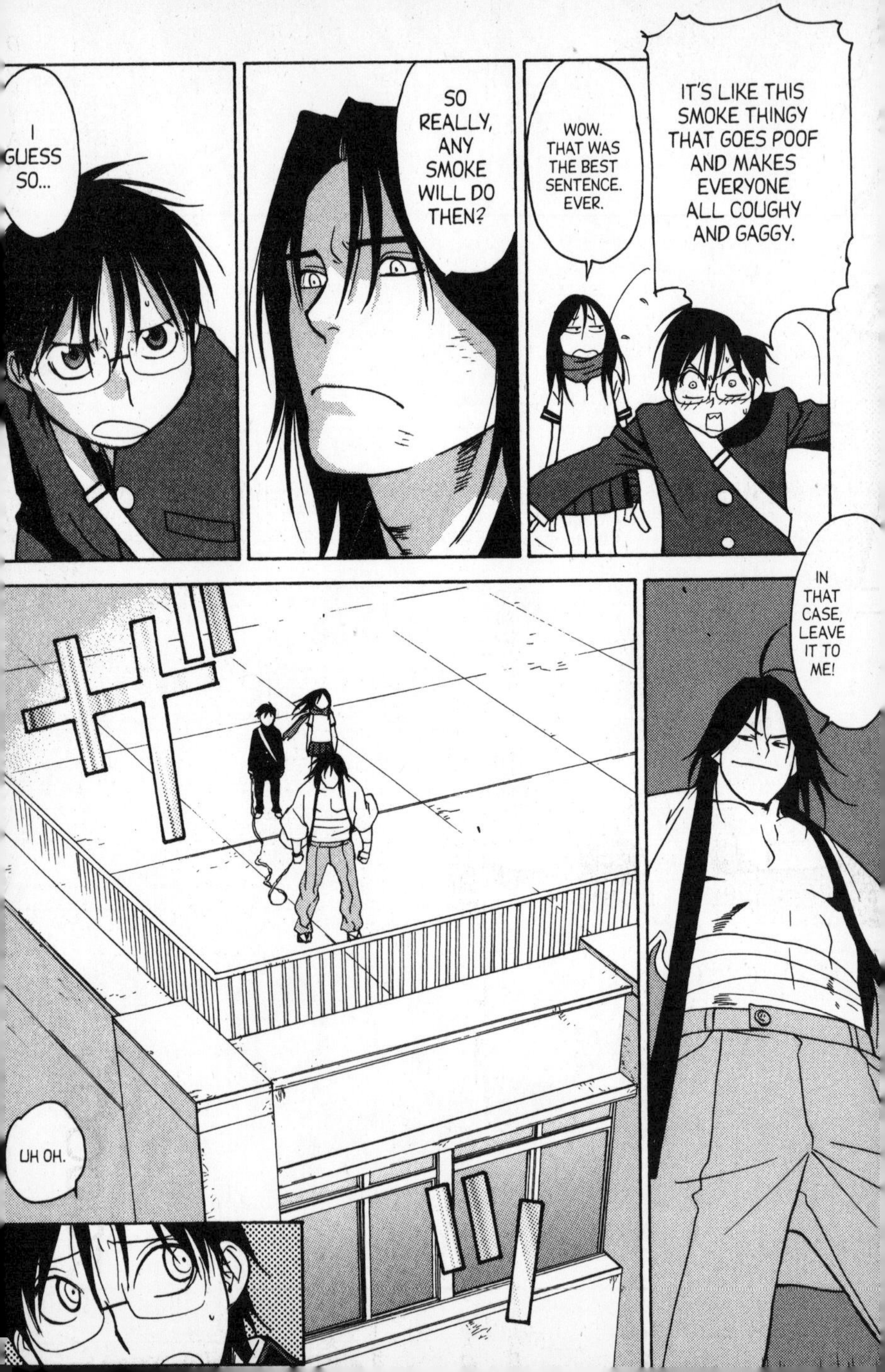
IT'S LIKE THIS SMOKE THINGY THAT GOES POOF AND MAKES EVERYONE ALL COUGHY AND GAGGY.
WOW. THAT WAS THE BEST SENTENCE. EVER.
SO REALLY, ANY SMOKE WILL DO THEN?
I GUESS SO...
IN THAT CASE, LEAVE IT TO ME!
UH OH.

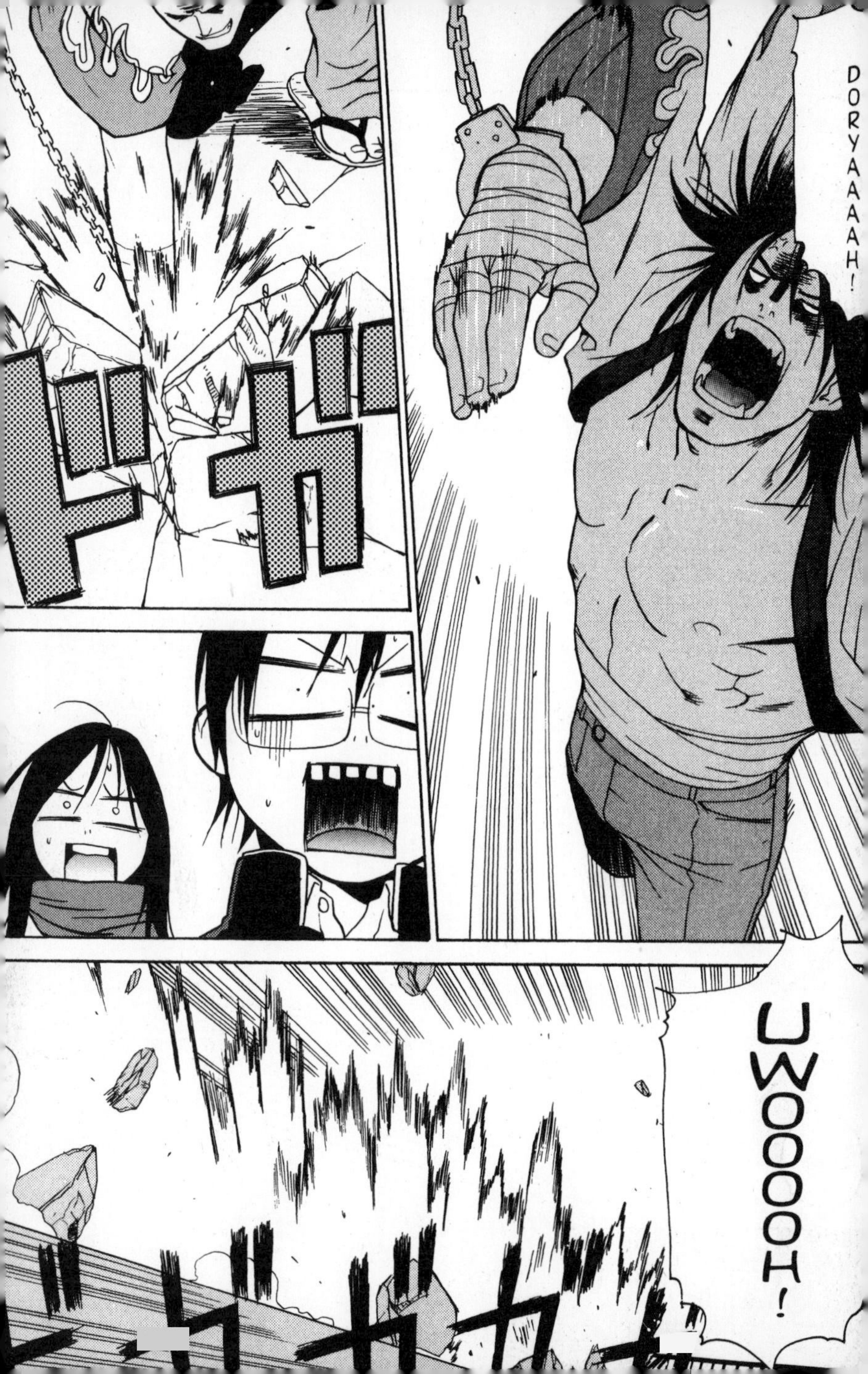
DORYAAAAAH!
ドガ
UWOOOOOH!

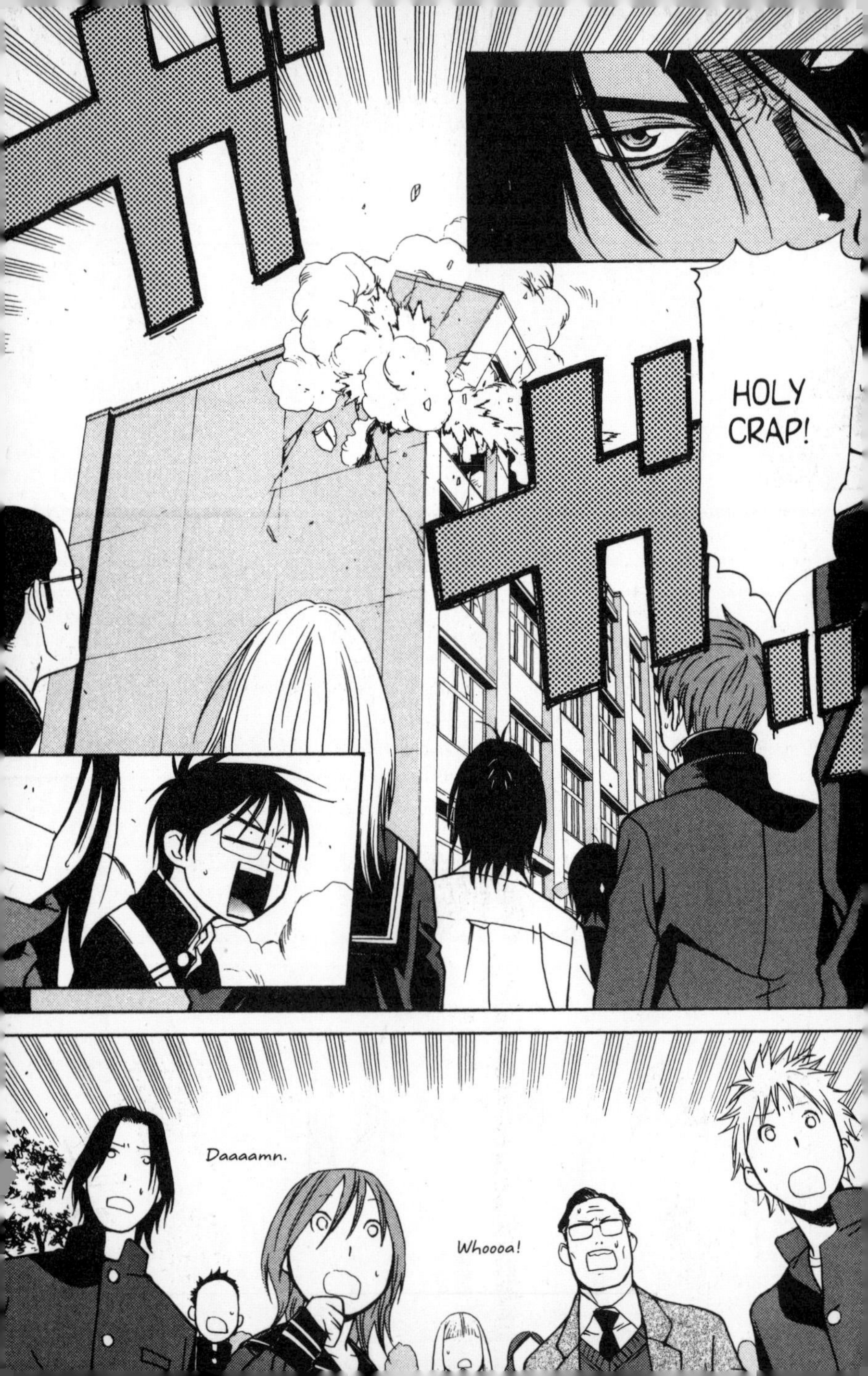
HOLY CRAP!
Daaaamn.
Whoooa!

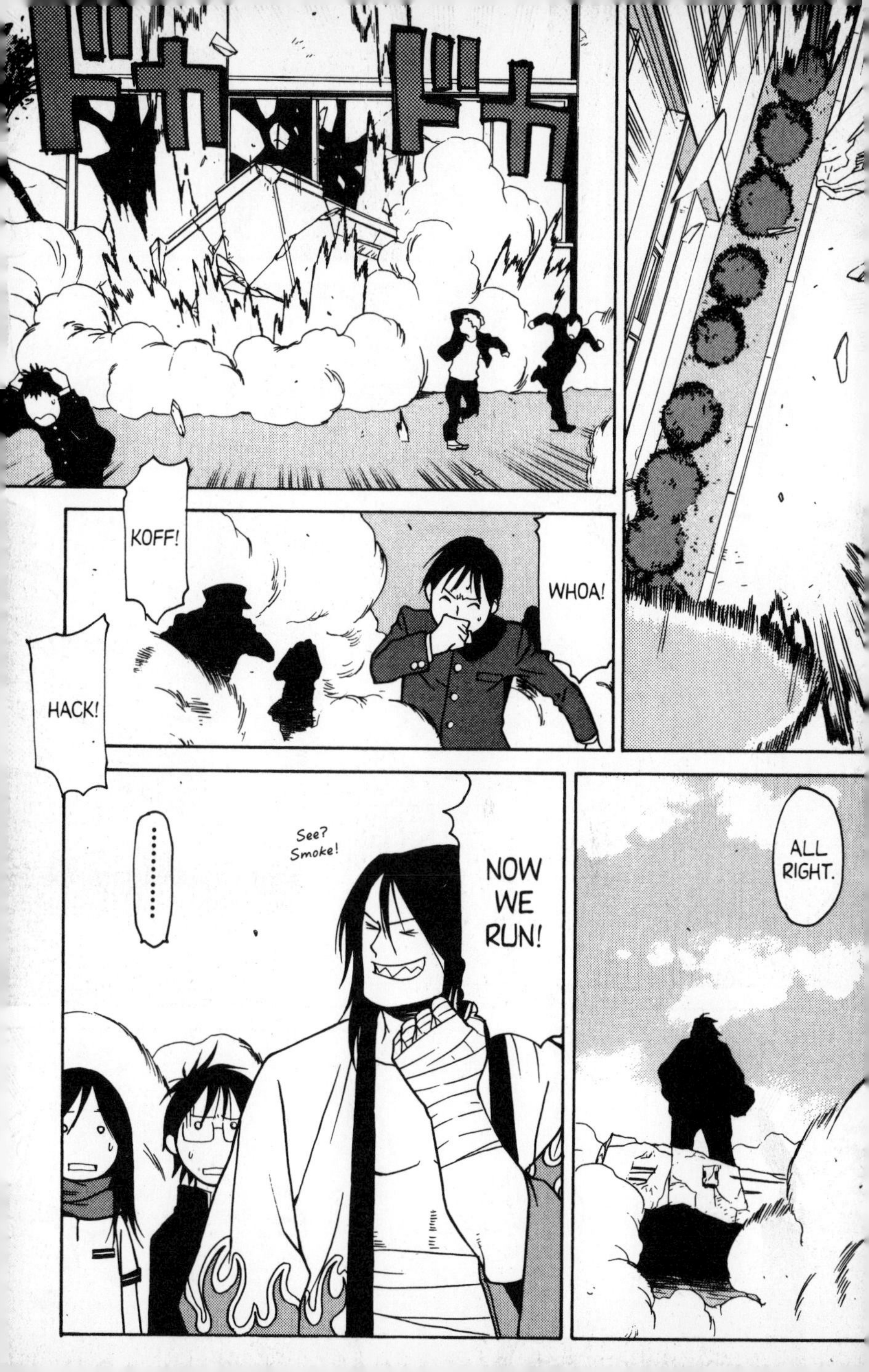
ドカ ドカ
WHOA!
KOFF!
HACK!
ALL RIGHT.
NOW WE RUN!
See? Smoke!
……

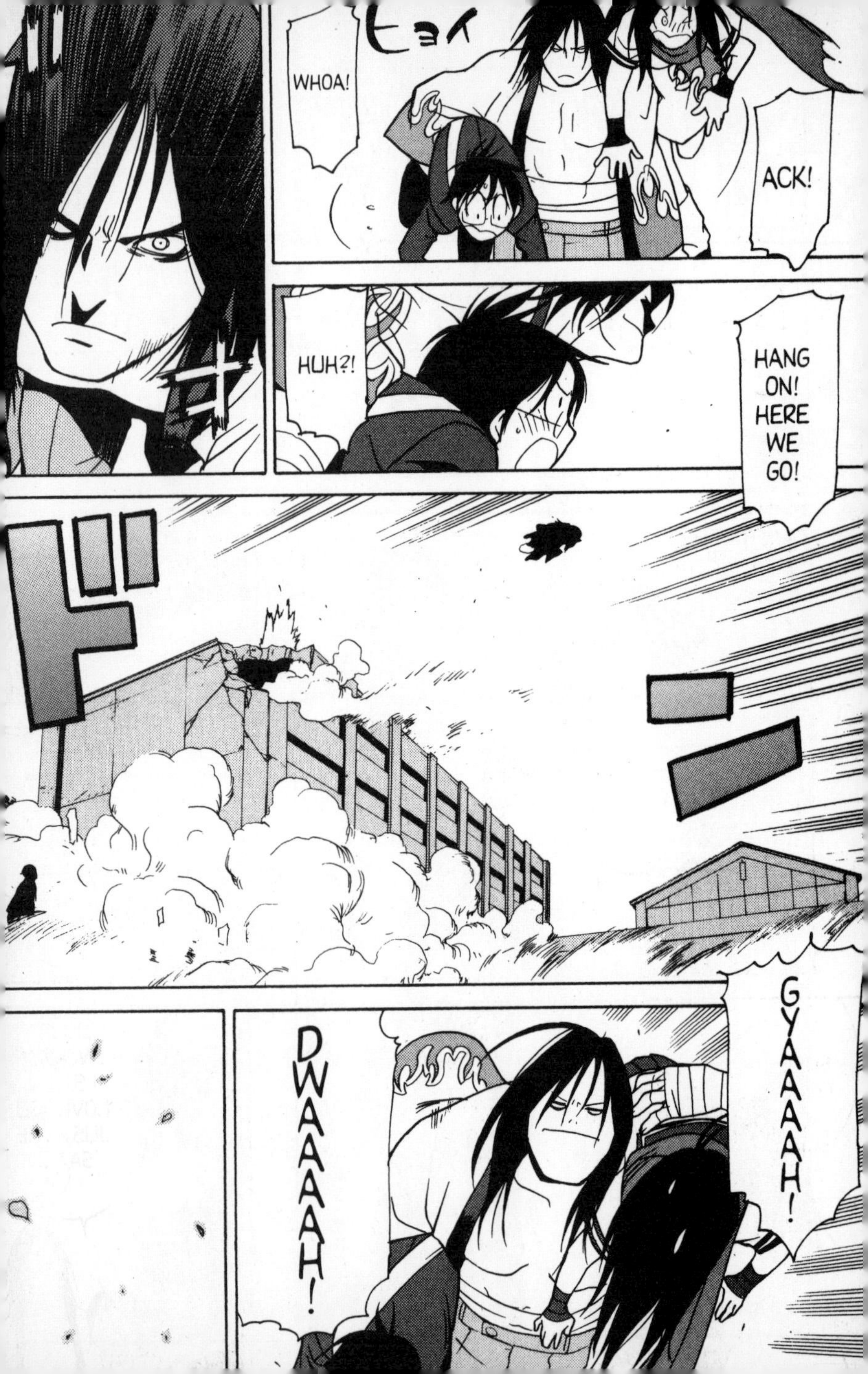
ヒョイ
WHOA!
ACK!
HANG ON! HERE WE GO!
HUH?!
ド
GYAAAAAH!
DWAAAAAH!

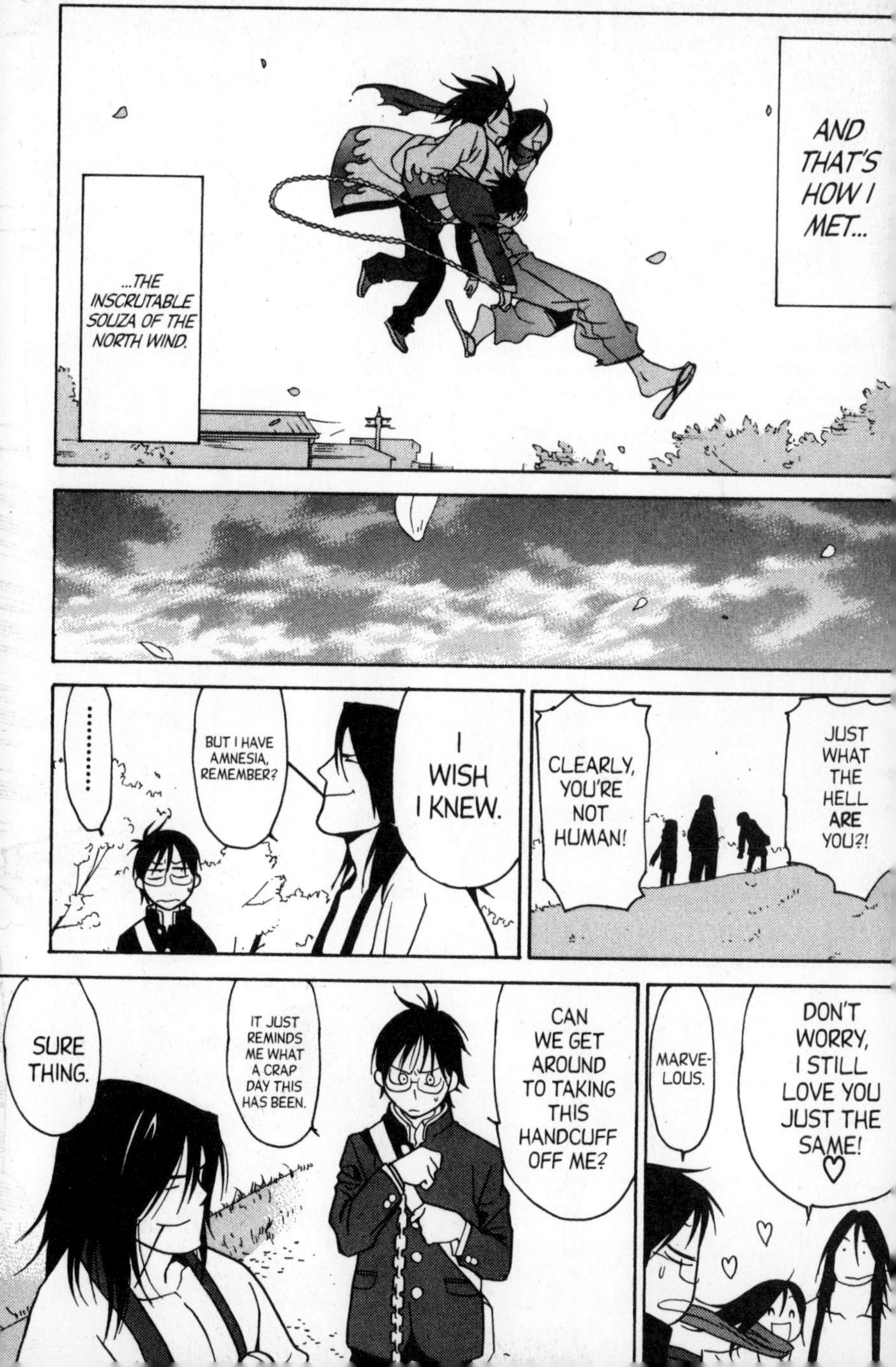
AND THAT'S HOW I MET...
...THE INSCRUTABLE SOUZA OF THE NORTH WIND.
JUST WHAT THE HELL ARE YOU?!
CLEARLY, YOU'RE NOT HUMAN!
I WISH I KNEW.
BUT I HAVE AMNESIA, REMEMBER?
....
DON'T WORRY, I STILL LOVE YOU JUST THE SAME! ♡
MARVE-LOUS.
CAN WE GET AROUND TO TAKING THIS HANDCUFF OFF ME?
IT JUST REMINDS ME WHAT A CRAP DAY THIS HAS BEEN.
SURE THING.

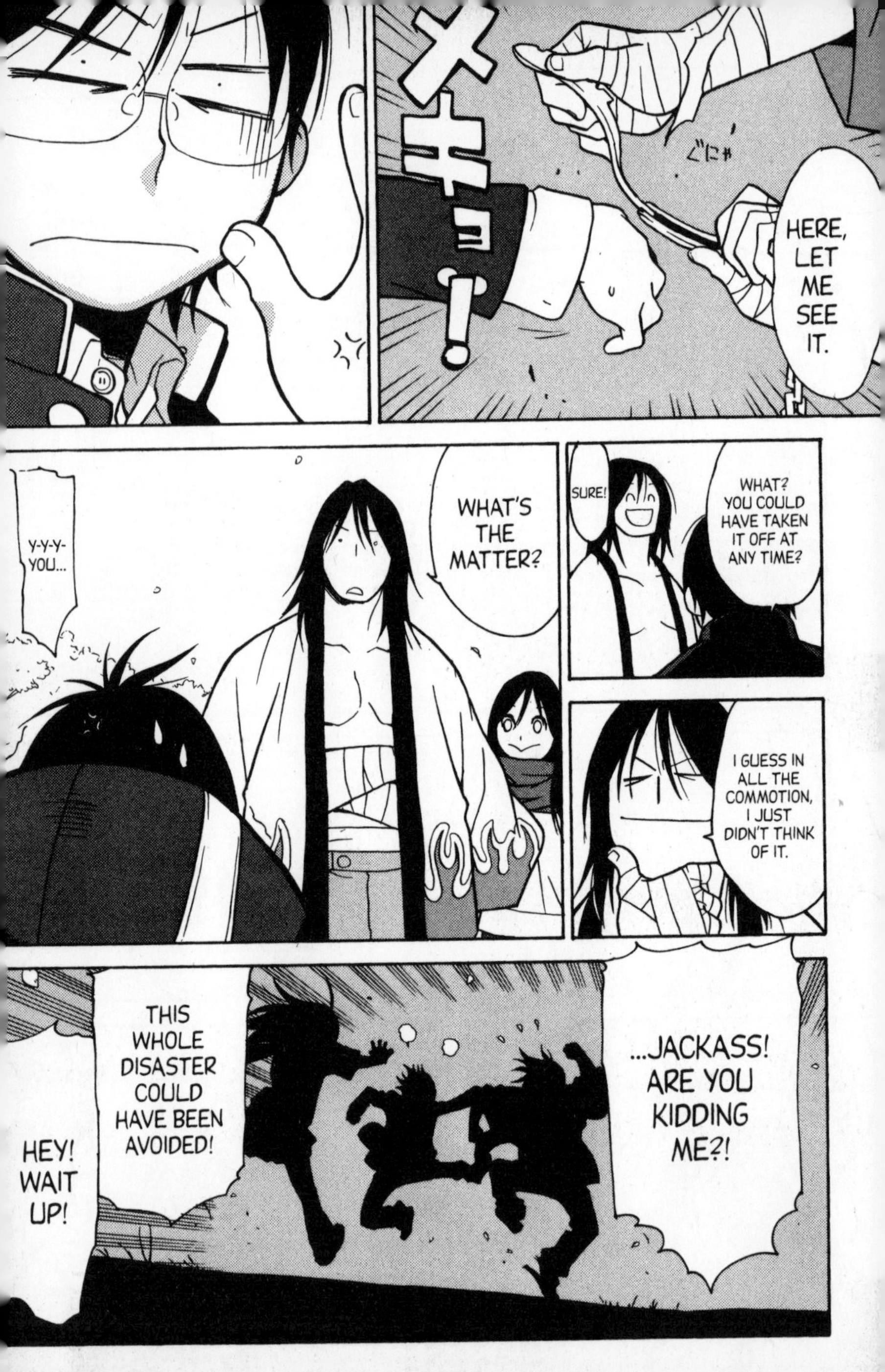

ぐにゃ
HERE, LET ME SEE IT.
メキョ!
WHAT? YOU COULD HAVE TAKEN IT OFF AT ANY TIME?
SURE!
I GUESS IN ALL THE COMMOTION, I JUST DIDN'T THINK OF IT.
WHAT'S THE MATTER?
Y-Y-Y-YOU...
...JACKASS! ARE YOU KIDDING ME?!
THIS WHOLE DISASTER COULD HAVE BEEN AVOIDED!
HEY! WAIT UP!

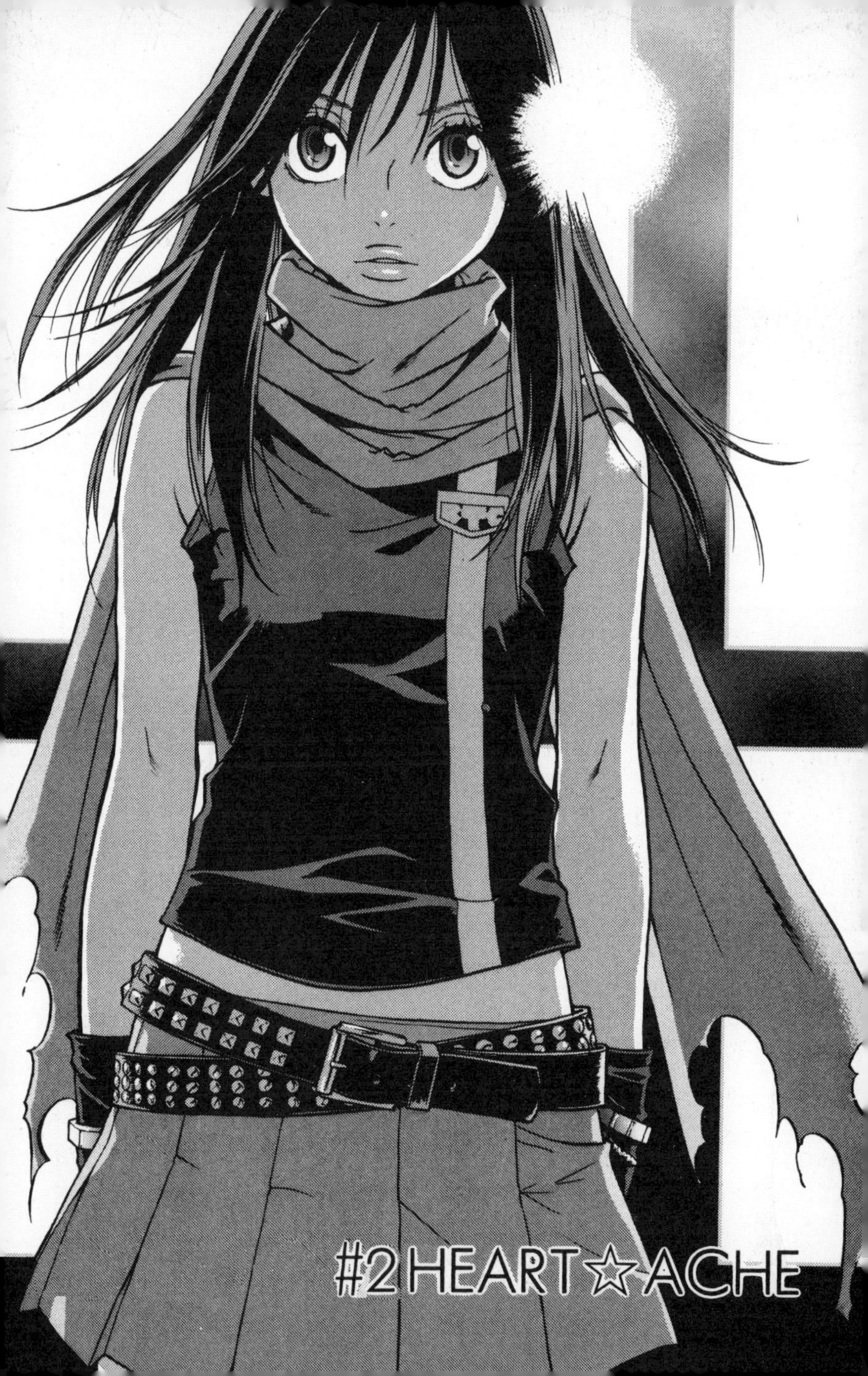
#2 HEART☆ACHE

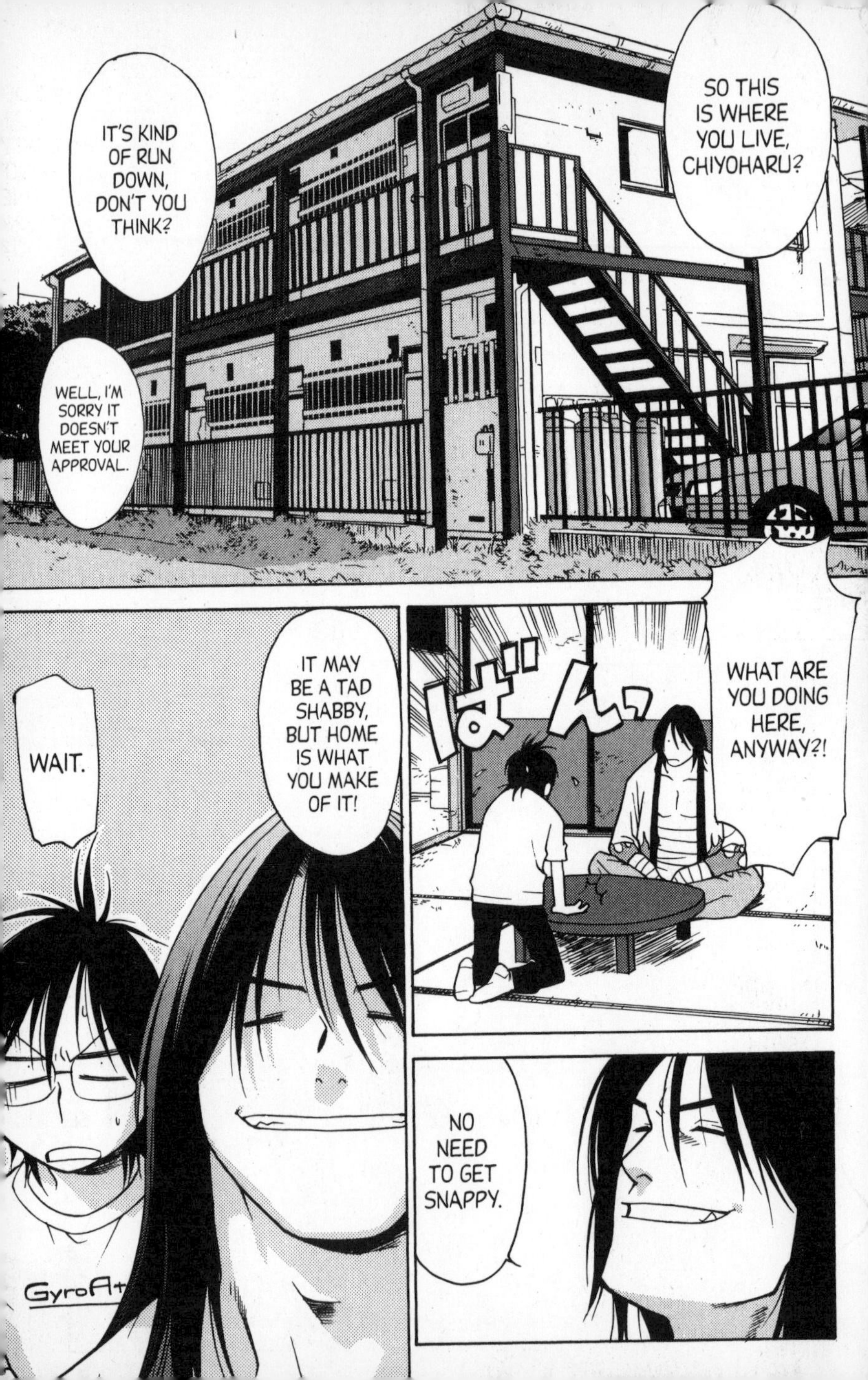
SO THIS IS WHERE YOU LIVE, CHIYOHARU?
IT'S KIND OF RUN DOWN, DON'T YOU THINK?
WELL, I'M SORRY IT DOESN'T MEET YOUR APPROVAL.
ばんっ
WHAT ARE YOU DOING HERE, ANYWAY?!
NO NEED TO GET SNAPPY.
IT MAY BE A TAD SHABBY, BUT HOME IS WHAT YOU MAKE OF IT!
WAIT.

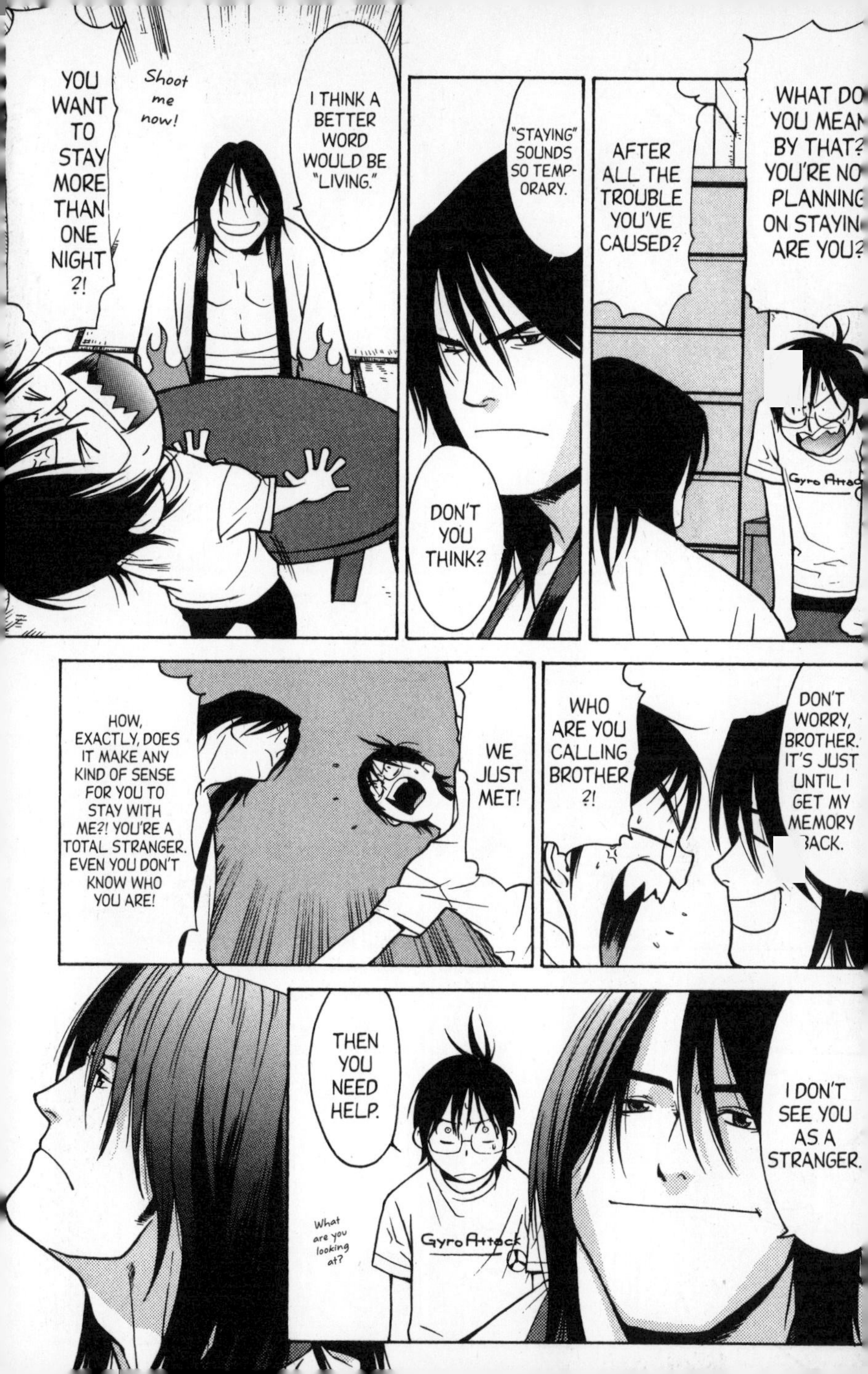
WHAT DO YOU MEAN BY THAT? YOU'RE NO PLANNING ON STAYIN ARE YOU?
AFTER ALL THE TROUBLE YOU'VE CAUSED?
"STAYING" SOUNDS SO TEMPORARY.
DON'T YOU THINK?
I THINK A BETTER WORD WOULD BE "LIVING."
YOU WANT TO STAY MORE THAN ONE NIGHT?!
Shoot me now!
DON'T WORRY, BROTHER. IT'S JUST UNTIL I GET MY MEMORY BACK.
WHO ARE YOU CALLING BROTHER?!
WE JUST MET!
HOW, EXACTLY, DOES IT MAKE ANY KIND OF SENSE FOR YOU TO STAY WITH ME?! YOU'RE A TOTAL STRANGER. EVEN YOU DON'T KNOW WHO YOU ARE!
I DON'T SEE YOU AS A STRANGER.
THEN YOU NEED HELP.
What are you looking at?
Gyro Attack

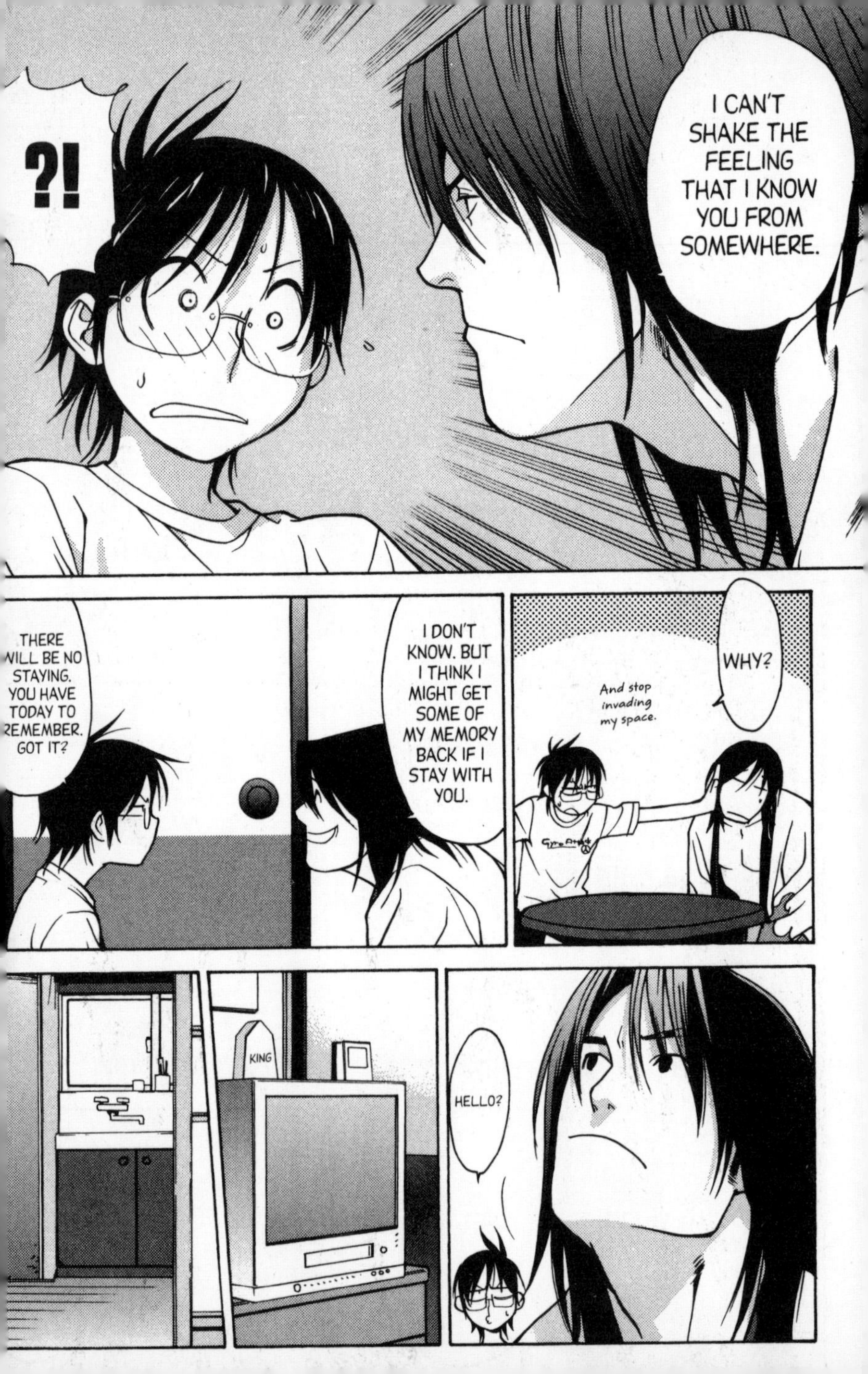
I CAN'T SHAKE THE FEELING THAT I KNOW YOU FROM SOMEWHERE.
?!
WHY?
And stop invading my space.
I DON'T KNOW. BUT I THINK I MIGHT GET SOME OF MY MEMORY BACK IF I STAY WITH YOU.
THERE WILL BE NO STAYING. YOU HAVE TODAY TO REMEMBER. GOT IT?
HELLO?
KING

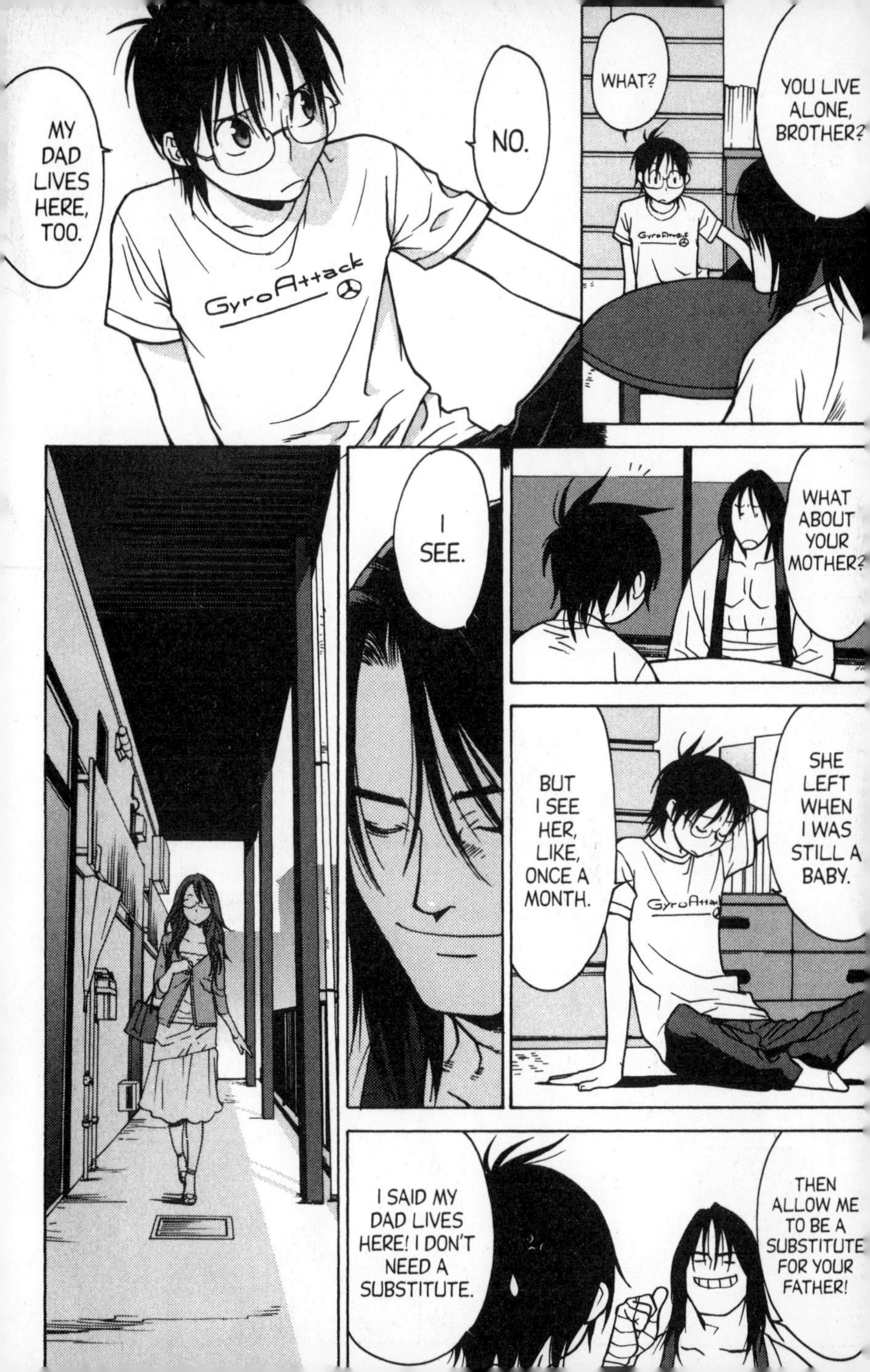
YOU LIVE ALONE, BROTHER?
WHAT?
GyroAttack
NO.
MY DAD LIVES HERE, TOO.
GyroAttack
WHAT ABOUT YOUR MOTHER?
SHE LEFT WHEN I WAS STILL A BABY.
BUT I SEE HER, LIKE, ONCE A MONTH.
GyroAttack
I SEE.
THEN ALLOW ME TO BE A SUBSTITUTE FOR YOUR FATHER!
I SAID MY DAD LIVES HERE! I DON'T NEED A SUBSTITUTE.

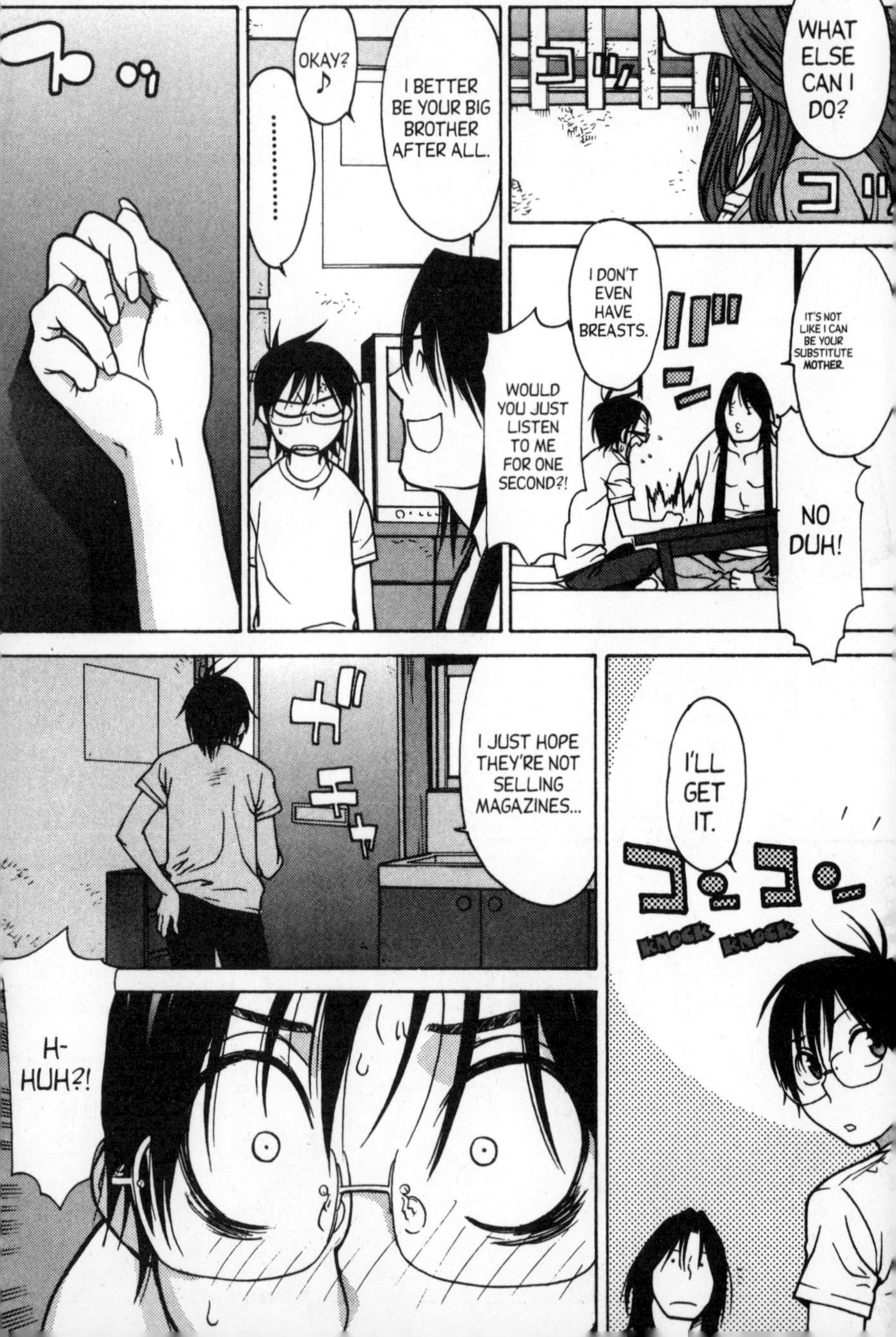
WHAT ELSE CAN I DO?
コッ
コッ
IT'S NOT LIKE I CAN BE YOUR SUBSTITUTE MOTHER.
I DON'T EVEN HAVE BREASTS.
NO DUH!
WOULD YOU JUST LISTEN TO ME FOR ONE SECOND?!
I BETTER BE YOUR BIG BROTHER AFTER ALL.
OKAY? ♪
......
I'LL GET IT.
KNOCK KNOCK
I JUST HOPE THEY'RE NOT SELLING MAGAZINES...
H-HUH?!

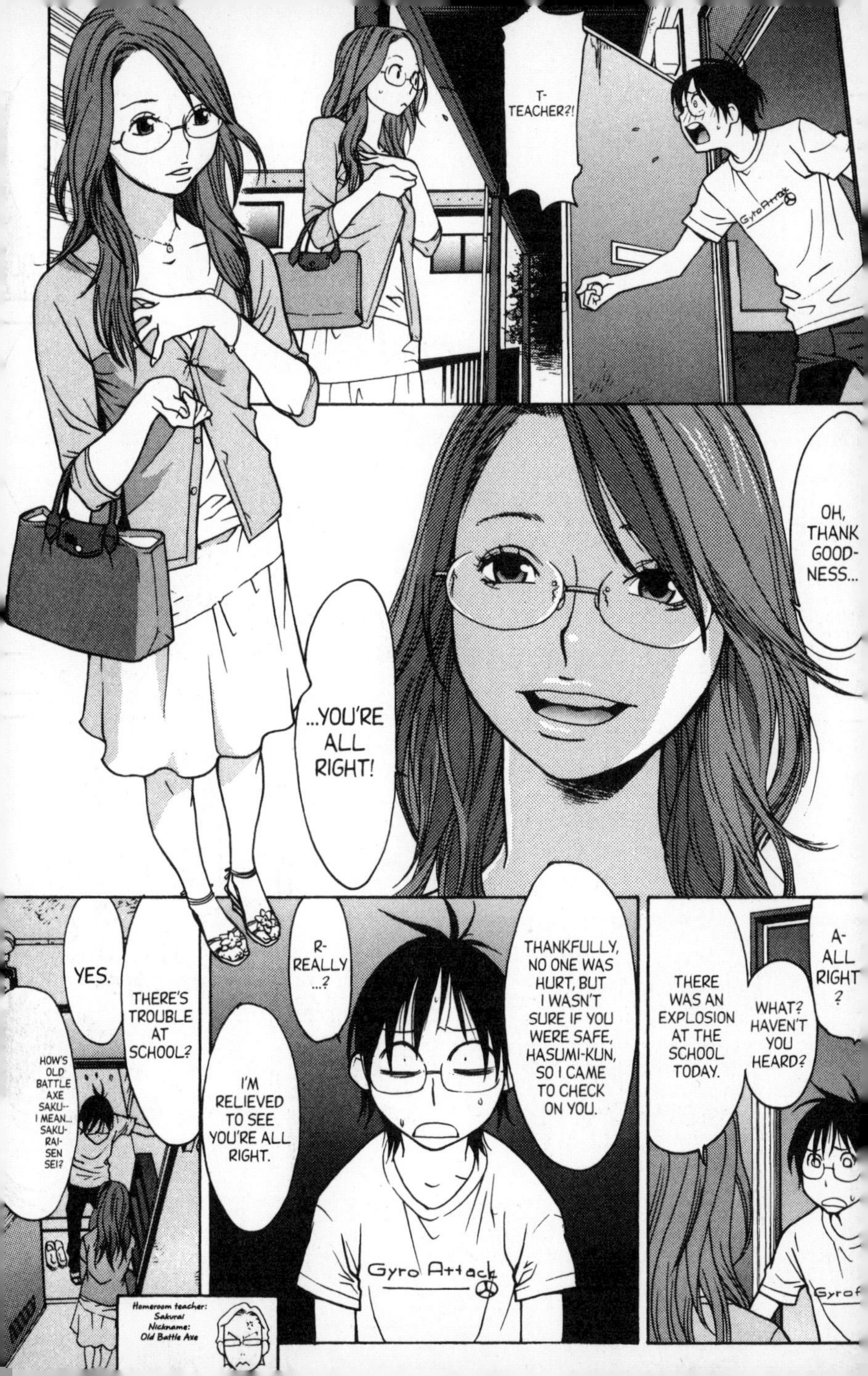
T-
TEACHER?!
OH, THANK GOODNESS...
...YOU'RE ALL RIGHT!
A- ALL RIGHT?
WHAT? HAVEN'T YOU HEARD?
THERE WAS AN EXPLOSION AT THE SCHOOL TODAY.
THANKFULLY, NO ONE WAS HURT, BUT I WASN'T SURE IF YOU WERE SAFE, HASUMI-KUN, SO I CAME TO CHECK ON YOU.
R- REALLY ...?
I'M RELIEVED TO SEE YOU'RE ALL RIGHT.
THERE'S TROUBLE AT SCHOOL?
YES.
HOW'S OLD BATTLE AXE SAKU-- I MEAN... SAKURAI-SEN SEI?
Homeroom teacher: Sakurai Nickname: Old Battle Axe
Gyro Attack

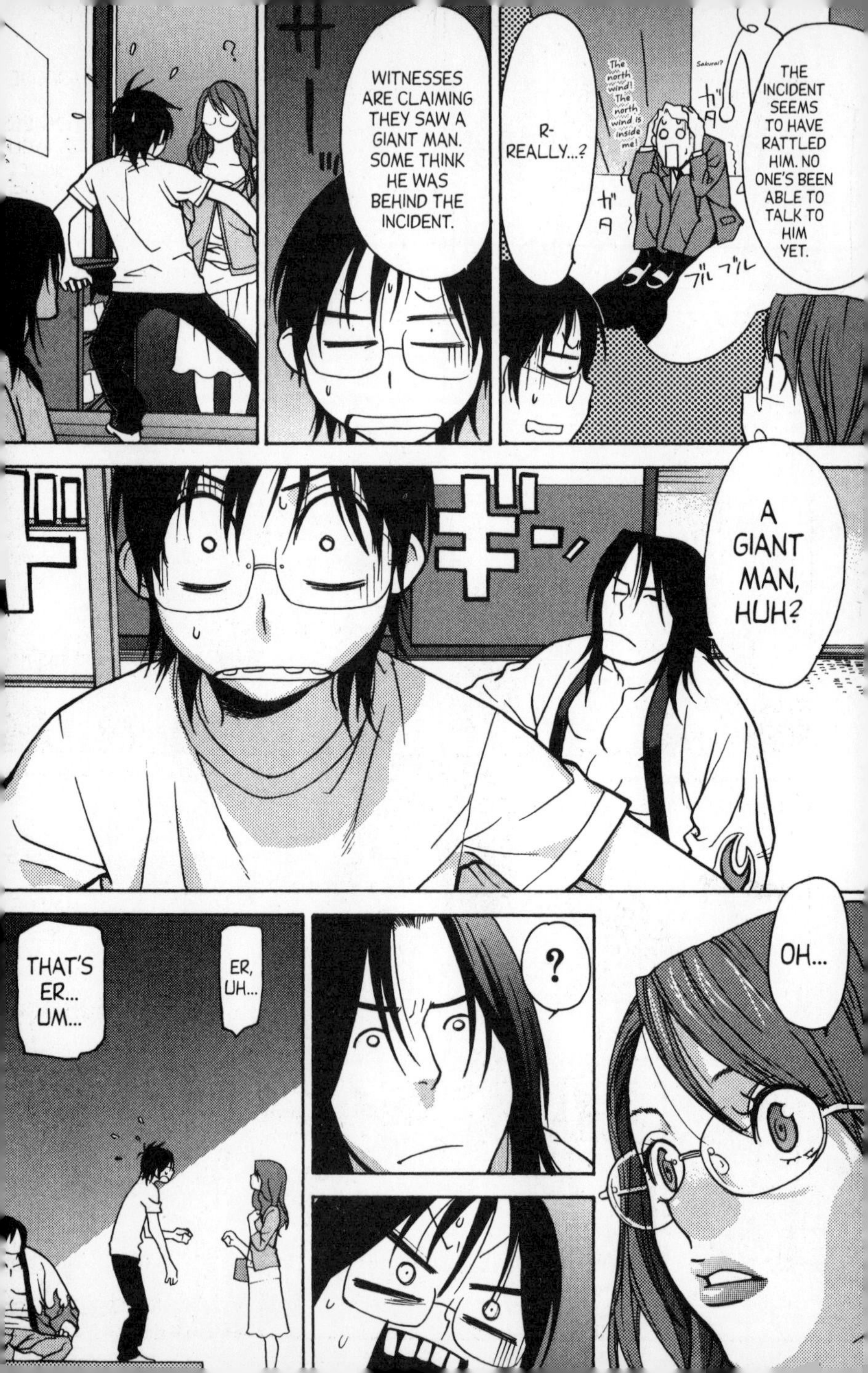
Sakurai?
THE INCIDENT SEEMS TO HAVE RATTLED HIM. NO ONE'S BEEN ABLE TO TALK TO HIM YET.
The north wind! The north wind is inside me!
ガタ
ブルブル
R- REALLY...?
WITNESSES ARE CLAIMING THEY SAW A GIANT MAN. SOME THINK HE WAS BEHIND THE INCIDENT.
A GIANT MAN, HUH?
OH...
?
ER, UH...
THAT'S ER... UM...

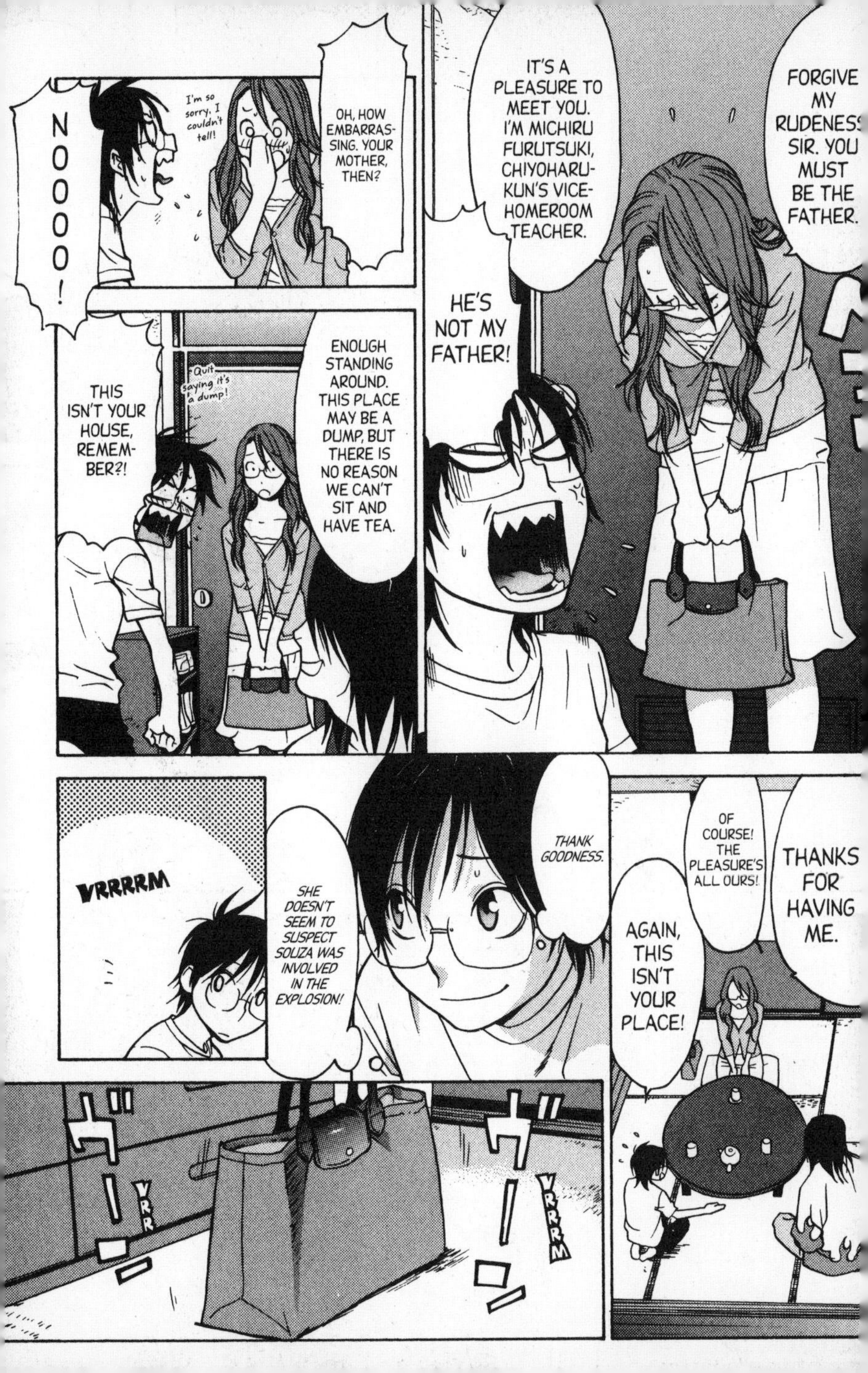
FORGIVE MY RUDENESS SIR. YOU MUST BE THE FATHER.
IT'S A PLEASURE TO MEET YOU. I'M MICHIRU FURUTSUKI, CHIYOHARU-KUN'S VICE-HOMEROOM TEACHER.
HE'S NOT MY FATHER!
OH, HOW EMBARRASSING. YOUR MOTHER, THEN?
I'm so sorry. I couldn't tell!
NOOOO!
ENOUGH STANDING AROUND. THIS PLACE MAY BE A DUMP, BUT THERE IS NO REASON WE CAN'T SIT AND HAVE TEA.
Quit saying it's a dump!
THIS ISN'T YOUR HOUSE, REMEMBER?!
THANKS FOR HAVING ME.
OF COURSE! THE PLEASURE'S ALL OURS!
AGAIN, THIS ISN'T YOUR PLACE!
THANK GOODNESS.
SHE DOESN'T SEEM TO SUSPECT SOUZA WAS INVOLVED IN THE EXPLOSION!
VRRRRM
VRRRRM
VRR

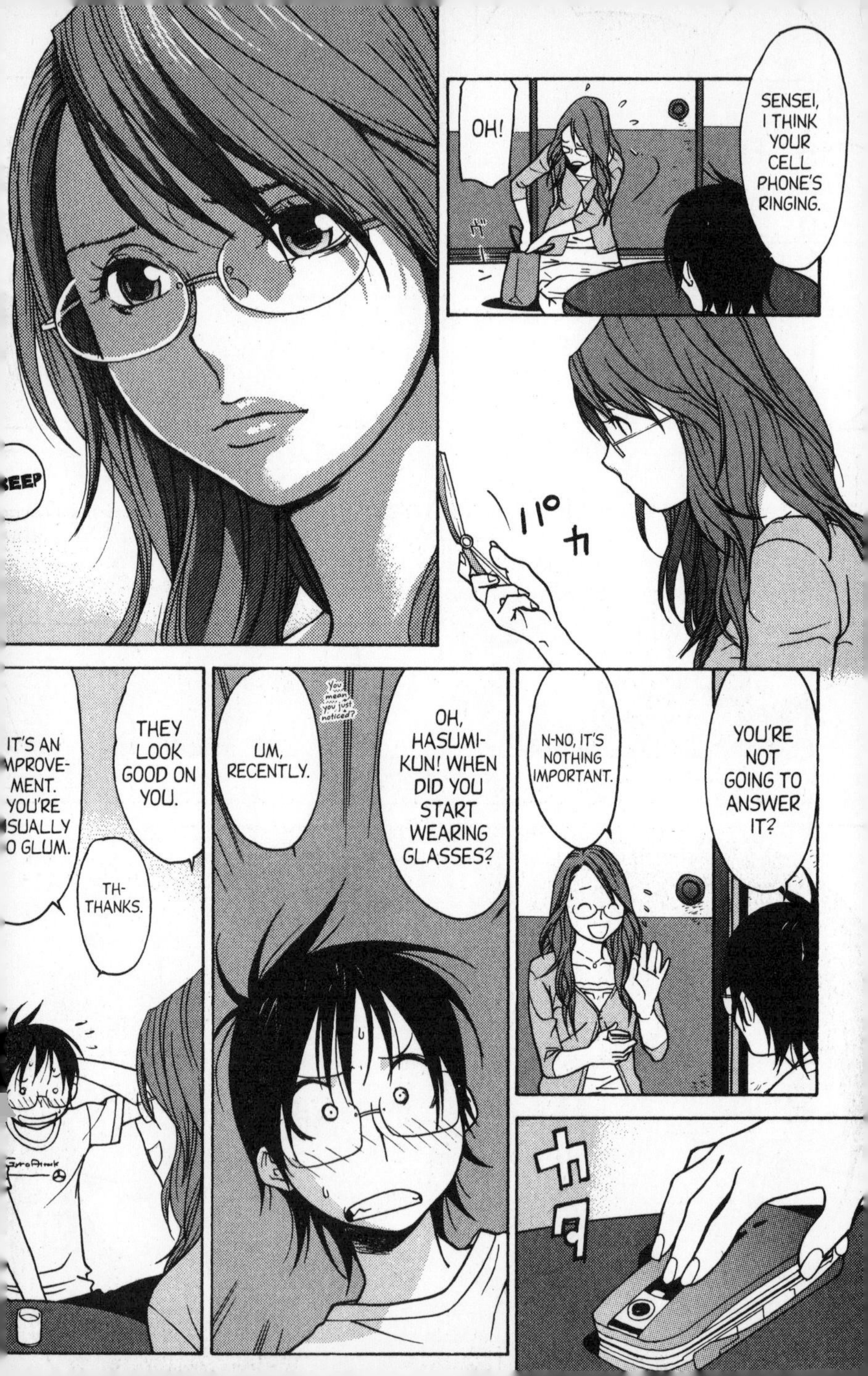
SENSEI, I THINK YOUR CELL PHONE'S RINGING.
OH!
パカ
YOU'RE NOT GOING TO ANSWER IT?
N-NO, IT'S NOTHING IMPORTANT.
カタ
OH, HASUMI-KUN! WHEN DID YOU START WEARING GLASSES?
You mean you just noticed?
UM, RECENTLY.
THEY LOOK GOOD ON YOU.
IT'S AN MPROVE-MENT. YOU'RE SUALLY O GLUM.
TH-THANKS.

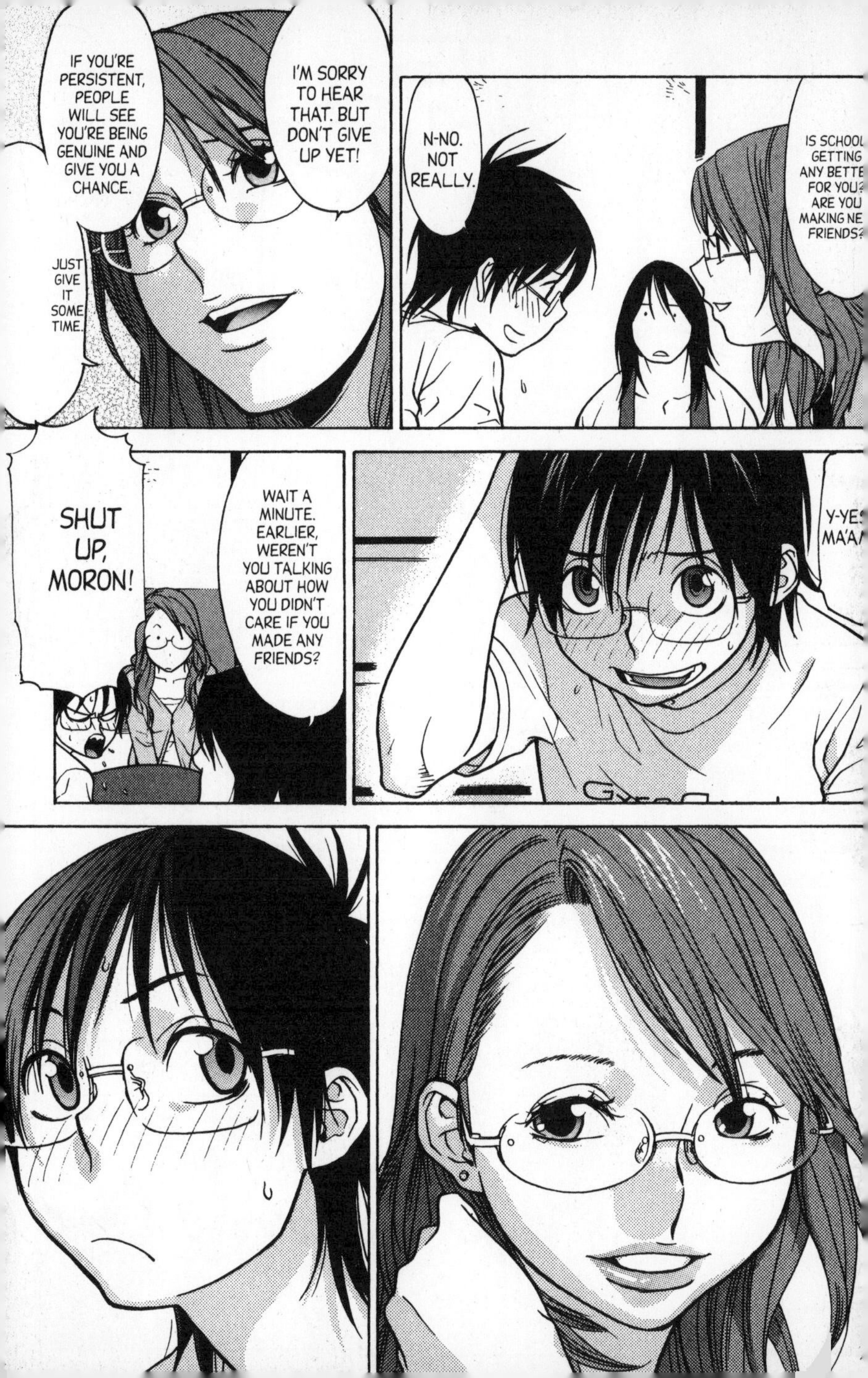
IS SCHOOL GETTING ANY BETTE FOR YOU? ARE YOU MAKING NE FRIENDS?
N-NO. NOT REALLY.
I'M SORRY TO HEAR THAT. BUT DON'T GIVE UP YET!
IF YOU'RE PERSISTENT, PEOPLE WILL SEE YOU'RE BEING GENUINE AND GIVE YOU A CHANCE.
JUST GIVE IT SOME TIME.
Y-YES MA'A
WAIT A MINUTE. EARLIER, WEREN'T YOU TALKING ABOUT HOW YOU DIDN'T CARE IF YOU MADE ANY FRIENDS?
SHUT UP, MORON!

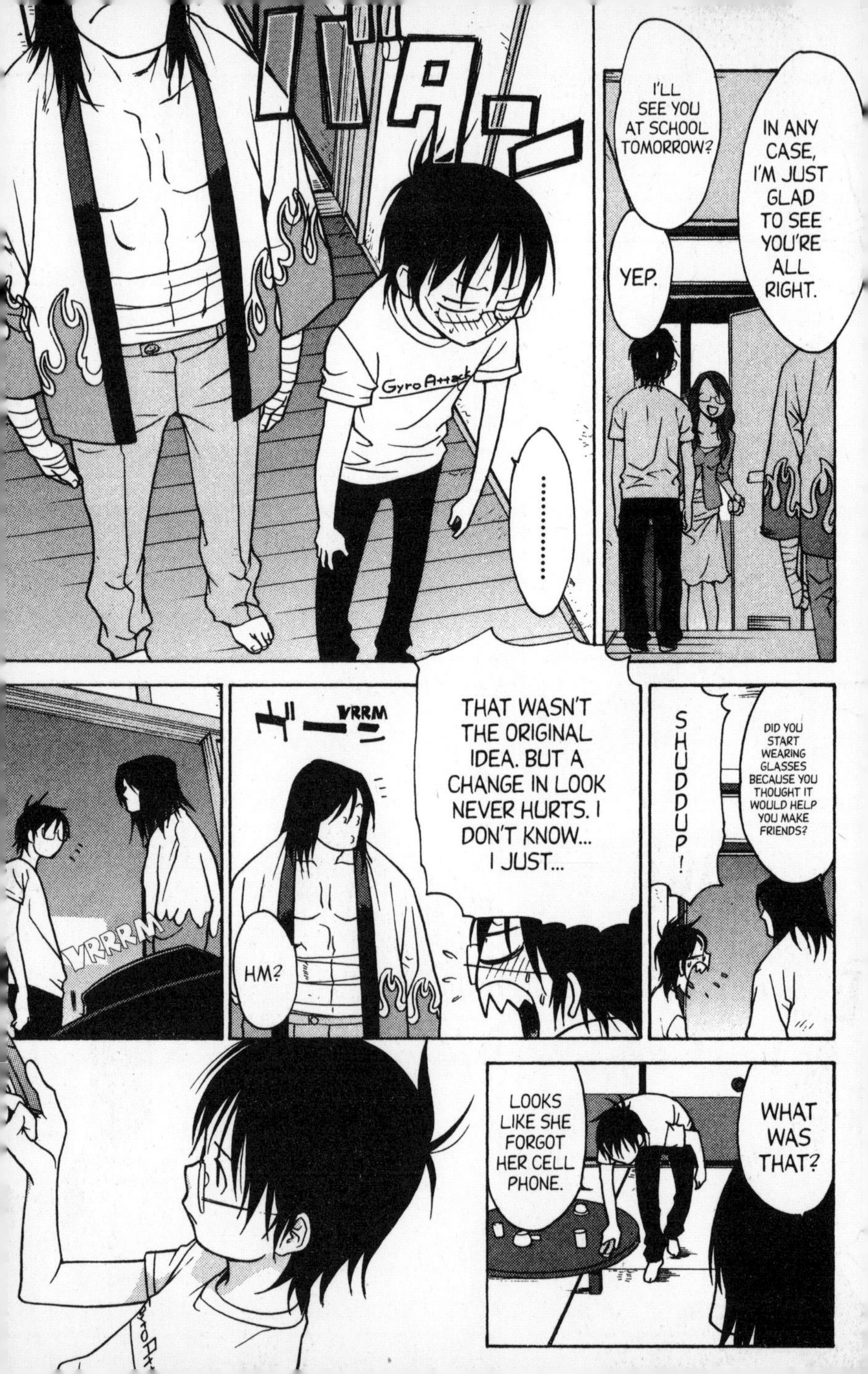
IN ANY CASE, I'M JUST GLAD TO SEE YOU'RE ALL RIGHT.
I'LL SEE YOU AT SCHOOL TOMORROW?
YEP.
……………
DID YOU START WEARING GLASSES BECAUSE YOU THOUGHT IT WOULD HELP YOU MAKE FRIENDS?
SHUDDUP!
THAT WASN'T THE ORIGINAL IDEA. BUT A CHANGE IN LOOK NEVER HURTS. I DON'T KNOW... I JUST...
VRRM
HM?
VRRRM
WHAT WAS THAT?
LOOKS LIKE SHE FORGOT HER CELL PHONE.

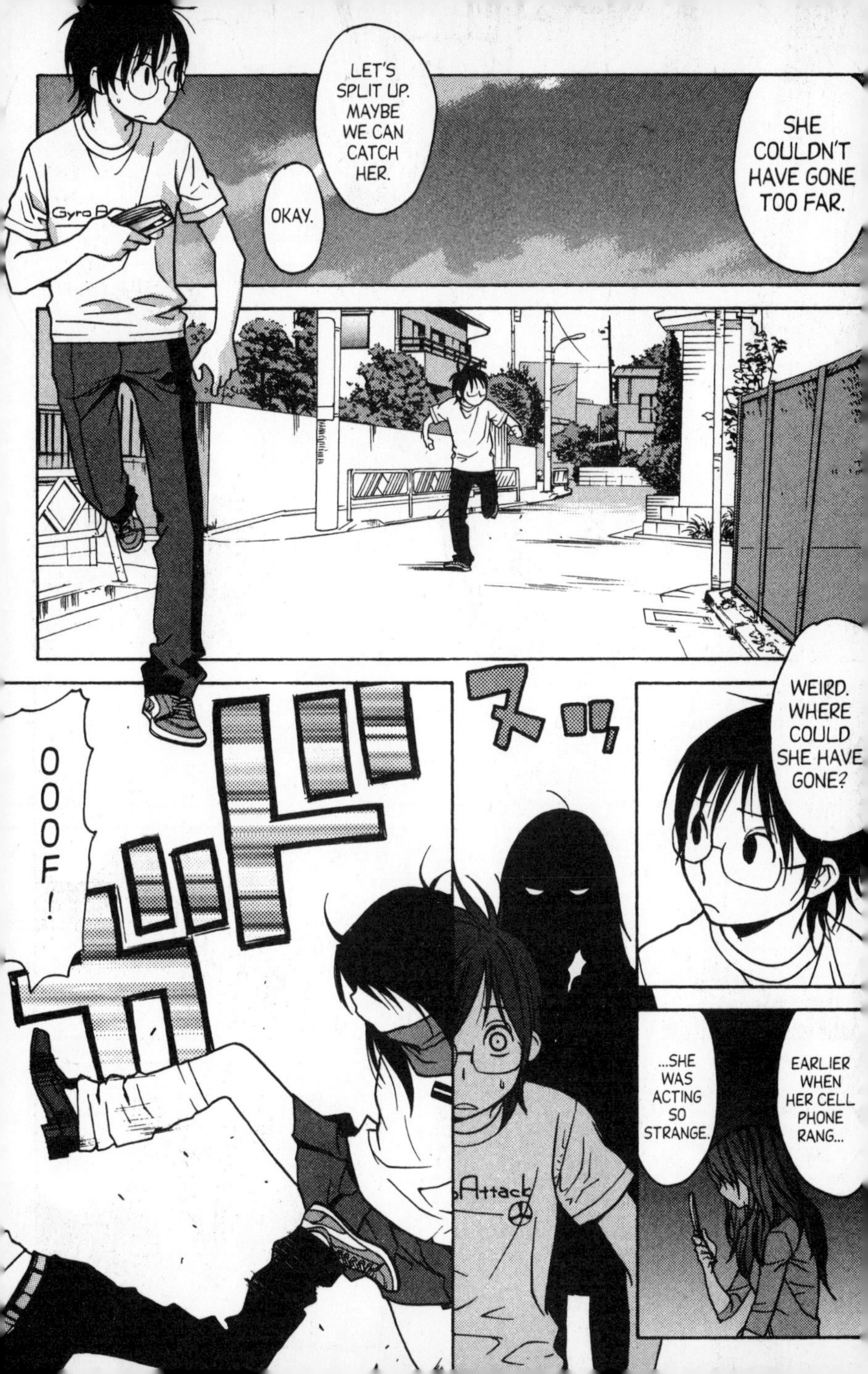
SHE COULDN'T HAVE GONE TOO FAR.
LET'S SPLIT UP. MAYBE WE CAN CATCH HER.
OKAY.
WEIRD. WHERE COULD SHE HAVE GONE?
EARLIER WHEN HER CELL PHONE RANG...
...SHE WAS ACTING SO STRANGE.
ヌッ
OOOF!

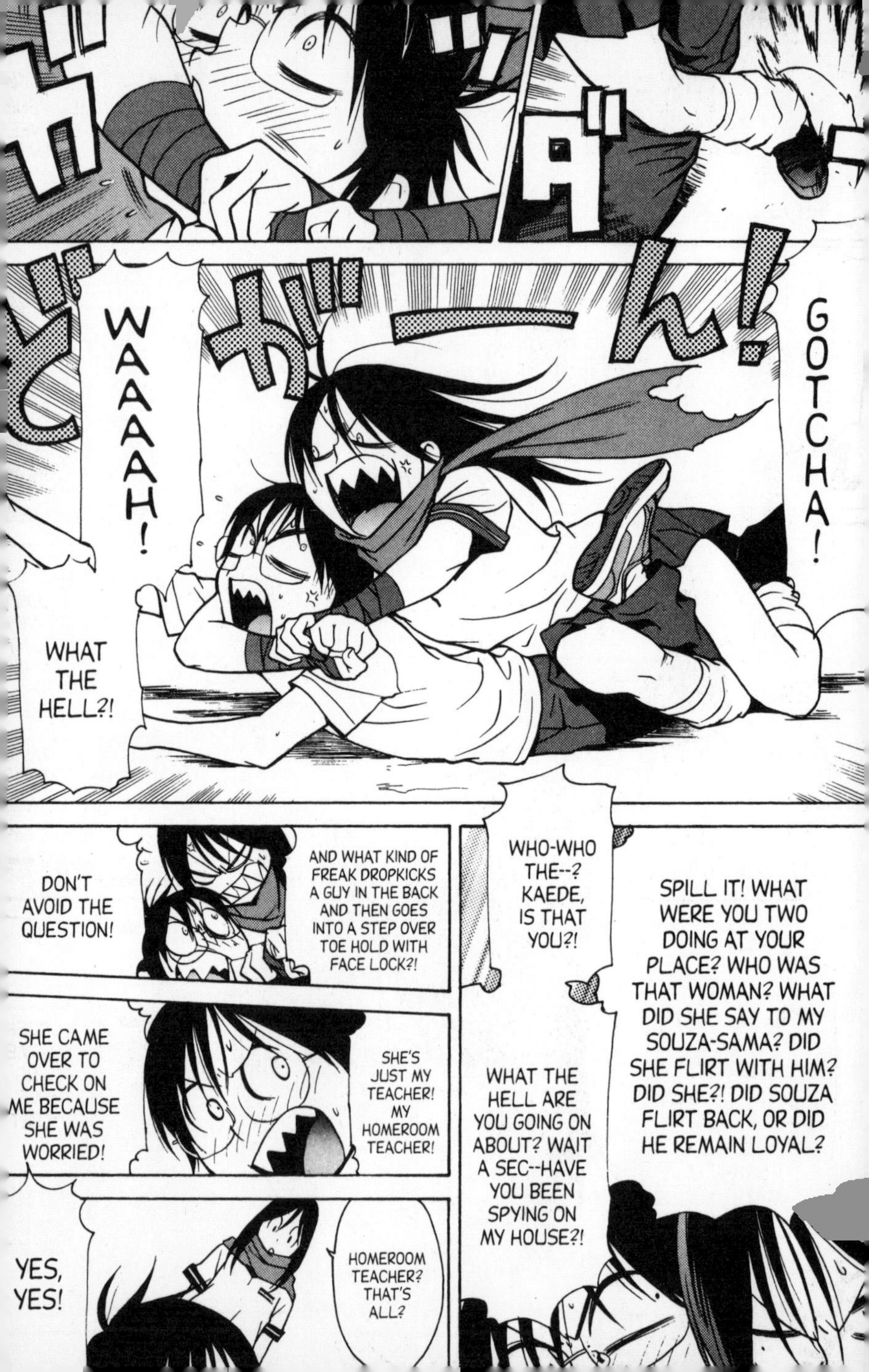
GOTCHA!
WAAAAH!
WHAT THE HELL?!
WHO-WHO THE--? KAEDE, IS THAT YOU?!
SPILL IT! WHAT WERE YOU TWO DOING AT YOUR PLACE? WHO WAS THAT WOMAN? WHAT DID SHE SAY TO MY SOUZA-SAMA? DID SHE FLIRT WITH HIM? DID SHE?! DID SOUZA FLIRT BACK, OR DID HE REMAIN LOYAL?
WHAT THE HELL ARE YOU GOING ON ABOUT? WAIT A SEC--HAVE YOU BEEN SPYING ON MY HOUSE?!
AND WHAT KIND OF FREAK DROPKICKS A GUY IN THE BACK AND THEN GOES INTO A STEP OVER TOE HOLD WITH FACE LOCK?!
DON'T AVOID THE QUESTION!
SHE'S JUST MY TEACHER! MY HOMEROOM TEACHER!
SHE CAME OVER TO CHECK ON ME BECAUSE SHE WAS WORRIED!
HOMEROOM TEACHER? THAT'S ALL?
YES, YES!

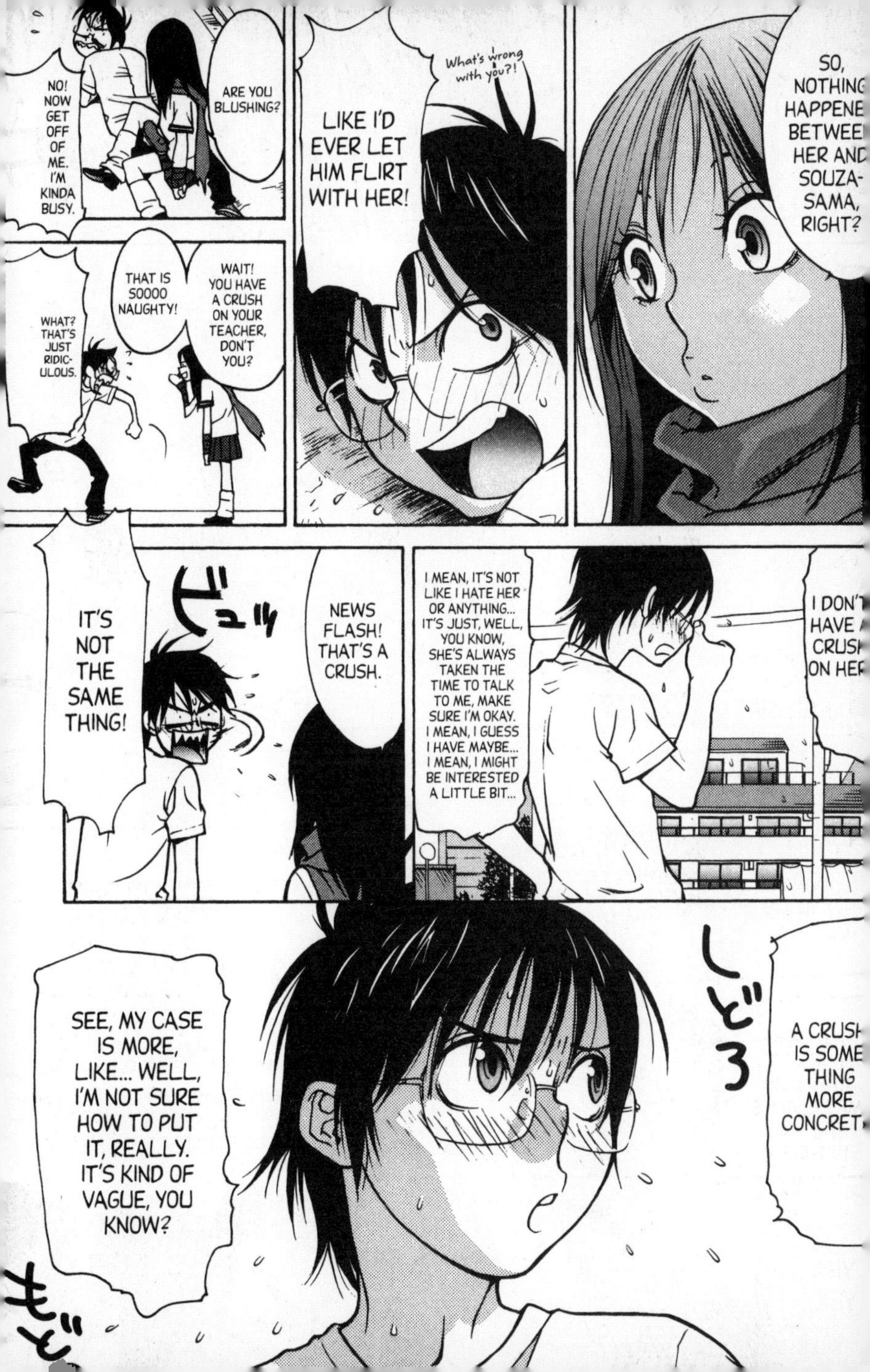
SO, NOTHING HAPPENE BETWEE HER AND SOUZA-SAMA, RIGHT?
LIKE I'D EVER LET HIM FLIRT WITH HER!
What's wrong with you?!
ARE YOU BLUSHING?
NO! NOW GET OFF OF ME. I'M KINDA BUSY.
WAIT! YOU HAVE A CRUSH ON YOUR TEACHER, DON'T YOU?
THAT IS SOOOO NAUGHTY!
WHAT? THAT'S JUST RIDIC-ULOUS.
I DON'T HAVE A CRUSH ON HER
I MEAN, IT'S NOT LIKE I HATE HER OR ANYTHING... IT'S JUST, WELL, YOU KNOW, SHE'S ALWAYS TAKEN THE TIME TO TALK TO ME, MAKE SURE I'M OKAY. I MEAN, I GUESS I HAVE MAYBE... I MEAN, I MIGHT BE INTERESTED A LITTLE BIT...
NEWS FLASH! THAT'S A CRUSH.
ビュッ
IT'S NOT THE SAME THING!
A CRUSH IS SOME THING MORE CONCRET
しどろ
SEE, MY CASE IS MORE, LIKE... WELL, I'M NOT SURE HOW TO PUT IT, REALLY. IT'S KIND OF VAGUE, YOU KNOW?
もど

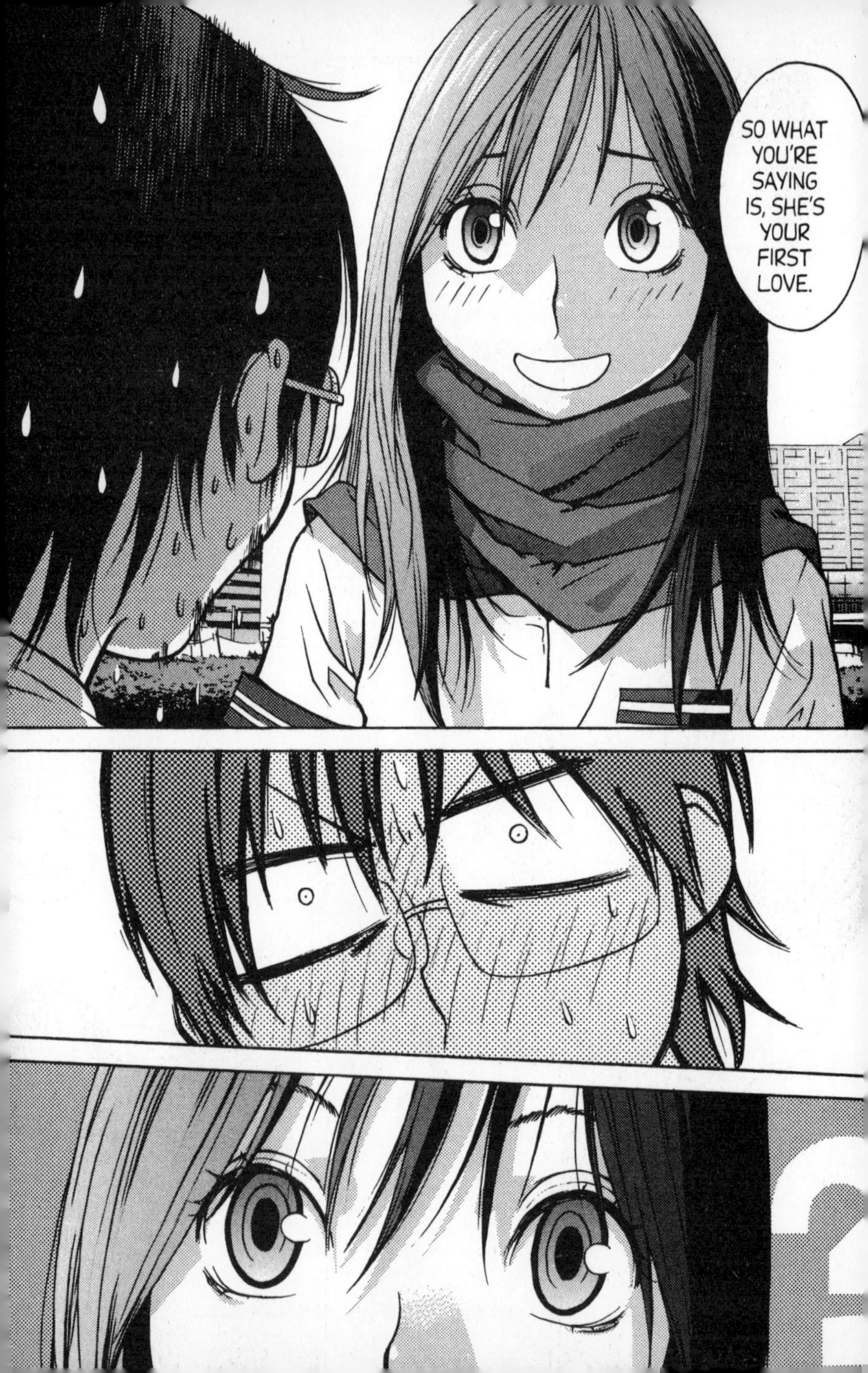
SO WHAT YOU'RE SAYING IS, SHE'S YOUR FIRST LOVE.

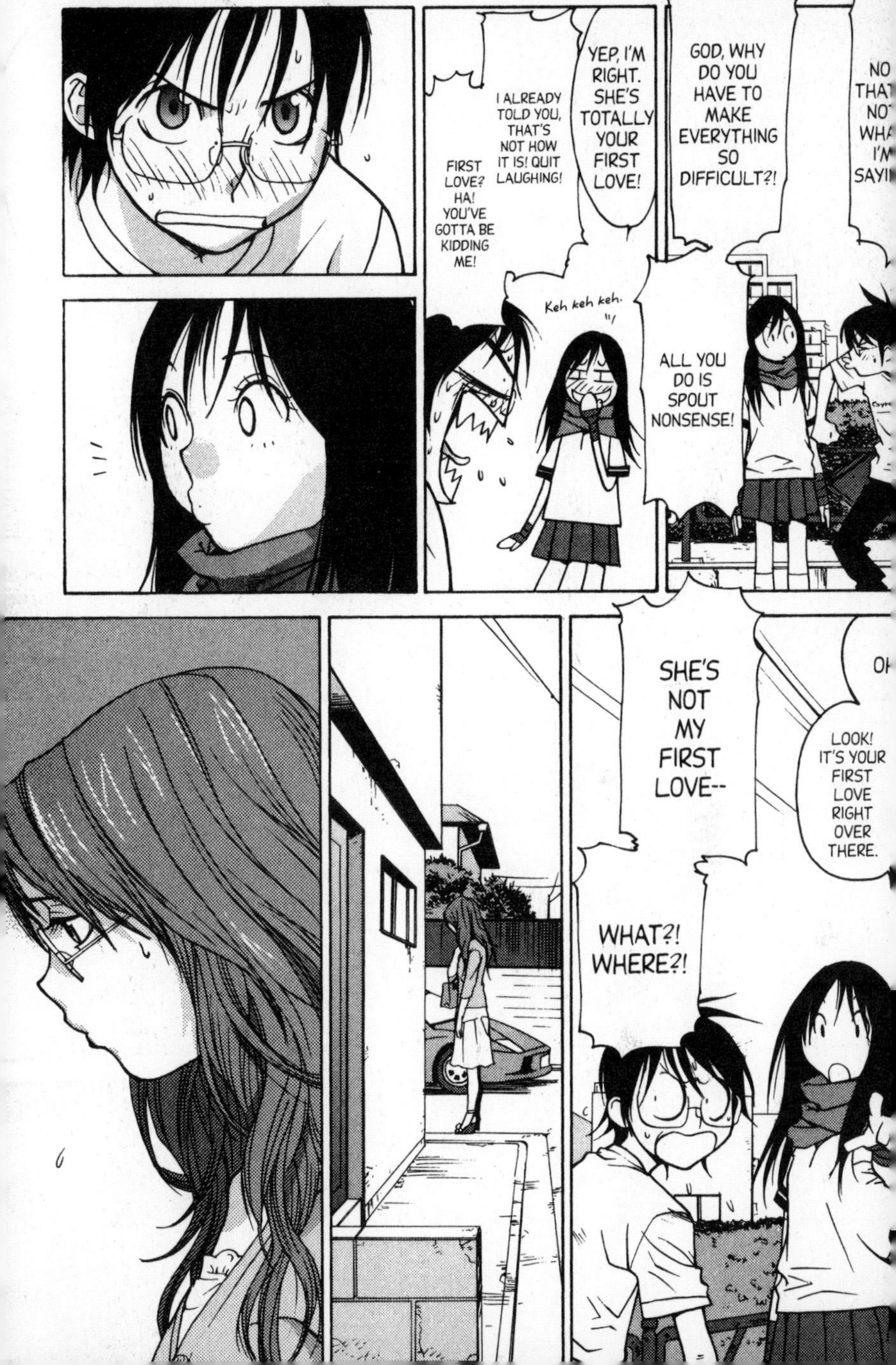
NO THAT NOT WHA I'M SAYI
GOD, WHY DO YOU HAVE TO MAKE EVERYTHING SO DIFFICULT?!
ALL YOU DO IS SPOUT NONSENSE!
YEP, I'M RIGHT. SHE'S TOTALLY YOUR FIRST LOVE!
I ALREADY TOLD YOU, THAT'S NOT HOW IT IS! QUIT LAUGHING!
FIRST LOVE? HA! YOU'VE GOTTA BE KIDDING ME!
Keh keh keh.
LOOK! IT'S YOUR FIRST LOVE RIGHT OVER THERE.
SHE'S NOT MY FIRST LOVE--
WHAT?! WHERE?!

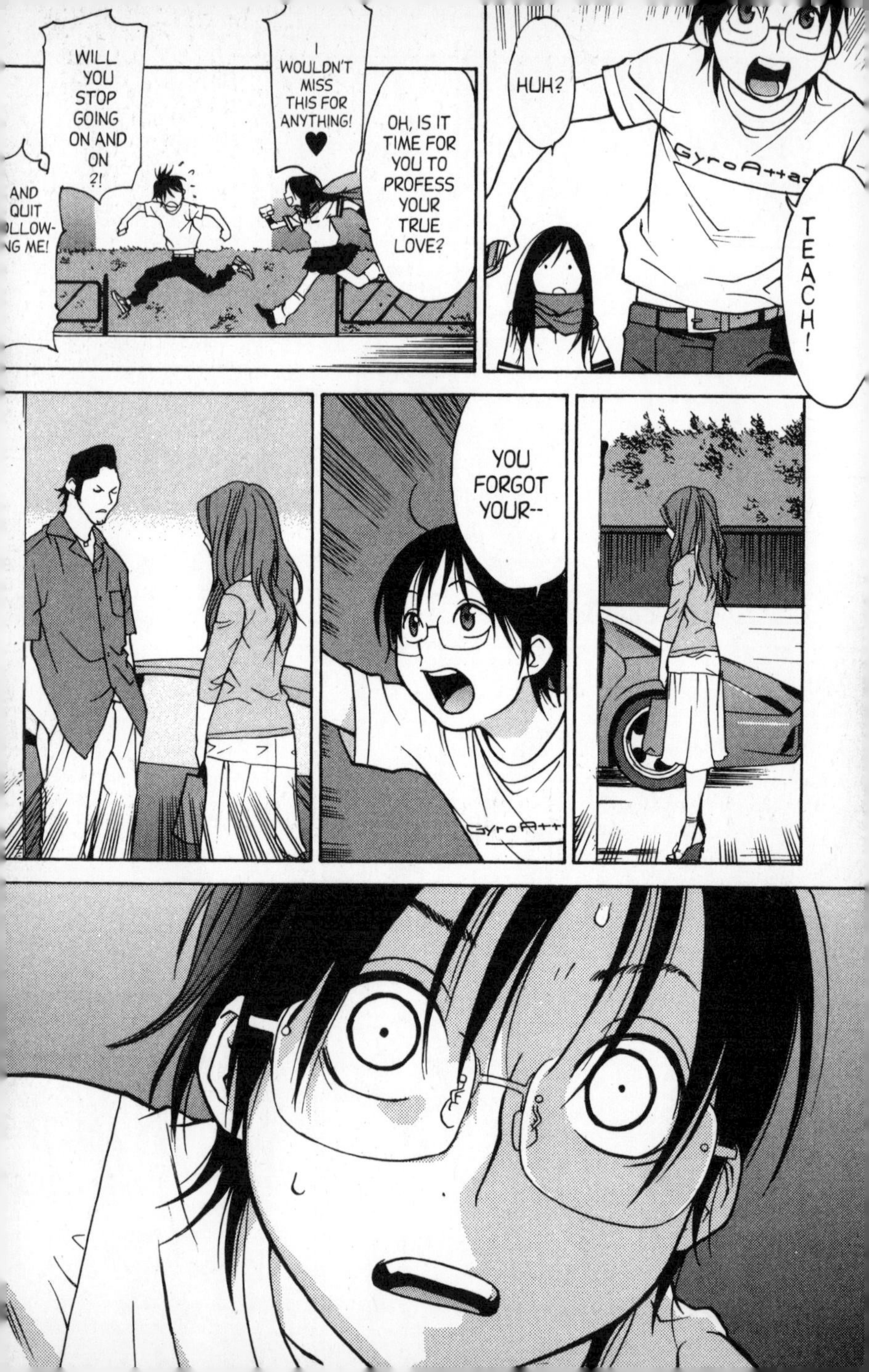
TEACH!
HUH?
OH, IS IT TIME FOR YOU TO PROFESS YOUR TRUE LOVE?
I WOULDN'T MISS THIS FOR ANYTHING! ♥
WILL YOU STOP GOING ON AND ON ?!
AND QUIT OLLOW- NG ME!
YOU FORGOT YOUR--

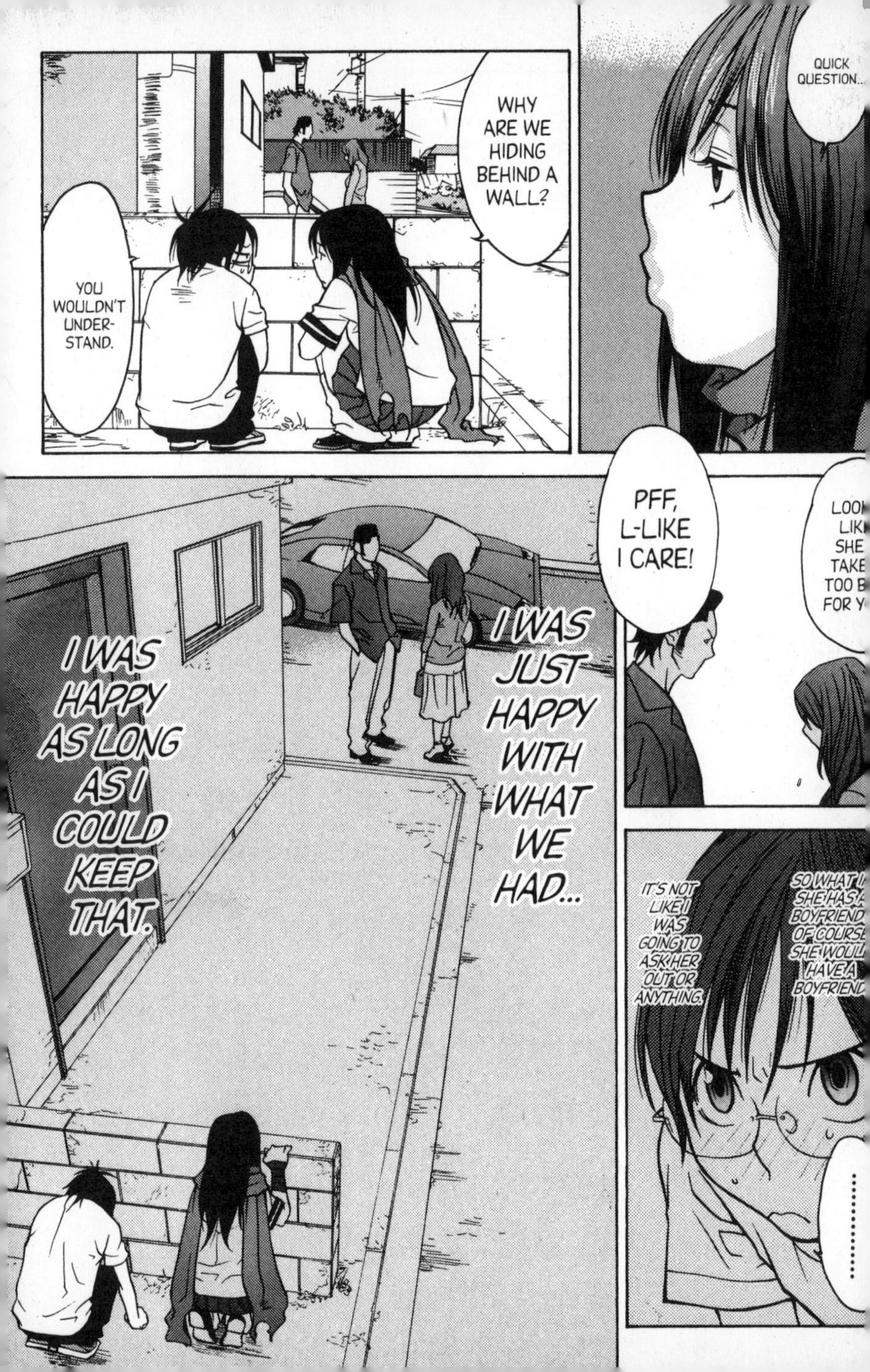
QUICK QUESTION...
WHY ARE WE HIDING BEHIND A WALL?
YOU WOULDN'T UNDER-STAND.
LOO LIK SHE TAKE TOO B FOR Y
PFF, L-LIKE I CARE!
SO WHAT I SHE HAS A BOYFRIEND OF COURSE SHE WOUL HAVE A BOYFRIEND
IT'S NOT LIKE I WAS GOING TO ASK HER OUT OR ANYTHING.
......
I WAS JUST HAPPY WITH WHAT WE HAD...
I WAS HAPPY AS LONG AS I COULD KEEP THAT.

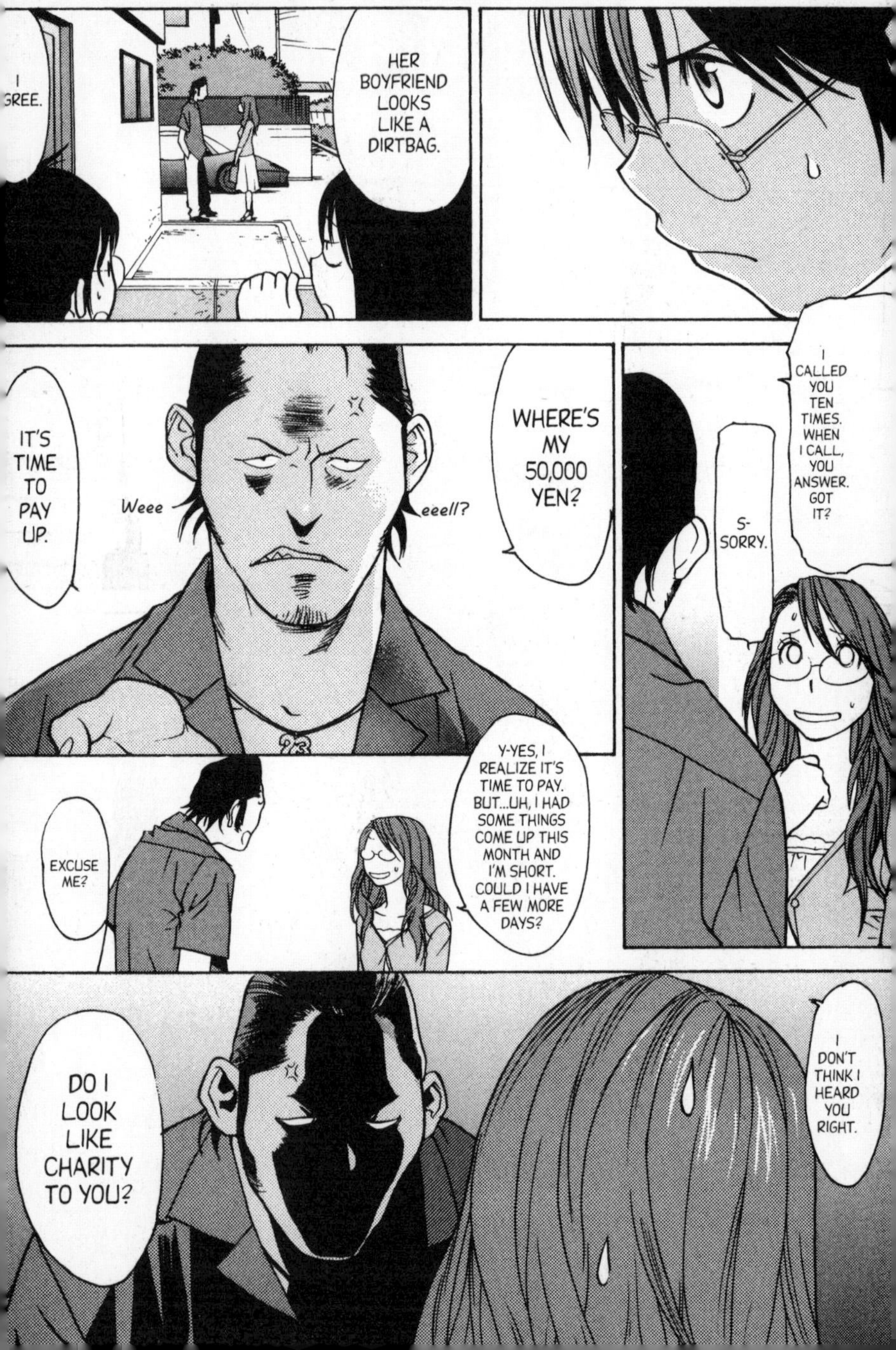
HER BOYFRIEND LOOKS LIKE A DIRTBAG.
I GREE.
I CALLED YOU TEN TIMES. WHEN I CALL, YOU ANSWER. GOT IT?
S-SORRY.
WHERE'S MY 50,000 YEN?
Weee eeell?
IT'S TIME TO PAY UP.
Y-YES, I REALIZE IT'S TIME TO PAY. BUT...UH, I HAD SOME THINGS COME UP THIS MONTH AND I'M SHORT. COULD I HAVE A FEW MORE DAYS?
EXCUSE ME?
I DON'T THINK I HEARD YOU RIGHT.
DO I LOOK LIKE CHARITY TO YOU?

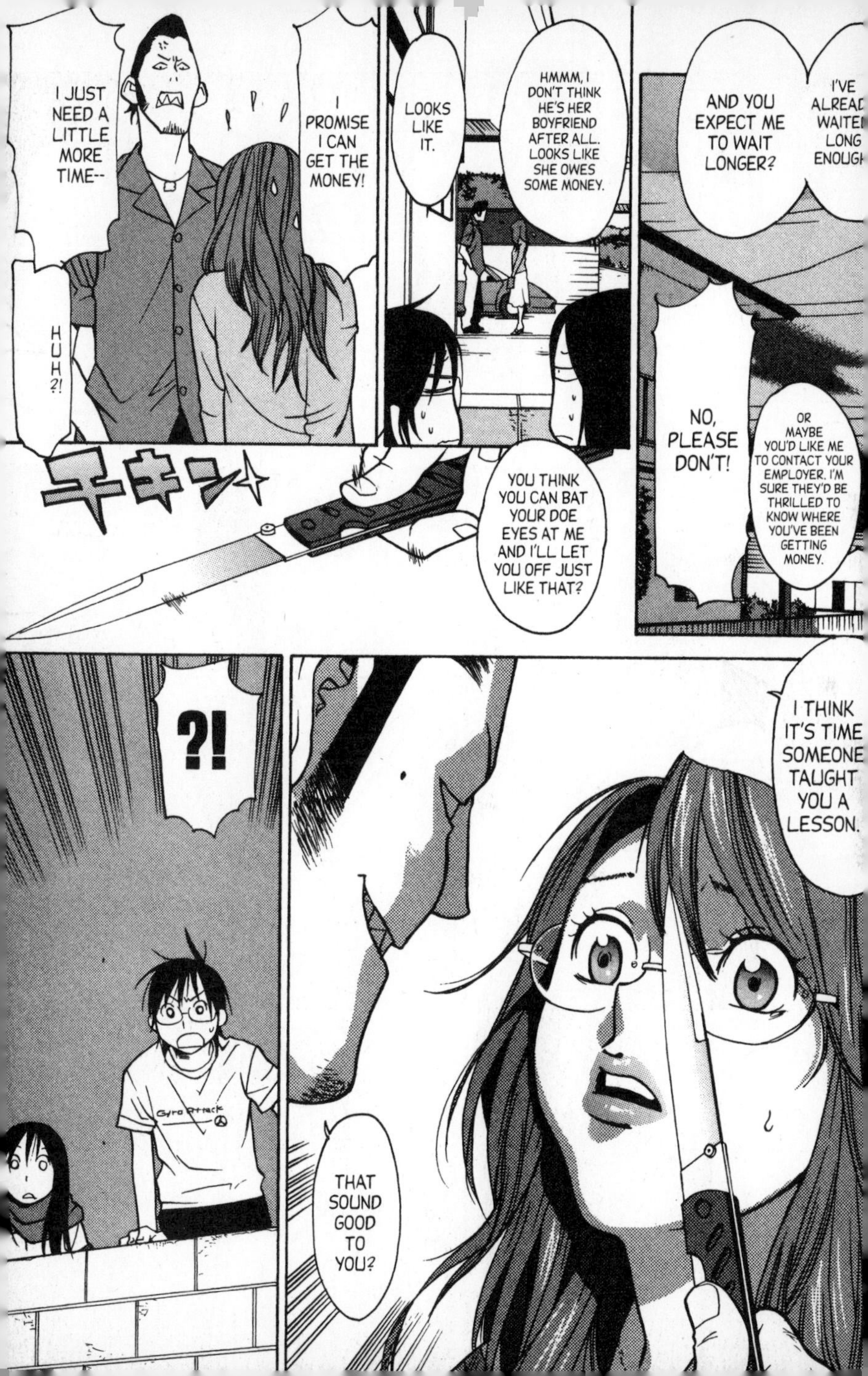
I'VE ALREAD WAITE LONG ENOUGH
AND YOU EXPECT ME TO WAIT LONGER?
OR MAYBE YOU'D LIKE ME TO CONTACT YOUR EMPLOYER. I'M SURE THEY'D BE THRILLED TO KNOW WHERE YOU'VE BEEN GETTING MONEY.
NO, PLEASE DON'T!
HMMM, I DON'T THINK HE'S HER BOYFRIEND AFTER ALL. LOOKS LIKE SHE OWES SOME MONEY.
LOOKS LIKE IT.
I PROMISE I CAN GET THE MONEY!
I JUST NEED A LITTLE MORE TIME--
HUH?!
YOU THINK YOU CAN BAT YOUR DOE EYES AT ME AND I'LL LET YOU OFF JUST LIKE THAT?
I THINK IT'S TIME SOMEONE TAUGHT YOU A LESSON.
THAT SOUND GOOD TO YOU?
?!

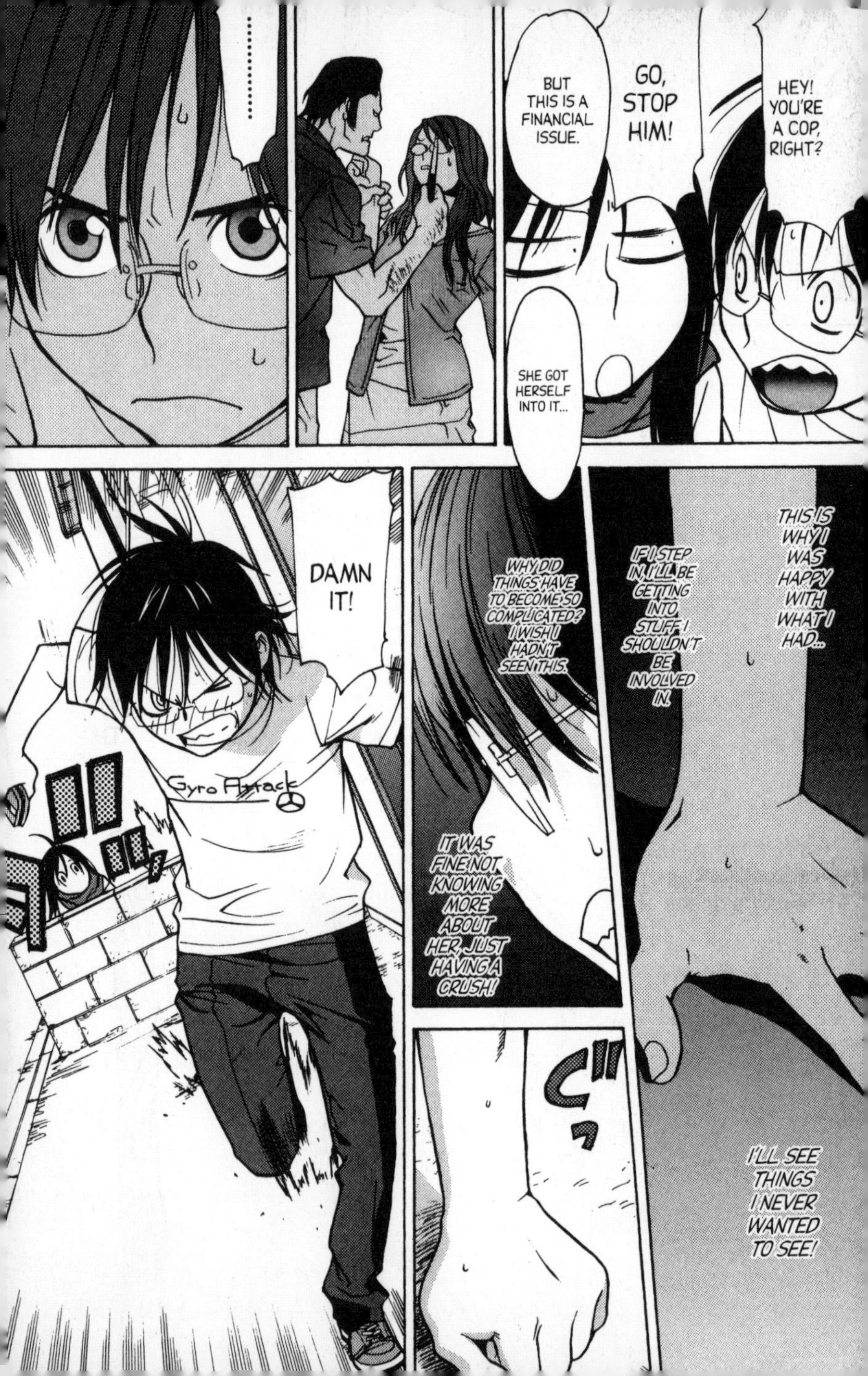
HEY! YOU'RE A COP, RIGHT?
GO, STOP HIM!
BUT THIS IS A FINANCIAL ISSUE.
SHE GOT HERSELF INTO IT...
……
THIS IS WHY I WAS HAPPY WITH WHAT I HAD...
IF I STEP IN, I'LL BE GETTING INTO STUFF I SHOULDN'T BE INVOLVED IN.
I'LL SEE THINGS I NEVER WANTED TO SEE!
WHY DID THINGS HAVE TO BECOME SO COMPLICATED? I WISH I HADN'T SEEN THIS.
IT WAS FINE NOT KNOWING MORE ABOUT HER, JUST HAVING A CRUSH!
DAMN IT!
Gyro Attack

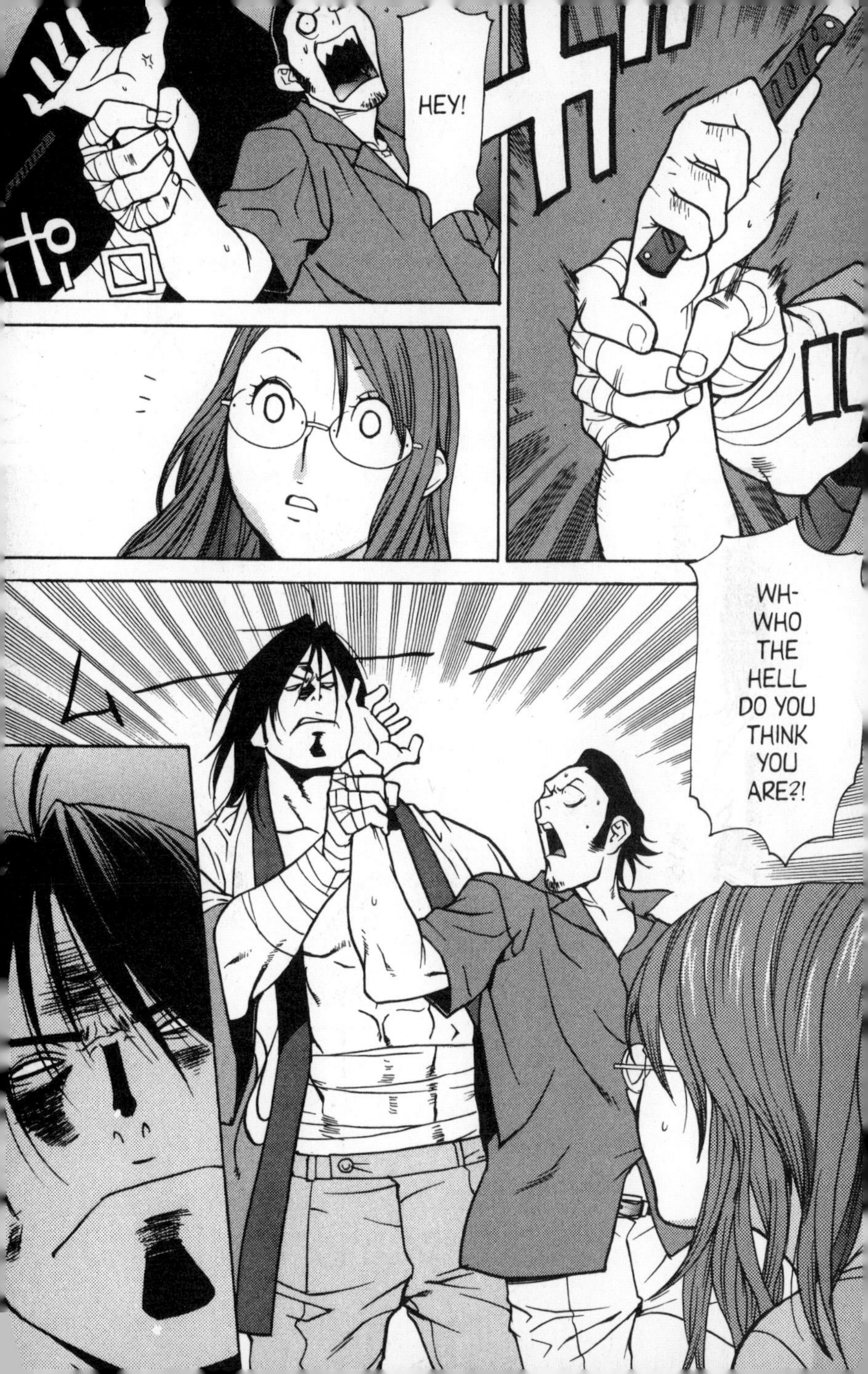
HEY!
WH- WHO THE HELL DO YOU THINK YOU ARE?!

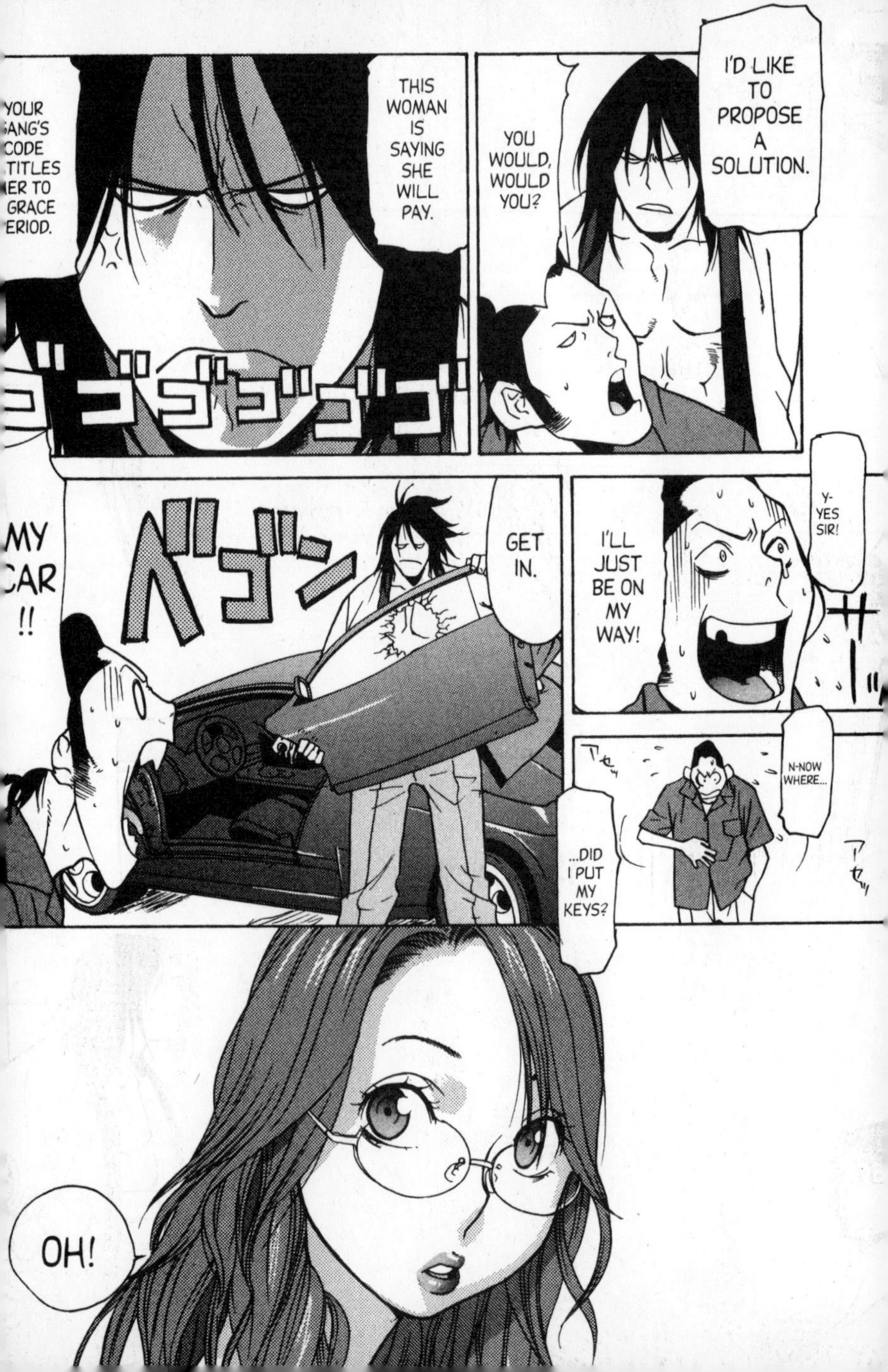
I'D LIKE TO PROPOSE A SOLUTION.
YOU WOULD, WOULD YOU?
THIS WOMAN IS SAYING SHE WILL PAY.
YOUR
ANG'S CODE
TITLES
ER TO
GRACE
ERIOD.
ゴゴゴゴゴ
Y-YES SIR!
I'LL JUST BE ON MY WAY!
GET IN.
ベゴン
MY
AR
!!
N-NOW WHERE...
...DID I PUT MY KEYS?
OH!

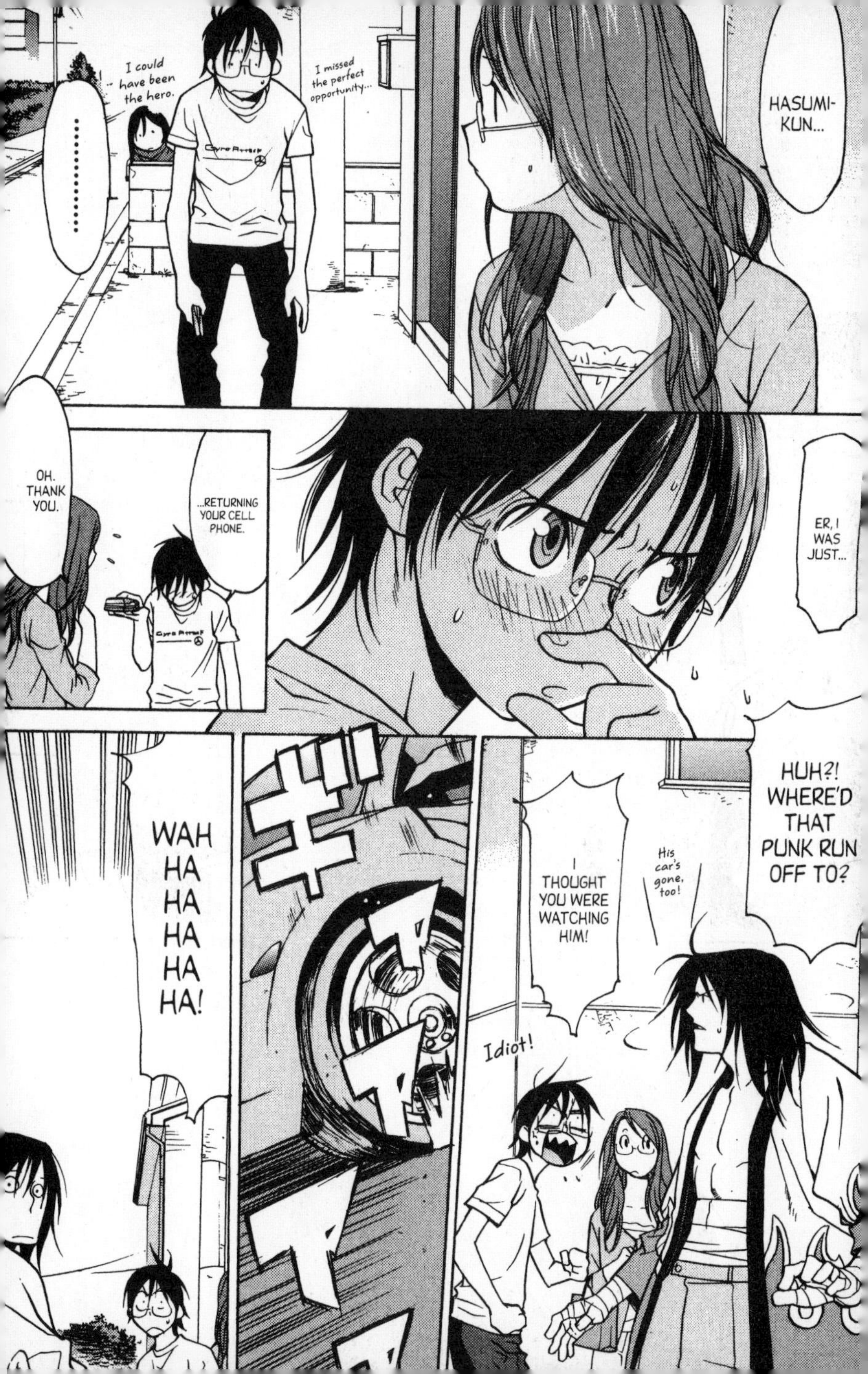
HASUMI-KUN...
I missed the perfect opportunity...
I could have been the hero.
......
ER, I WAS JUST...
...RETURNING YOUR CELL PHONE.
OH. THANK YOU.
HUH?! WHERE'D THAT PUNK RUN OFF TO?
His car's gone, too!
I THOUGHT YOU WERE WATCHING HIM!
Idiot!
WAH HA HA HA HA HA!

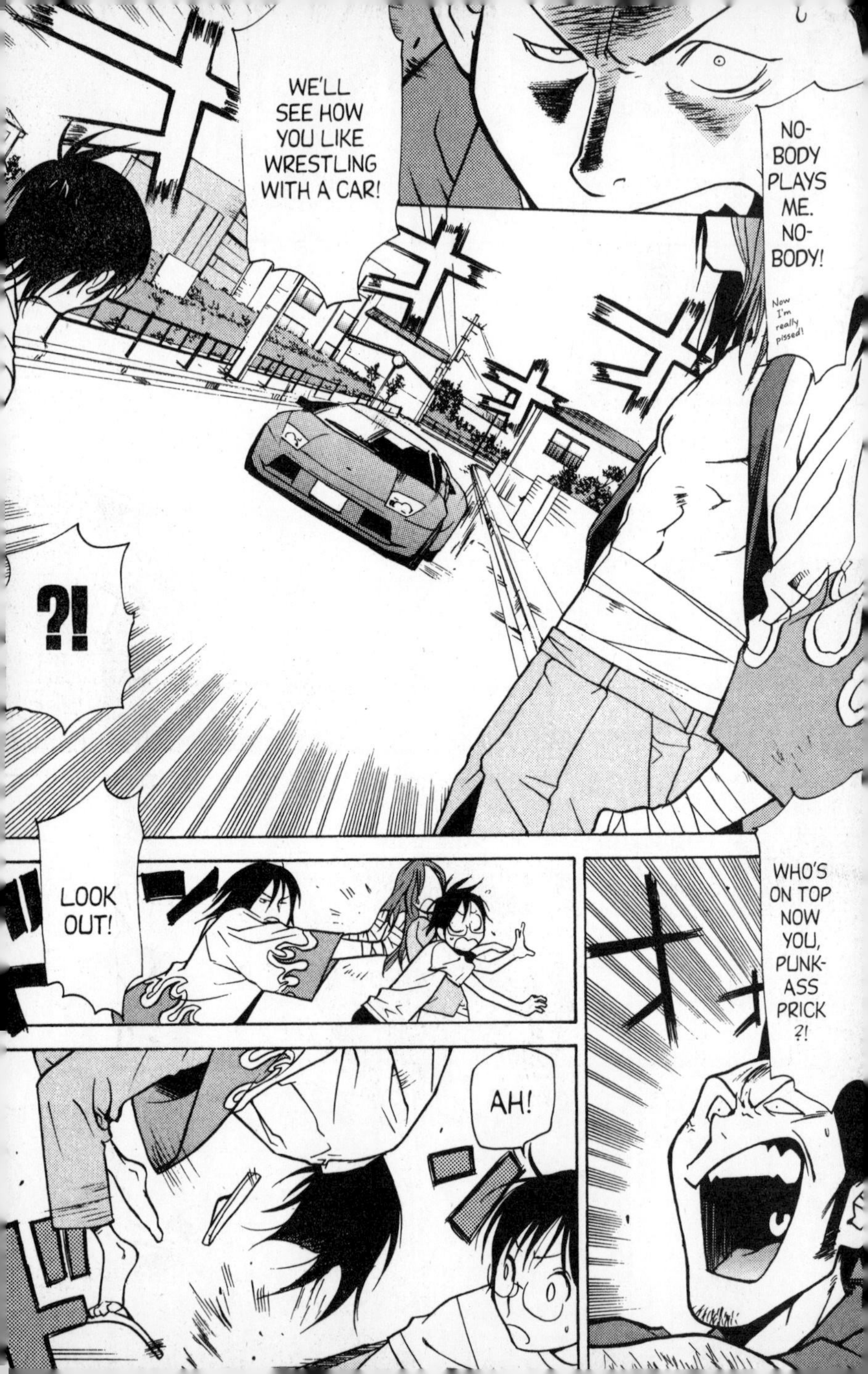
NO-BODY PLAYS ME. NO-BODY!
Now I'm really pissed!
WE'LL SEE HOW YOU LIKE WRESTLING WITH A CAR!
?!
WHO'S ON TOP NOW YOU, PUNK-ASS PRICK ?!
LOOK OUT!
AH!

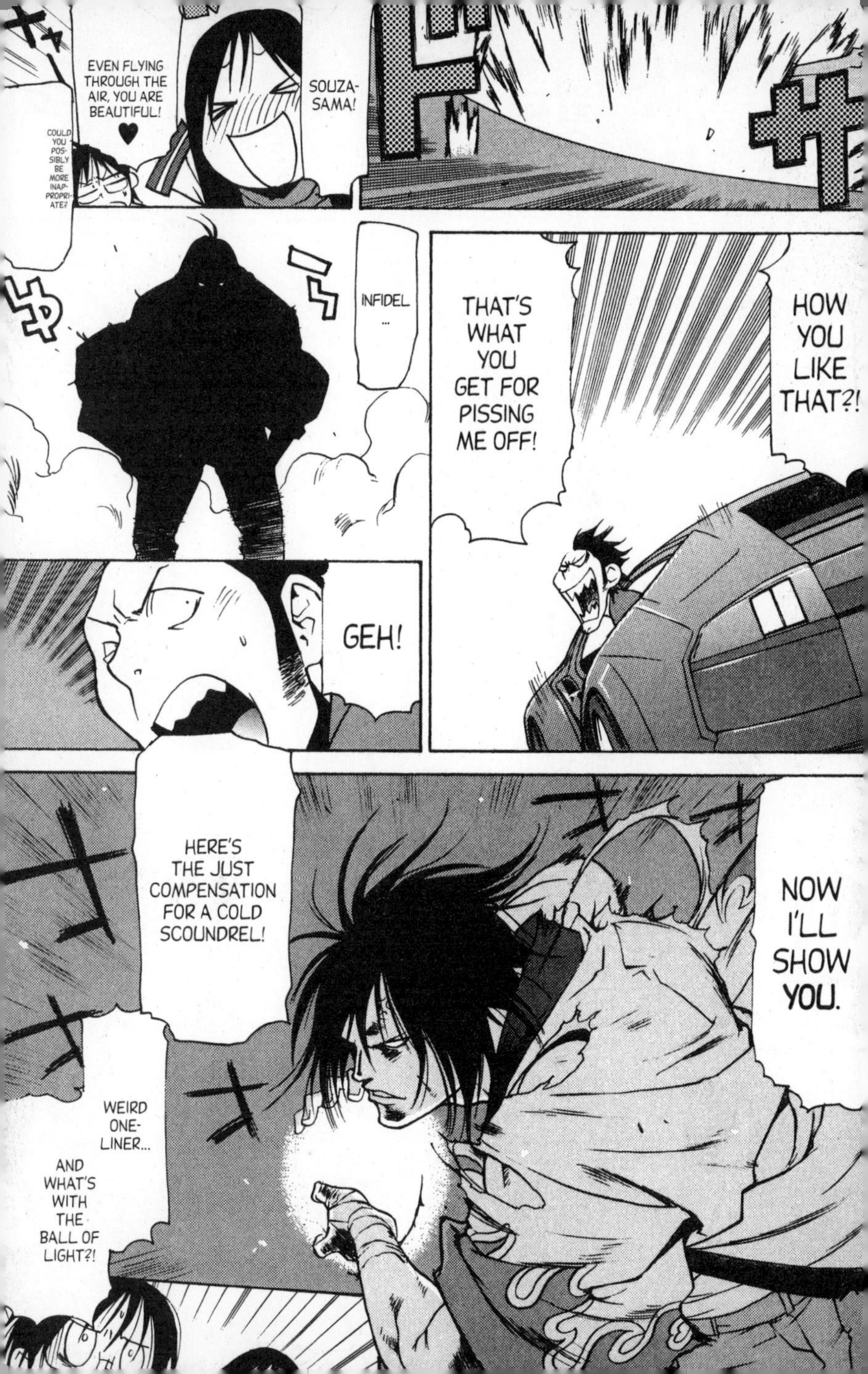
SOUZA-SAMA!
EVEN FLYING THROUGH THE AIR, YOU ARE BEAUTIFUL!
COULD YOU POS-SIBLY BE MORE INAP-PROPRI-ATE?
HOW YOU LIKE THAT?!
THAT'S WHAT YOU GET FOR PISSING ME OFF!
INFIDEL ...
GEH!
NOW I'LL SHOW YOU.
HERE'S THE JUST COMPENSATION FOR A COLD SCOUNDREL!
WEIRD ONE-LINER...
AND WHAT'S WITH THE BALL OF LIGHT?!

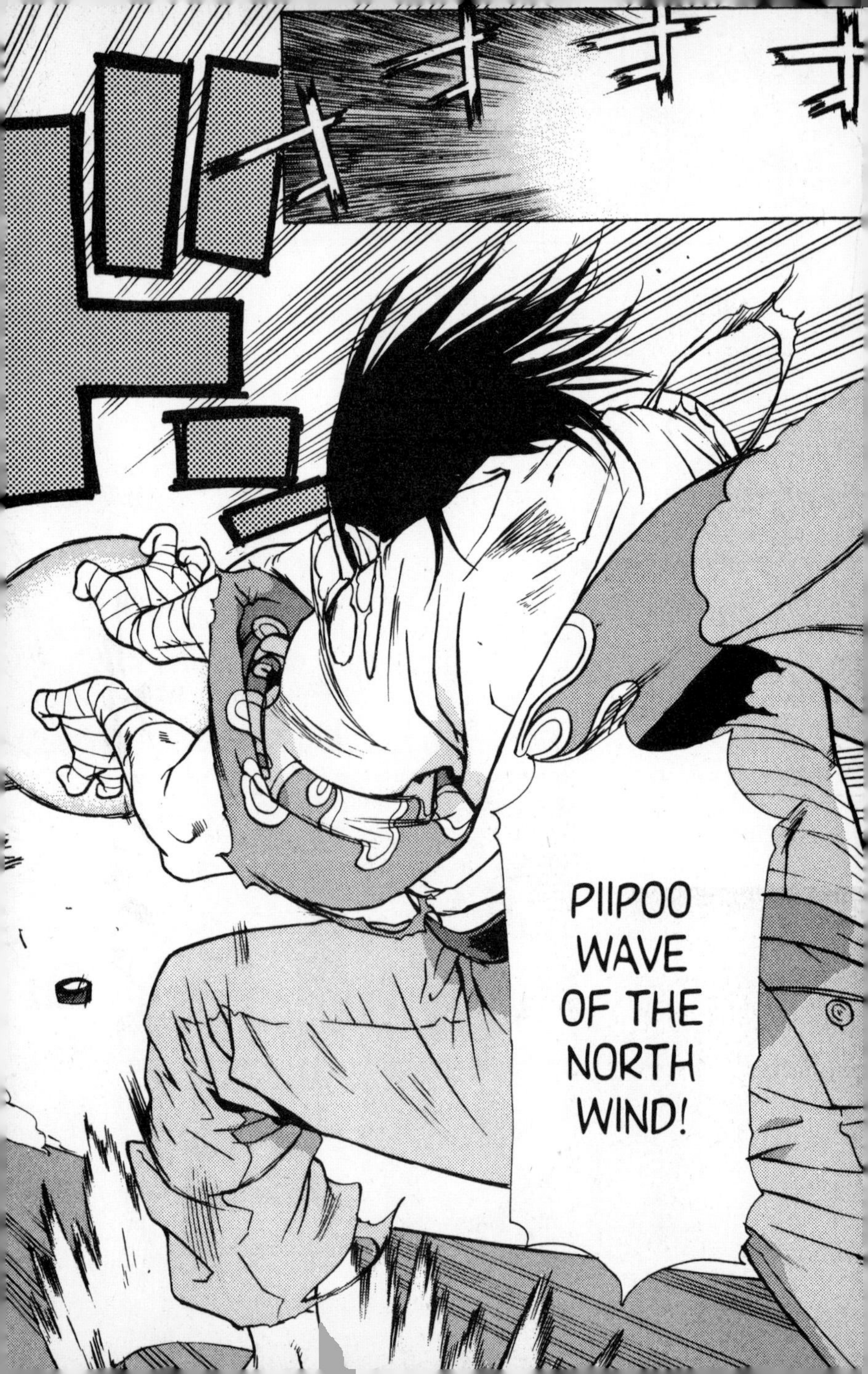
PIIPOO
WAVE
OF THE
NORTH
WIND!

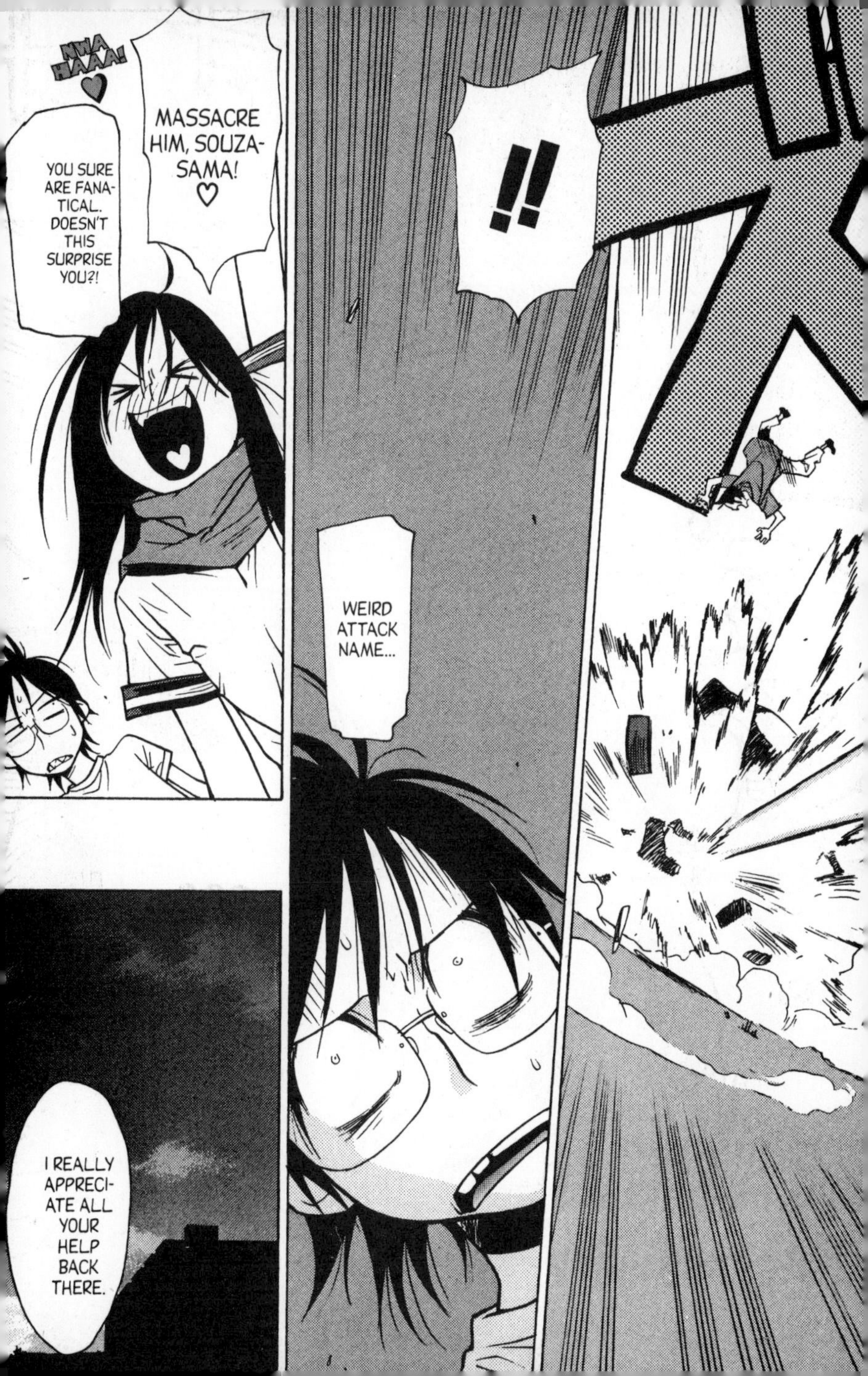
!!
WEIRD ATTACK NAME...
MASSACRE HIM, SOUZA-SAMA! ♡
NWA HAAA! ♡
YOU SURE ARE FANATICAL. DOESN'T THIS SURPRISE YOU?!
I REALLY APPRECIATE ALL YOUR HELP BACK THERE.

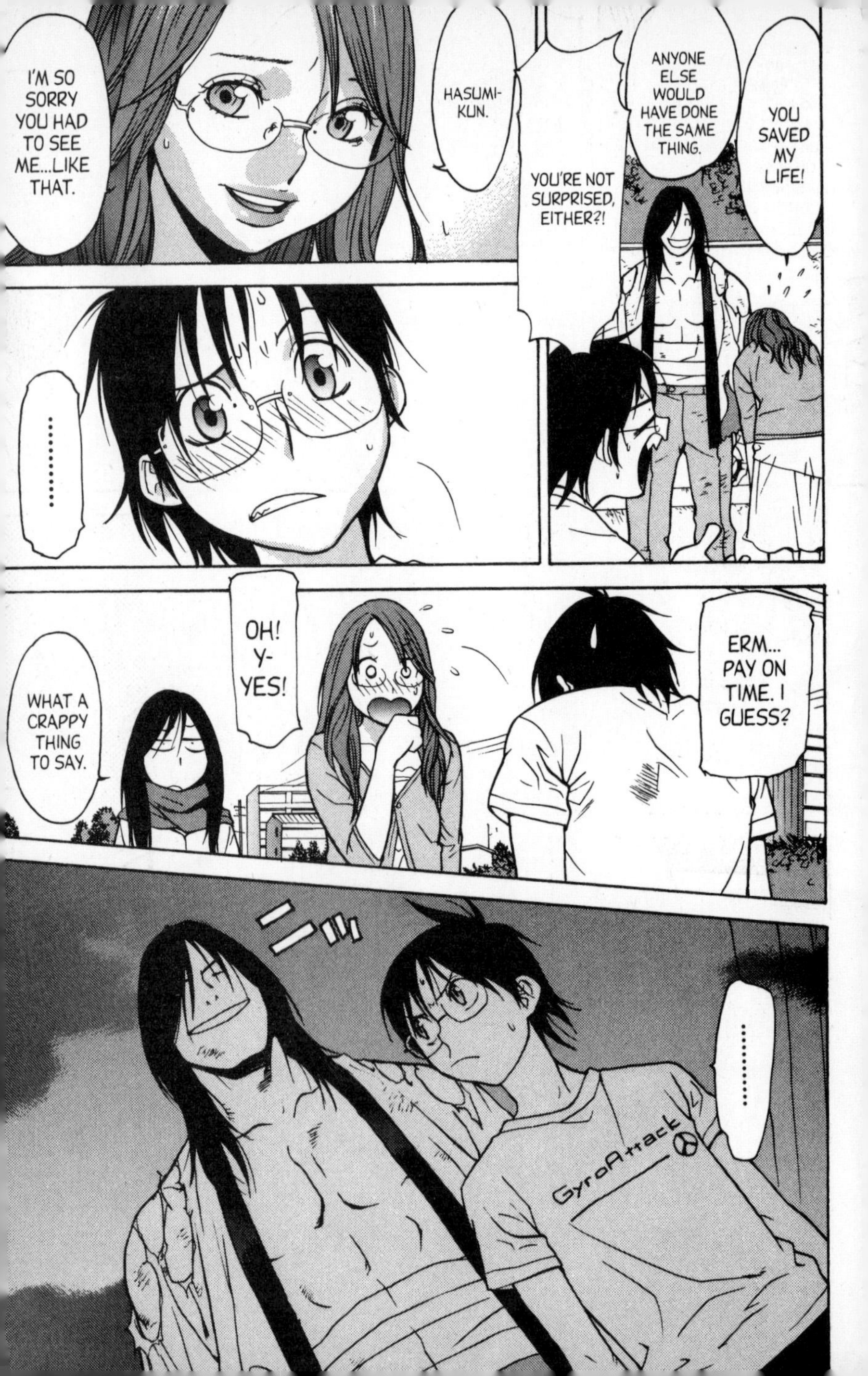
YOU SAVED MY LIFE!
ANYONE ELSE WOULD HAVE DONE THE SAME THING.
YOU'RE NOT SURPRISED, EITHER?!
HASUMI-KUN.
I'M SO SORRY YOU HAD TO SEE ME...LIKE THAT.
....
ERM... PAY ON TIME. I GUESS?
OH! Y-YES!
WHAT A CRAPPY THING TO SAY.
....

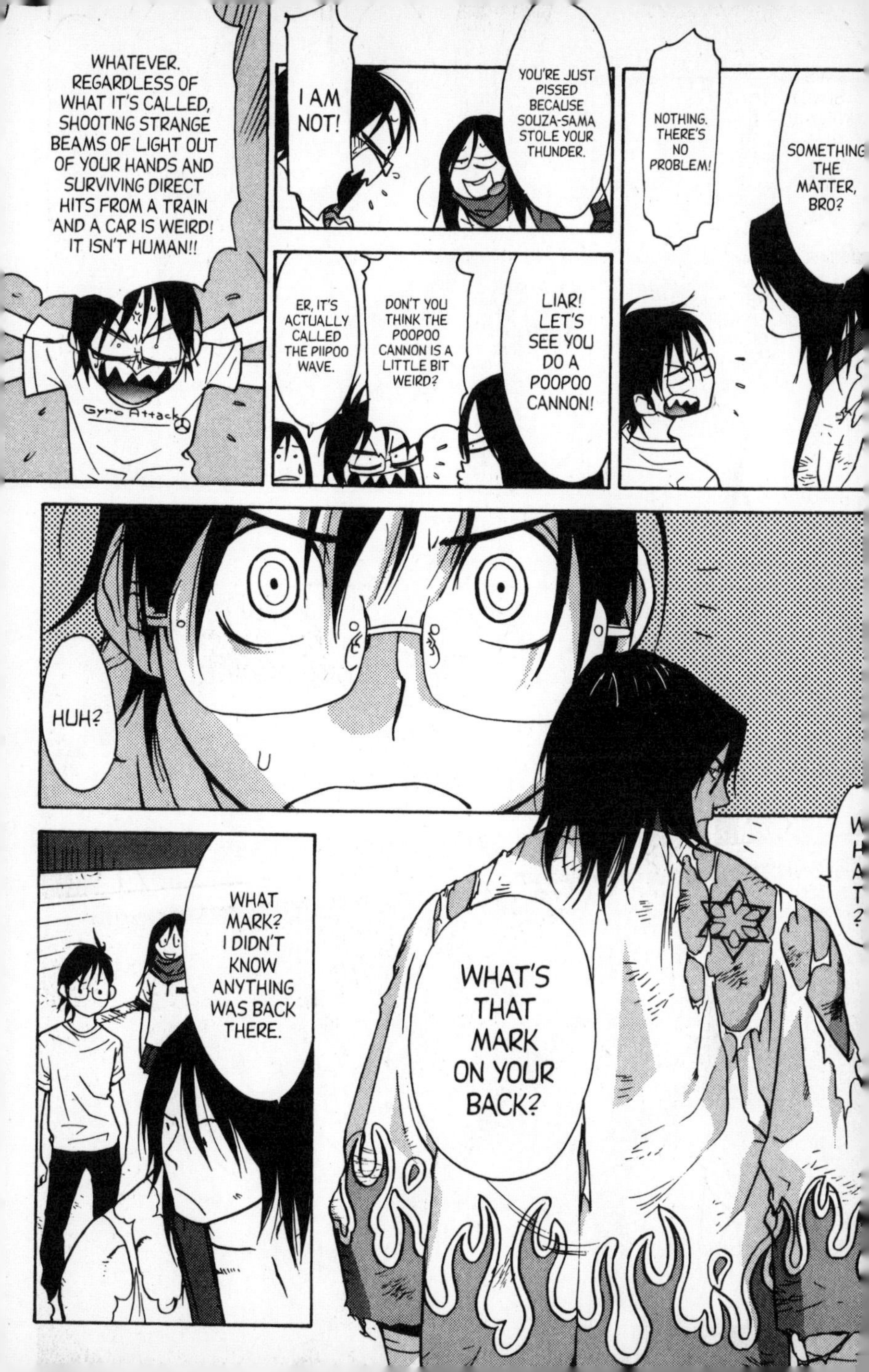
SOMETHING THE MATTER, BRO?
NOTHING. THERE'S NO PROBLEM!
YOU'RE JUST PISSED BECAUSE SOUZA-SAMA STOLE YOUR THUNDER.
I AM NOT!
LIAR! LET'S SEE YOU DO A POOPOO CANNON!
DON'T YOU THINK THE POOPOO CANNON IS A LITTLE BIT WEIRD?
ER, IT'S ACTUALLY CALLED THE PIIPOO WAVE.
WHATEVER. REGARDLESS OF WHAT IT'S CALLED, SHOOTING STRANGE BEAMS OF LIGHT OUT OF YOUR HANDS AND SURVIVING DIRECT HITS FROM A TRAIN AND A CAR IS WEIRD! IT ISN'T HUMAN!!
Gyro Attack
HUH?
WHAT?
WHAT'S THAT MARK ON YOUR BACK?
WHAT MARK? I DIDN'T KNOW ANYTHING WAS BACK THERE.

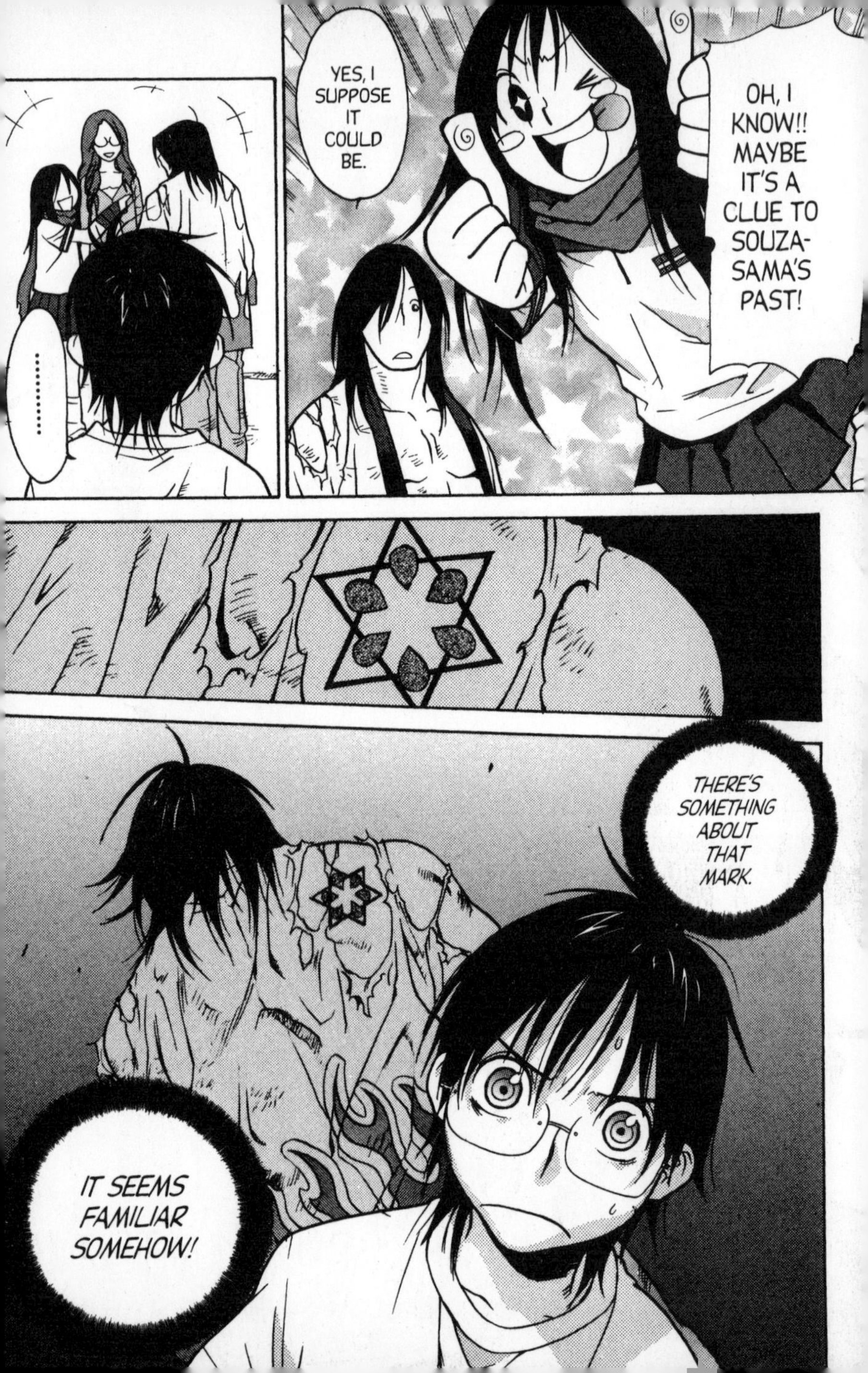
OH, I KNOW!! MAYBE IT'S A CLUE TO SOUZA-SAMA'S PAST!
YES, I SUPPOSE IT COULD BE.
....
THERE'S SOMETHING ABOUT THAT MARK.
IT SEEMS FAMILIAR SOMEHOW!

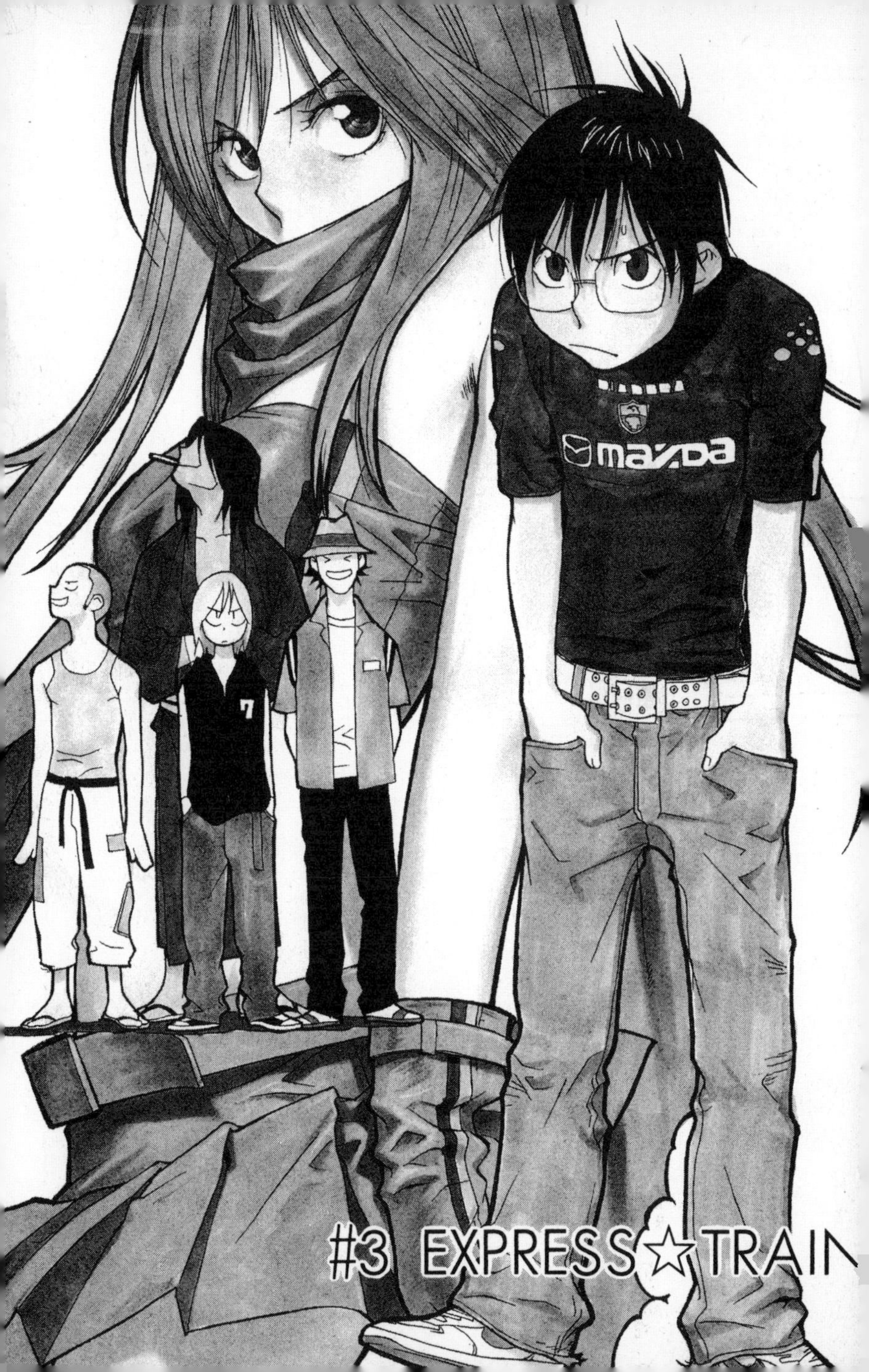
mazda
7
#3 EXPRESS☆TRAIN

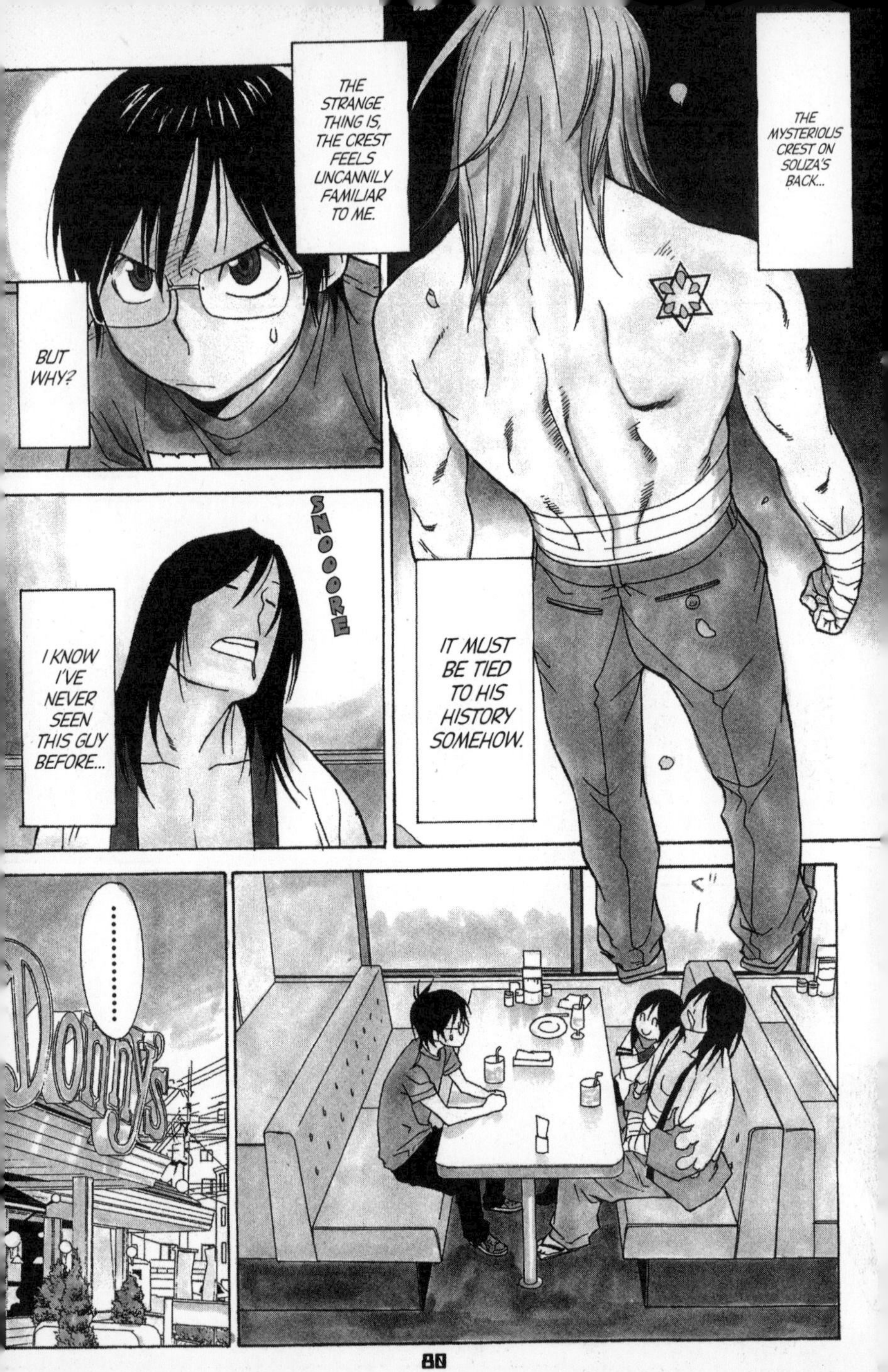
THE MYSTERIOUS CREST ON SOUZA'S BACK...
THE STRANGE THING IS, THE CREST FEELS UNCANNILY FAMILIAR TO ME.
IT MUST BE TIED TO HIS HISTORY SOMEHOW.
BUT WHY?
SNOOORE
I KNOW I'VE NEVER SEEN THIS GUY BEFORE...
......

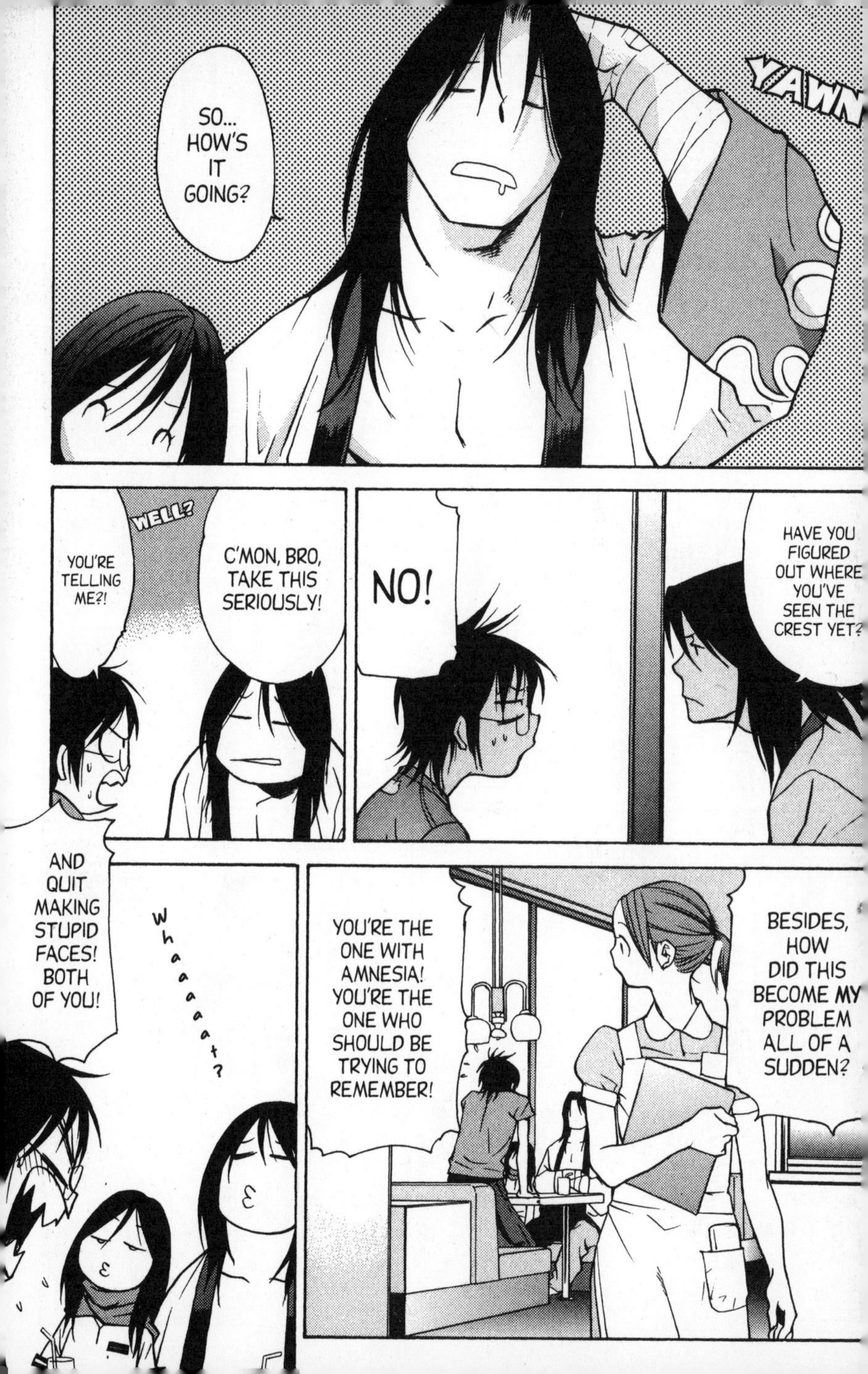
YAWN
SO... HOW'S IT GOING?
HAVE YOU FIGURED OUT WHERE YOU'VE SEEN THE CREST YET?
NO!
C'MON, BRO, TAKE THIS SERIOUSLY!
WELL?
YOU'RE TELLING ME?!
BESIDES, HOW DID THIS BECOME **MY** PROBLEM ALL OF A SUDDEN?
YOU'RE THE ONE WITH AMNESIA! YOU'RE THE ONE WHO SHOULD BE TRYING TO REMEMBER!
AND QUIT MAKING STUPID FACES! BOTH OF YOU!
Whaaaaaat?

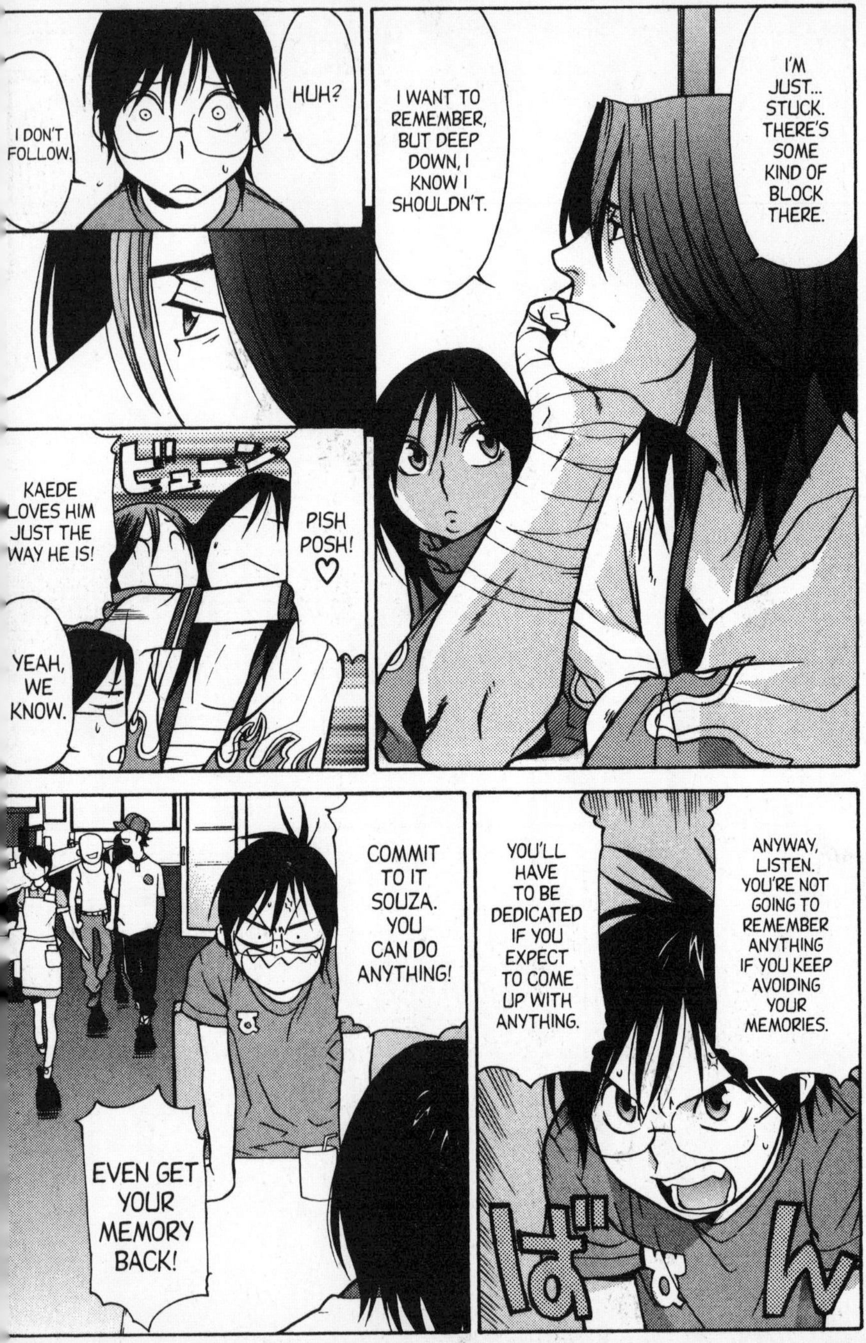
I'M JUST... STUCK. THERE'S SOME KIND OF BLOCK THERE.
I WANT TO REMEMBER, BUT DEEP DOWN, I KNOW I SHOULDN'T.
HUH?
I DON'T FOLLOW.
KAEDE LOVES HIM JUST THE WAY HE IS!
PISH POSH! ♥
YEAH, WE KNOW.
ANYWAY, LISTEN. YOU'RE NOT GOING TO REMEMBER ANYTHING IF YOU KEEP AVOIDING YOUR MEMORIES.
YOU'LL HAVE TO BE DEDICATED IF YOU EXPECT TO COME UP WITH ANYTHING.
COMMIT TO IT SOUZA. YOU CAN DO ANYTHING!
EVEN GET YOUR MEMORY BACK!

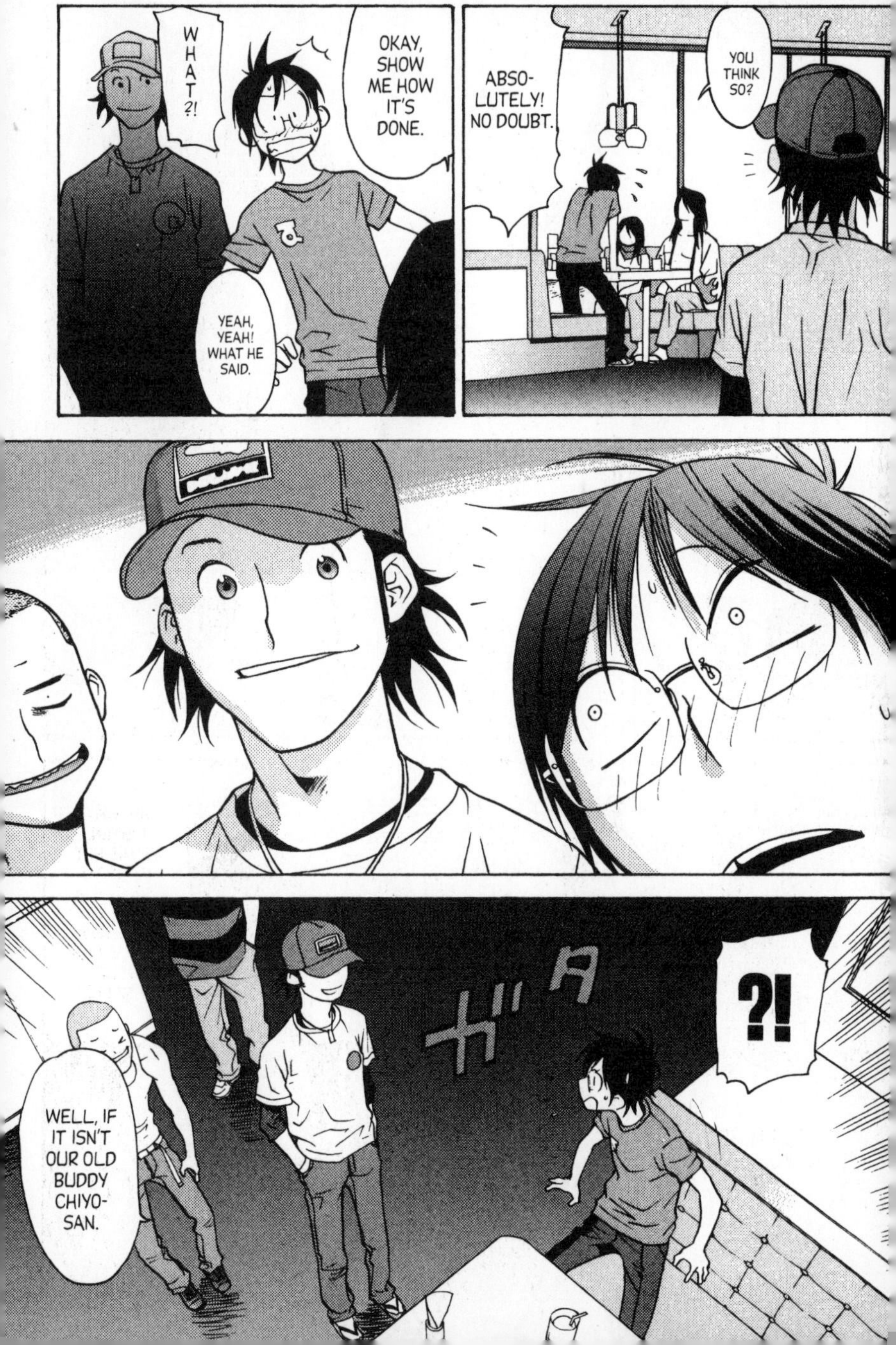
YOU THINK SO?
ABSO-LUTELY! NO DOUBT.
OKAY, SHOW ME HOW IT'S DONE.
WHAT?!
YEAH, YEAH! WHAT HE SAID.
?!
WELL, IF IT ISN'T OUR OLD BUDDY CHIYO-SAN.

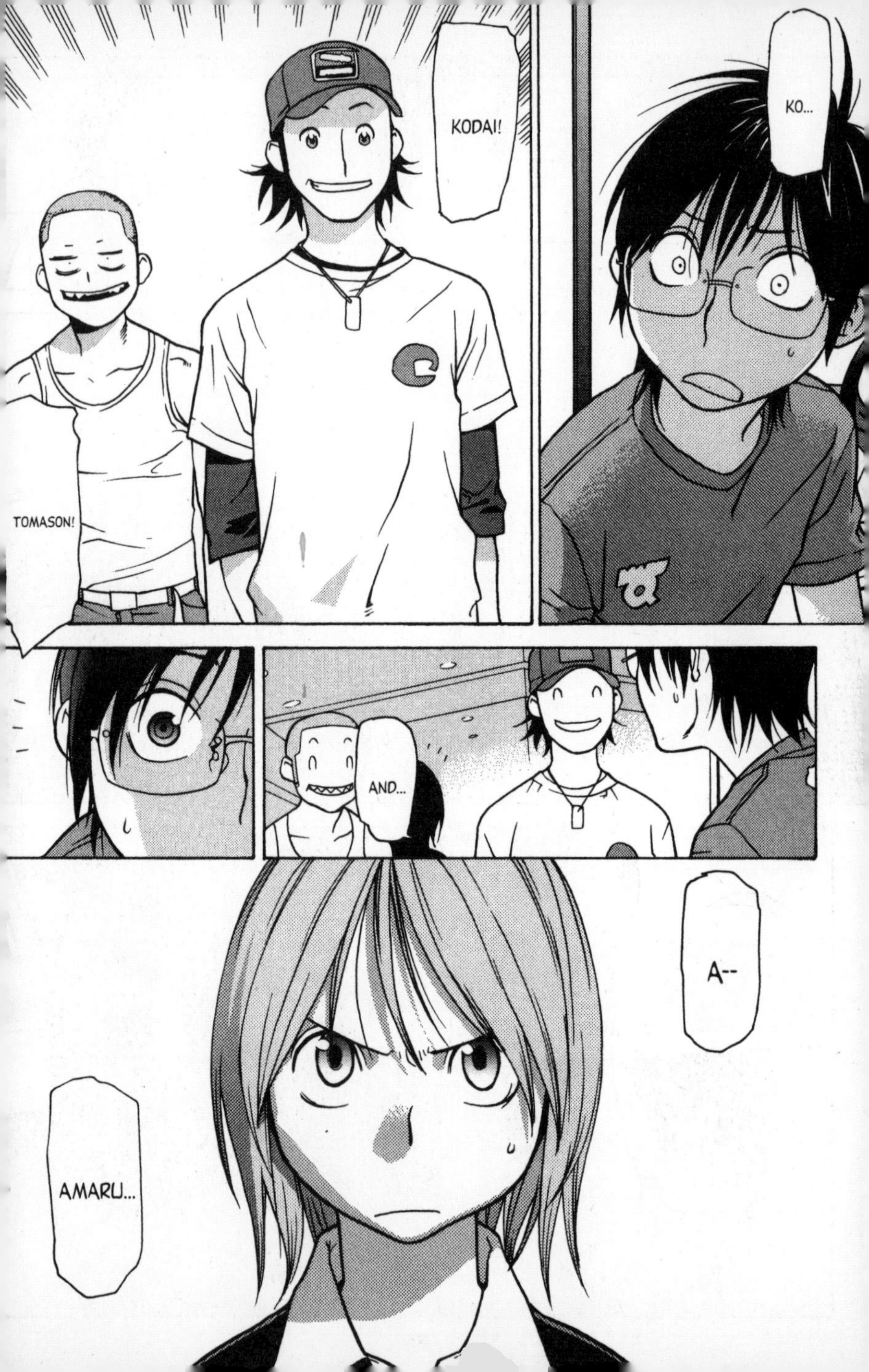
KO...
KODAI!
TOMASON!
AND...
A--
AMARU...

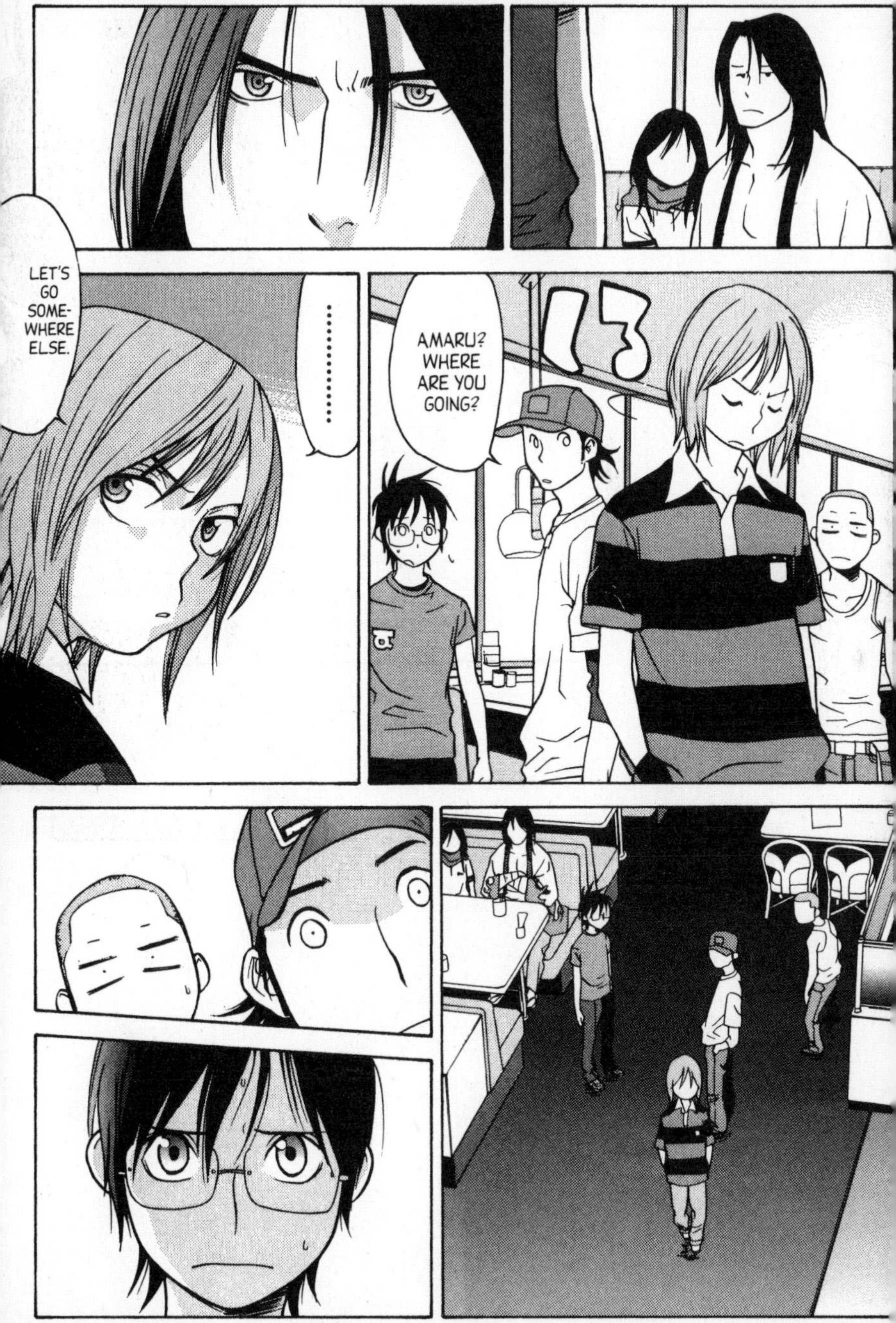
AMARU? WHERE ARE YOU GOING?
......
LET'S GO SOMEWHERE ELSE.

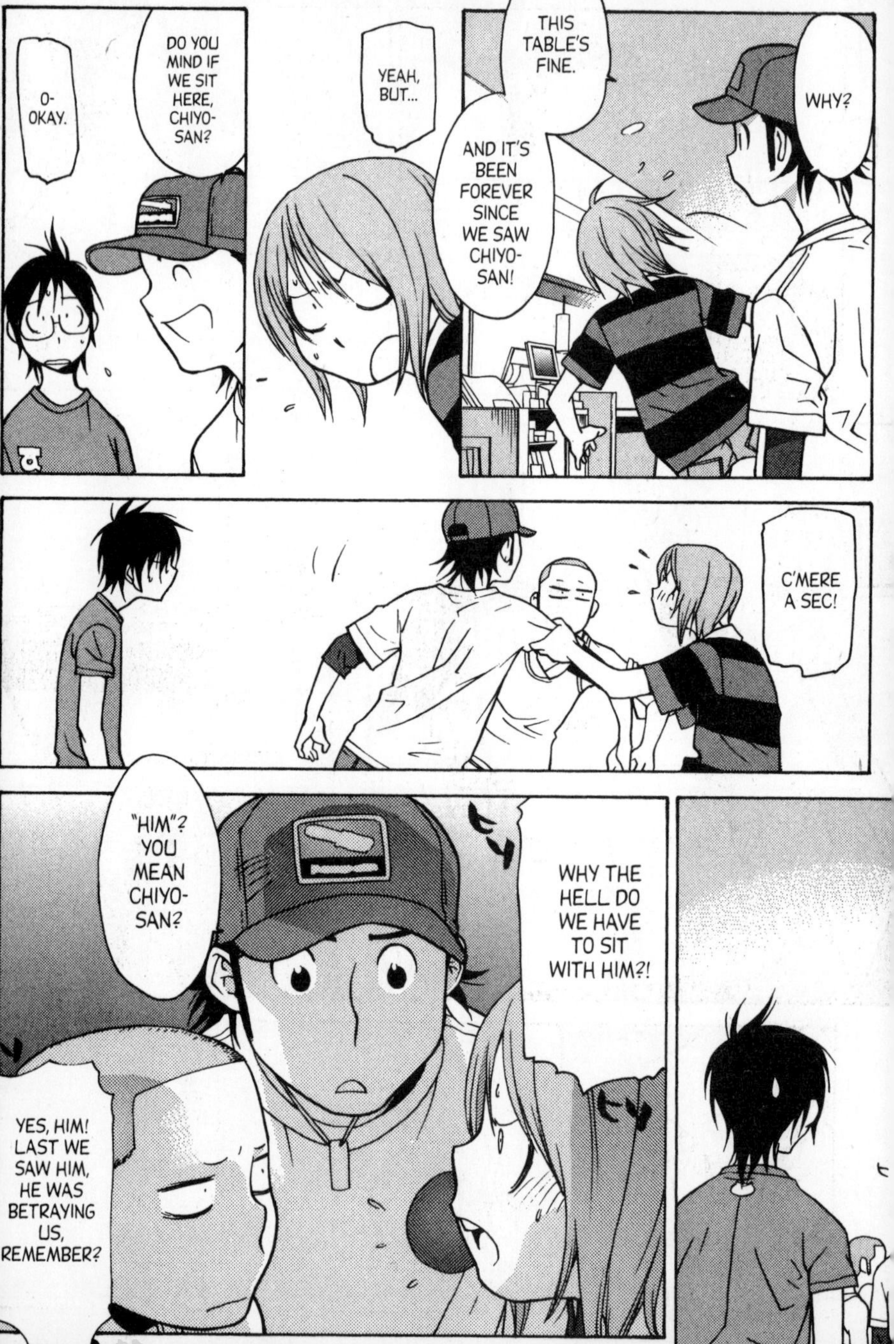
WHY?
THIS TABLE'S FINE.
AND IT'S BEEN FOREVER SINCE WE SAW CHIYO-SAN!
YEAH, BUT...
DO YOU MIND IF WE SIT HERE, CHIYO-SAN?
O-OKAY.
C'MERE A SEC!
WHY THE HELL DO WE HAVE TO SIT WITH HIM?!
"HIM"? YOU MEAN CHIYO-SAN?
YES, HIM! LAST WE SAW HIM, HE WAS BETRAYING US, REMEMBER?

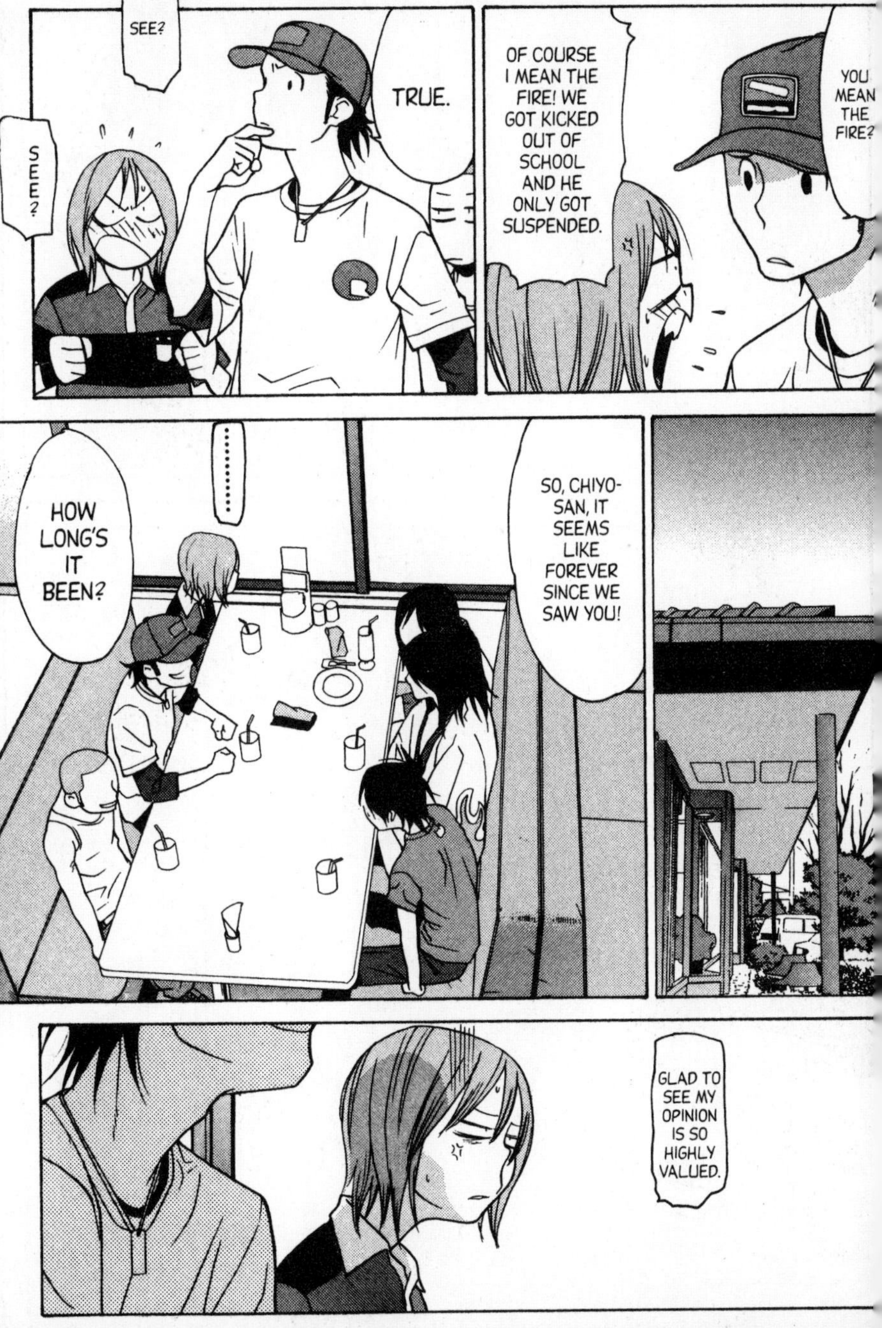
YOU MEAN THE FIRE?
OF COURSE I MEAN THE FIRE! WE GOT KICKED OUT OF SCHOOL AND HE ONLY GOT SUSPENDED.
TRUE.
SEE?
SEE?
SO, CHIYO-SAN, IT SEEMS LIKE FOREVER SINCE WE SAW YOU!
....
HOW LONG'S IT BEEN?
GLAD TO SEE MY OPINION IS SO HIGHLY VALUED.

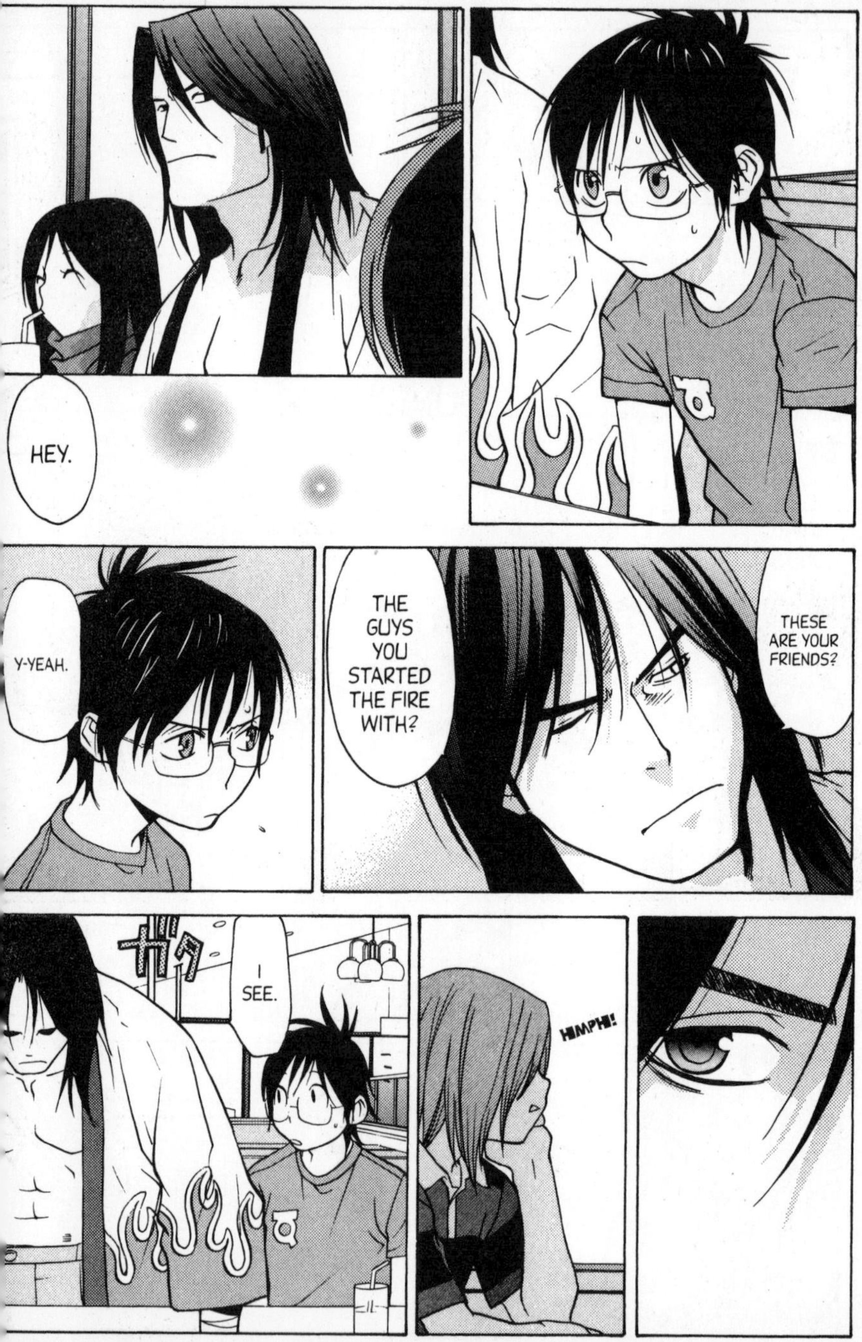
HEY.
THESE ARE YOUR FRIENDS?
THE GUYS YOU STARTED THE FIRE WITH?
Y-YEAH.
HMPH!
I SEE.

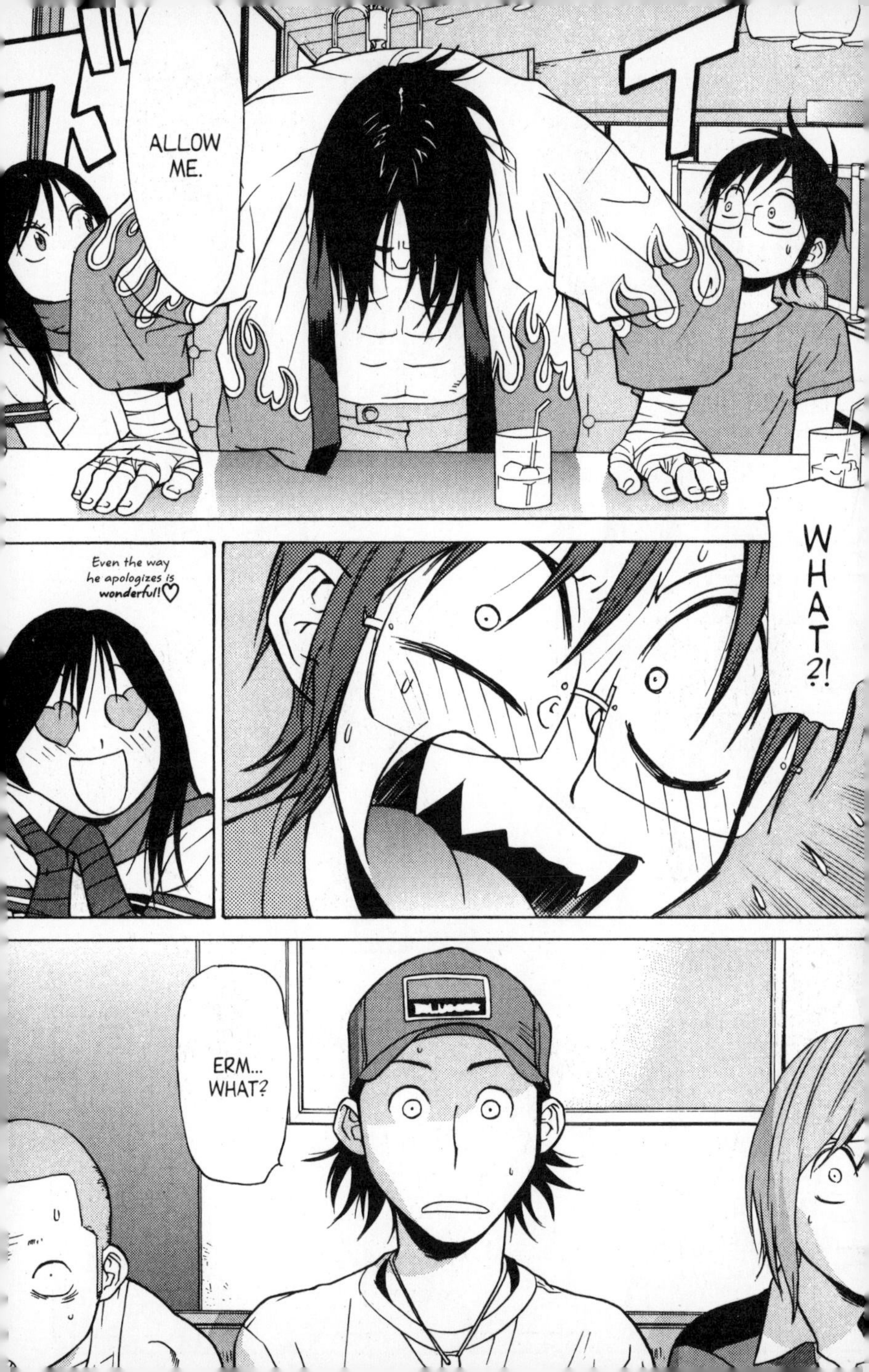
ALLOW ME.
WHAT?!
Even the way he apologizes is **wonderful!**♡
ERM... WHAT?

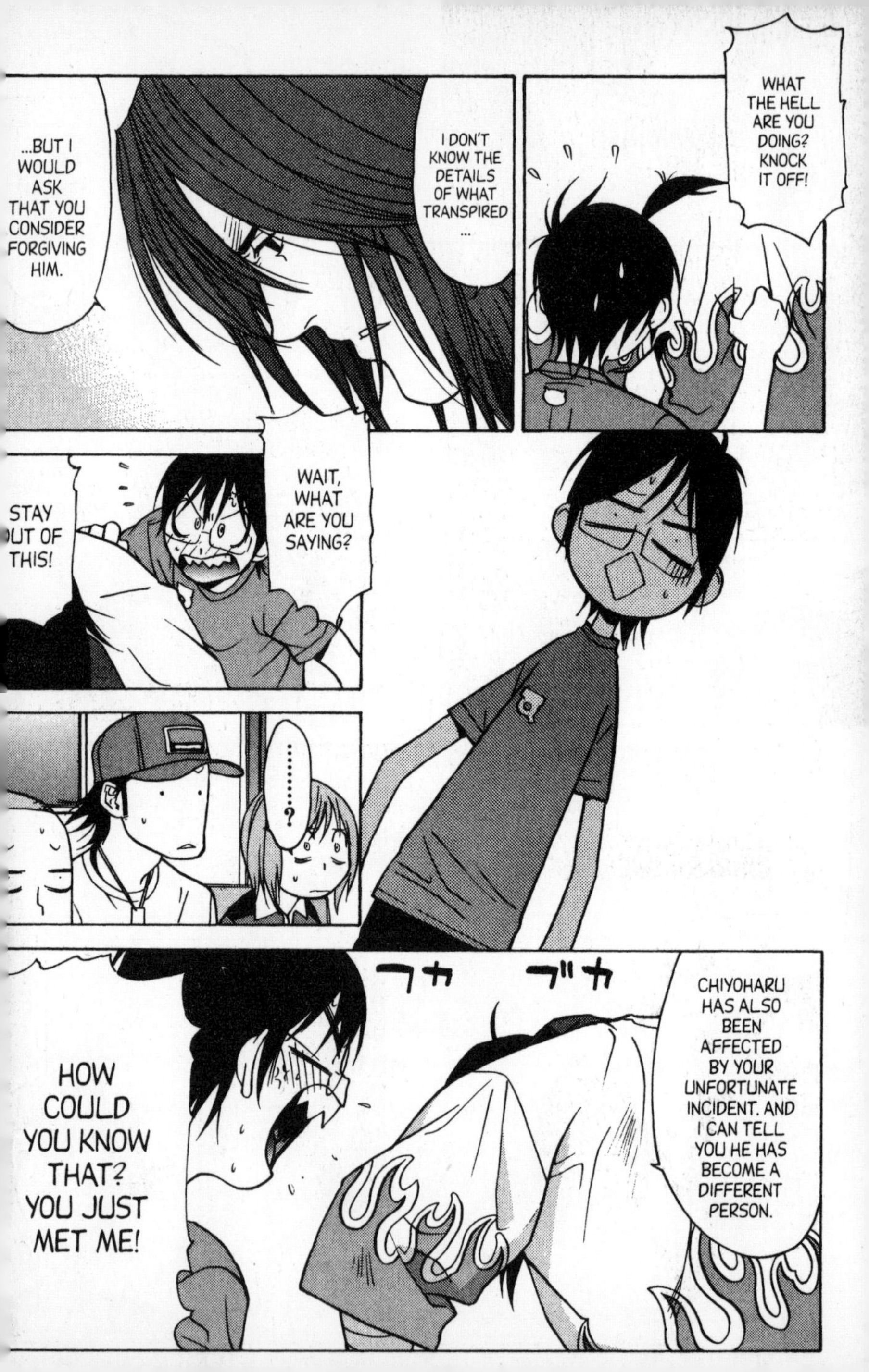
WHAT THE HELL ARE YOU DOING? KNOCK IT OFF!
I DON'T KNOW THE DETAILS OF WHAT TRANSPIRED ...
...BUT I WOULD ASK THAT YOU CONSIDER FORGIVING HIM.
WAIT, WHAT ARE YOU SAYING?
STAY OUT OF THIS!
.........?
CHIYOHARU HAS ALSO BEEN AFFECTED BY YOUR UNFORTUNATE INCIDENT. AND I CAN TELL YOU HE HAS BECOME A DIFFERENT PERSON.
ブカ
フカ
HOW COULD YOU KNOW THAT? YOU JUST MET ME!

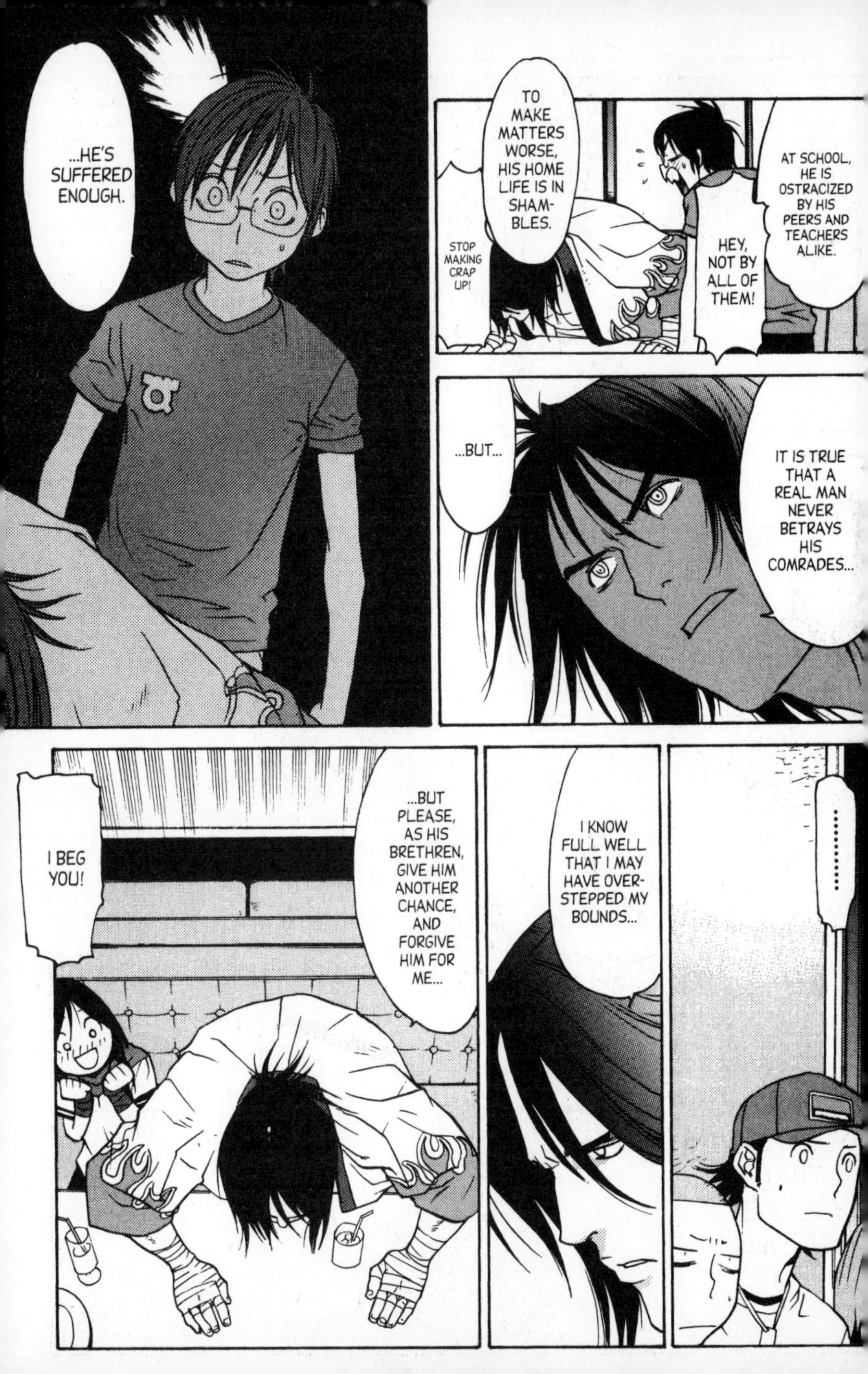
AT SCHOOL, HE IS OSTRACIZED BY HIS PEERS AND TEACHERS ALIKE.
HEY, NOT BY ALL OF THEM!
TO MAKE MATTERS WORSE, HIS HOME LIFE IS IN SHAMBLES.
STOP MAKING CRAP UP!
IT IS TRUE THAT A REAL MAN NEVER BETRAYS HIS COMRADES...
...BUT...
...HE'S SUFFERED ENOUGH.
......
I KNOW FULL WELL THAT I MAY HAVE OVER-STEPPED MY BOUNDS...
...BUT PLEASE, AS HIS BRETHREN, GIVE HIM ANOTHER CHANCE, AND FORGIVE HIM FOR ME...
I BEG YOU!

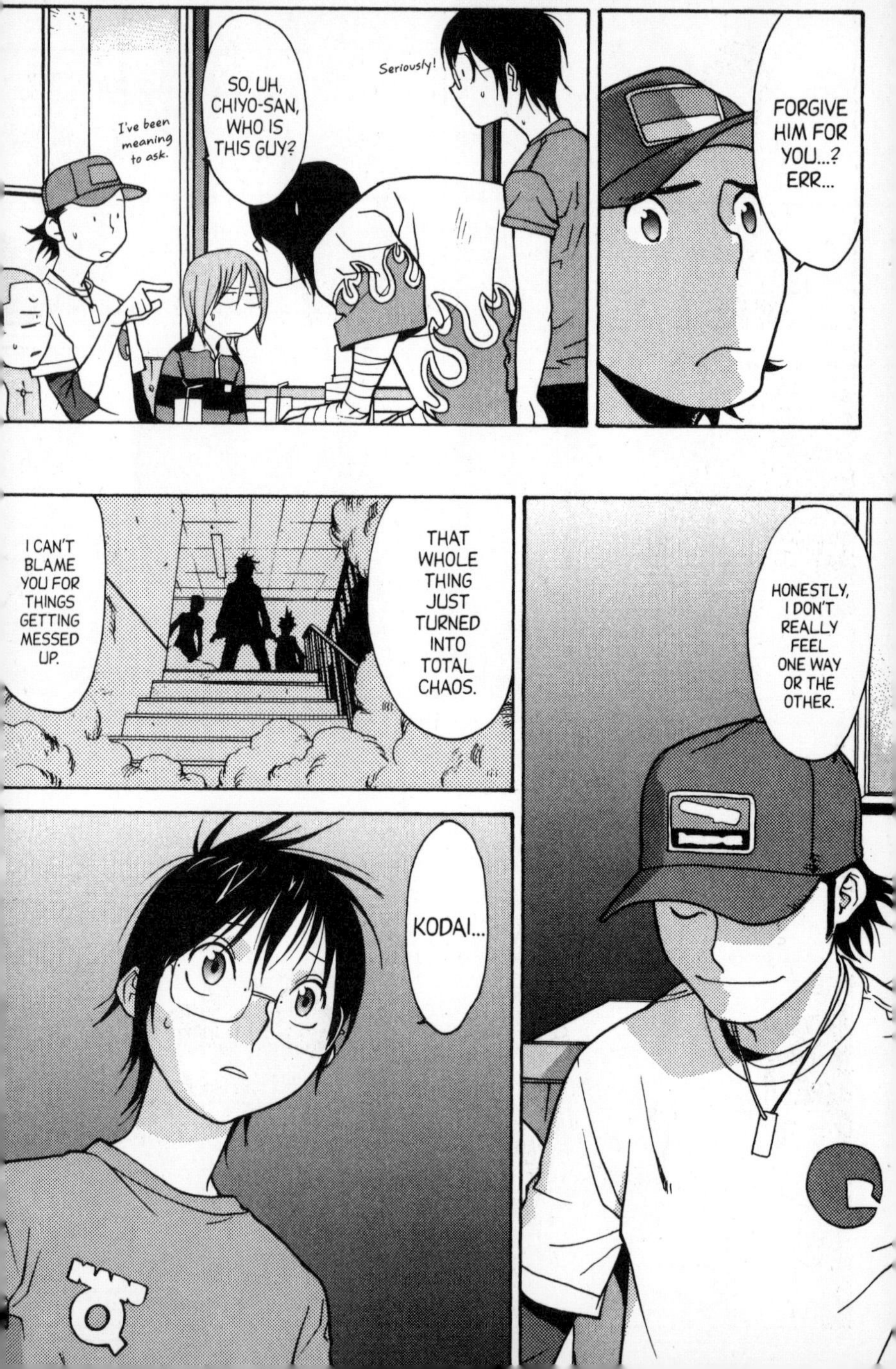
FORGIVE HIM FOR YOU...? ERR...
SO, UH, CHIYO-SAN, WHO IS THIS GUY?
Seriously!
I've been meaning to ask.
HONESTLY, I DON'T REALLY FEEL ONE WAY OR THE OTHER.
THAT WHOLE THING JUST TURNED INTO TOTAL CHAOS.
I CAN'T BLAME YOU FOR THINGS GETTING MESSED UP.
KODAI...

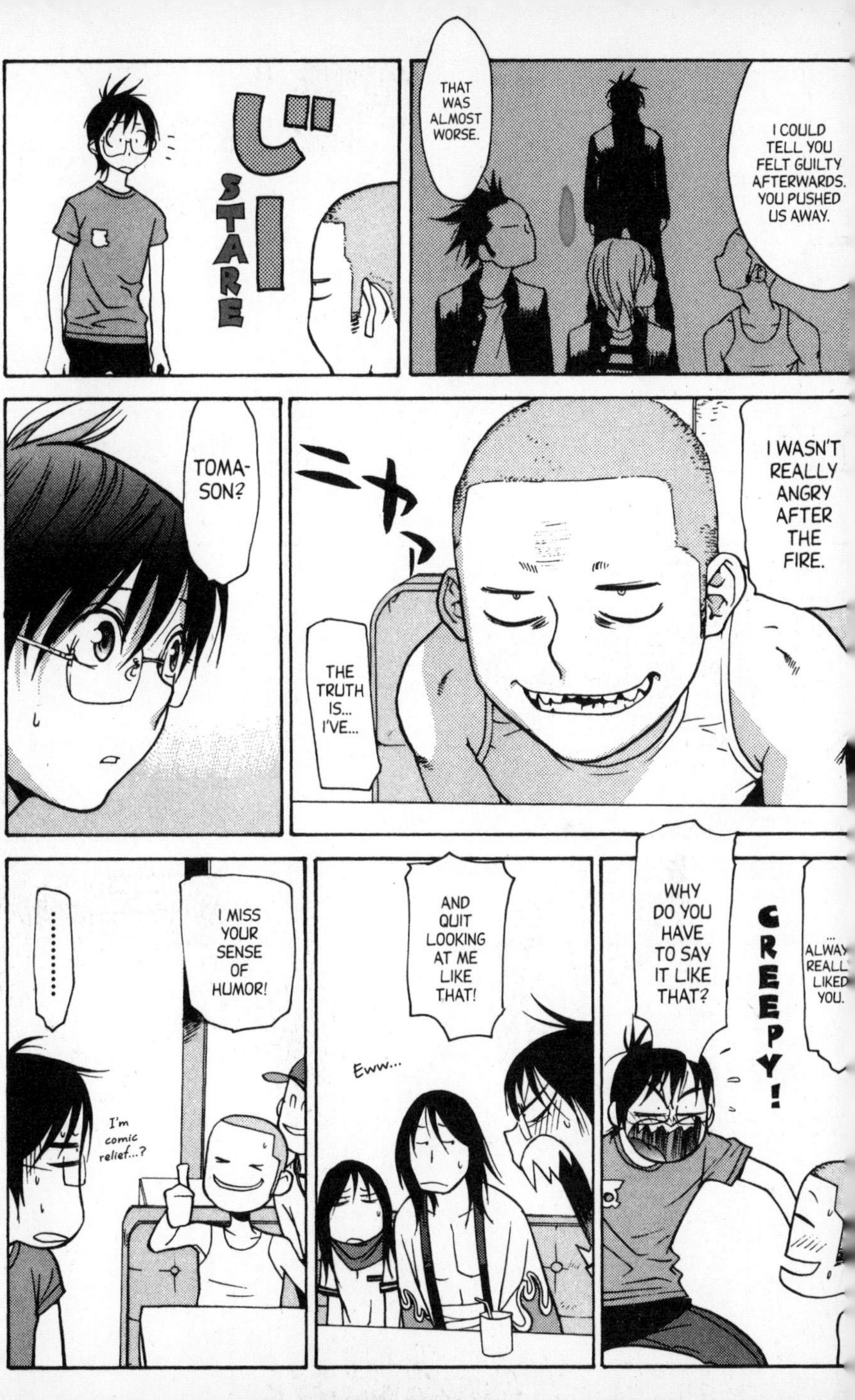
I COULD TELL YOU FELT GUILTY AFTERWARDS. YOU PUSHED US AWAY.
THAT WAS ALMOST WORSE.
じー
STARE
I WASN'T REALLY ANGRY AFTER THE FIRE.
ニヤ
THE TRUTH IS... I'VE...
TOMA-SON?
... ALWAY REALL LIKED YOU.
CREEPY!
WHY DO YOU HAVE TO SAY IT LIKE THAT?
AND QUIT LOOKING AT ME LIKE THAT!
Eww...
I MISS YOUR SENSE OF HUMOR!
....
I'm comic relief...?

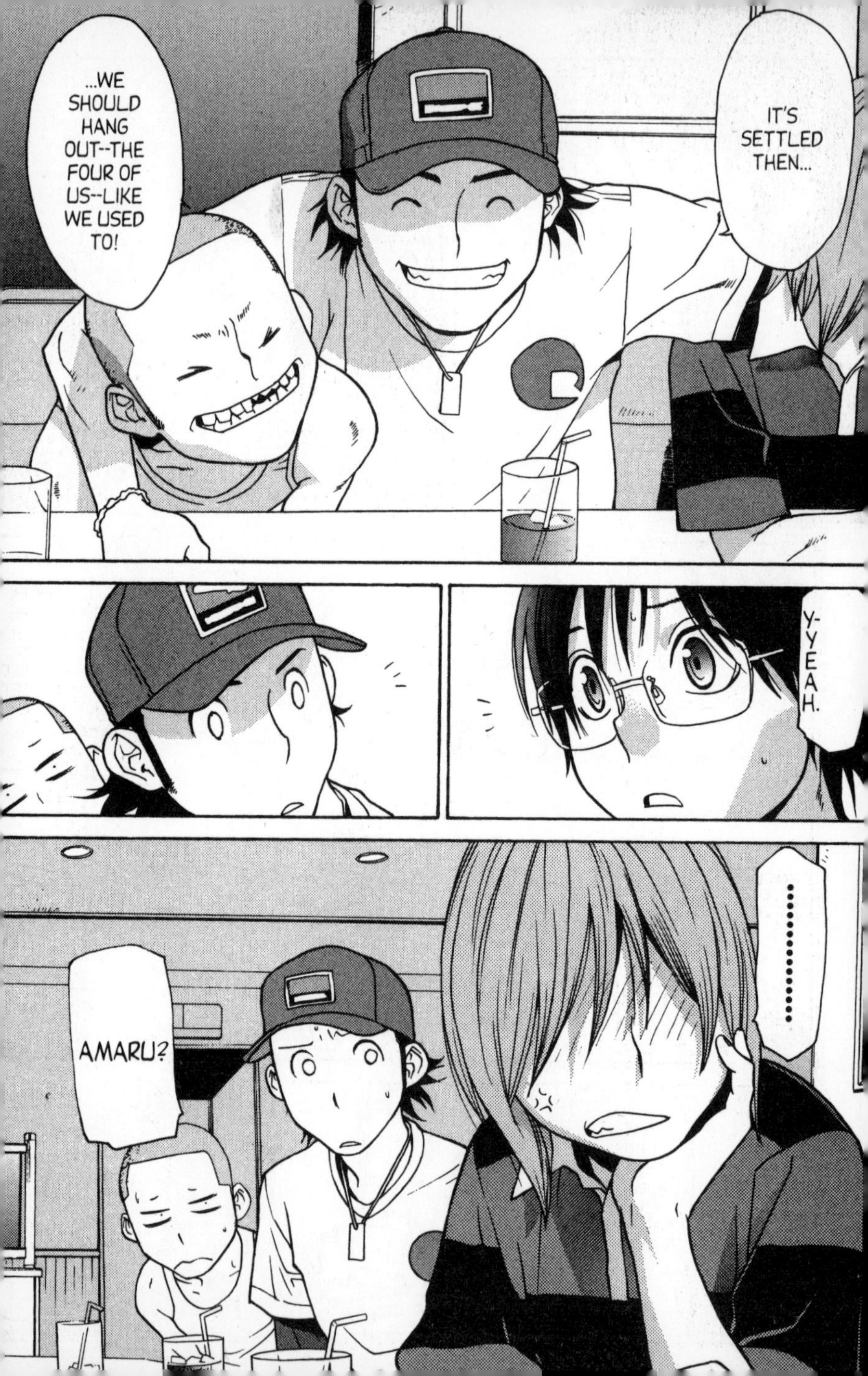
IT'S SETTLED THEN...
...WE SHOULD HANG OUT--THE FOUR OF US--LIKE WE USED TO!
Y-YEAH.
....
AMARU?

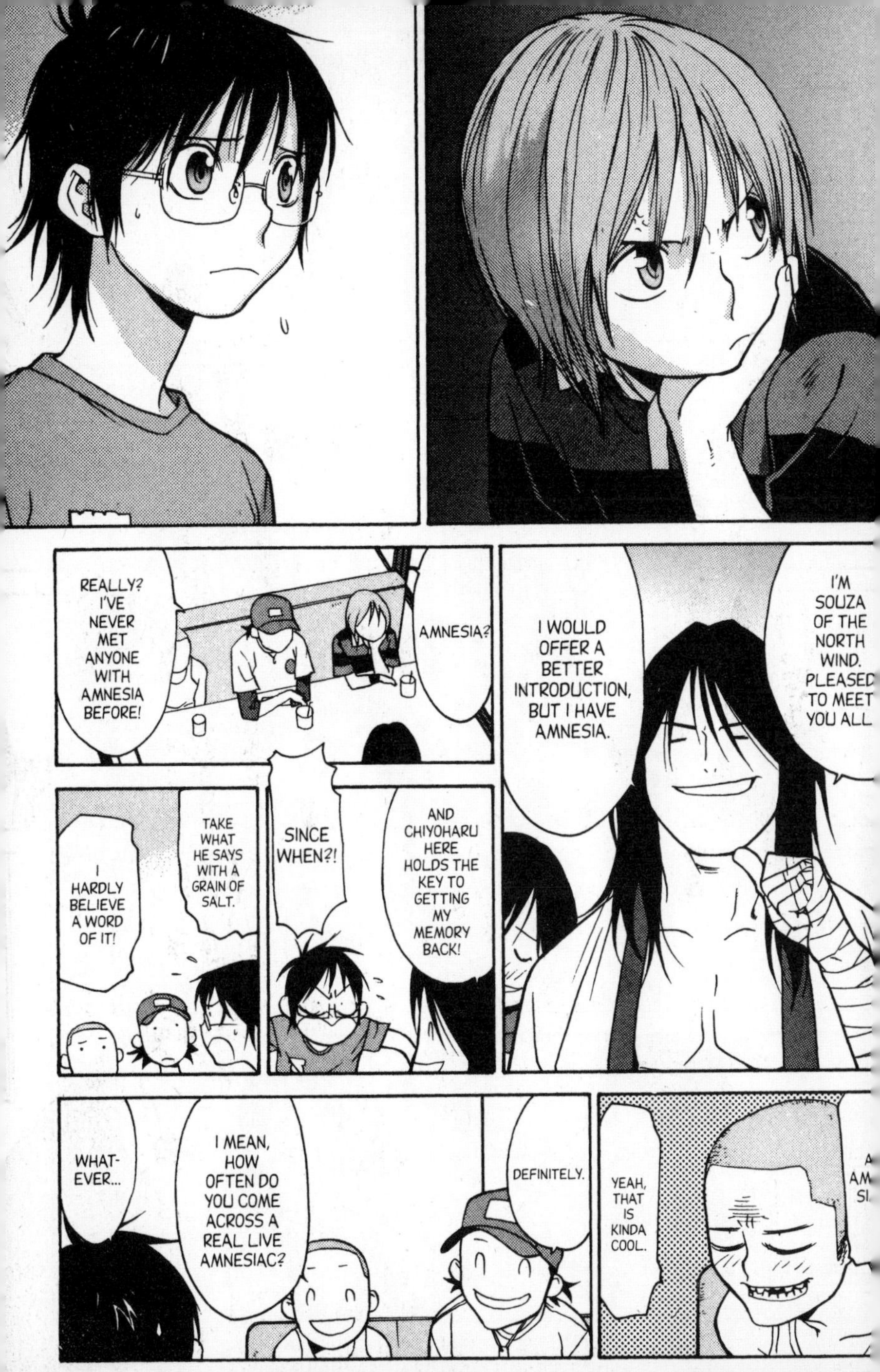
I'M SOUZA OF THE NORTH WIND. PLEASED TO MEET YOU ALL.
I WOULD OFFER A BETTER INTRODUCTION, BUT I HAVE AMNESIA.
AMNESIA?
REALLY? I'VE NEVER MET ANYONE WITH AMNESIA BEFORE!
AND CHIYOHARU HERE HOLDS THE KEY TO GETTING MY MEMORY BACK!
SINCE WHEN?!
TAKE WHAT HE SAYS WITH A GRAIN OF SALT.
I HARDLY BELIEVE A WORD OF IT!
YEAH, THAT IS KINDA COOL.
DEFINITELY.
I MEAN, HOW OFTEN DO YOU COME ACROSS A REAL LIVE AMNESIAC?
WHAT-EVER...

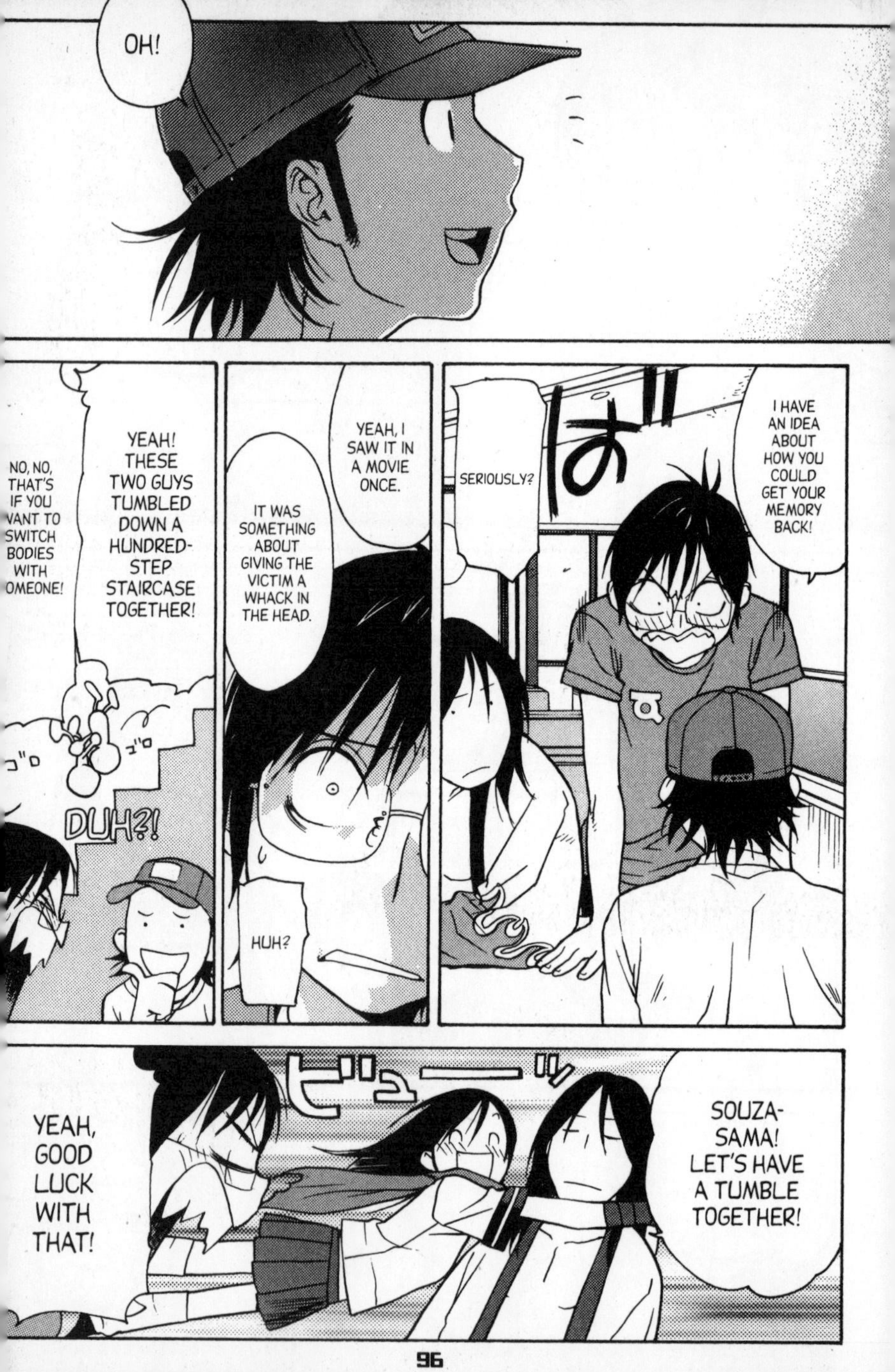
OH!
I HAVE AN IDEA ABOUT HOW YOU COULD GET YOUR MEMORY BACK!
SERIOUSLY?
YEAH, I SAW IT IN A MOVIE ONCE.
IT WAS SOMETHING ABOUT GIVING THE VICTIM A WHACK IN THE HEAD.
HUH?
YEAH! THESE TWO GUYS TUMBLED DOWN A HUNDRED-STEP STAIRCASE TOGETHER!
DUH?!
NO, NO, THAT'S IF YOU VANT TO SWITCH BODIES WITH OMEONE!
SOUZA-SAMA! LET'S HAVE A TUMBLE TOGETHER!
YEAH, GOOD LUCK WITH THAT!

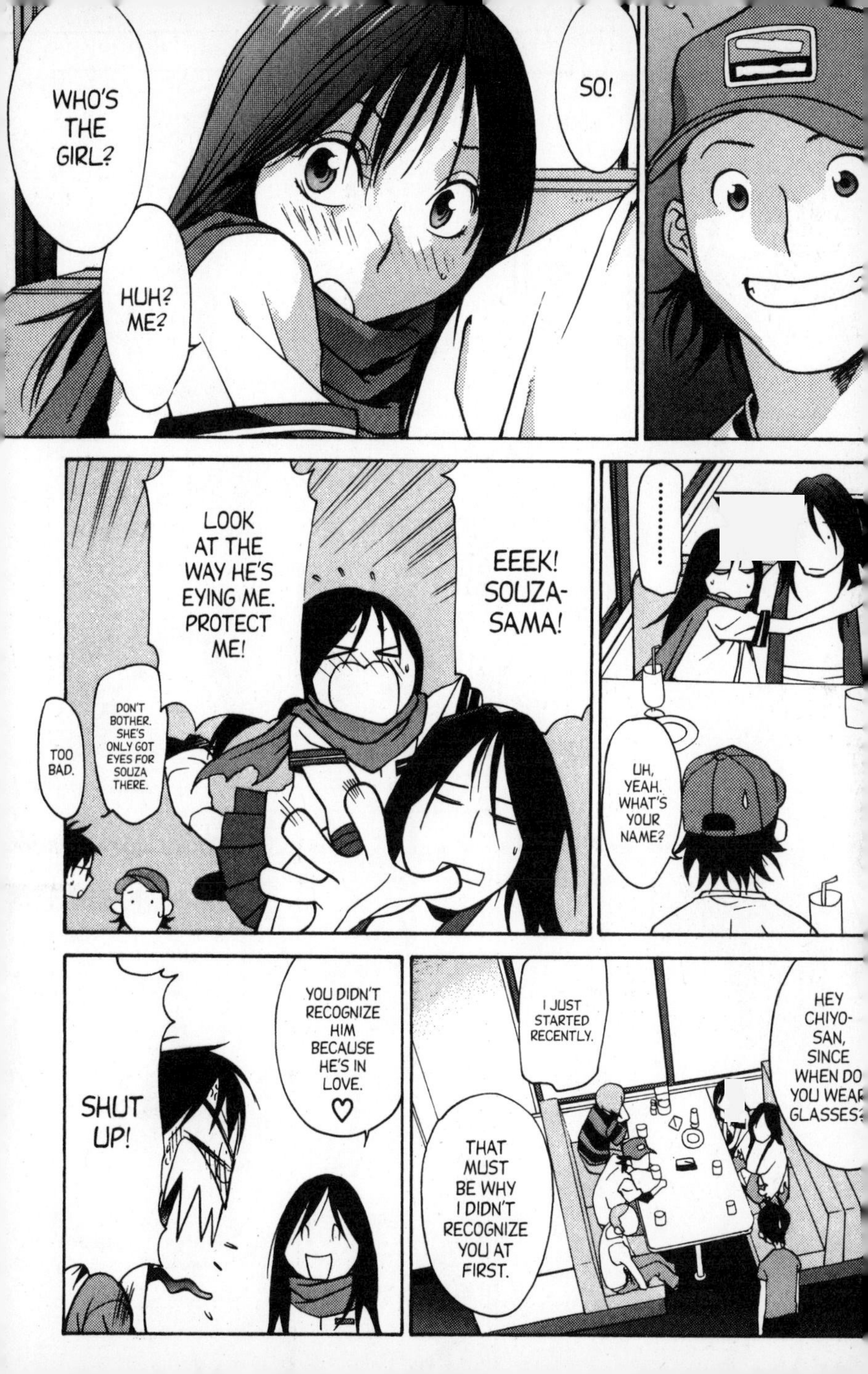
SO!
WHO'S THE GIRL?
HUH? ME?
......
UH, YEAH. WHAT'S YOUR NAME?
EEEK! SOUZA-SAMA!
LOOK AT THE WAY HE'S EYING ME. PROTECT ME!
DON'T BOTHER. SHE'S ONLY GOT EYES FOR SOUZA THERE.
TOO BAD.
HEY CHIYO-SAN, SINCE WHEN DO YOU WEAR GLASSES?
I JUST STARTED RECENTLY.
THAT MUST BE WHY I DIDN'T RECOGNIZE YOU AT FIRST.
YOU DIDN'T RECOGNIZE HIM BECAUSE HE'S IN LOVE. ♡
SHUT UP!

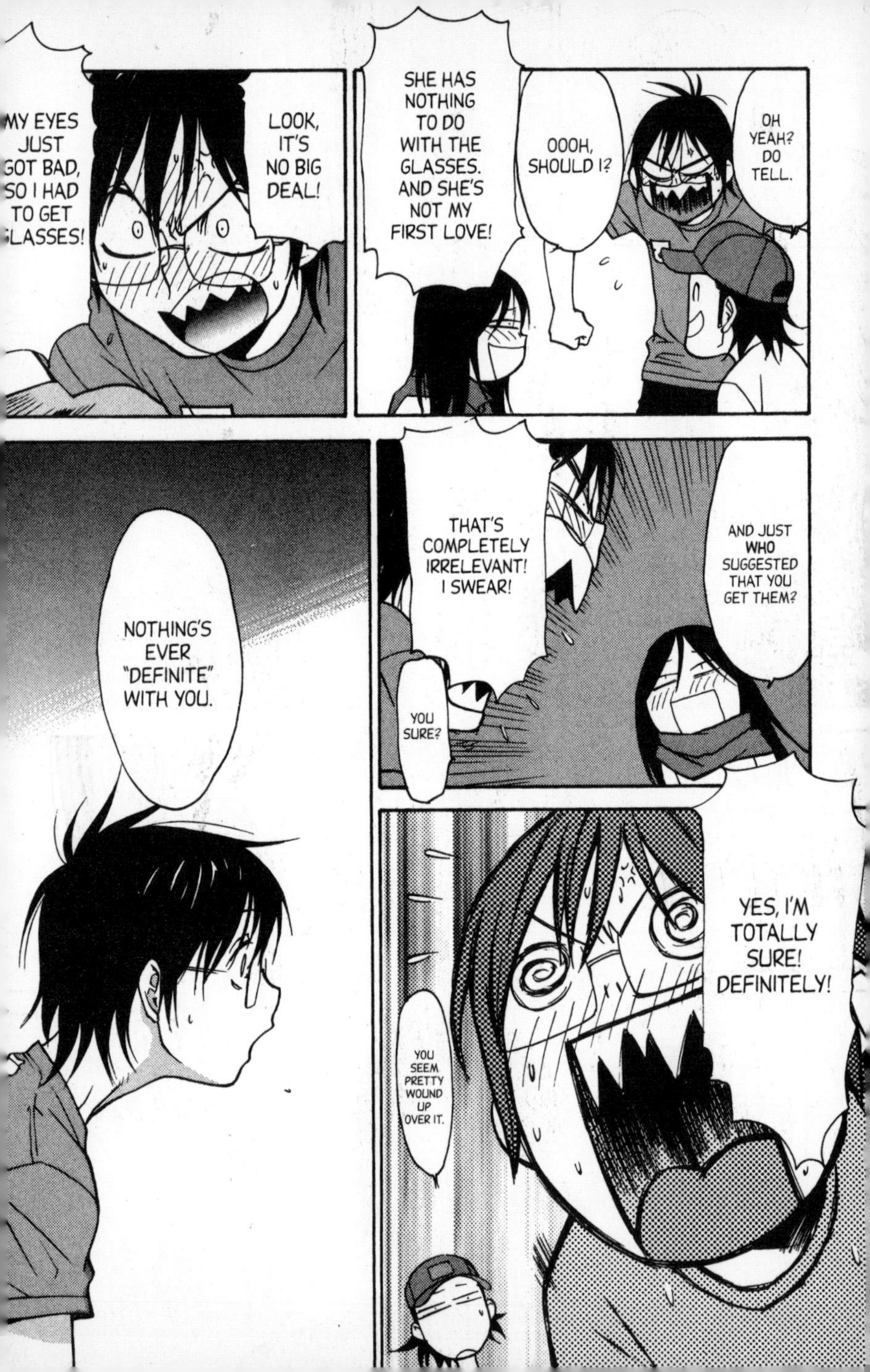
OH YEAH? DO TELL.
OOOH, SHOULD I?
SHE HAS NOTHING TO DO WITH THE GLASSES. AND SHE'S NOT MY FIRST LOVE!
LOOK, IT'S NO BIG DEAL!
MY EYES JUST GOT BAD, SO I HAD TO GET GLASSES!
AND JUST WHO SUGGESTED THAT YOU GET THEM?
THAT'S COMPLETELY IRRELEVANT! I SWEAR!
YOU SURE?
YES, I'M TOTALLY SURE! DEFINITELY!
YOU SEEM PRETTY WOUND UP OVER IT.
NOTHING'S EVER "DEFINITE" WITH YOU.

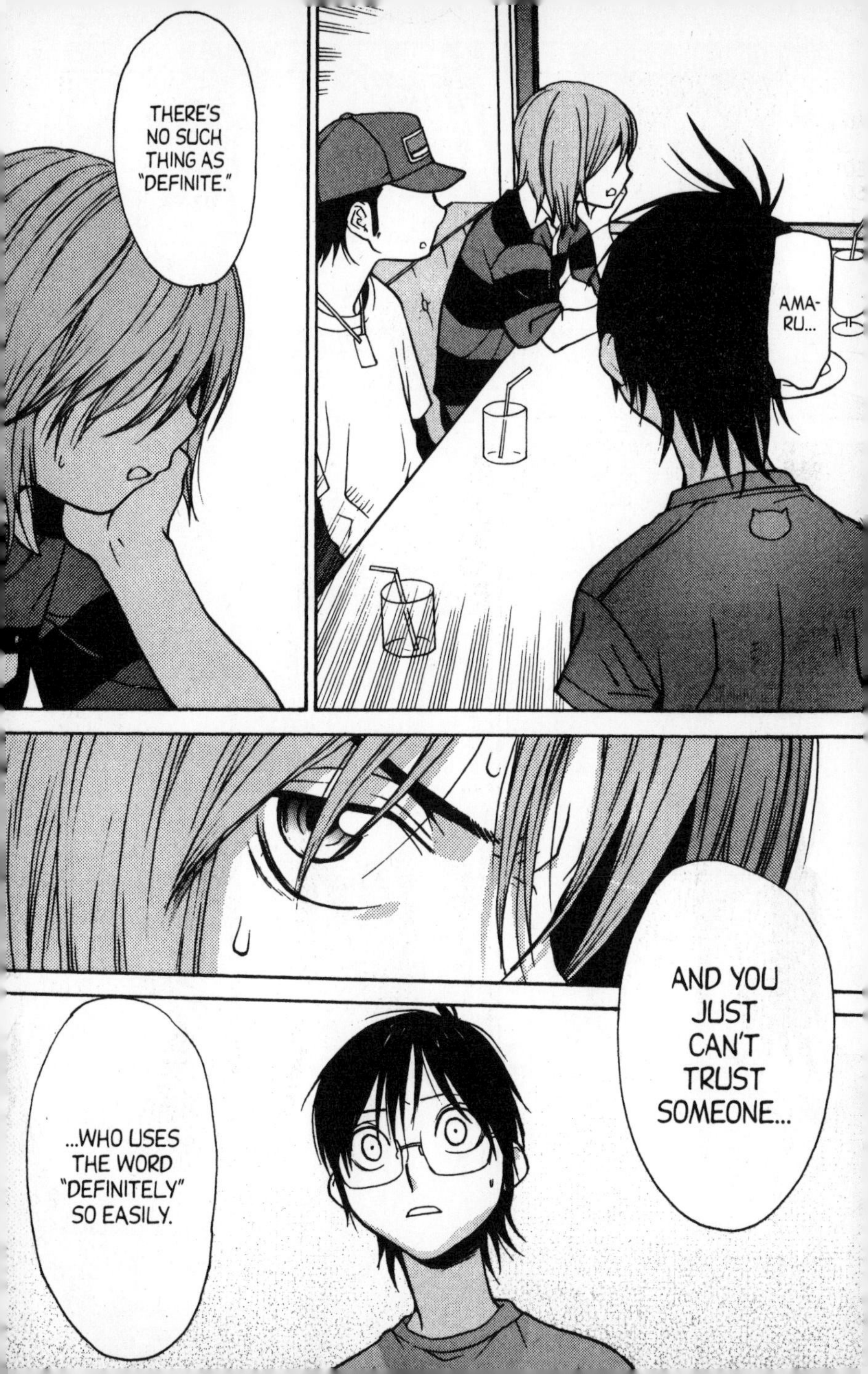
AMA-RU...
THERE'S NO SUCH THING AS "DEFINITE."
AND YOU JUST CAN'T TRUST SOMEONE...
...WHO USES THE WORD "DEFINITELY" SO EASILY.

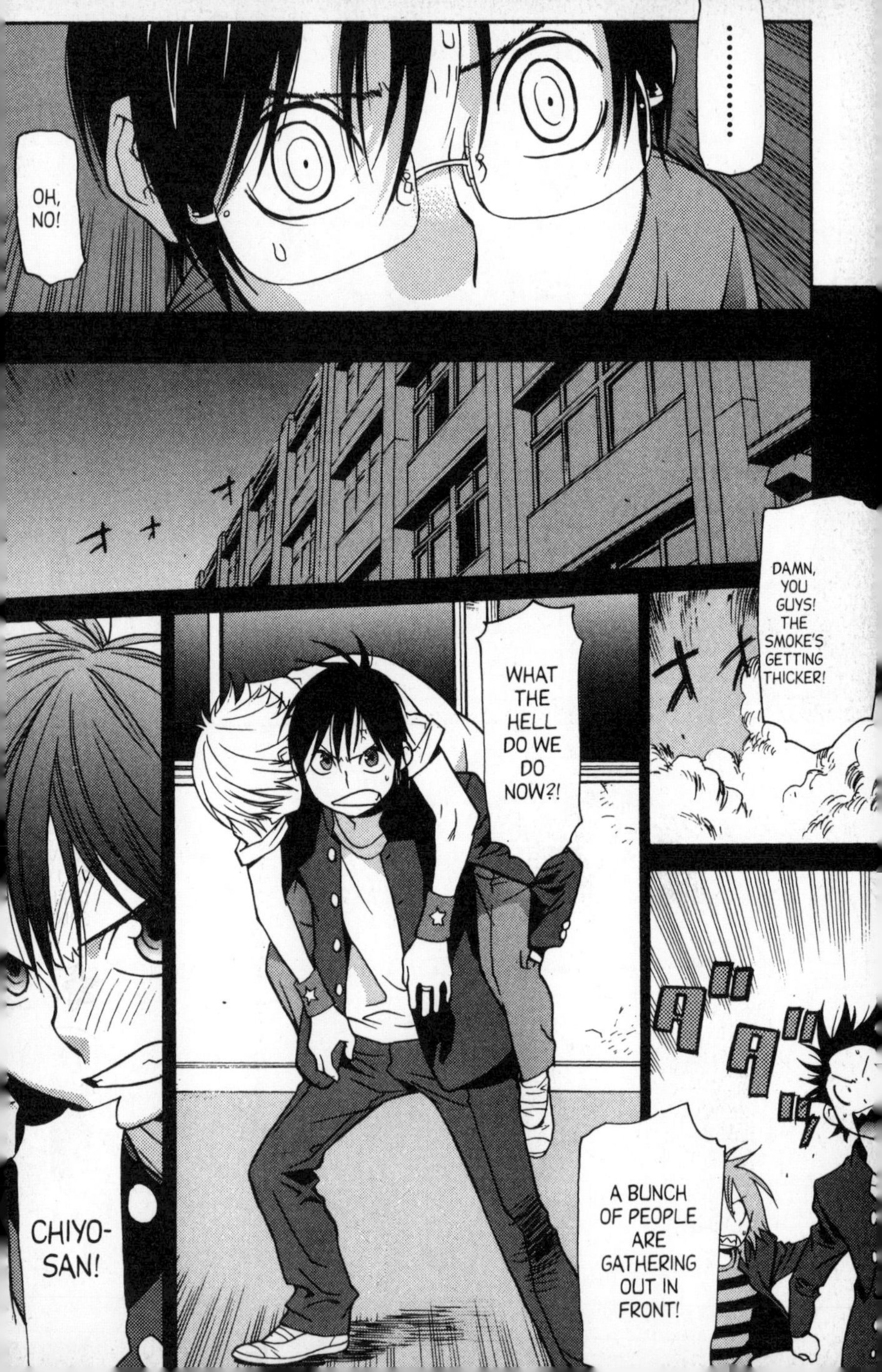

......
OH, NO!
DAMN, YOU GUYS! THE SMOKE'S GETTING THICKER!
A BUNCH OF PEOPLE ARE GATHERING OUT IN FRONT!
WHAT THE HELL DO WE DO NOW?!
CHIYO-SAN!

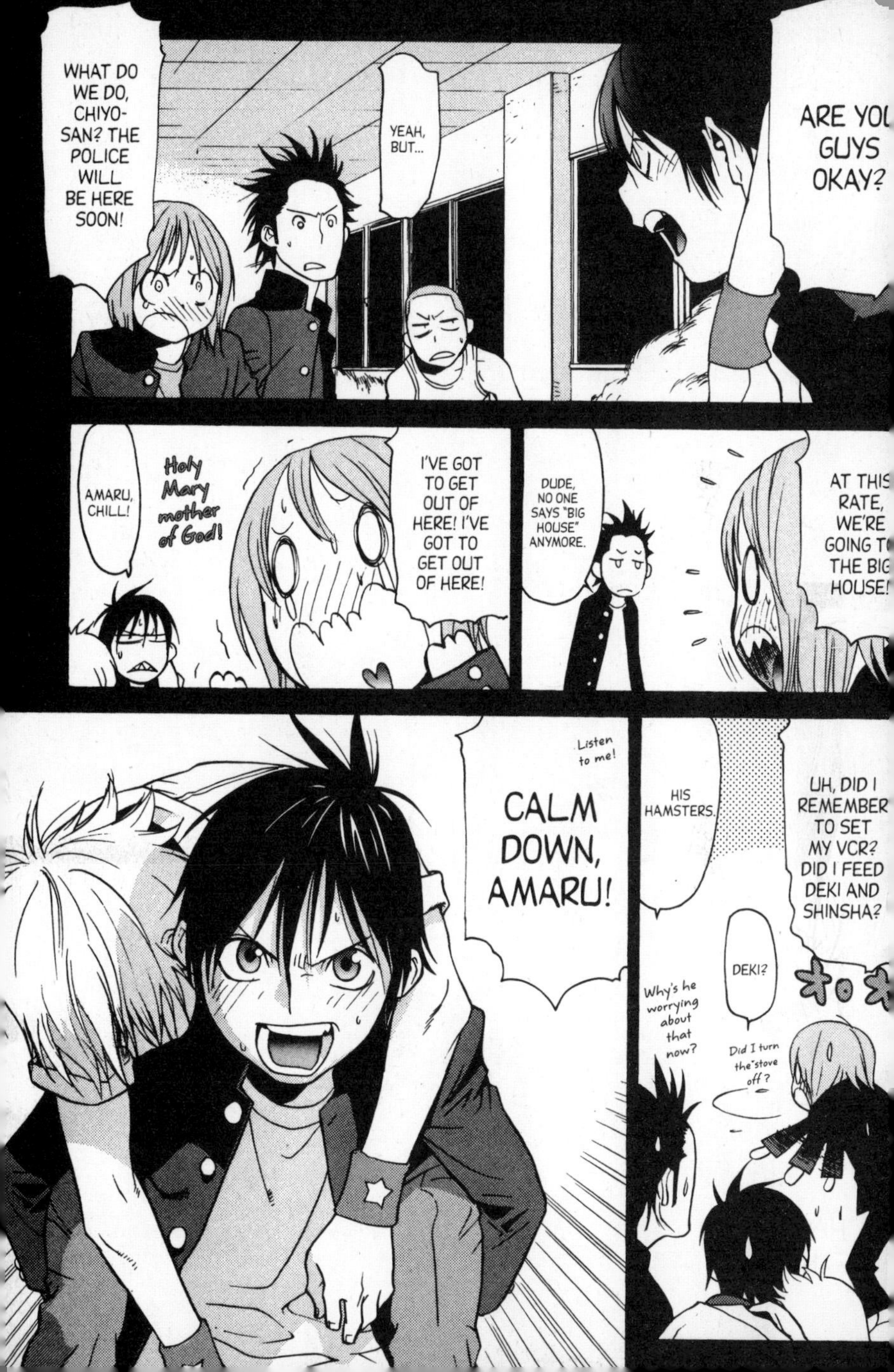
ARE YOU GUYS OKAY?
YEAH, BUT...
WHAT DO WE DO, CHIYO-SAN? THE POLICE WILL BE HERE SOON!
AT THIS RATE, WE'RE GOING TO THE BIG HOUSE!
DUDE, NO ONE SAYS "BIG HOUSE" ANYMORE.
I'VE GOT TO GET OUT OF HERE! I'VE GOT TO GET OUT OF HERE!
Holy Mary mother of God!
AMARU, CHILL!
UH, DID I REMEMBER TO SET MY VCR? DID I FEED DEKI AND SHINSHA?
HIS HAMSTERS.
DEKI?
Did I turn the stove off?
Why's he worrying about that now?
Listen to me!
CALM DOWN, AMARU!

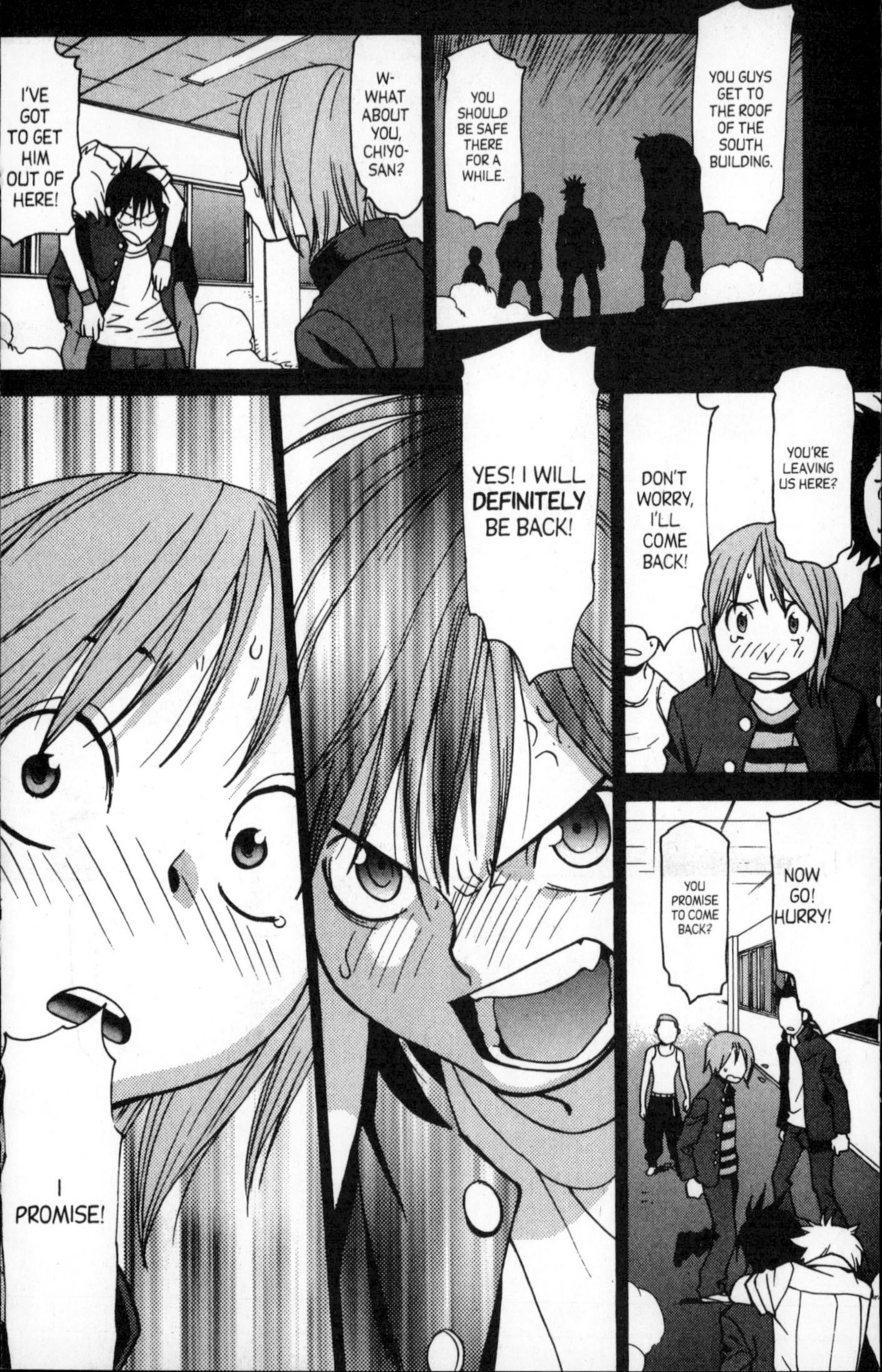
YOU GUYS GET TO THE ROOF OF THE SOUTH BUILDING.
YOU SHOULD BE SAFE THERE FOR A WHILE.
W-WHAT ABOUT YOU, CHIYO-SAN?
I'VE GOT TO GET HIM OUT OF HERE!
YOU'RE LEAVING US HERE?
DON'T WORRY, I'LL COME BACK!
NOW GO! HURRY!
YOU PROMISE TO COME BACK?
YES! I WILL **DEFINITELY** BE BACK!
I PROMISE!

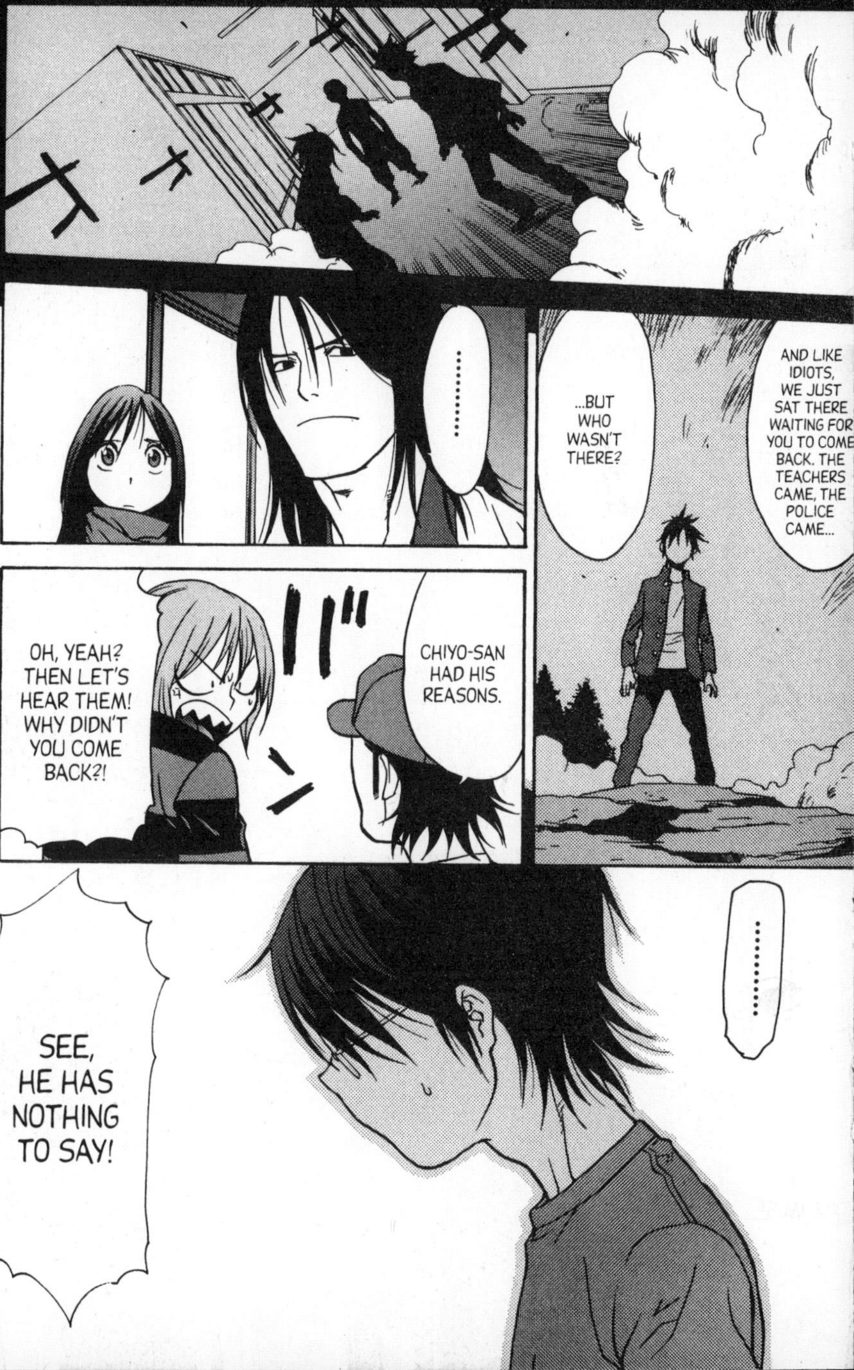
AND LIKE IDIOTS, WE JUST SAT THERE WAITING FOR YOU TO COME BACK. THE TEACHERS CAME, THE POLICE CAME...
...BUT WHO WASN'T THERE?
....
CHIYO-SAN HAD HIS REASONS.
OH, YEAH? THEN LET'S HEAR THEM! WHY DIDN'T YOU COME BACK?!
....
SEE, HE HAS NOTHING TO SAY!

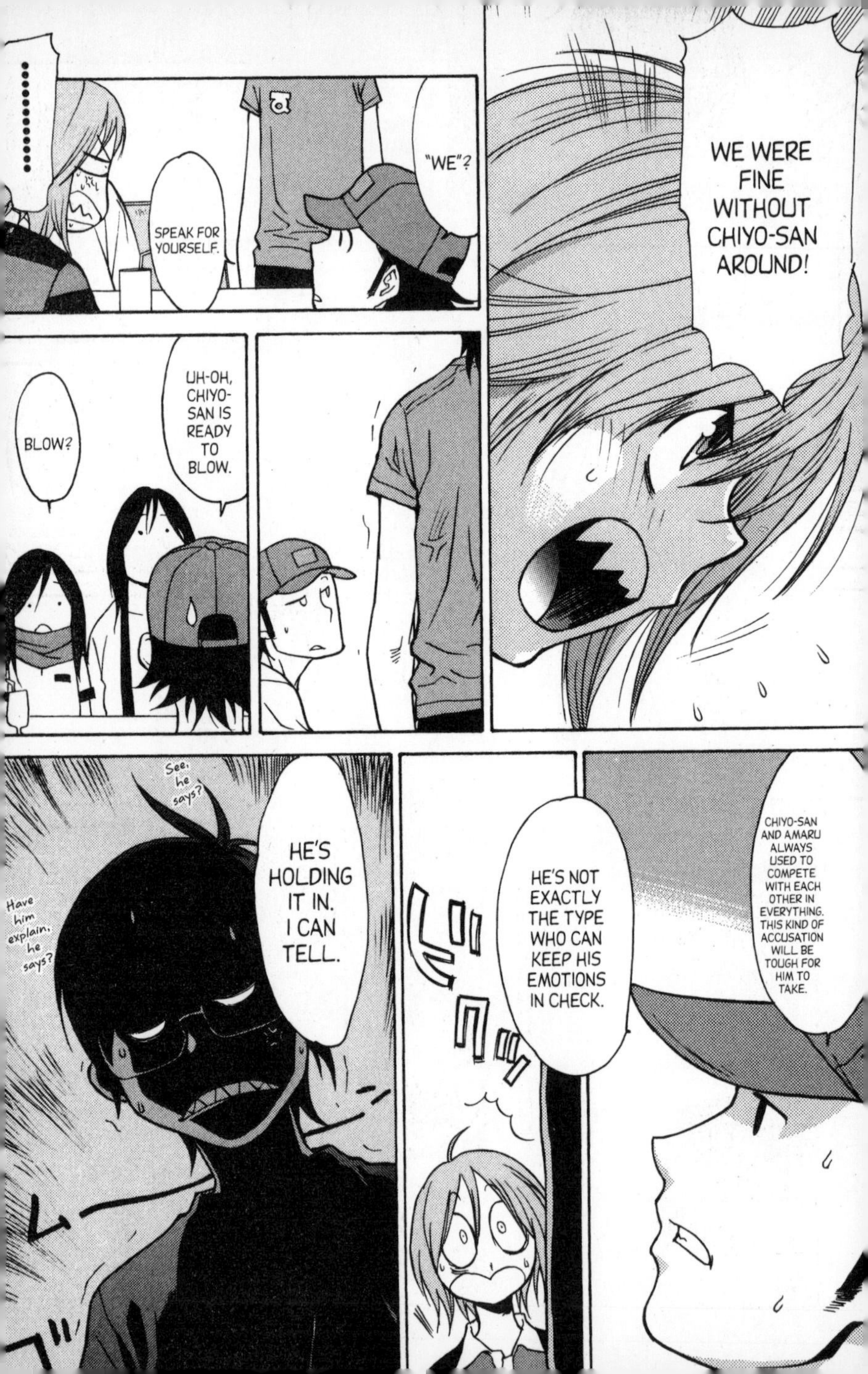
WE WERE FINE WITHOUT CHIYO-SAN AROUND!
"WE"?
SPEAK FOR YOURSELF.
UH-OH, CHIYO-SAN IS READY TO BLOW.
BLOW?
CHIYO-SAN AND AMARU ALWAYS USED TO COMPETE WITH EACH OTHER IN EVERYTHING. THIS KIND OF ACCUSATION WILL BE TOUGH FOR HIM TO TAKE.
HE'S NOT EXACTLY THE TYPE WHO CAN KEEP HIS EMOTIONS IN CHECK.
HE'S HOLDING IT IN. I CAN TELL.
See, he says?
Have him explain, he says?

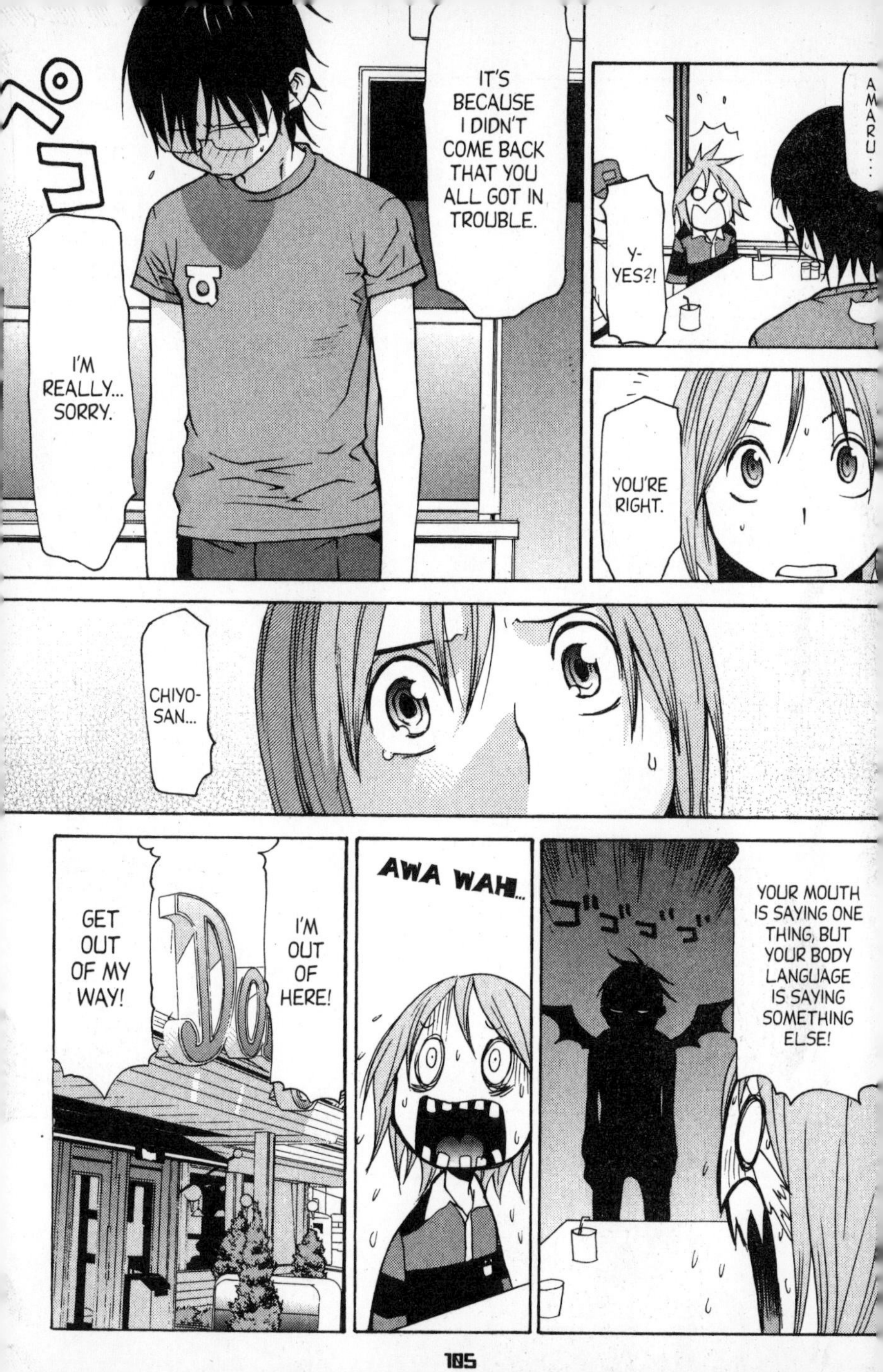
AMARU...
Y- YES?!
YOU'RE RIGHT.
IT'S BECAUSE I DIDN'T COME BACK THAT YOU ALL GOT IN TROUBLE.
ペコ
I'M REALLY... SORRY.
CHIYO-SAN...
ゴゴゴゴ
YOUR MOUTH IS SAYING ONE THING, BUT YOUR BODY LANGUAGE IS SAYING SOMETHING ELSE!
AWA WAH...
I'M OUT OF HERE!
GET OUT OF MY WAY!

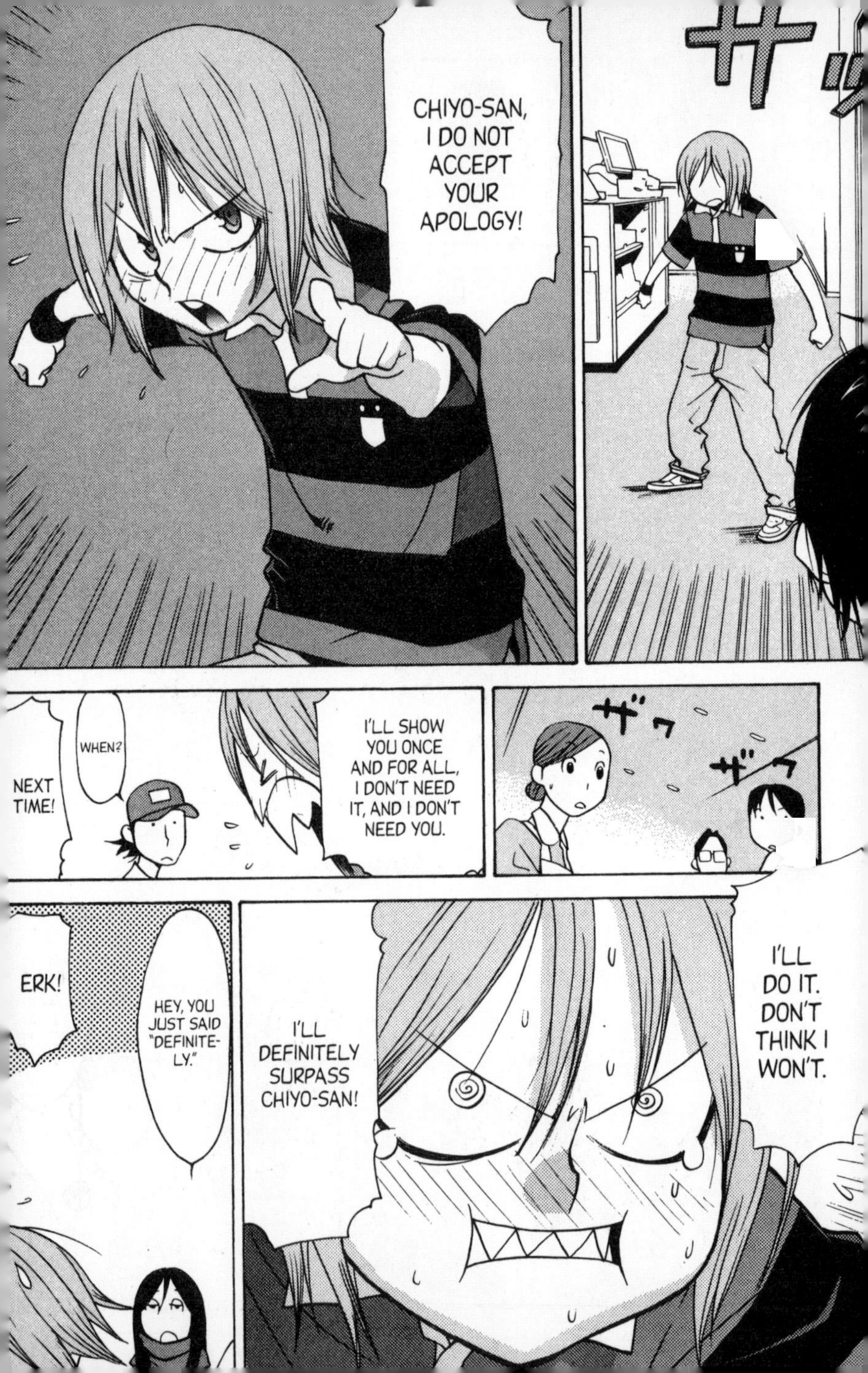
CHIYO-SAN, I DO NOT ACCEPT YOUR APOLOGY!
I'LL SHOW YOU ONCE AND FOR ALL, I DON'T NEED IT, AND I DON'T NEED YOU.
WHEN?
NEXT TIME!
I'LL DO IT. DON'T THINK I WON'T.
I'LL DEFINITELY SURPASS CHIYO-SAN!
HEY, YOU JUST SAID "DEFINITE-LY."
ERK!

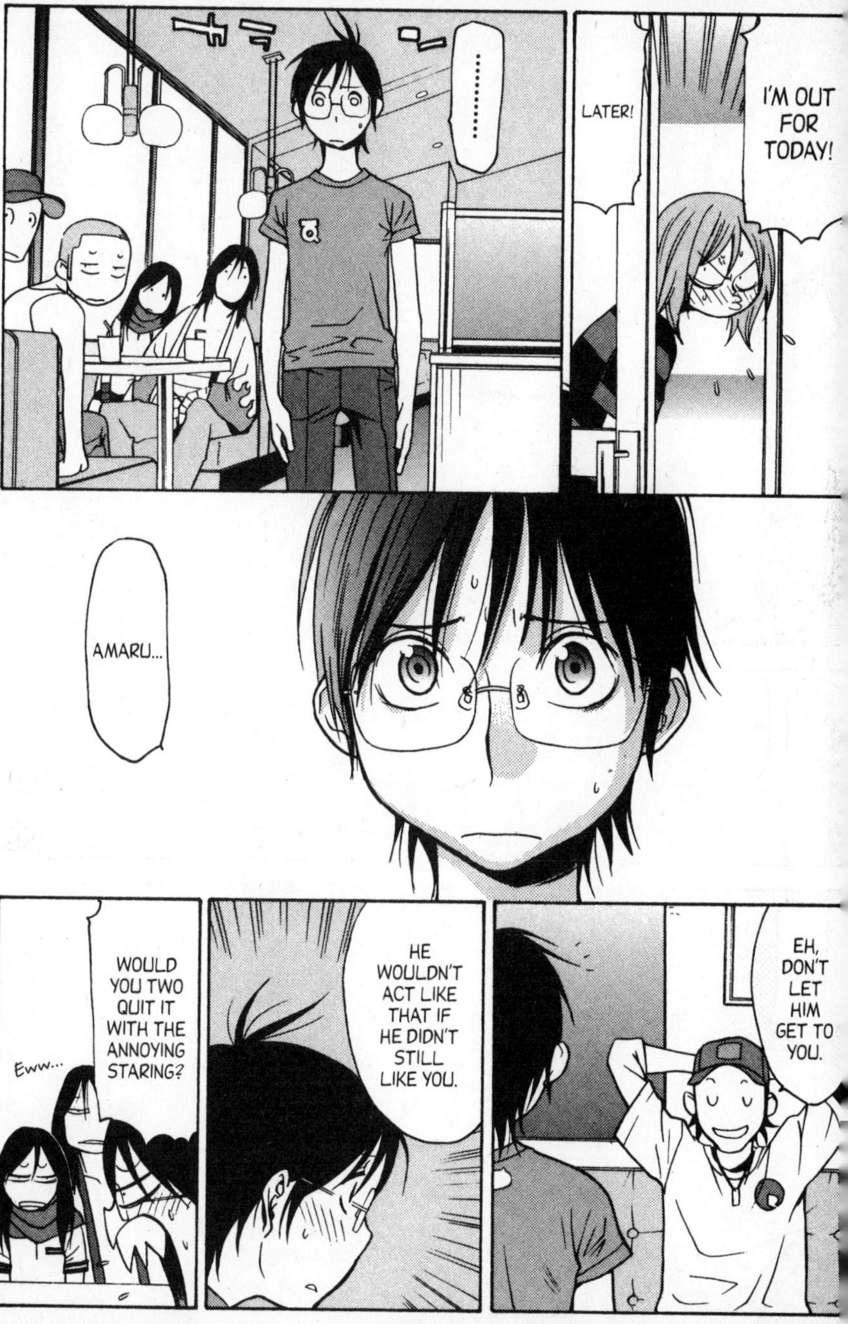
I'M OUT FOR TODAY!
LATER!
......
AMARU...
EH, DON'T LET HIM GET TO YOU.
HE WOULDN'T ACT LIKE THAT IF HE DIDN'T STILL LIKE YOU.
WOULD YOU TWO QUIT IT WITH THE ANNOYING STARING?
Eww...

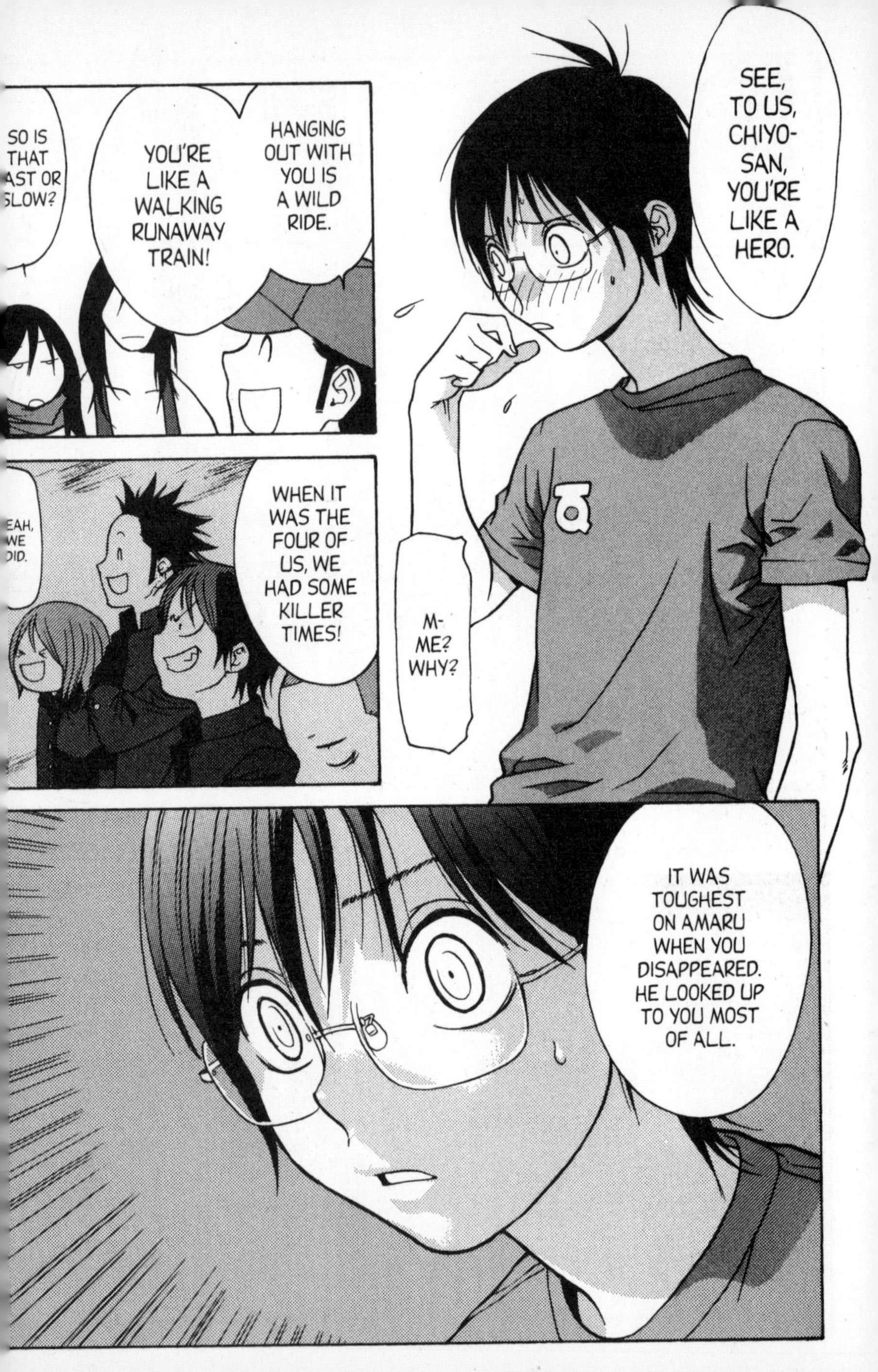
SEE, TO US, CHIYO-SAN, YOU'RE LIKE A HERO.
M-ME? WHY?
HANGING OUT WITH YOU IS A WILD RIDE.
YOU'RE LIKE A WALKING RUNAWAY TRAIN!
SO IS THAT AST OR SLOW?
WHEN IT WAS THE FOUR OF US, WE HAD SOME KILLER TIMES!
EAH, WE DID.
IT WAS TOUGHEST ON AMARU WHEN YOU DISAPPEARED. HE LOOKED UP TO YOU MOST OF ALL.

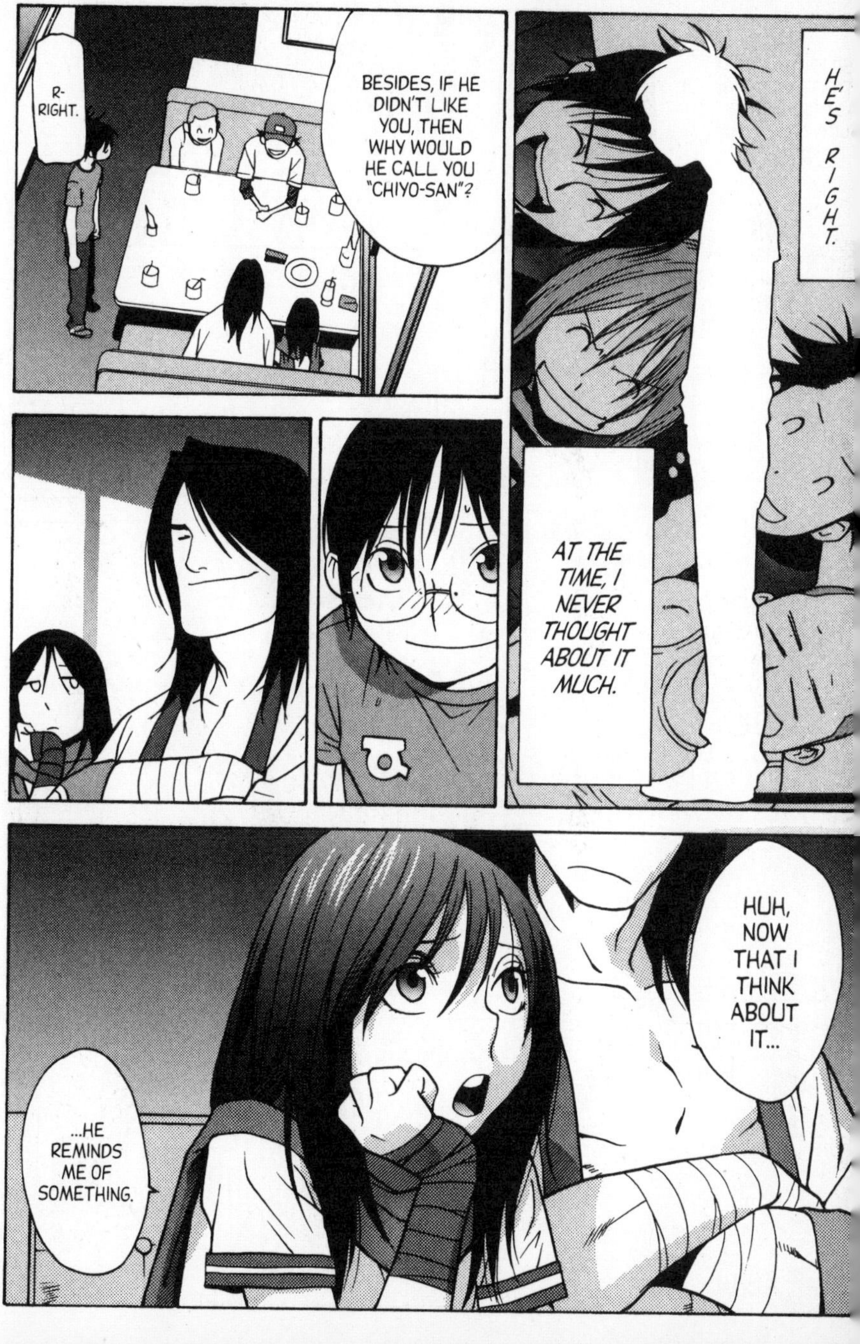
HE'S RIGHT.
AT THE TIME, I NEVER THOUGHT ABOUT IT MUCH.
BESIDES, IF HE DIDN'T LIKE YOU, THEN WHY WOULD HE CALL YOU "CHIYO-SAN"?
R-RIGHT.
HUH, NOW THAT I THINK ABOUT IT...
...HE REMINDS ME OF SOMETHING.

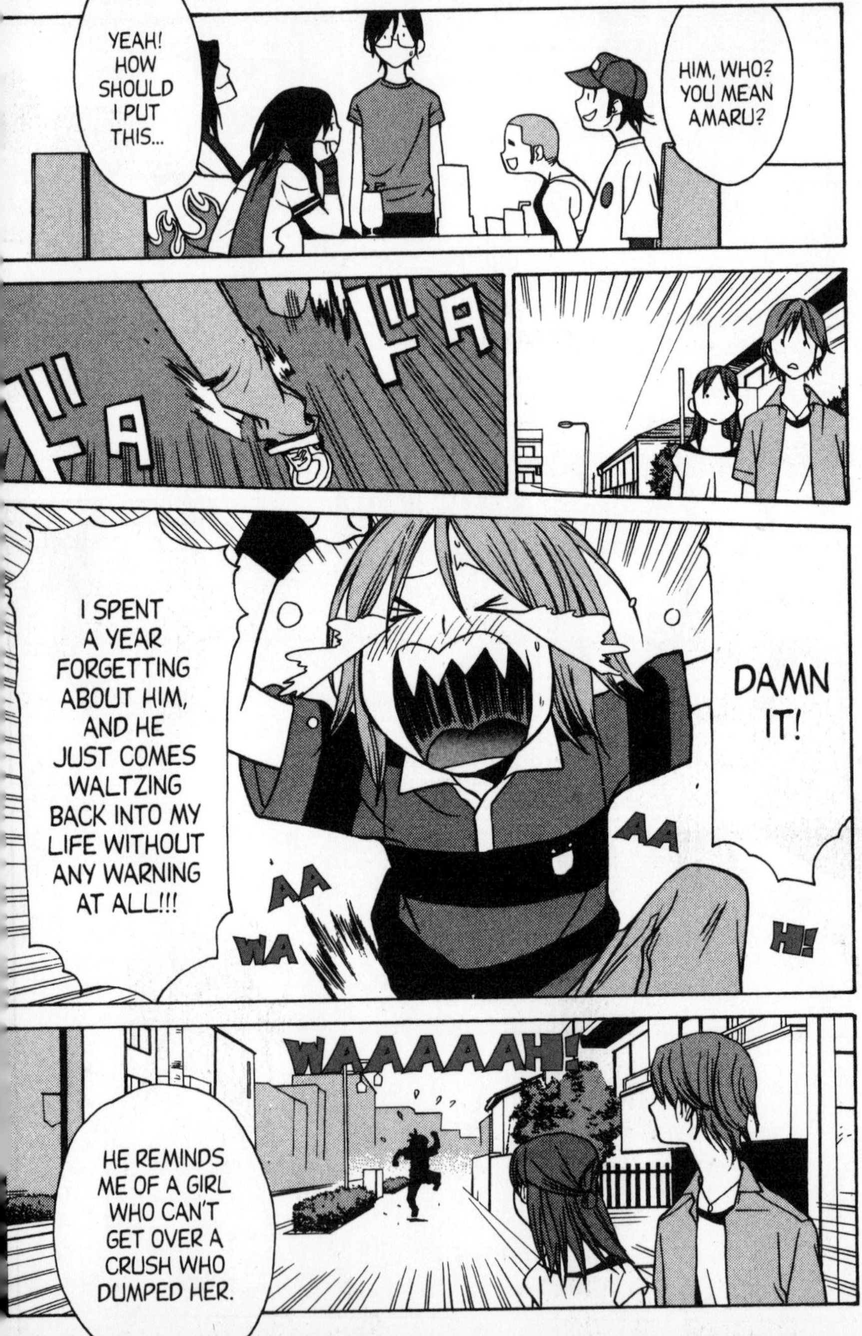
HIM, WHO? YOU MEAN AMARU?
YEAH! HOW SHOULD I PUT THIS...
DAMN IT!
I SPENT A YEAR FORGETTING ABOUT HIM, AND HE JUST COMES WALTZING BACK INTO MY LIFE WITHOUT ANY WARNING AT ALL!!!
WA AA AA H!
WAAAAAH!
HE REMINDS ME OF A GIRL WHO CAN'T GET OVER A CRUSH WHO DUMPED HER.

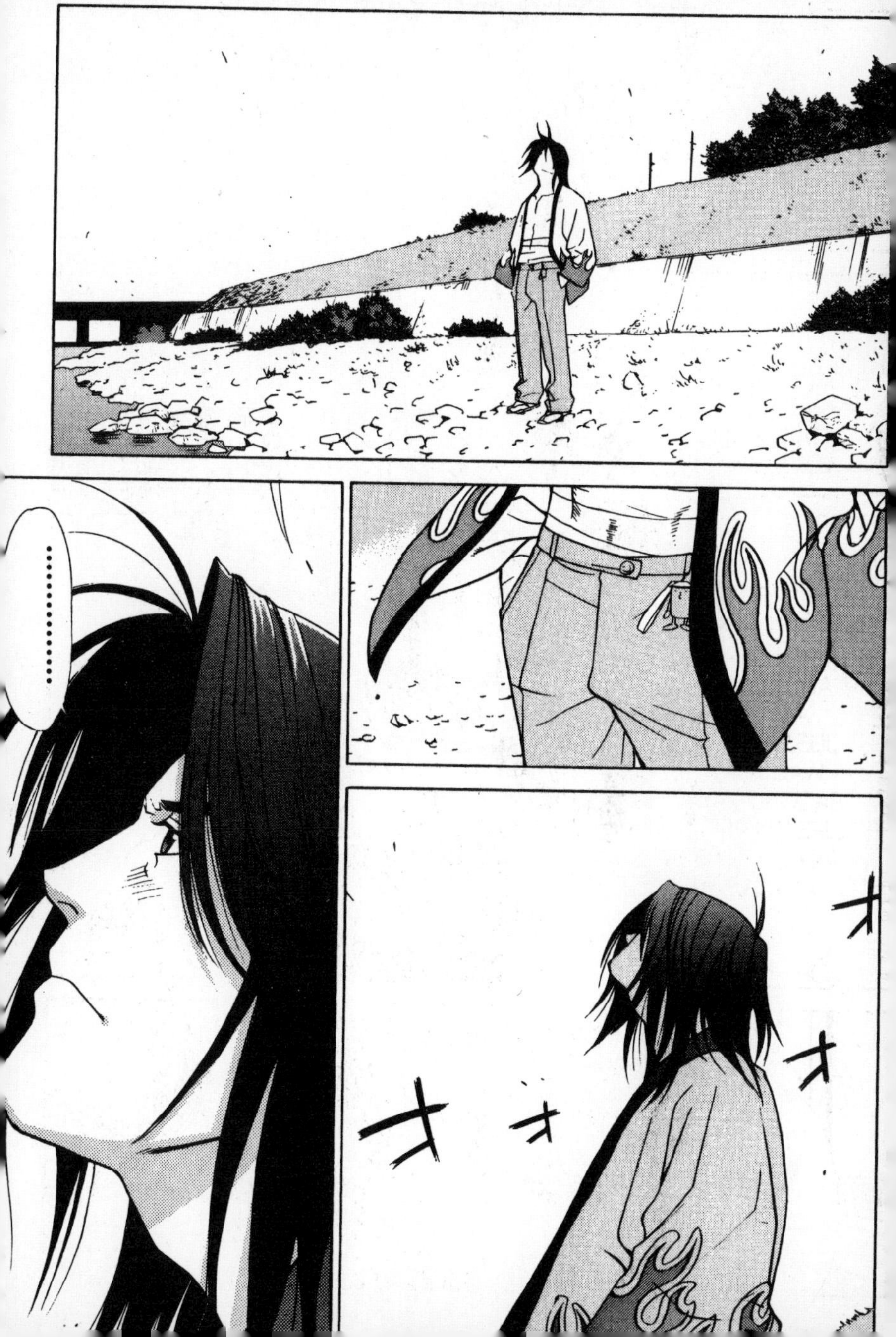
オ オ オ オ
……

#4 STRAP☆TRAP

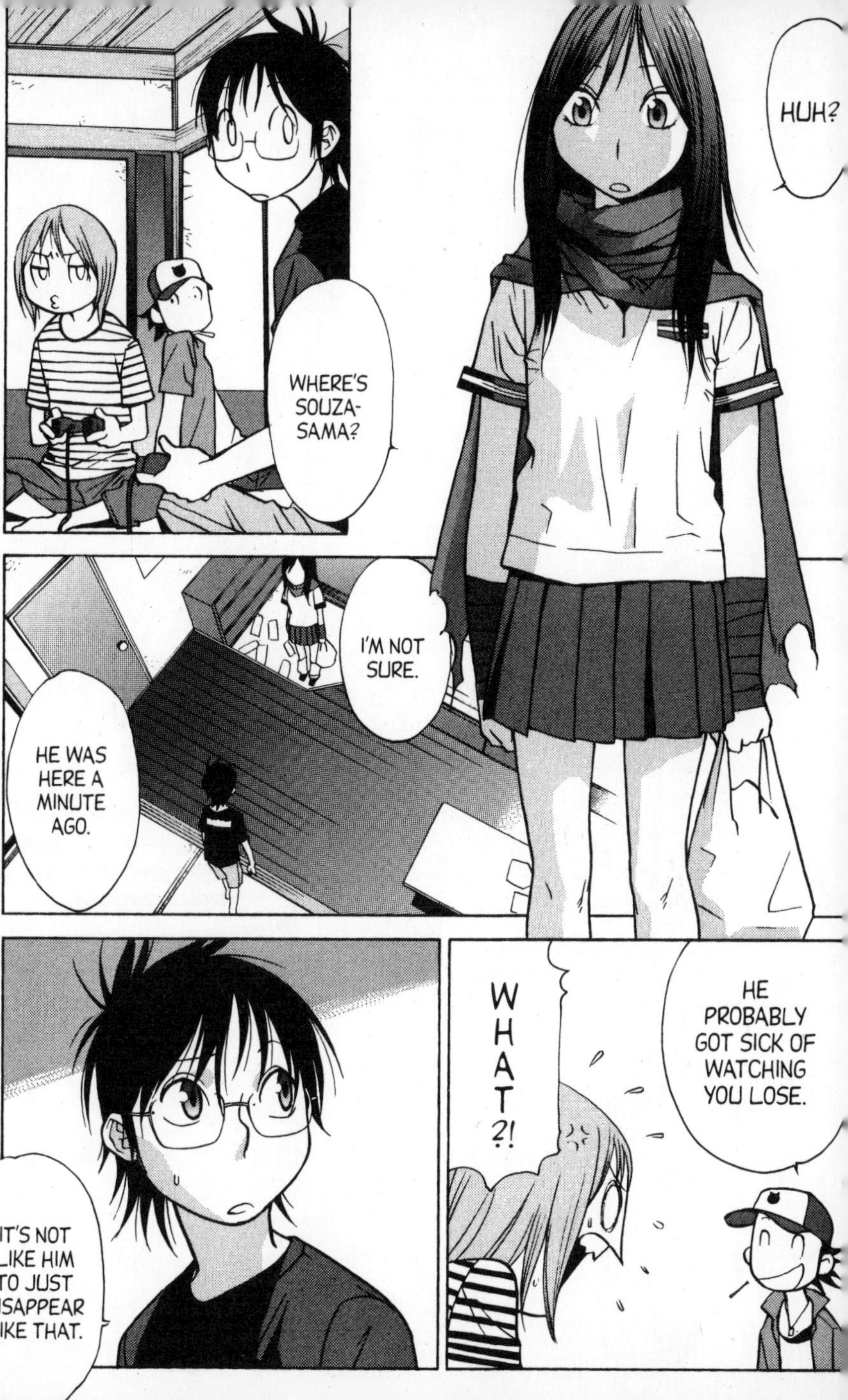
HUH?
WHERE'S SOUZA-SAMA?
I'M NOT SURE.
HE WAS HERE A MINUTE AGO.
HE PROBABLY GOT SICK OF WATCHING YOU LOSE.
WHAT?!
IT'S NOT LIKE HIM TO JUST DISAPPEAR LIKE THAT.

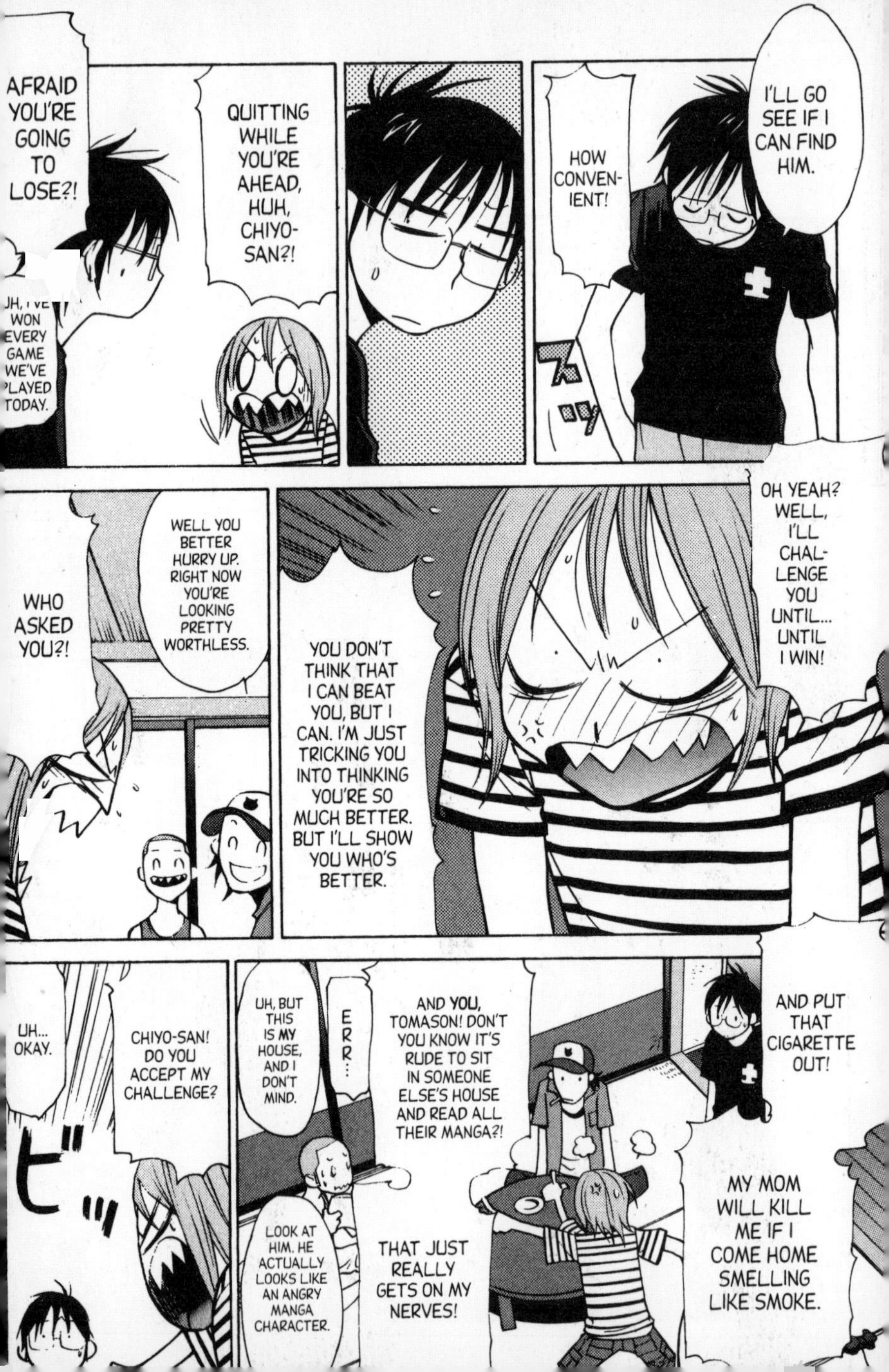

I'LL GO SEE IF I CAN FIND HIM.
ズッ
HOW CONVEN-IENT!
QUITTING WHILE YOU'RE AHEAD, HUH, CHIYO-SAN?!
AFRAID YOU'RE GOING TO LOSE?!
UH, I'VE WON EVERY GAME WE'VE PLAYED TODAY.
OH YEAH? WELL, I'LL CHAL-LENGE YOU UNTIL... UNTIL I WIN!
YOU DON'T THINK THAT I CAN BEAT YOU, BUT I CAN. I'M JUST TRICKING YOU INTO THINKING YOU'RE SO MUCH BETTER. BUT I'LL SHOW YOU WHO'S BETTER.
WELL YOU BETTER HURRY UP. RIGHT NOW YOU'RE LOOKING PRETTY WORTHLESS.
WHO ASKED YOU?!
AND YOU, TOMASON! DON'T YOU KNOW IT'S RUDE TO SIT IN SOMEONE ELSE'S HOUSE AND READ ALL THEIR MANGA?!
AND PUT THAT CIGARETTE OUT!
MY MOM WILL KILL ME IF I COME HOME SMELLING LIKE SMOKE.
THAT JUST REALLY GETS ON MY NERVES!
ERR...
UH, BUT THIS IS MY HOUSE, AND I DON'T MIND.
LOOK AT HIM. HE ACTUALLY LOOKS LIKE AN ANGRY MANGA CHARACTER.
CHIYO-SAN! DO YOU ACCEPT MY CHALLENGE?
ビッ
UH... OKAY.

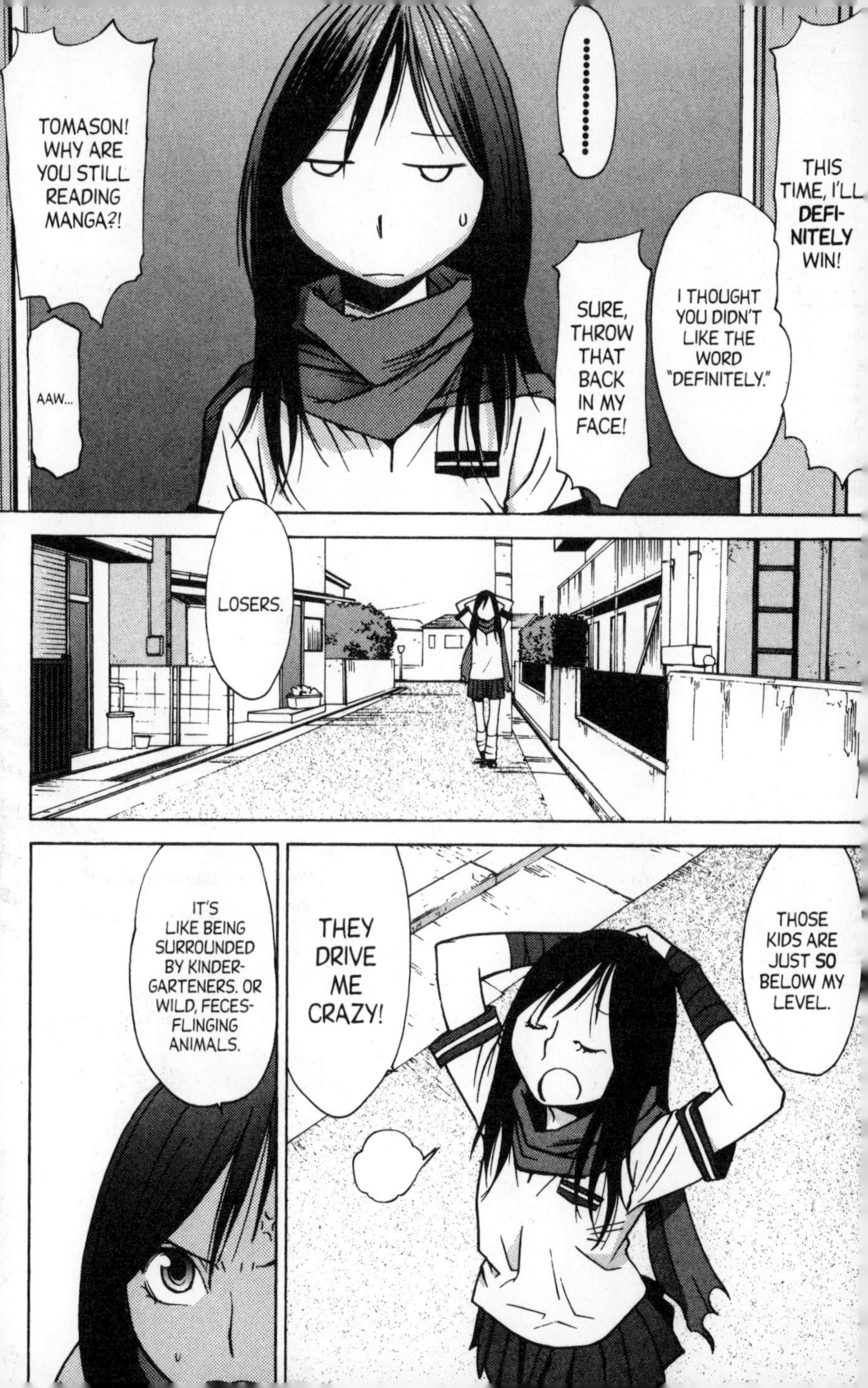
THIS TIME, I'LL **DEFINITELY** WIN!
I THOUGHT YOU DIDN'T LIKE THE WORD "DEFINITELY."
SURE, THROW THAT BACK IN MY FACE!
......
TOMASON! WHY ARE YOU STILL READING MANGA?!
AAW...
LOSERS.
THOSE KIDS ARE JUST **SO** BELOW MY LEVEL.
THEY DRIVE ME CRAZY!
IT'S LIKE BEING SURROUNDED BY KINDERGARTENERS. OR WILD, FECES-FLINGING ANIMALS.

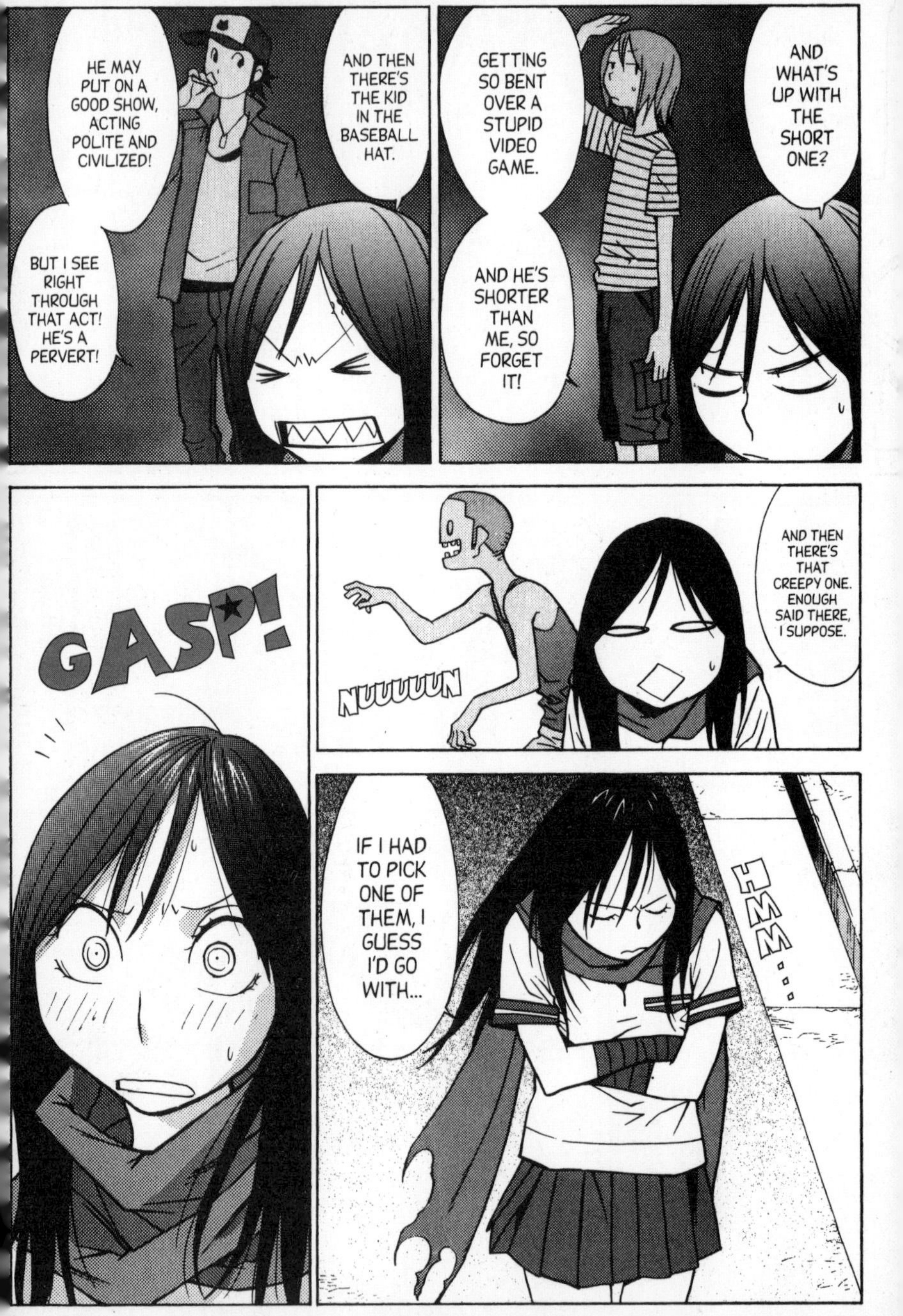
AND WHAT'S UP WITH THE SHORT ONE?
GETTING SO BENT OVER A STUPID VIDEO GAME.
AND HE'S SHORTER THAN ME, SO FORGET IT!
AND THEN THERE'S THE KID IN THE BASEBALL HAT.
HE MAY PUT ON A GOOD SHOW, ACTING POLITE AND CIVILIZED!
BUT I SEE RIGHT THROUGH THAT ACT! HE'S A PERVERT!
AND THEN THERE'S THAT CREEPY ONE. ENOUGH SAID THERE, I SUPPOSE.
NUUUUUN
HMM...
IF I HAD TO PICK ONE OF THEM, I GUESS I'D GO WITH...
GASP!

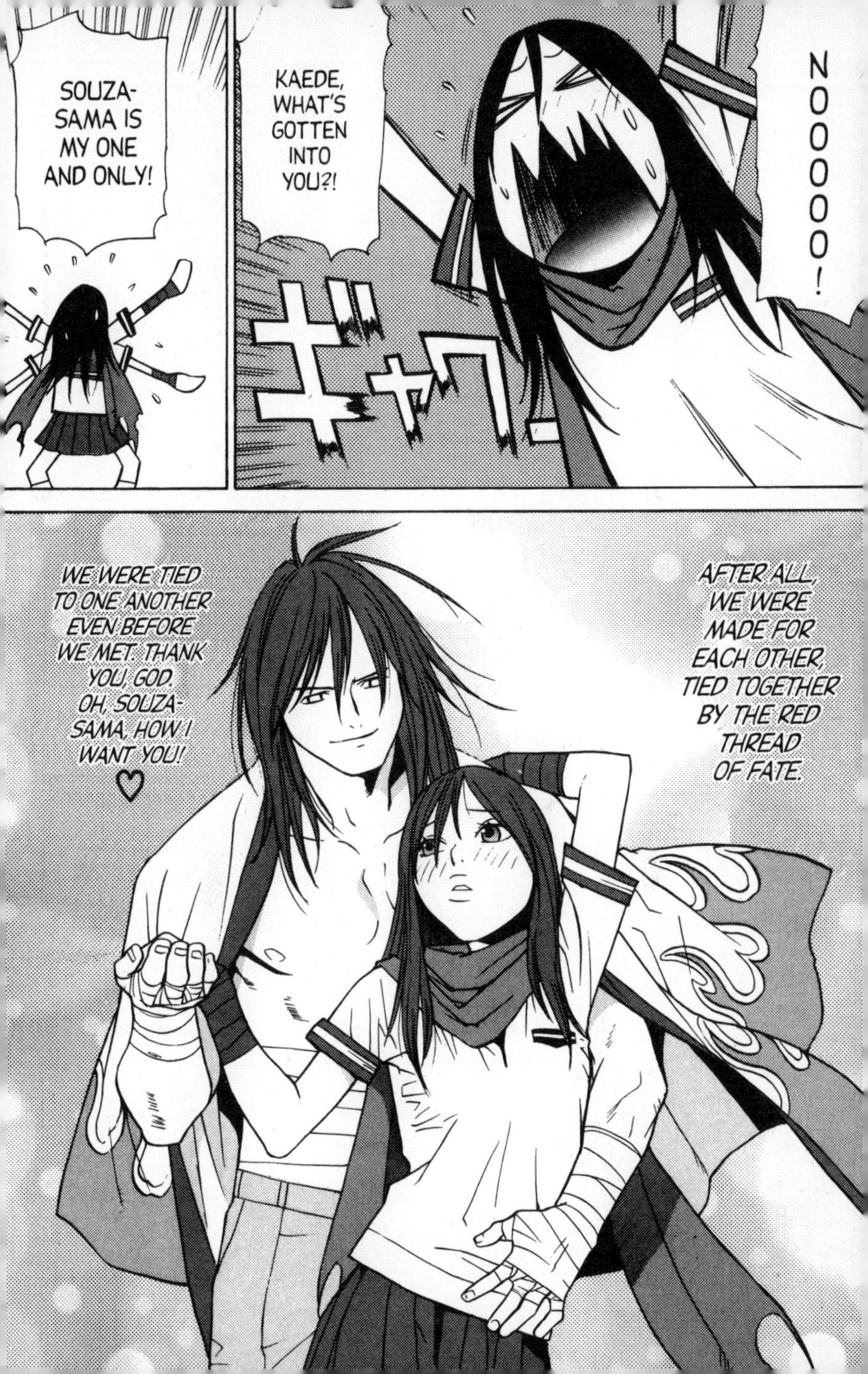
NOOOOO!
KAEDE, WHAT'S GOTTEN INTO YOU?!
ギャア!
SOUZA-SAMA IS MY ONE AND ONLY!
AFTER ALL, WE WERE MADE FOR EACH OTHER, TIED TOGETHER BY THE RED THREAD OF FATE.
WE WERE TIED TO ONE ANOTHER EVEN BEFORE WE MET. THANK YOU, GOD. OH, SOUZA-SAMA, HOW I WANT YOU! ♡

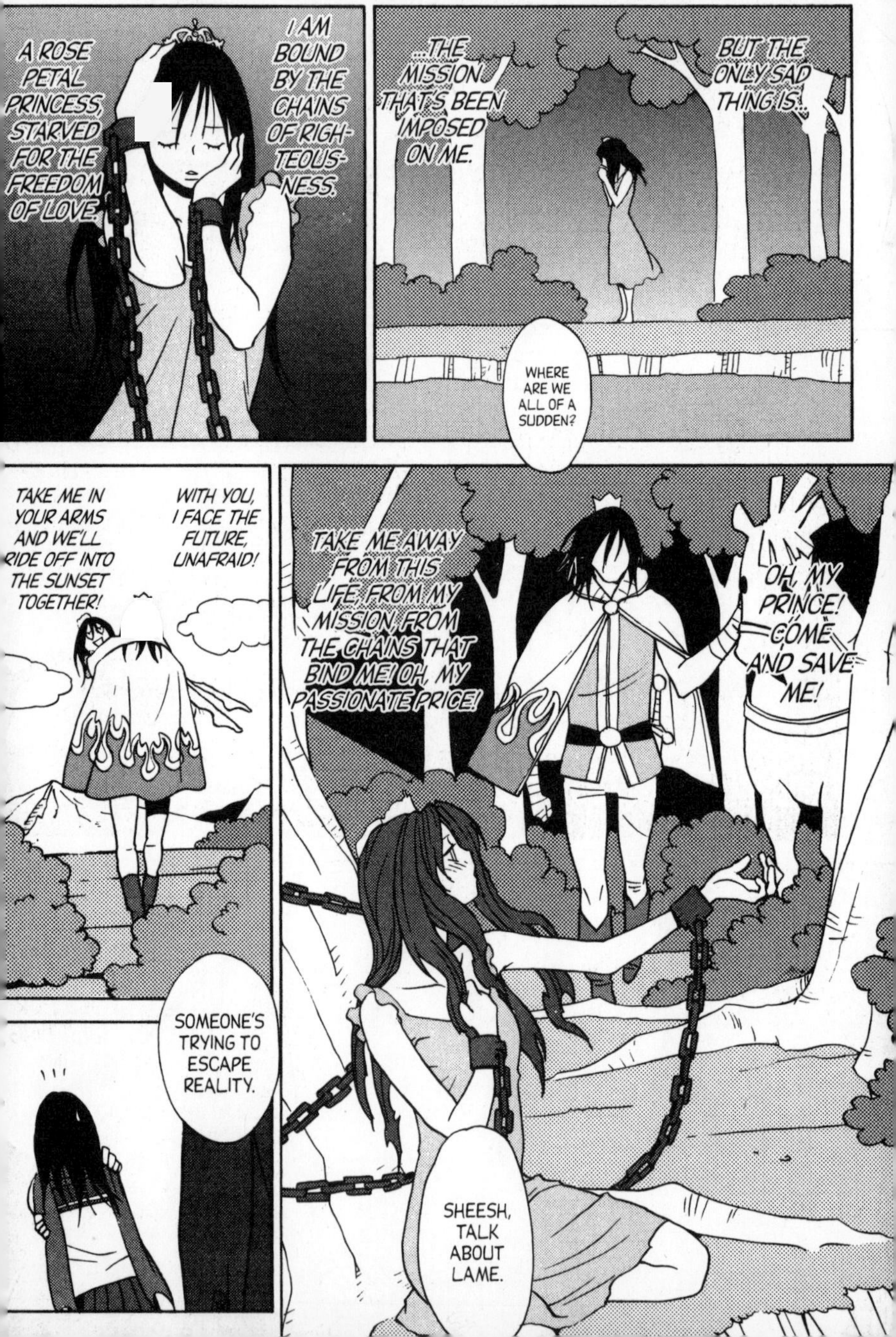
BUT THE ONLY SAD THING IS...
...THE MISSION THAT'S BEEN IMPOSED ON ME.
WHERE ARE WE ALL OF A SUDDEN?
I AM BOUND BY THE CHAINS OF RIGHTEOUSNESS.
A ROSE PETAL PRINCESS, STARVED FOR THE FREEDOM OF LOVE.
OH, MY PRINCE! COME AND SAVE ME!
TAKE ME AWAY FROM THIS LIFE, FROM MY MISSION, FROM THE CHAINS THAT BIND ME! OH, MY PASSIONATE PRICE!
SHEESH, TALK ABOUT LAME.
WITH YOU, I FACE THE FUTURE, UNAFRAID!
TAKE ME IN YOUR ARMS AND WE'LL RIDE OFF INTO THE SUNSET TOGETHER!
SOMEONE'S TRYING TO ESCAPE REALITY.

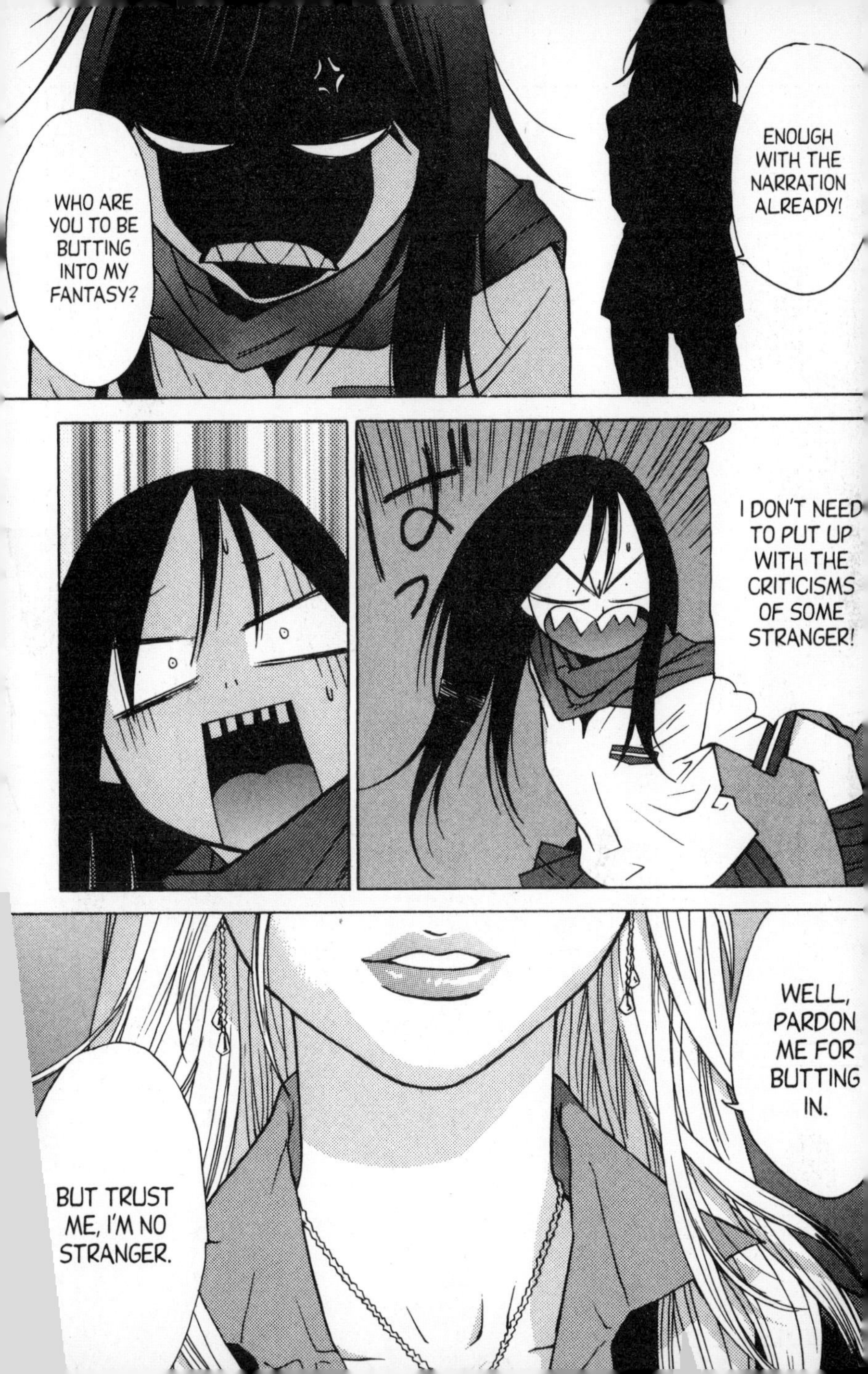
ENOUGH WITH THE NARRATION ALREADY!
WHO ARE YOU TO BE BUTTING INTO MY FANTASY?
I DON'T NEED TO PUT UP WITH THE CRITICISMS OF SOME STRANGER!
WELL, PARDON ME FOR BUTTING IN.
BUT TRUST ME, I'M NO STRANGER.

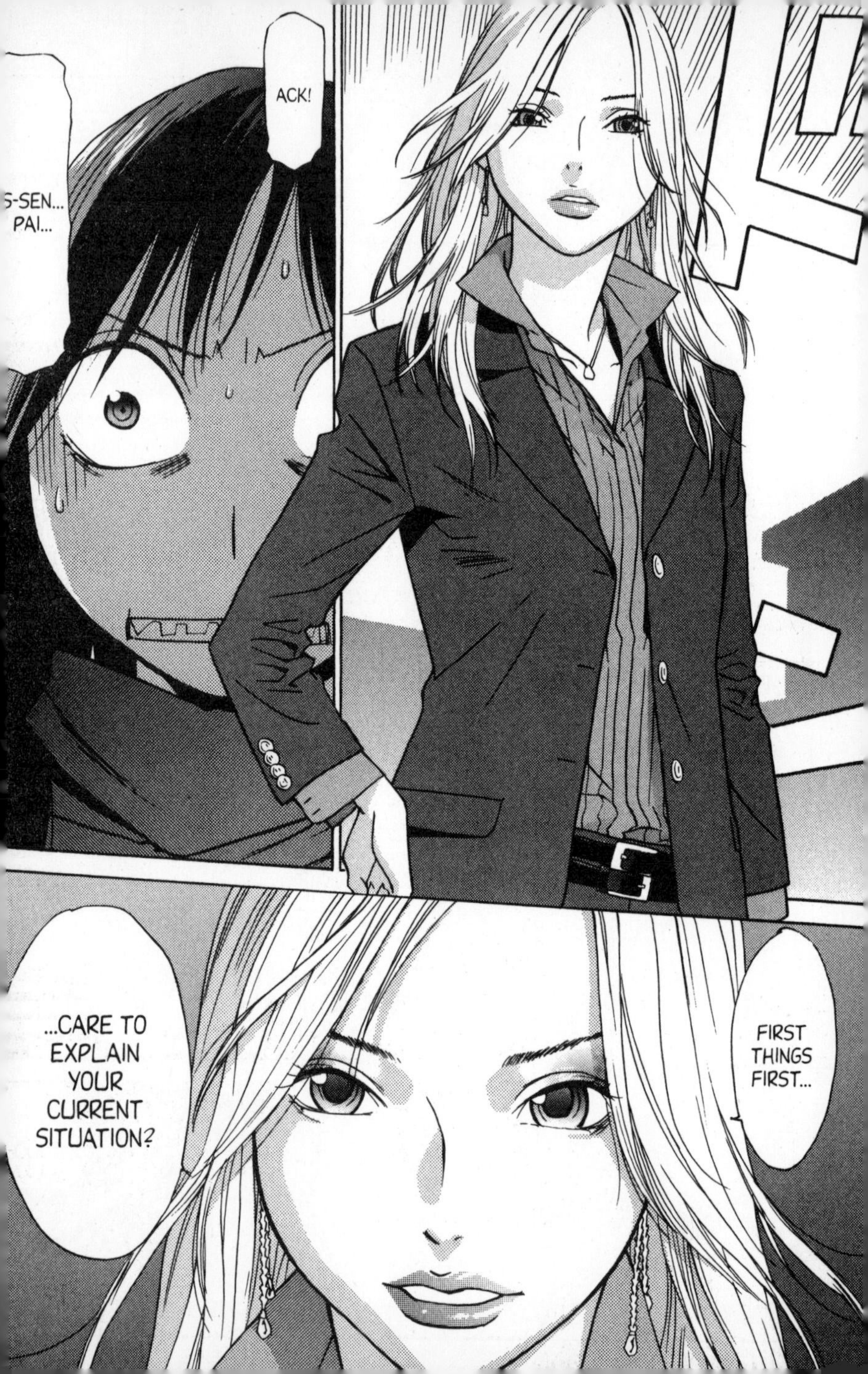
ACK!
S-SEN... PAI...
FIRST THINGS FIRST...
...CARE TO EXPLAIN YOUR CURRENT SITUATION?

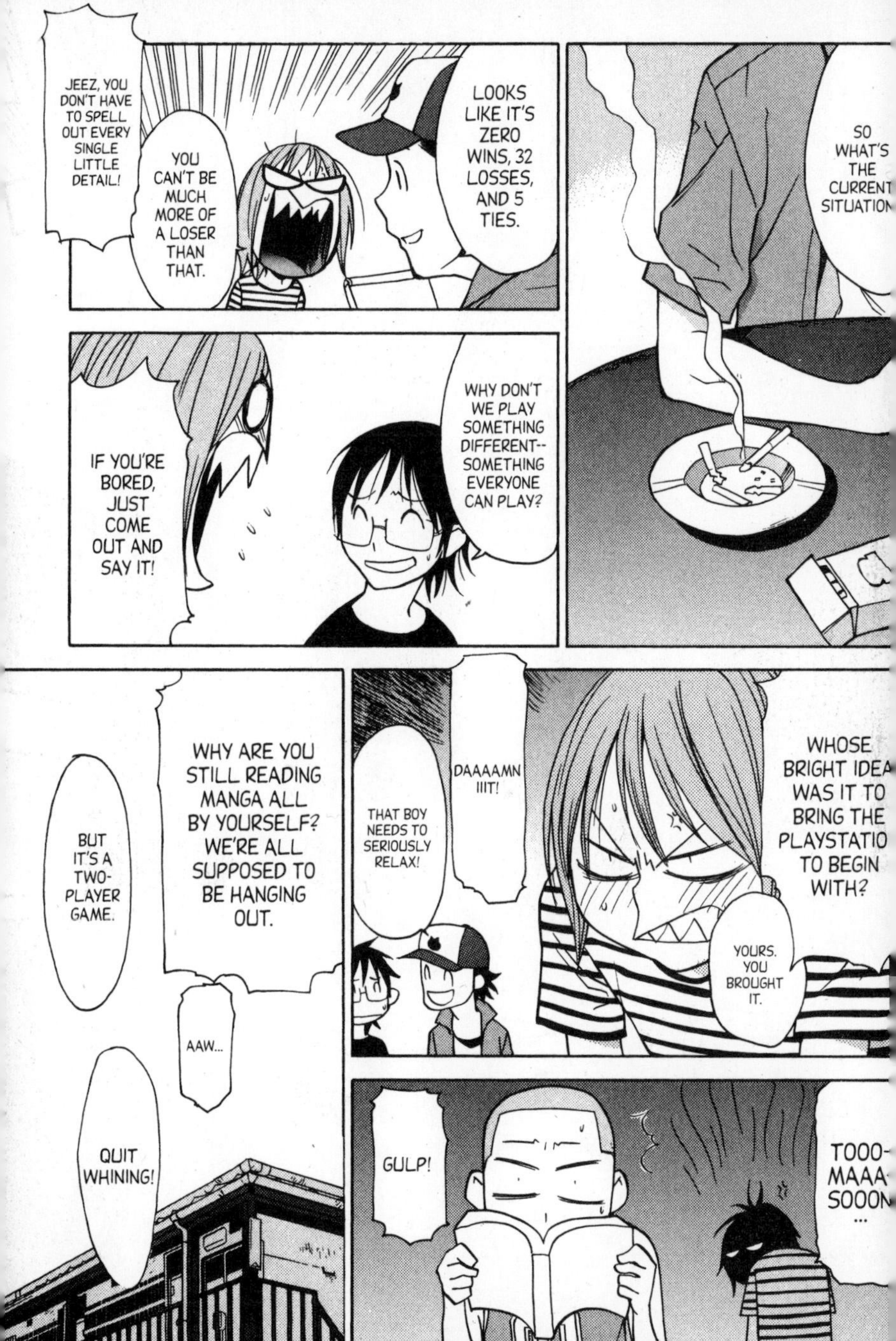
SO WHAT'S THE CURRENT SITUATION
LOOKS LIKE IT'S ZERO WINS, 32 LOSSES, AND 5 TIES.
YOU CAN'T BE MUCH MORE OF A LOSER THAN THAT.
JEEZ, YOU DON'T HAVE TO SPELL OUT EVERY SINGLE LITTLE DETAIL!
WHY DON'T WE PLAY SOMETHING DIFFERENT-- SOMETHING EVERYONE CAN PLAY?
IF YOU'RE BORED, JUST COME OUT AND SAY IT!
WHOSE BRIGHT IDEA WAS IT TO BRING THE PLAYSTATIO TO BEGIN WITH?
YOURS. YOU BROUGHT IT.
DAAAAMN IIIT!
THAT BOY NEEDS TO SERIOUSLY RELAX!
TOOO- MAAA- SOOON ...
GULP!
WHY ARE YOU STILL READING MANGA ALL BY YOURSELF? WE'RE ALL SUPPOSED TO BE HANGING OUT.
BUT IT'S A TWO-PLAYER GAME.
AAW...
QUIT WHINING!

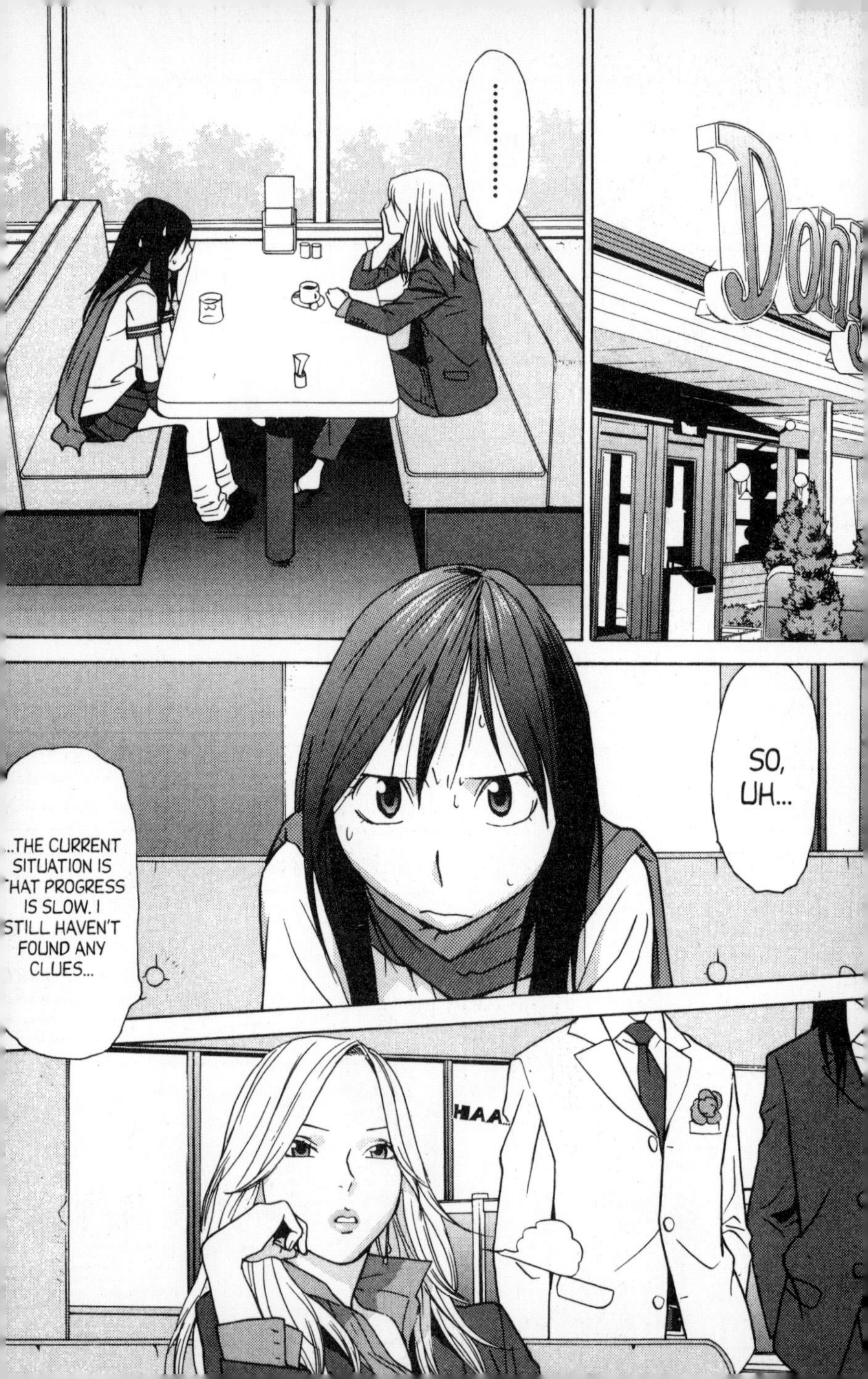
Don
……
SO, UH...
...THE CURRENT SITUATION IS THAT PROGRESS IS SLOW. I STILL HAVEN'T FOUND ANY CLUES...
HAA...

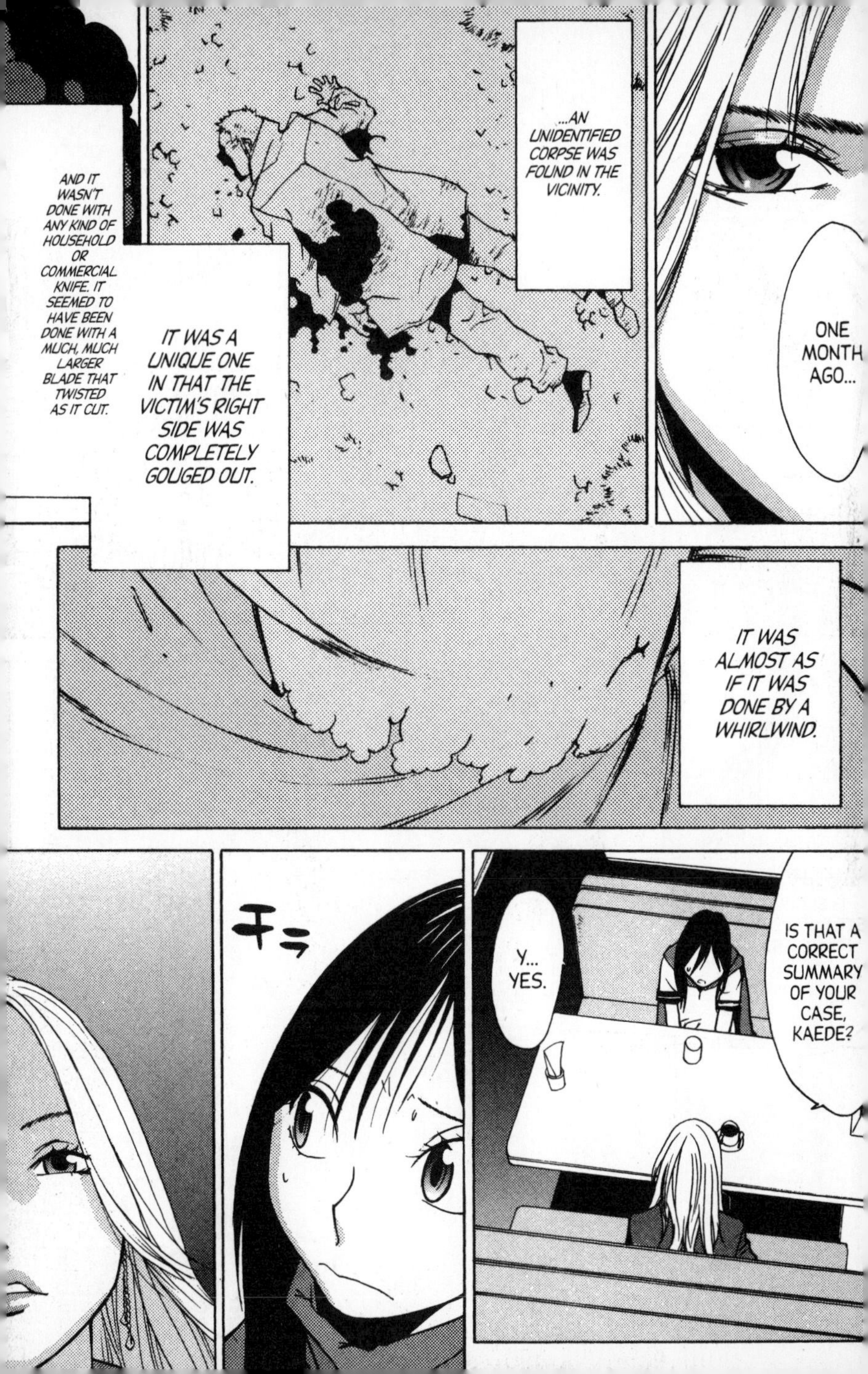
ONE MONTH AGO...
...AN UNIDENTIFIED CORPSE WAS FOUND IN THE VICINITY.
IT WAS A UNIQUE ONE IN THAT THE VICTIM'S RIGHT SIDE WAS COMPLETELY GOUGED OUT.
AND IT WASN'T DONE WITH ANY KIND OF HOUSEHOLD OR COMMERCIAL KNIFE. IT SEEMED TO HAVE BEEN DONE WITH A MUCH, MUCH LARGER BLADE THAT TWISTED AS IT CUT.
IT WAS ALMOST AS IF IT WAS DONE BY A WHIRLWIND.
IS THAT A CORRECT SUMMARY OF YOUR CASE, KAEDE?
Y... YES.
チラ

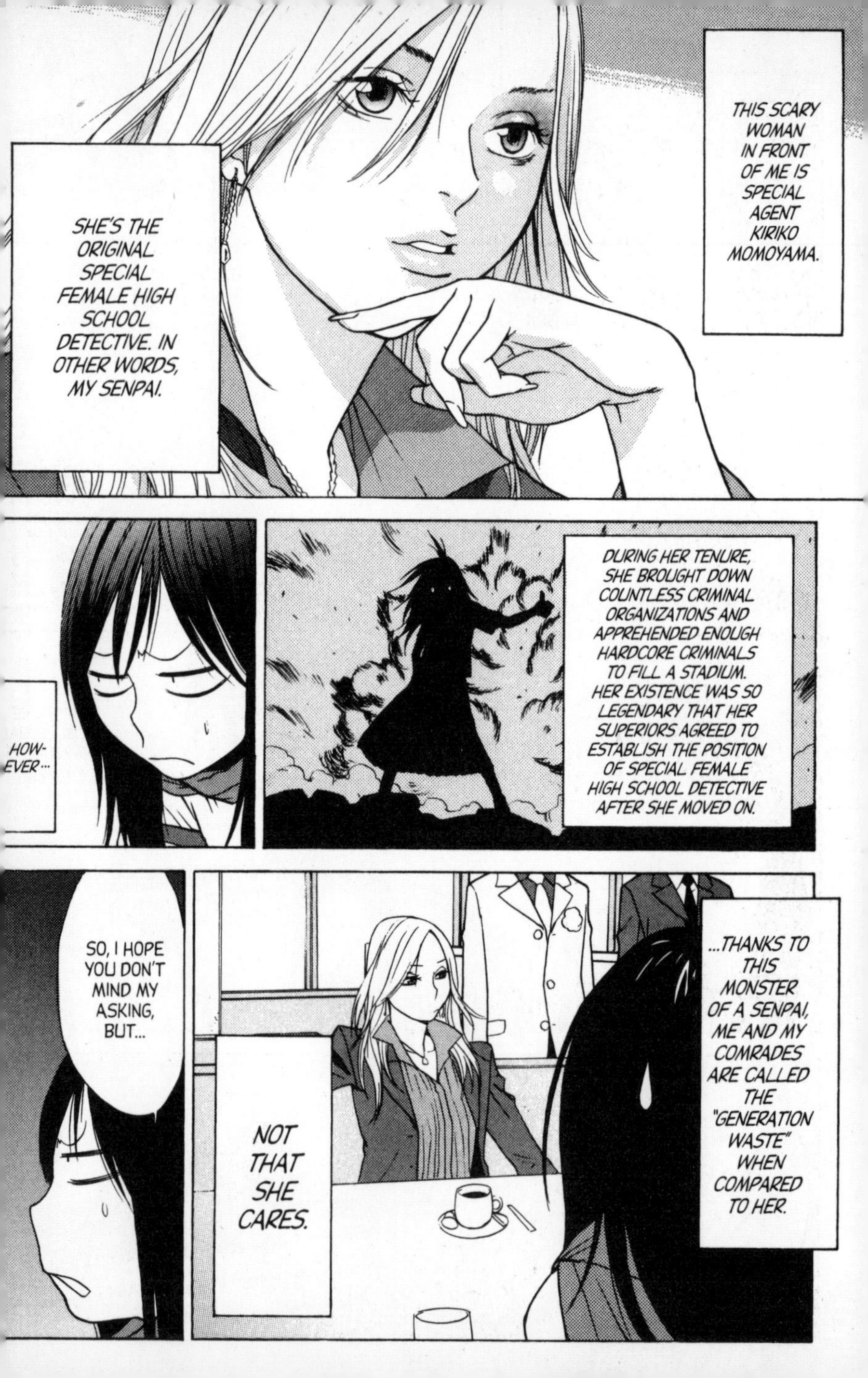
THIS SCARY WOMAN IN FRONT OF ME IS SPECIAL AGENT KIRIKO MOMOYAMA.
SHE'S THE ORIGINAL SPECIAL FEMALE HIGH SCHOOL DETECTIVE. IN OTHER WORDS, MY SENPAI.
DURING HER TENURE, SHE BROUGHT DOWN COUNTLESS CRIMINAL ORGANIZATIONS AND APPREHENDED ENOUGH HARDCORE CRIMINALS TO FILL A STADIUM. HER EXISTENCE WAS SO LEGENDARY THAT HER SUPERIORS AGREED TO ESTABLISH THE POSITION OF SPECIAL FEMALE HIGH SCHOOL DETECTIVE AFTER SHE MOVED ON.
HOW-EVER...
...THANKS TO THIS MONSTER OF A SENPAI, ME AND MY COMRADES ARE CALLED THE "GENERATION WASTE" WHEN COMPARED TO HER.
NOT THAT SHE CARES.
SO, I HOPE YOU DON'T MIND MY ASKING, BUT...

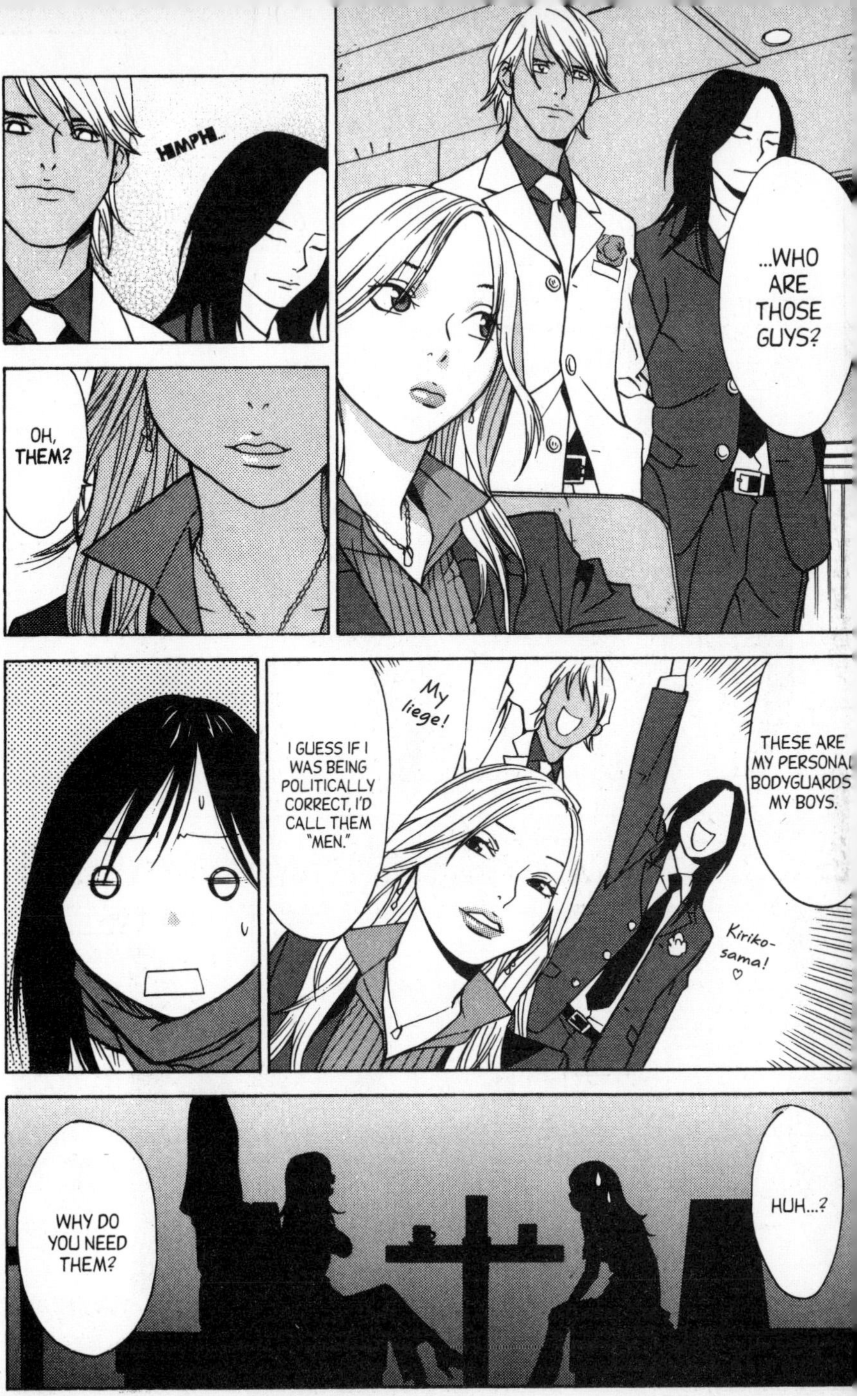
...WHO ARE THOSE GUYS?
HMPH...
OH, THEM?
THESE ARE MY PERSONAL BODYGUARDS MY BOYS.
Kiriko-sama! ♡
My liege!
I GUESS IF I WAS BEING POLITICALLY CORRECT, I'D CALL THEM "MEN."
HUH...?
WHY DO YOU NEED THEM?

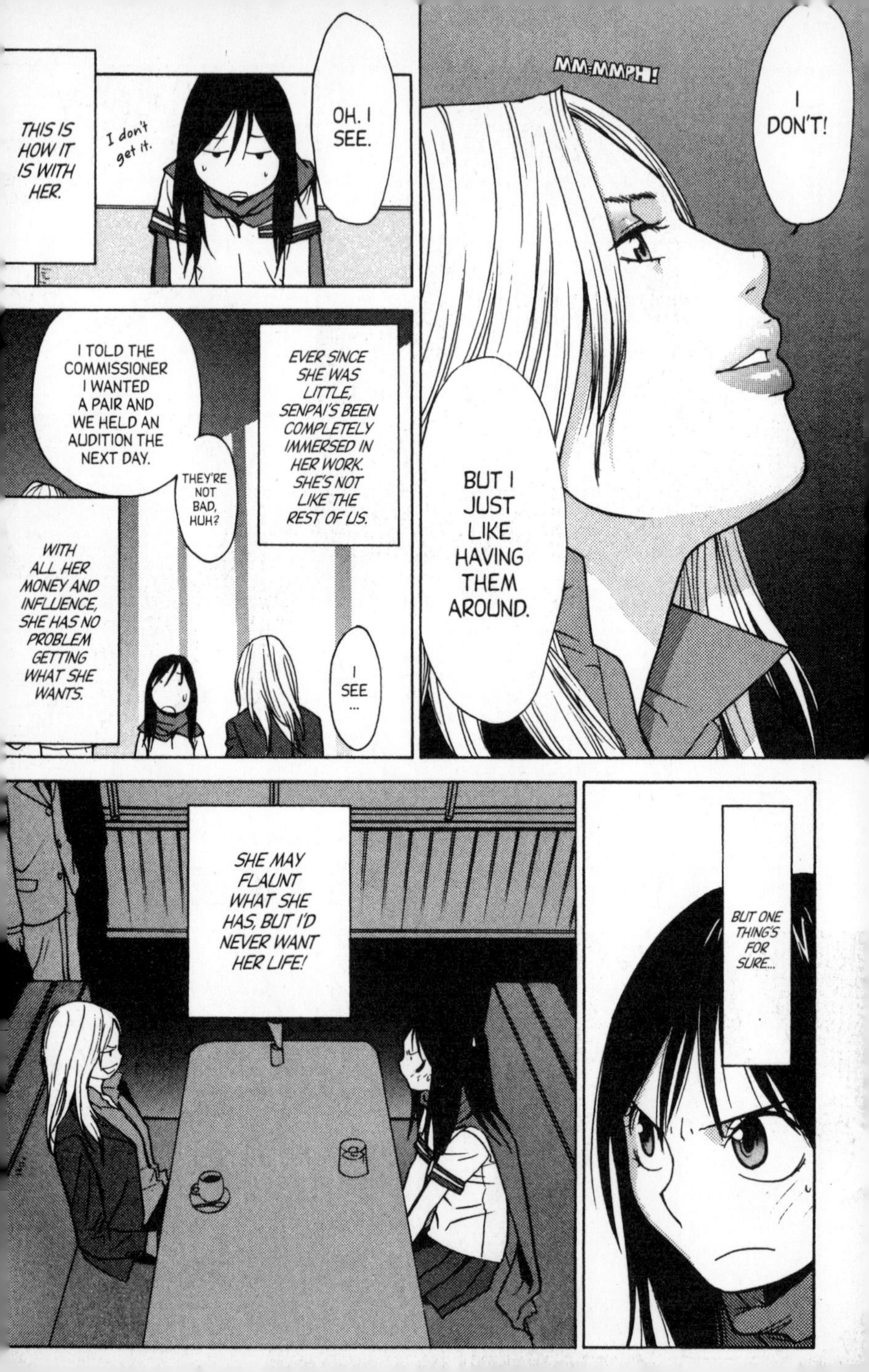
MM-MMPH!
I DON'T!
BUT I JUST LIKE HAVING THEM AROUND.
OH. I SEE.
I don't get it.
THIS IS HOW IT IS WITH HER.
EVER SINCE SHE WAS LITTLE, SENPAI'S BEEN COMPLETELY IMMERSED IN HER WORK. SHE'S NOT LIKE THE REST OF US.
I TOLD THE COMMISSIONER I WANTED A PAIR AND WE HELD AN AUDITION THE NEXT DAY.
THEY'RE NOT BAD, HUH?
I SEE...
WITH ALL HER MONEY AND INFLUENCE, SHE HAS NO PROBLEM GETTING WHAT SHE WANTS.
BUT ONE THING'S FOR SURE...
SHE MAY FLAUNT WHAT SHE HAS, BUT I'D NEVER WANT HER LIFE!

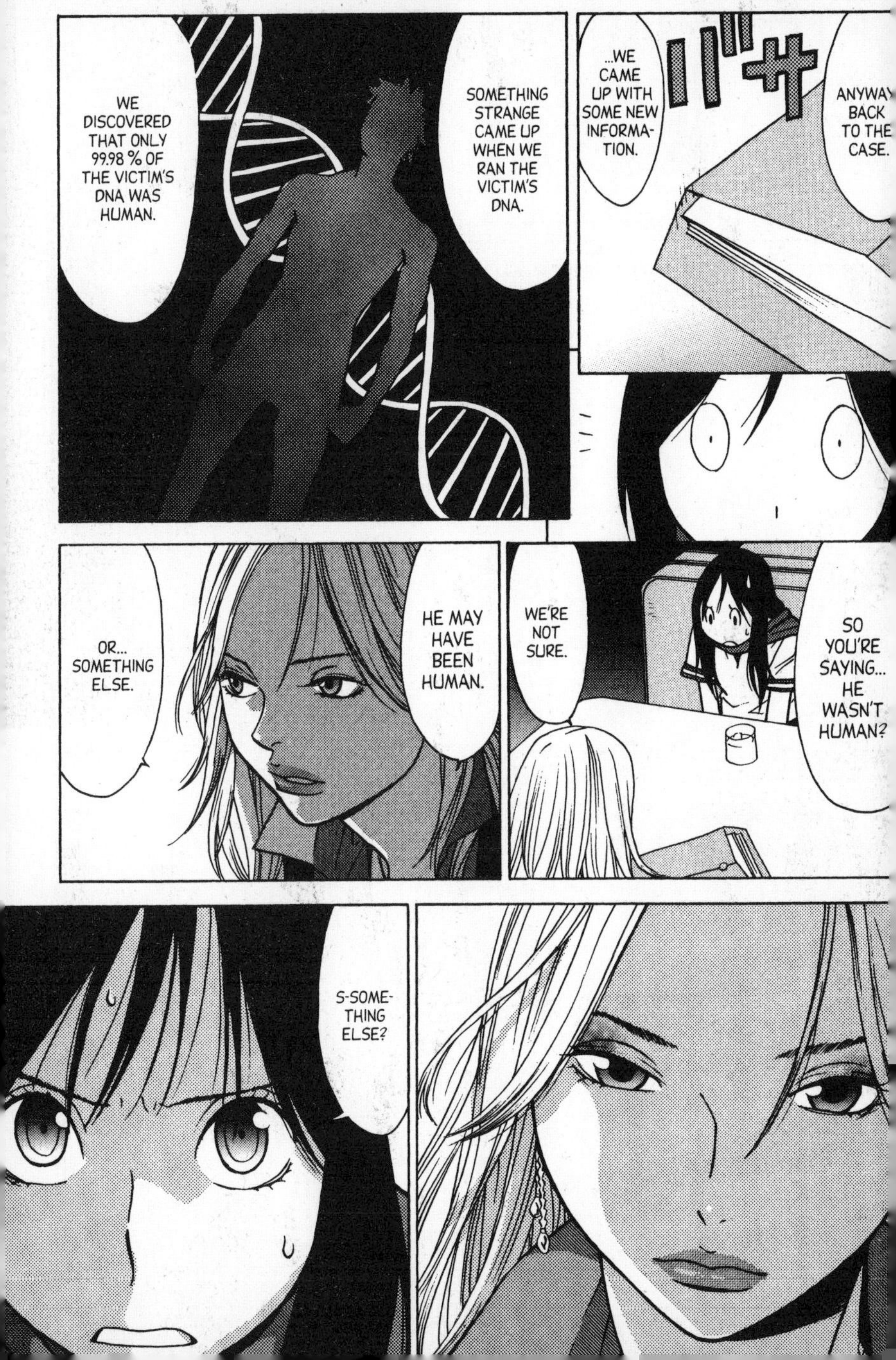
ANYWAY BACK TO THE CASE.
バサ
...WE CAME UP WITH SOME NEW INFORMA-TION.
SOMETHING STRANGE CAME UP WHEN WE RAN THE VICTIM'S DNA.
WE DISCOVERED THAT ONLY 99.98 % OF THE VICTIM'S DNA WAS HUMAN.
SO YOU'RE SAYING... HE WASN'T HUMAN?
WE'RE NOT SURE.
HE MAY HAVE BEEN HUMAN.
OR... SOMETHING ELSE.
S-SOME-THING ELSE?

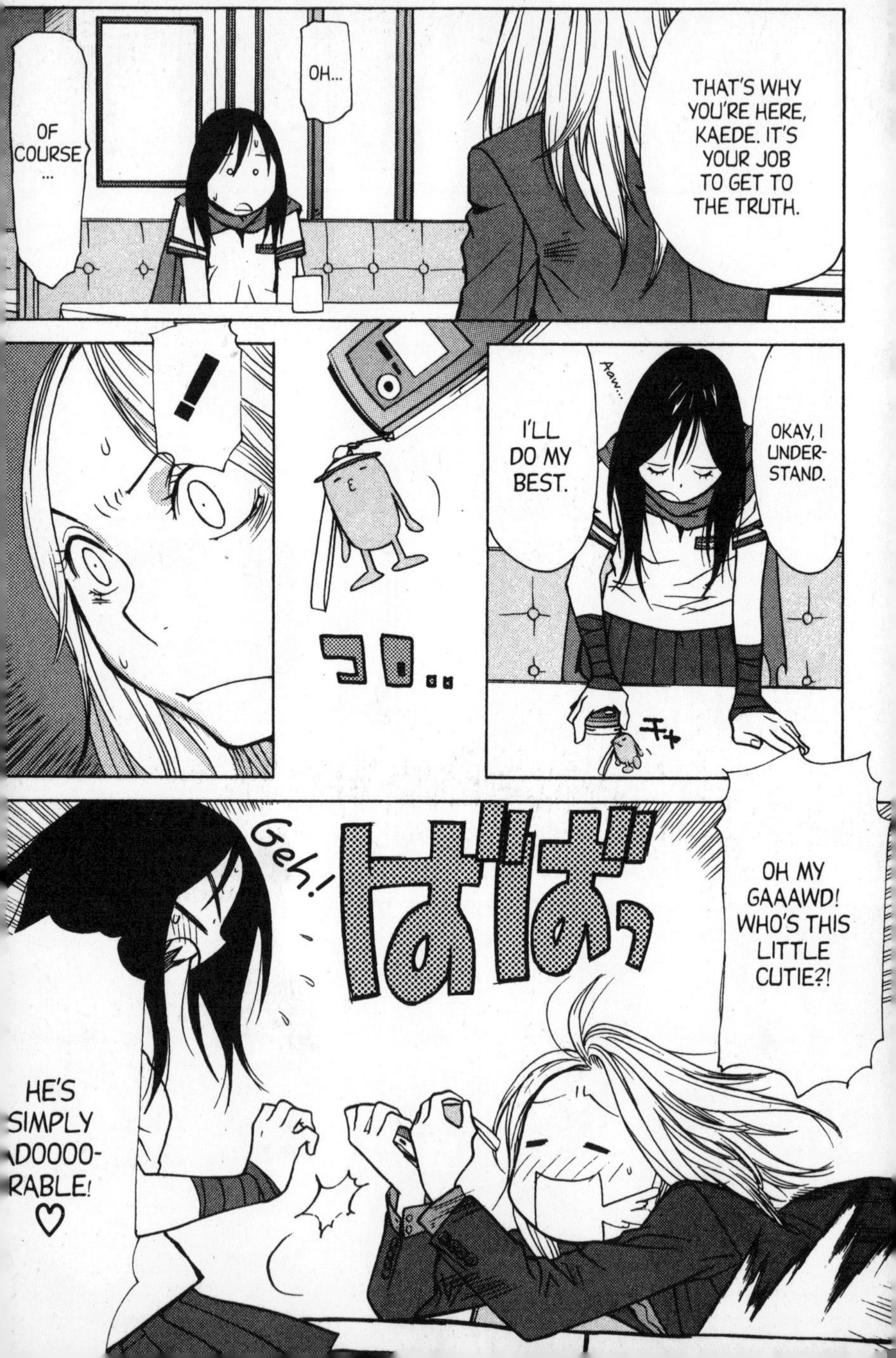
THAT'S WHY YOU'RE HERE, KAEDE. IT'S YOUR JOB TO GET TO THE TRUTH.
OH...
OF COURSE ...
OKAY, I UNDER-STAND.
Aaw...
I'LL DO MY BEST.
!
OH MY GAAAWD! WHO'S THIS LITTLE CUTIE?!
Geh!
HE'S SIMPLY ADOOOO-RABLE! ♡

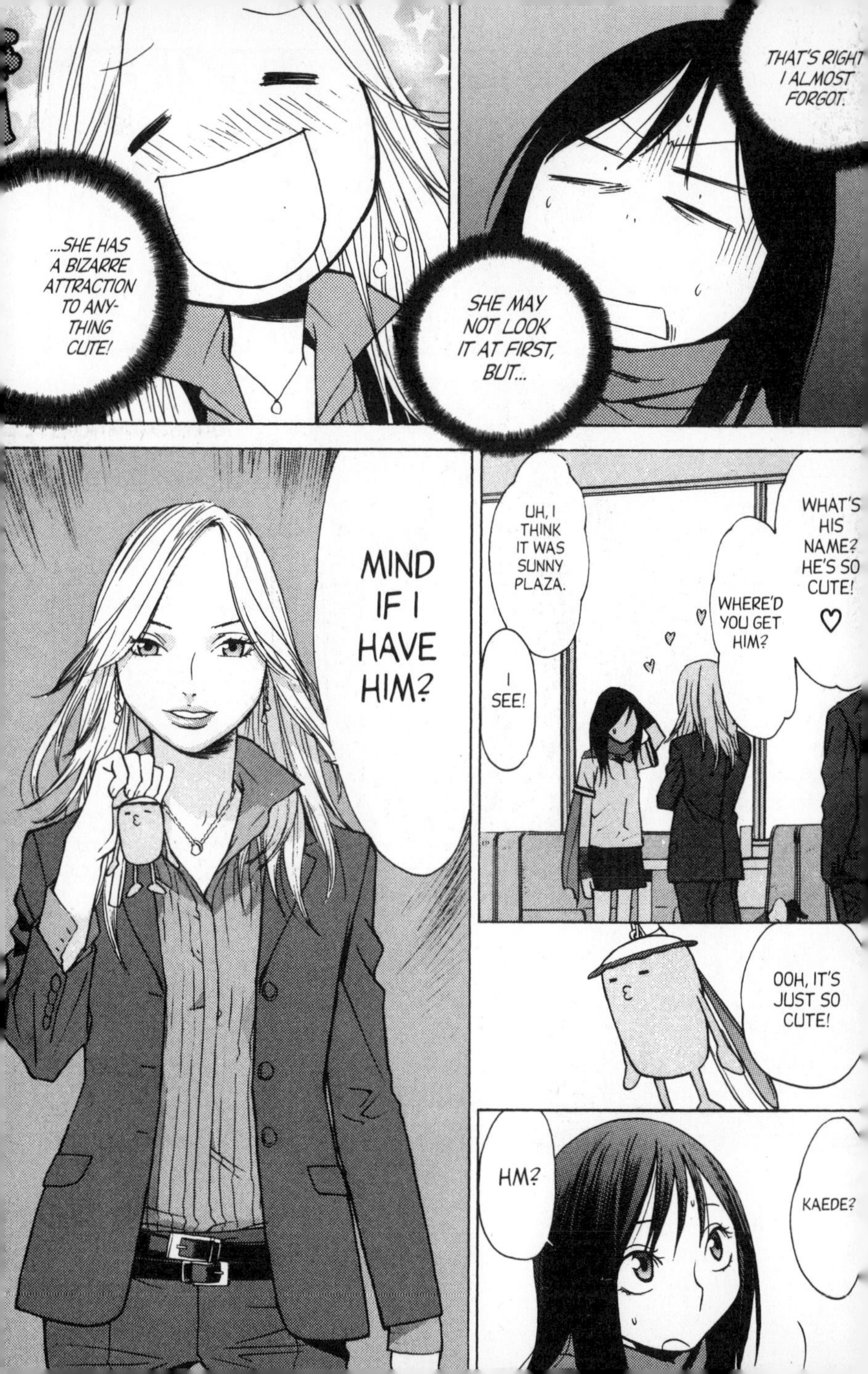
THAT'S RIGHT I ALMOST FORGOT.
SHE MAY NOT LOOK IT AT FIRST, BUT...
...SHE HAS A BIZARRE ATTRACTION TO ANY-THING CUTE!
WHAT'S HIS NAME? HE'S SO CUTE! ♡
WHERE'D YOU GET HIM?
UH, I THINK IT WAS SUNNY PLAZA.
I SEE!
OOH, IT'S JUST SO CUTE!
KAEDE?
HM?
MIND IF I HAVE HIM?

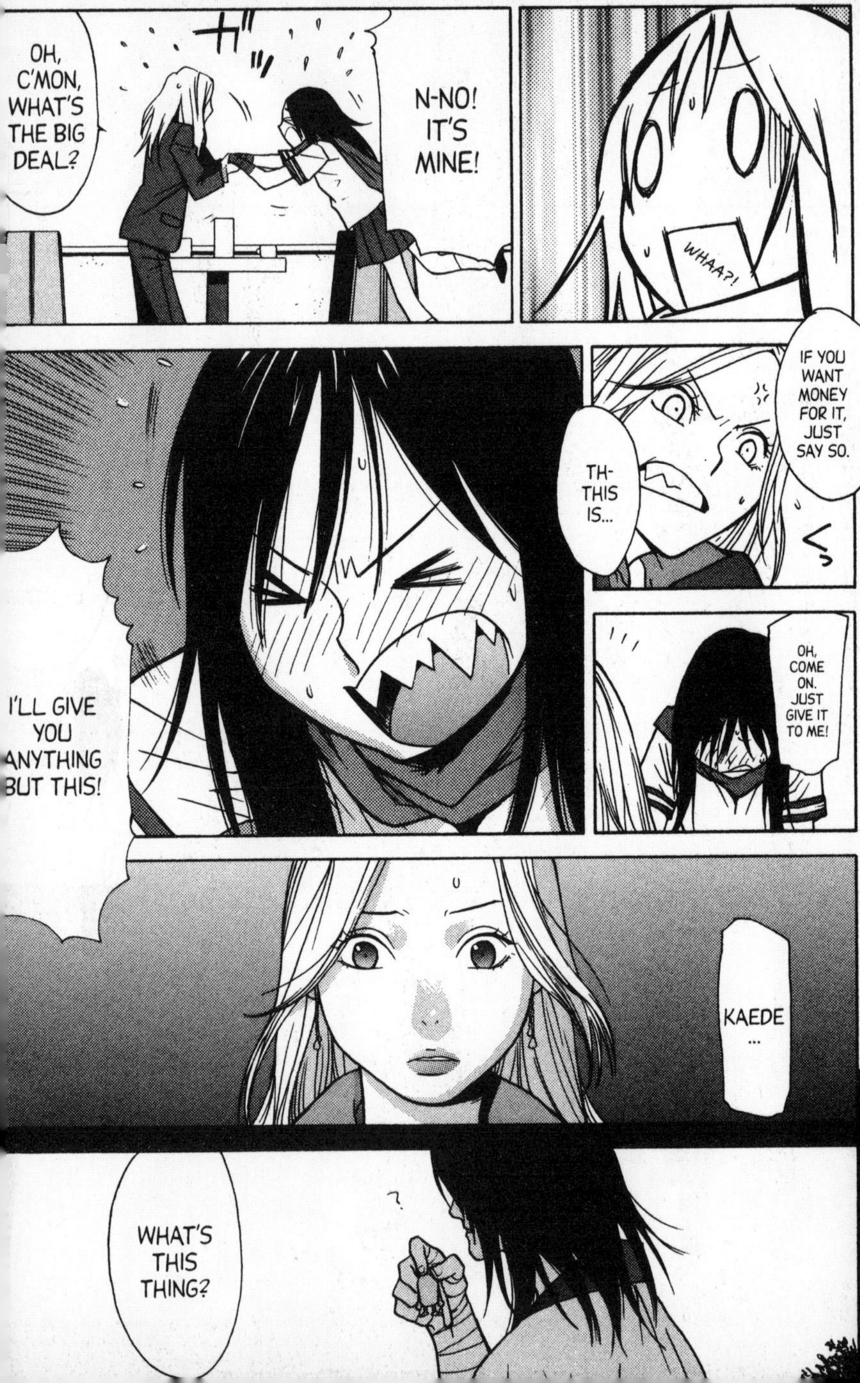
WHAA?!
N-NO! IT'S MINE!
OH, C'MON, WHAT'S THE BIG DEAL?
IF YOU WANT MONEY FOR IT, JUST SAY SO.
TH-THIS IS...
OH, COME ON. JUST GIVE IT TO ME!
I'LL GIVE YOU ANYTHING BUT THIS!
KAEDE ...
WHAT'S THIS THING?

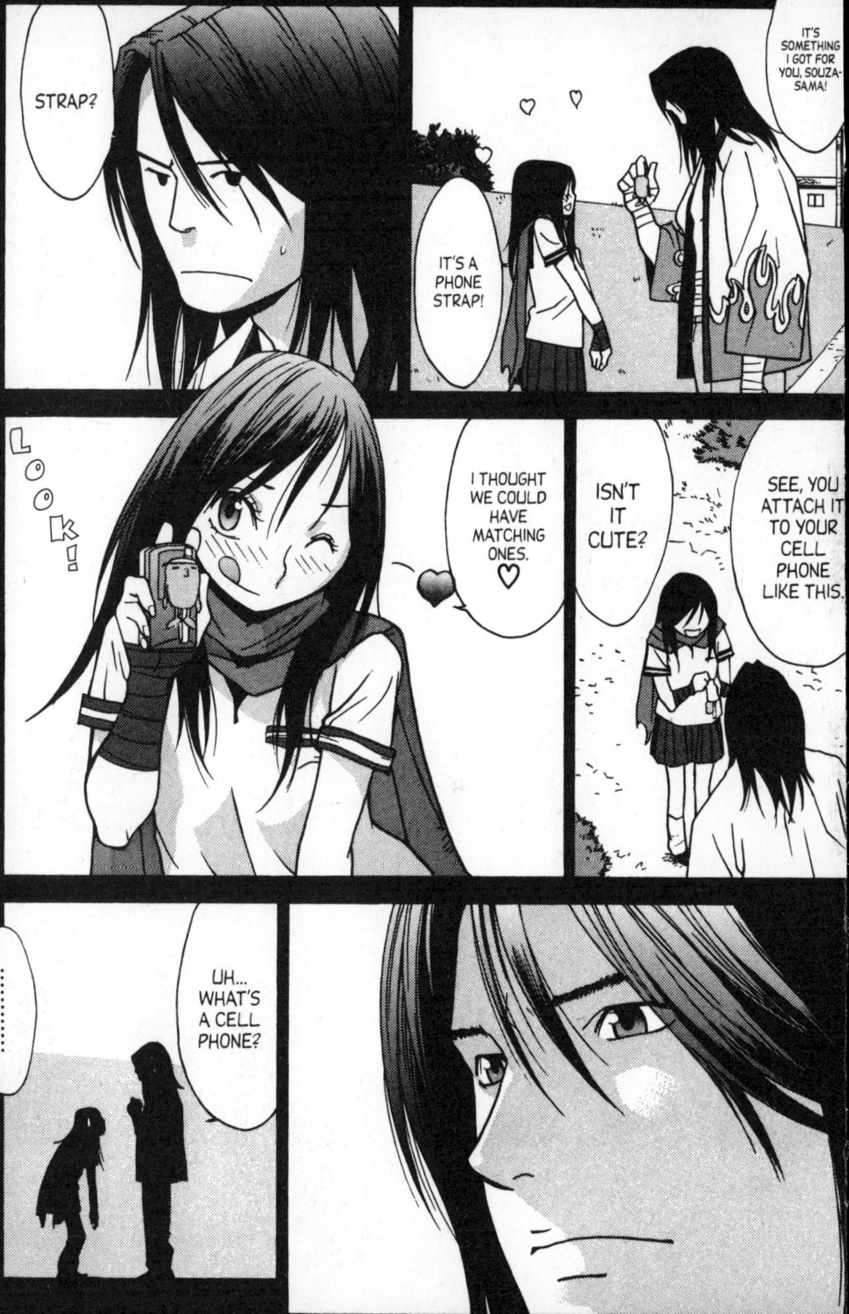
IT'S SOMETHING I GOT FOR YOU, SOUZA-SAMA!
IT'S A PHONE STRAP!
STRAP?
SEE, YOU ATTACH IT TO YOUR CELL PHONE LIKE THIS.
ISN'T IT CUTE?
I THOUGHT WE COULD HAVE MATCHING ONES. ♡
LOOK!
UH... WHAT'S A CELL PHONE?
......

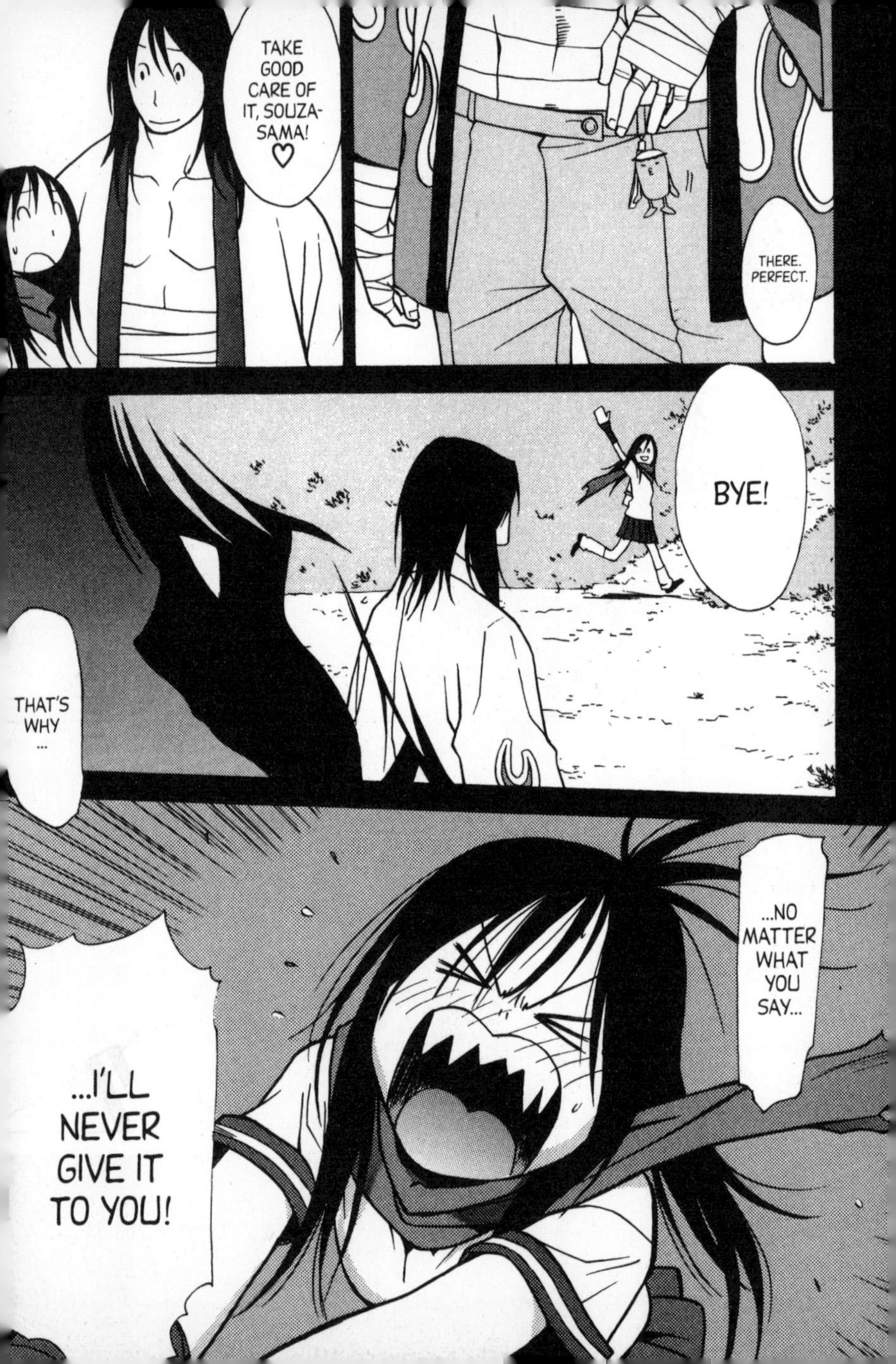
THERE. PERFECT.
TAKE GOOD CARE OF IT, SOUZA-SAMA! ♡
BYE!
THAT'S WHY...
...NO MATTER WHAT YOU SAY...
...I'LL NEVER GIVE IT TO YOU!

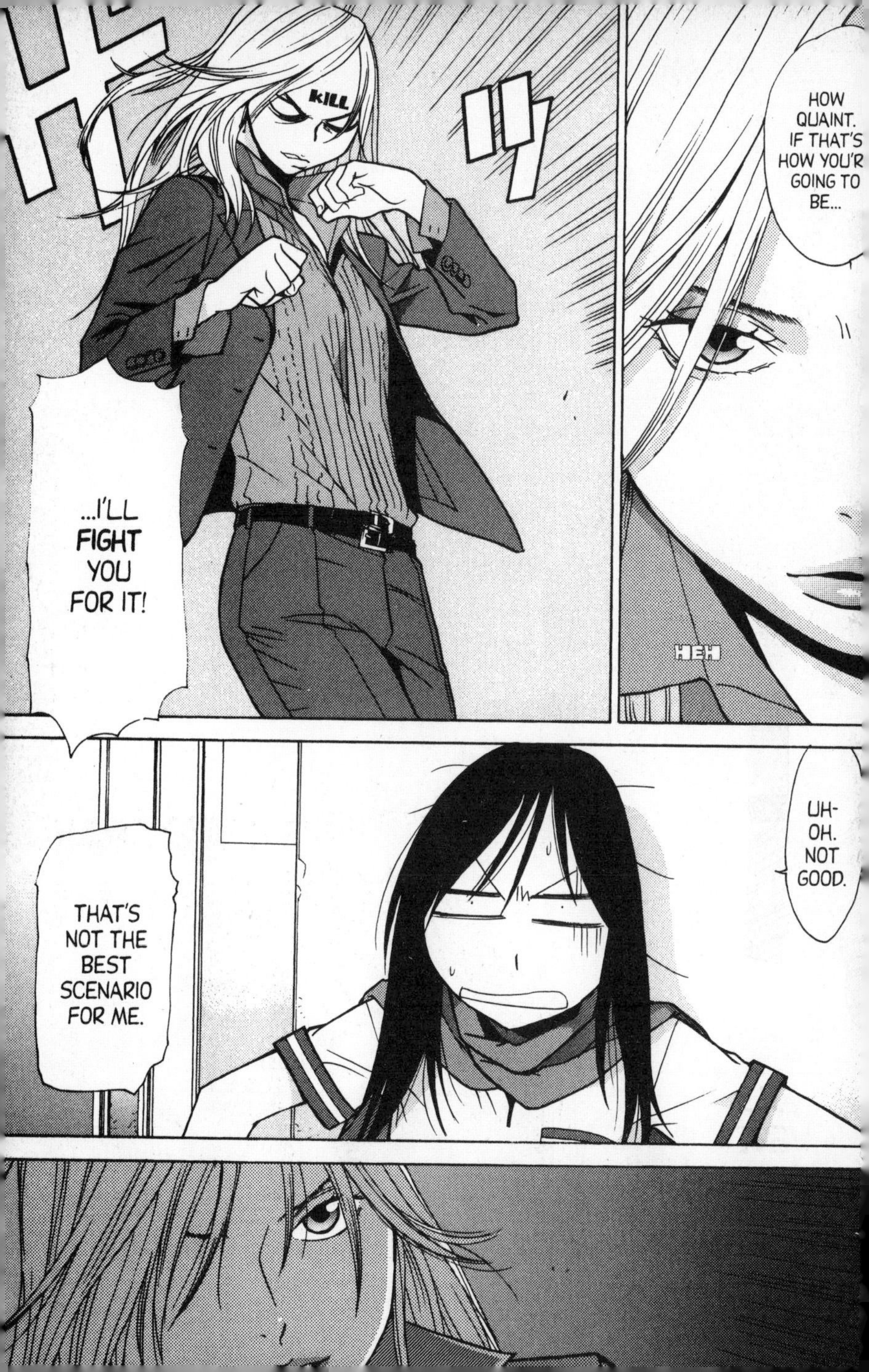
HOW QUAINT. IF THAT'S HOW YOU'R GOING TO BE...
HEH
KILL
...I'LL FIGHT YOU FOR IT!
UH-OH. NOT GOOD.
THAT'S NOT THE BEST SCENARIO FOR ME.

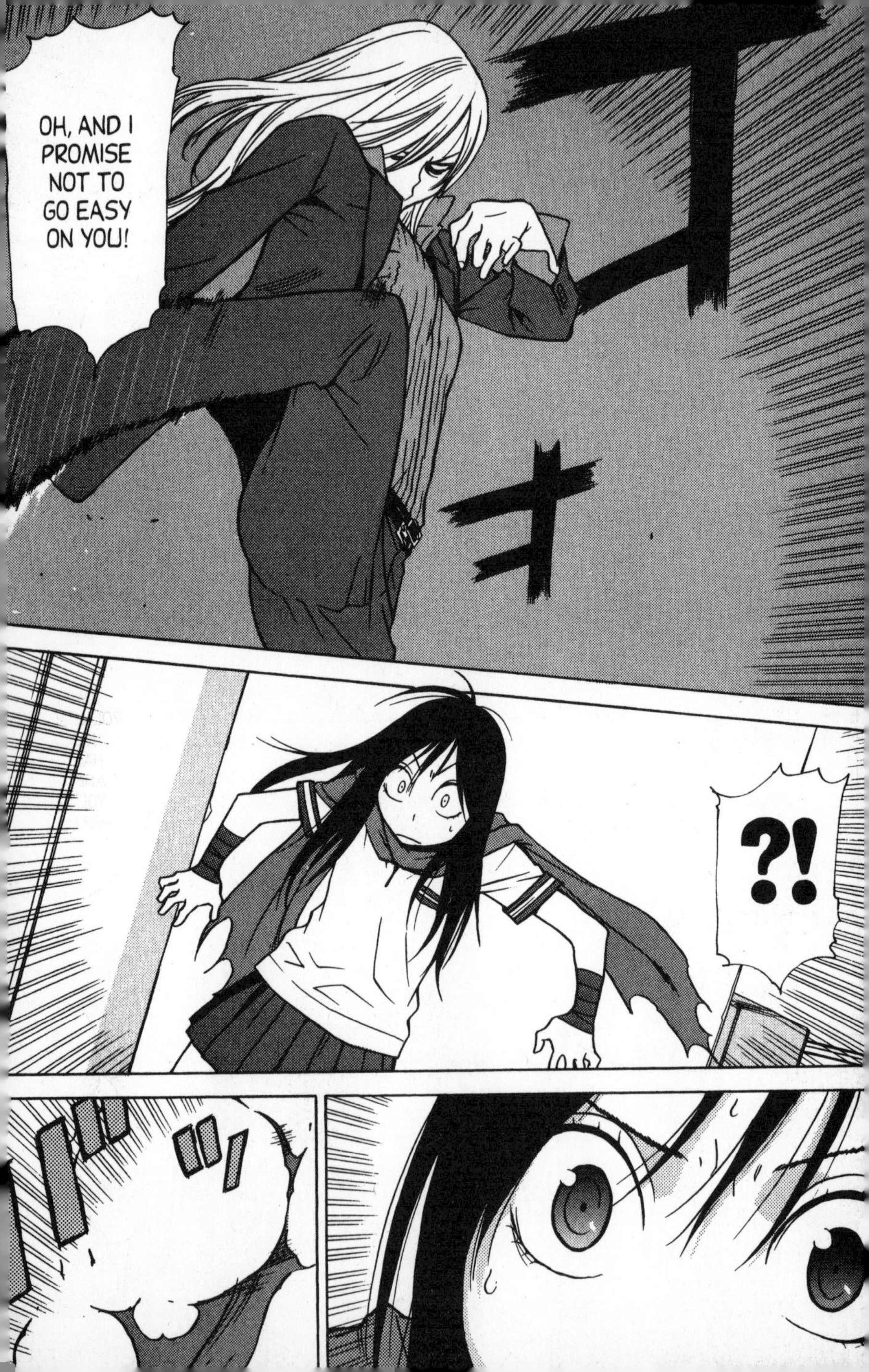
OH, AND I PROMISE NOT TO GO EASY ON YOU!
?!

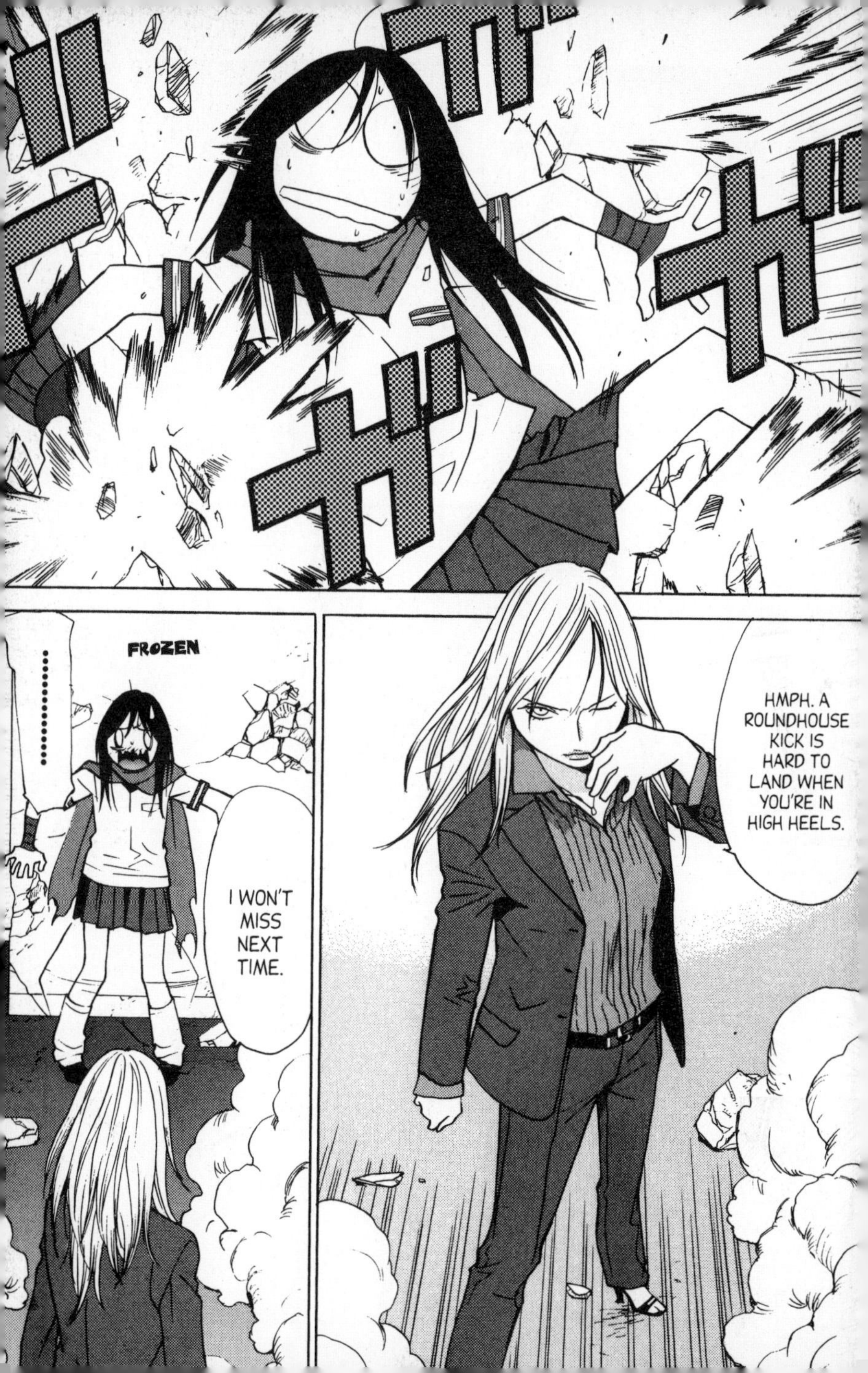
HMPH. A ROUNDHOUSE KICK IS HARD TO LAND WHEN YOU'RE IN HIGH HEELS.
FROZEN
....
I WON'T MISS NEXT TIME.

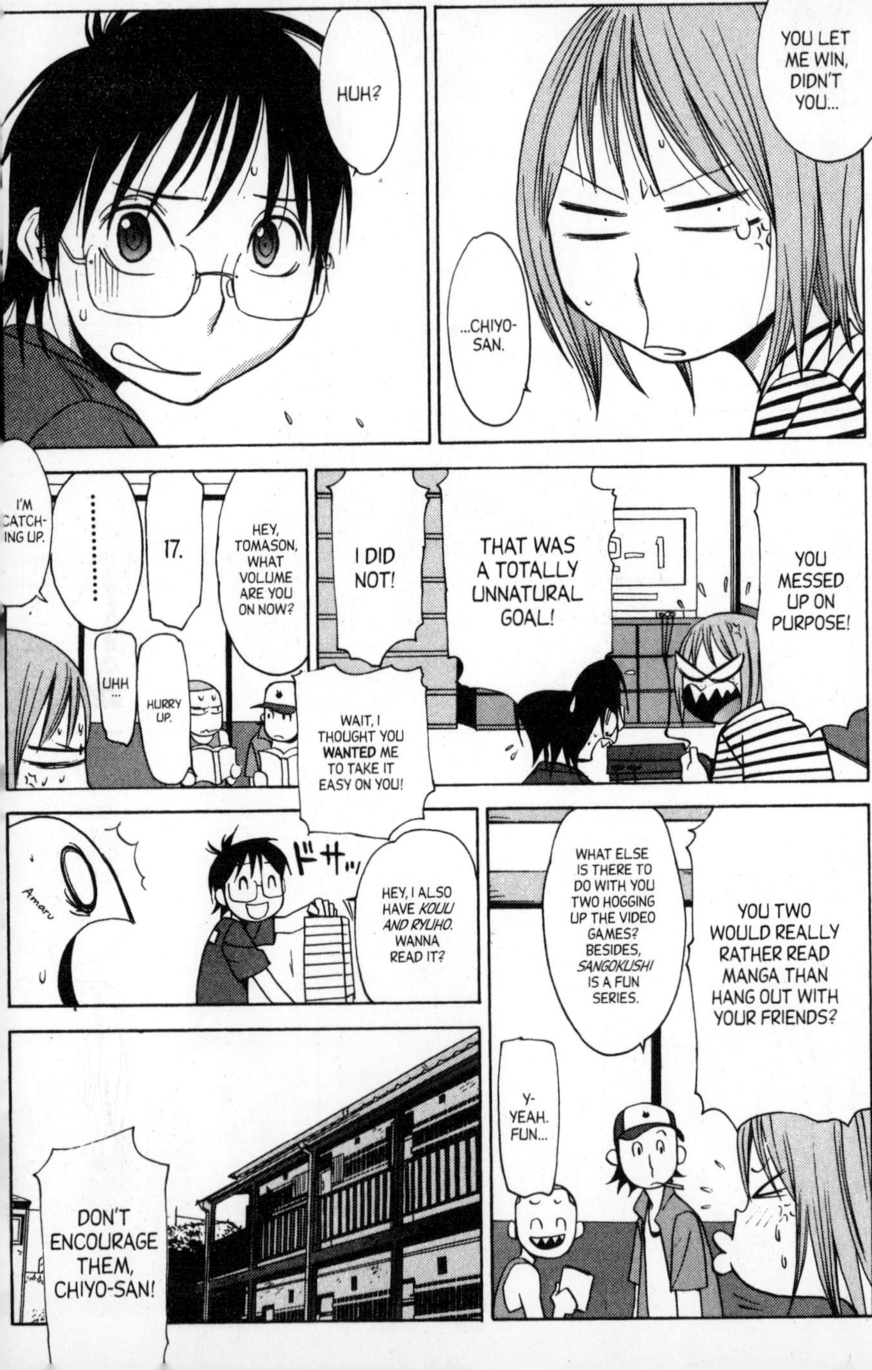
YOU LET ME WIN, DIDN'T YOU...
...CHIYO-SAN.
HUH?
YOU MESSED UP ON PURPOSE!
THAT WAS A TOTALLY UNNATURAL GOAL!
I DID NOT!
WAIT, I THOUGHT YOU WANTED ME TO TAKE IT EASY ON YOU!
HEY, TOMASON, WHAT VOLUME ARE YOU ON NOW?
17.
....
I'M CATCHING UP.
UHH...
HURRY UP.
YOU TWO WOULD REALLY RATHER READ MANGA THAN HANG OUT WITH YOUR FRIENDS?
WHAT ELSE IS THERE TO DO WITH YOU TWO HOGGING UP THE VIDEO GAMES? BESIDES, *SANGOKUSHI* IS A FUN SERIES.
Y-YEAH. FUN...
ドサッ
HEY, I ALSO HAVE *KOUU AND RYUHO*. WANNA READ IT?
Amaru
DON'T ENCOURAGE THEM, CHIYO-SAN!

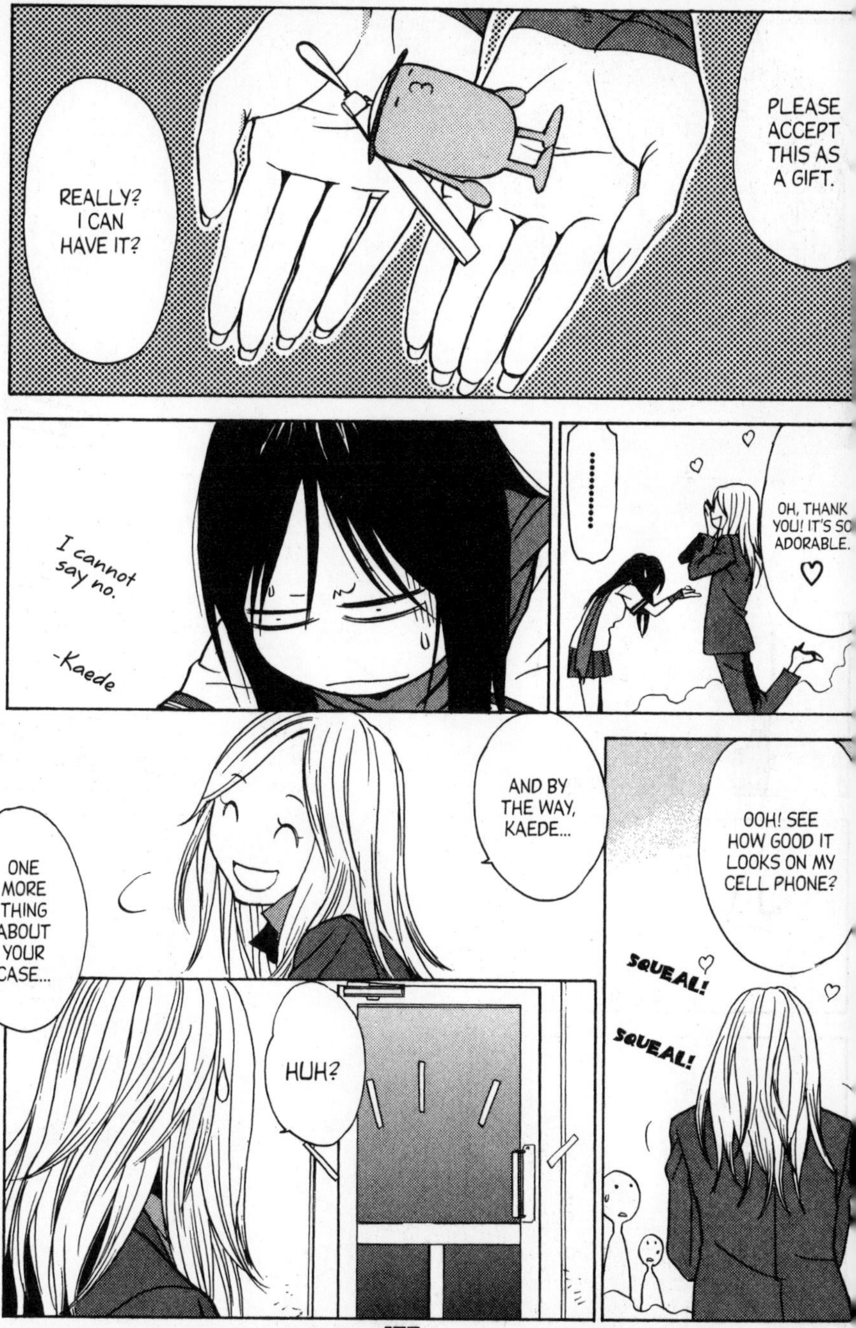
PLEASE ACCEPT THIS AS A GIFT.
REALLY? I CAN HAVE IT?
OH, THANK YOU! IT'S SO ADORABLE. ♡
......
I cannot say no. -Kaede
OOH! SEE HOW GOOD IT LOOKS ON MY CELL PHONE?
SQUEAL!
SQUEAL!
AND BY THE WAY, KAEDE...
ONE MORE THING ABOUT YOUR CASE...
HUH?

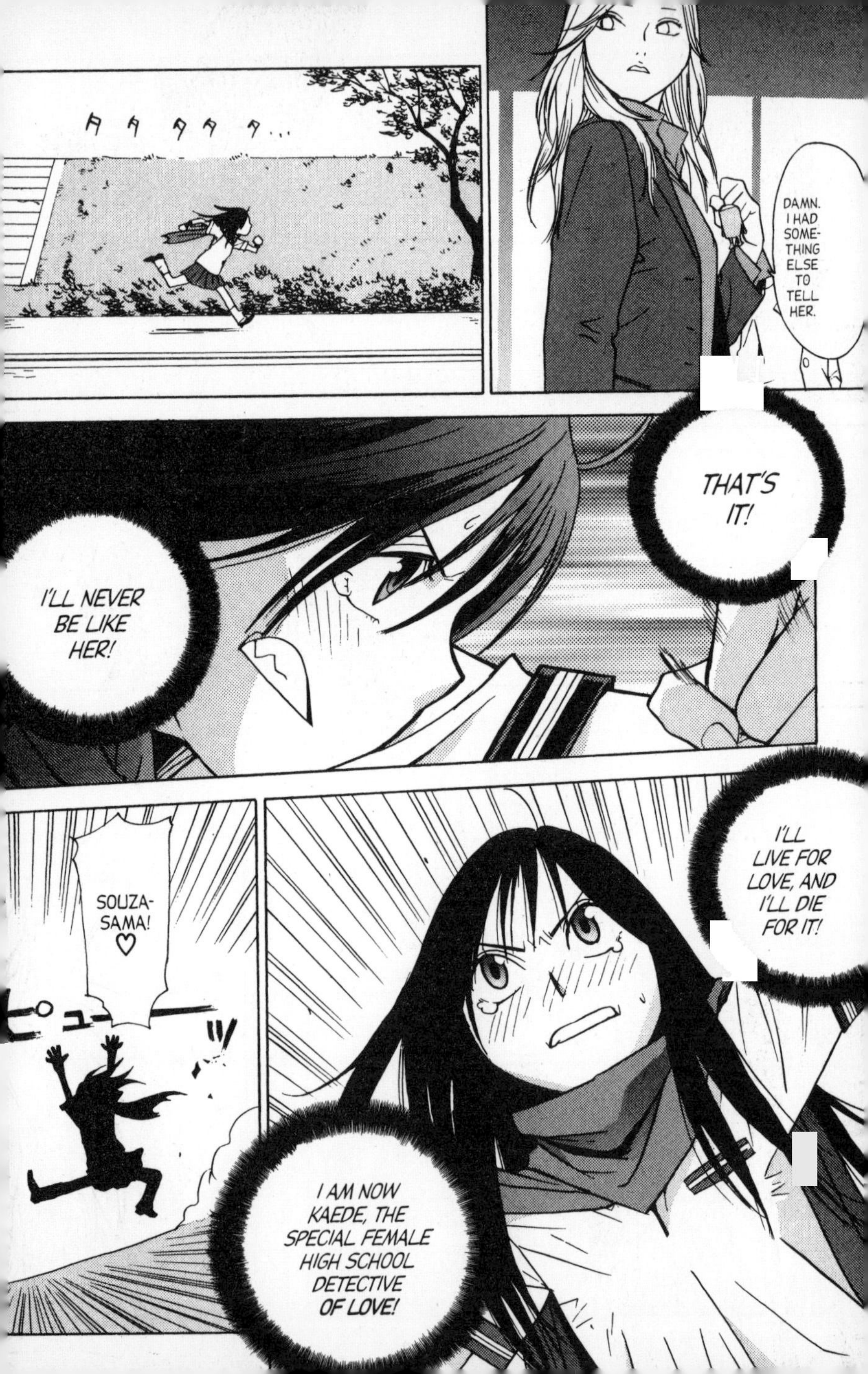
DAMN. I HAD SOMETHING ELSE TO TELL HER.
タタタタタ...
THAT'S IT!
I'LL NEVER BE LIKE HER!
I'LL LIVE FOR LOVE, AND I'LL DIE FOR IT!
I AM NOW KAEDE, THE SPECIAL FEMALE HIGH SCHOOL DETECTIVE OF LOVE!
SOUZA-SAMA! ♡
ピュー

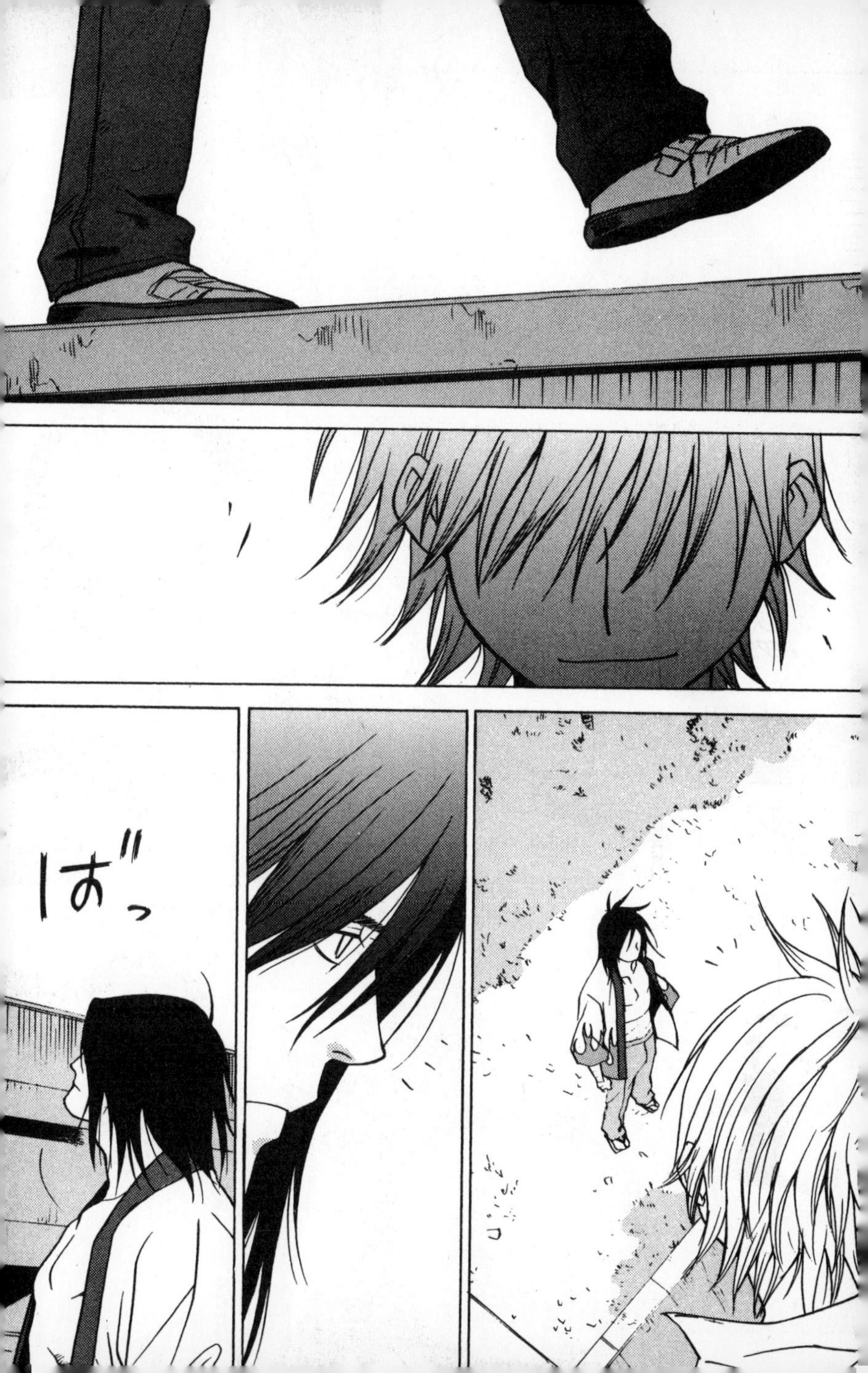
ばっ

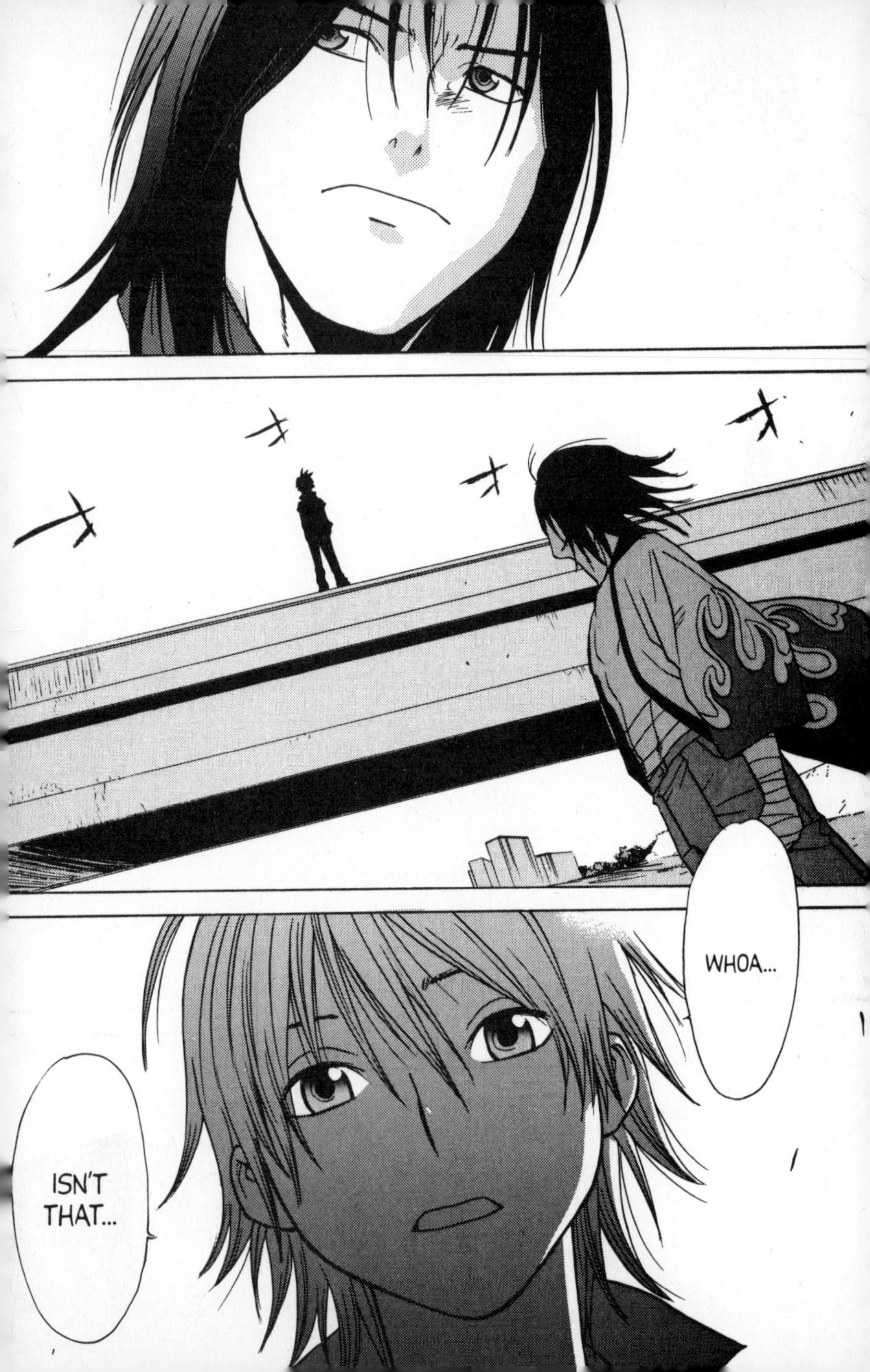
WHOA...
ISN'T THAT...

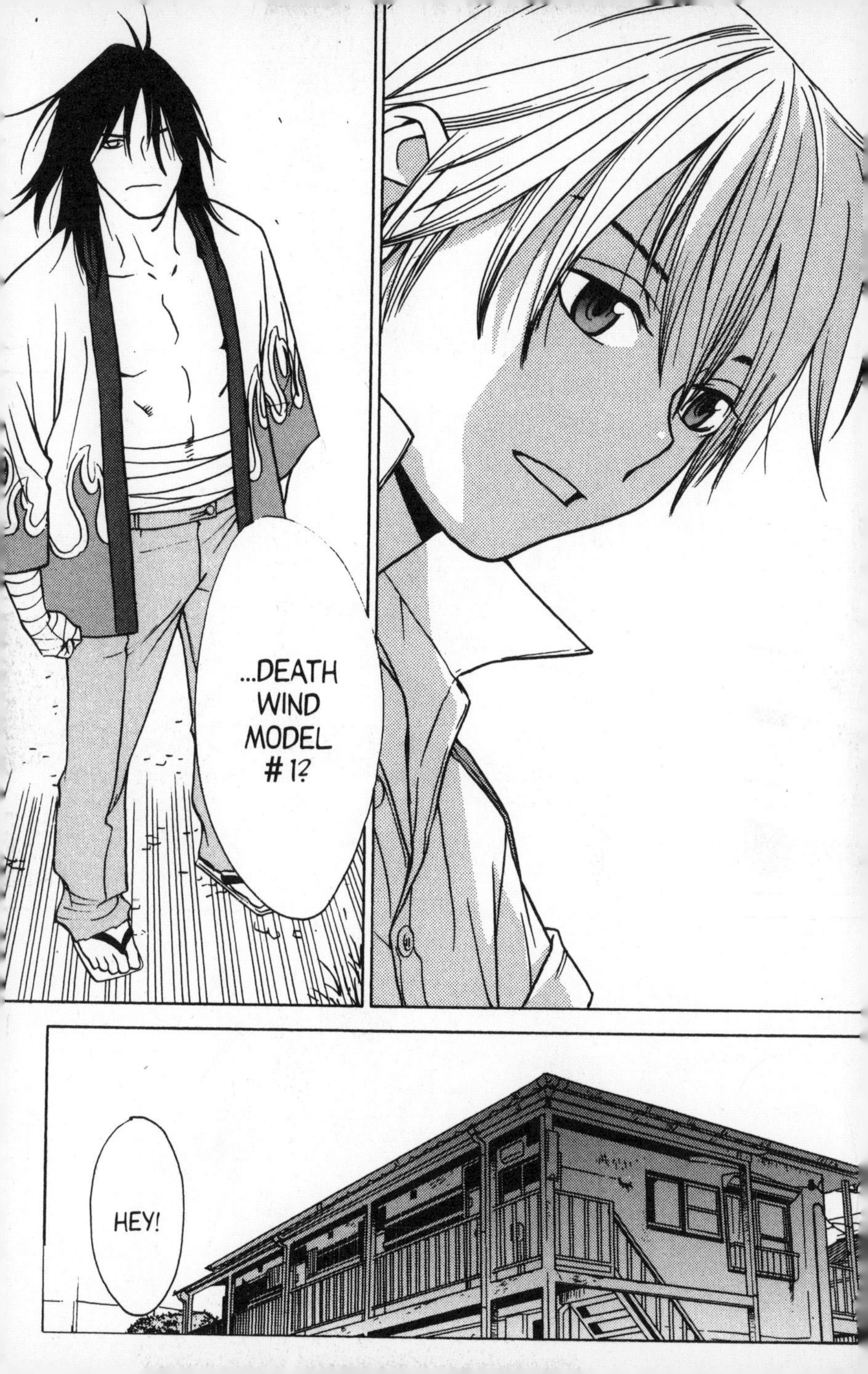
...DEATH WIND MODEL # 1?
HEY!

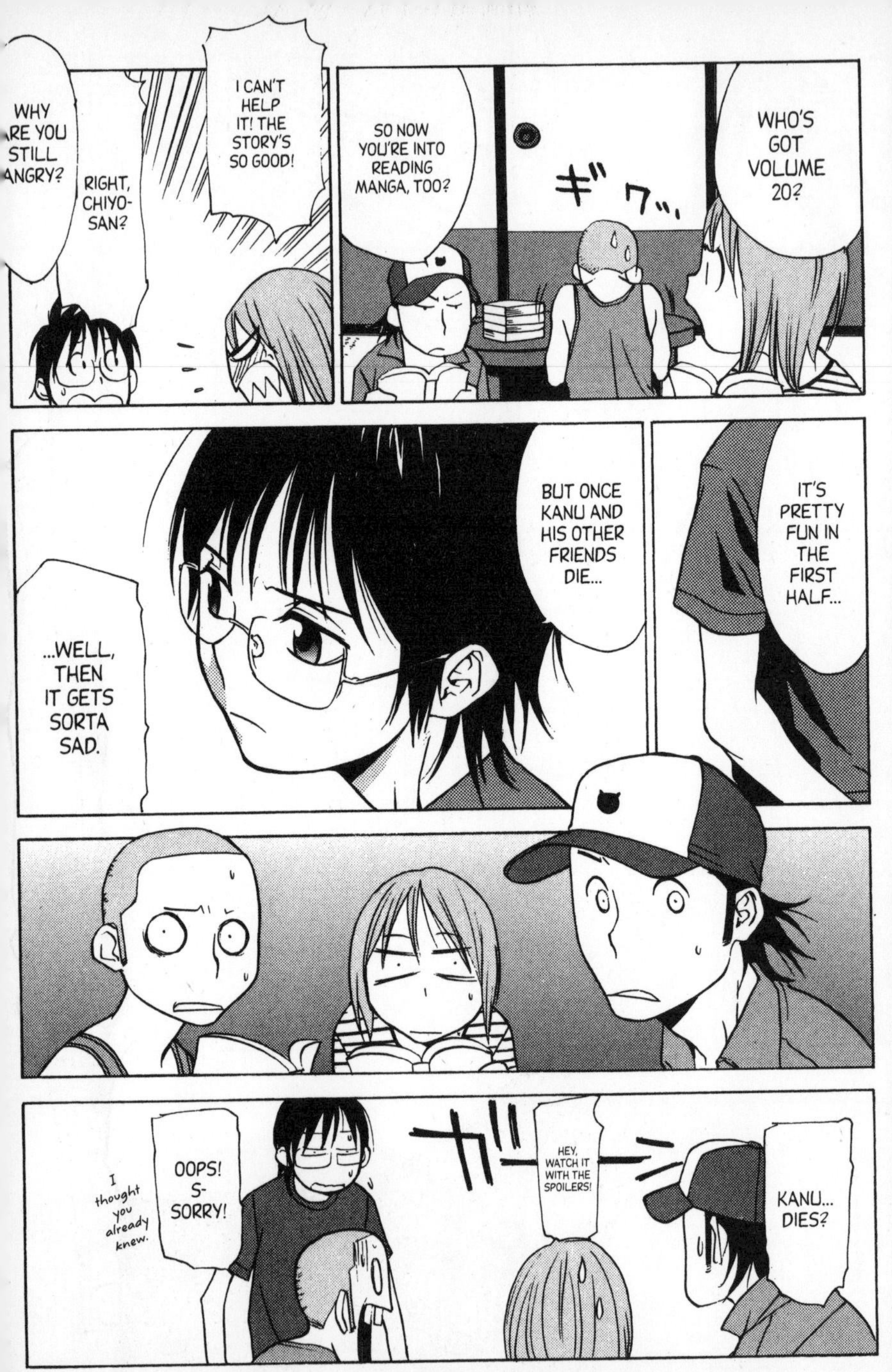
WHO'S GOT VOLUME 20?
ギクッ
SO NOW YOU'RE INTO READING MANGA, TOO?
I CAN'T HELP IT! THE STORY'S SO GOOD!
RIGHT, CHIYO-SAN?
WHY ARE YOU STILL ANGRY?
IT'S PRETTY FUN IN THE FIRST HALF...
BUT ONCE KANU AND HIS OTHER FRIENDS DIE...
...WELL, THEN IT GETS SORTA SAD.
KANU... DIES?
ガーン
HEY, WATCH IT WITH THE SPOILERS!
OOPS! S-SORRY!
I thought you already knew.

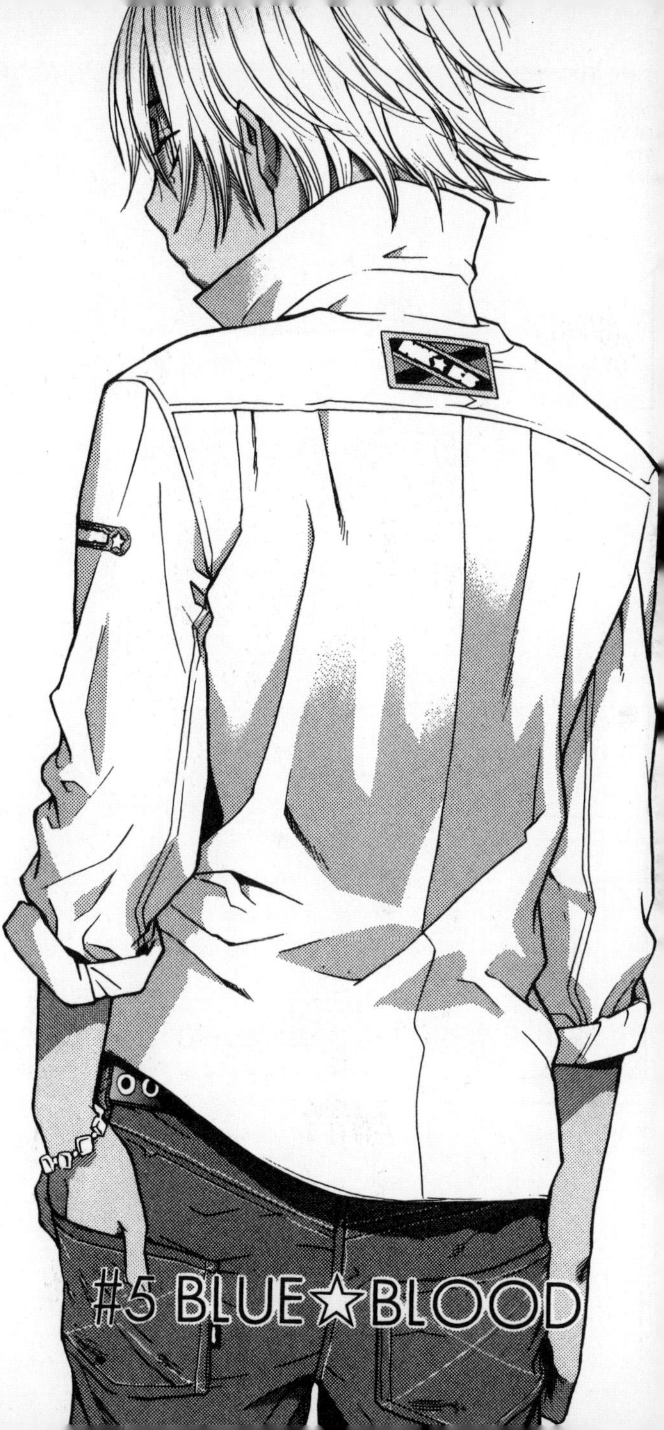
#5 BLUE☆BLOOD

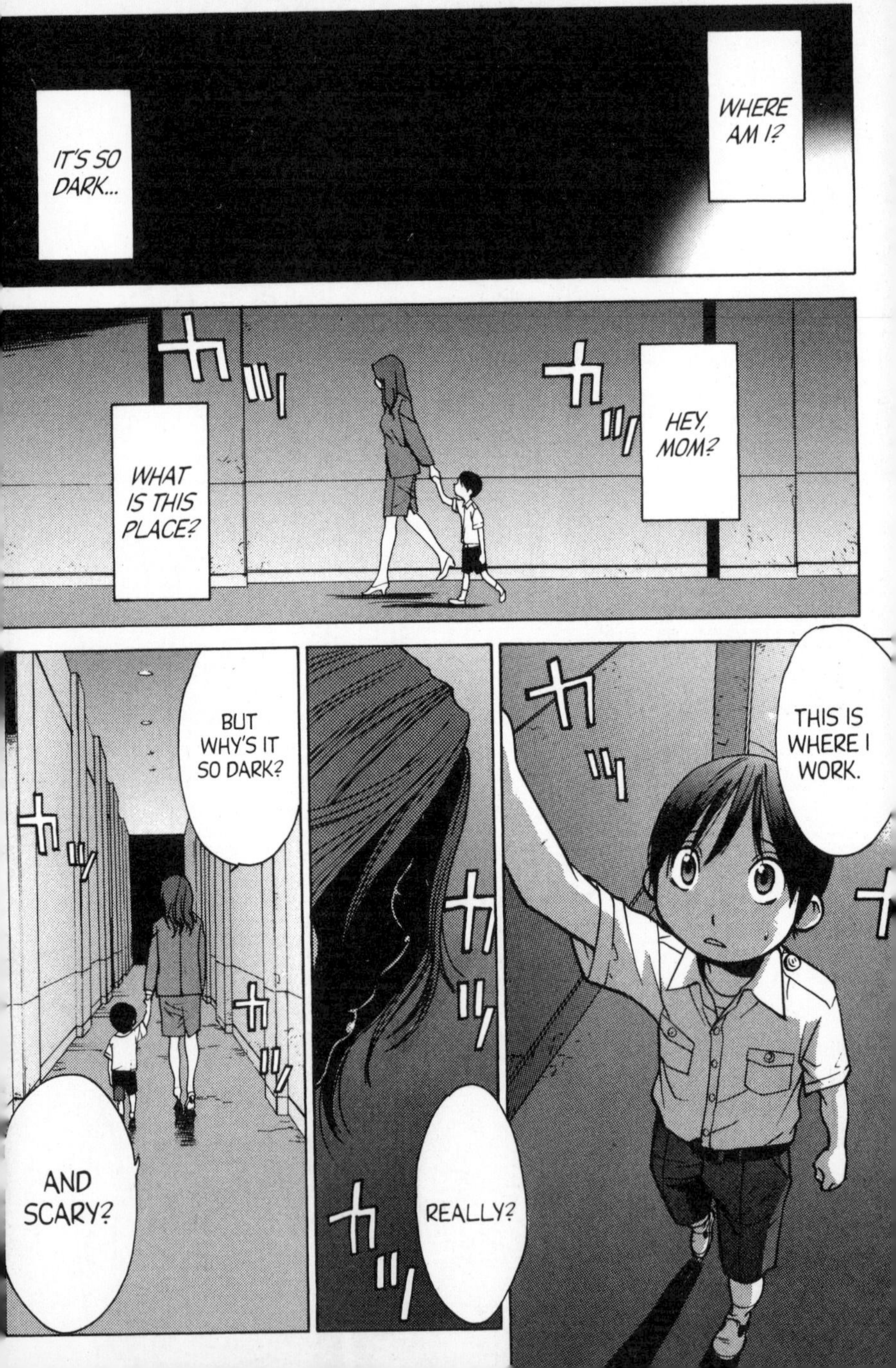
WHERE AM I?
IT'S SO DARK...
HEY, MOM?
WHAT IS THIS PLACE?
THIS IS WHERE I WORK.
REALLY?
BUT WHY'S IT SO DARK?
AND SCARY?

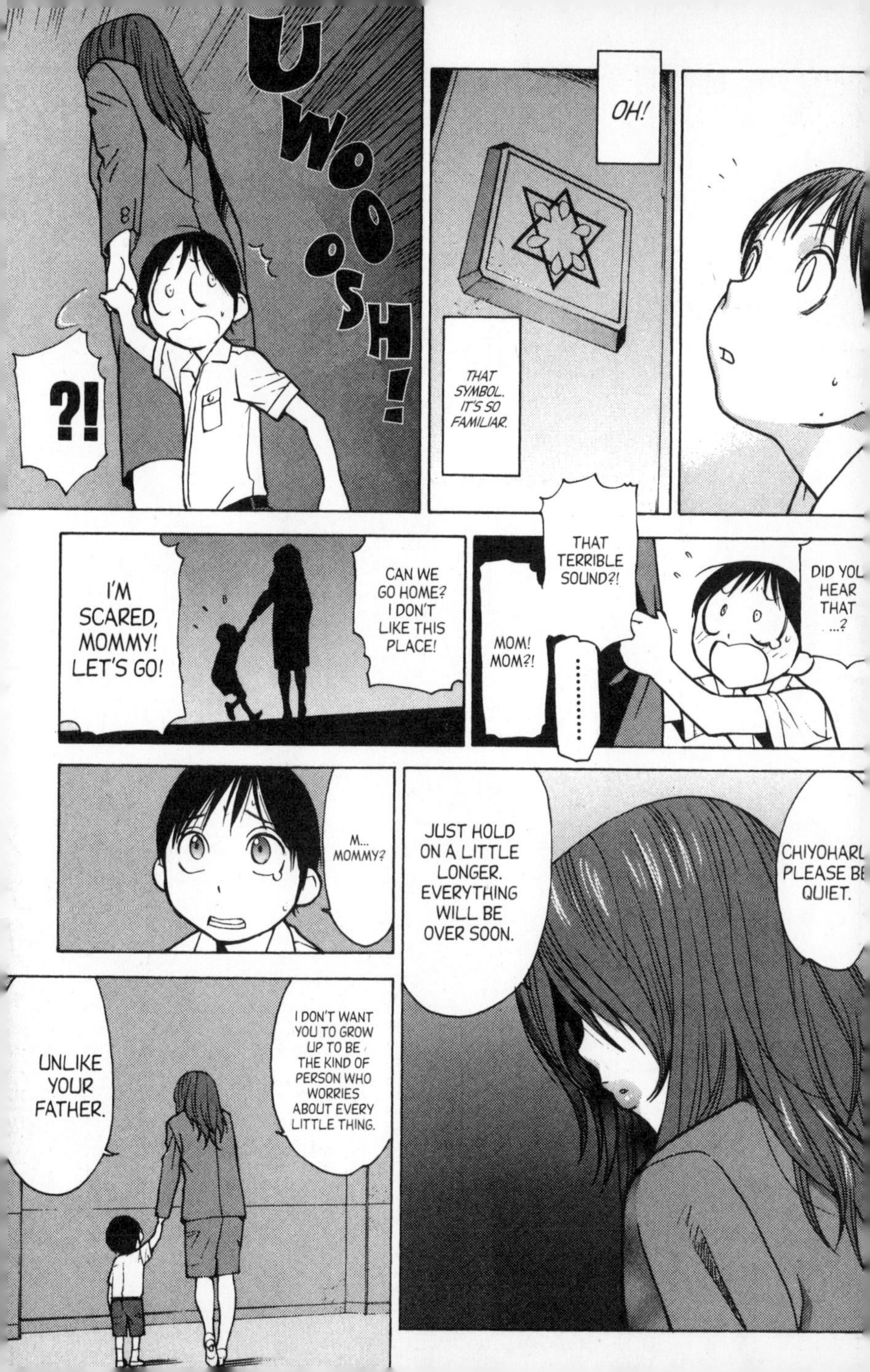
OH!
THAT SYMBOL. IT'S SO FAMILIAR.
UWOOOOSH!
?!
DID YOU HEAR THAT ...?
THAT TERRIBLE SOUND?!
MOM! MOM?!
......
CAN WE GO HOME? I DON'T LIKE THIS PLACE!
I'M SCARED, MOMMY! LET'S GO!
CHIYOHARU, PLEASE BE QUIET.
JUST HOLD ON A LITTLE LONGER. EVERYTHING WILL BE OVER SOON.
M... MOMMY?
I DON'T WANT YOU TO GROW UP TO BE THE KIND OF PERSON WHO WORRIES ABOUT EVERY LITTLE THING.
UNLIKE YOUR FATHER.

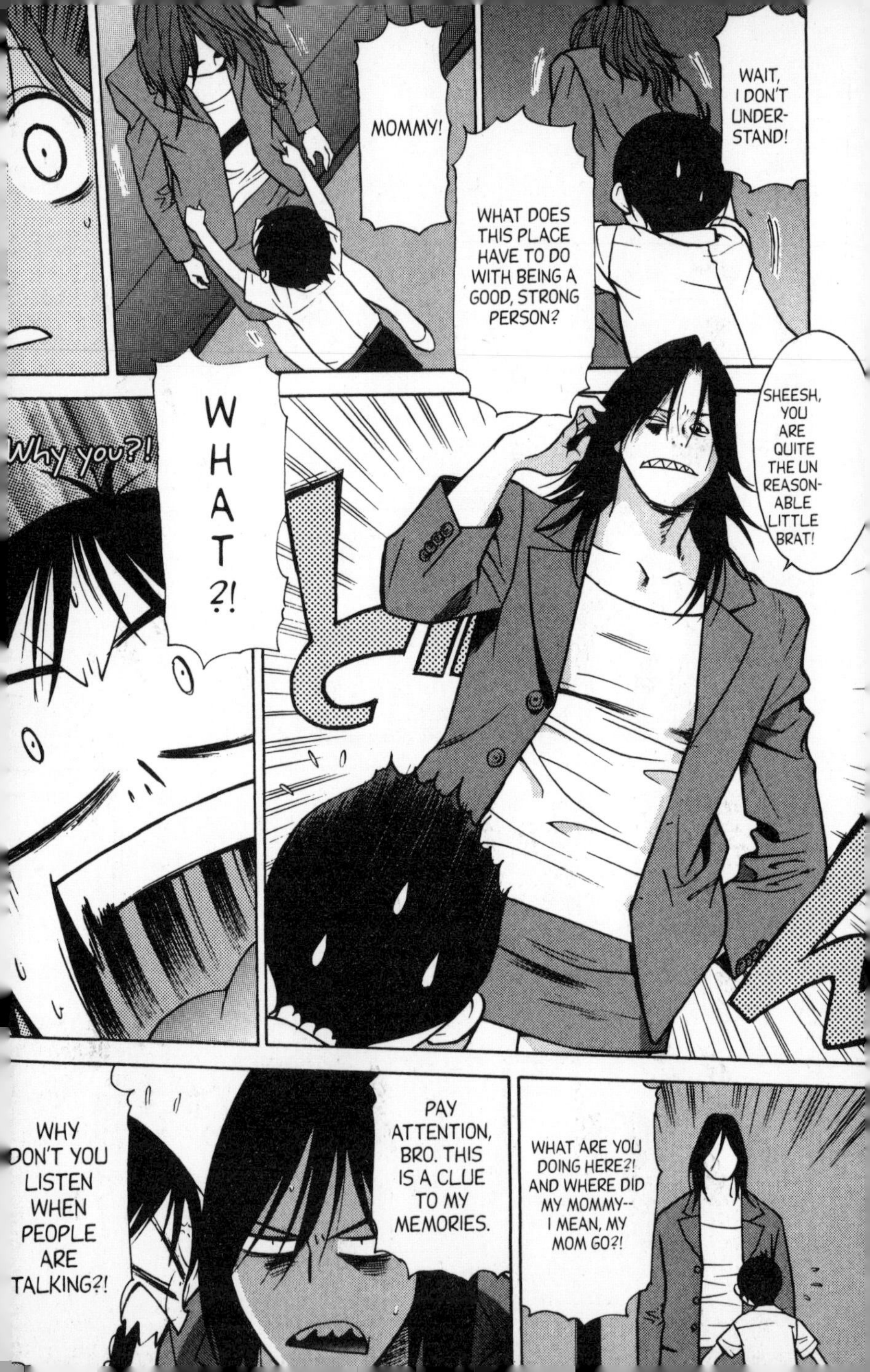
WAIT, I DON'T UNDER-STAND!
WHAT DOES THIS PLACE HAVE TO DO WITH BEING A GOOD, STRONG PERSON?
MOMMY!
SHEESH, YOU ARE QUITE THE UN REASON-ABLE LITTLE BRAT!
WHAT?!
Why you?!
WHAT ARE YOU DOING HERE?! AND WHERE DID MY MOMMY-- I MEAN, MY MOM GO?!
PAY ATTENTION, BRO. THIS IS A CLUE TO MY MEMORIES.
WHY DON'T YOU LISTEN WHEN PEOPLE ARE TALKING?!

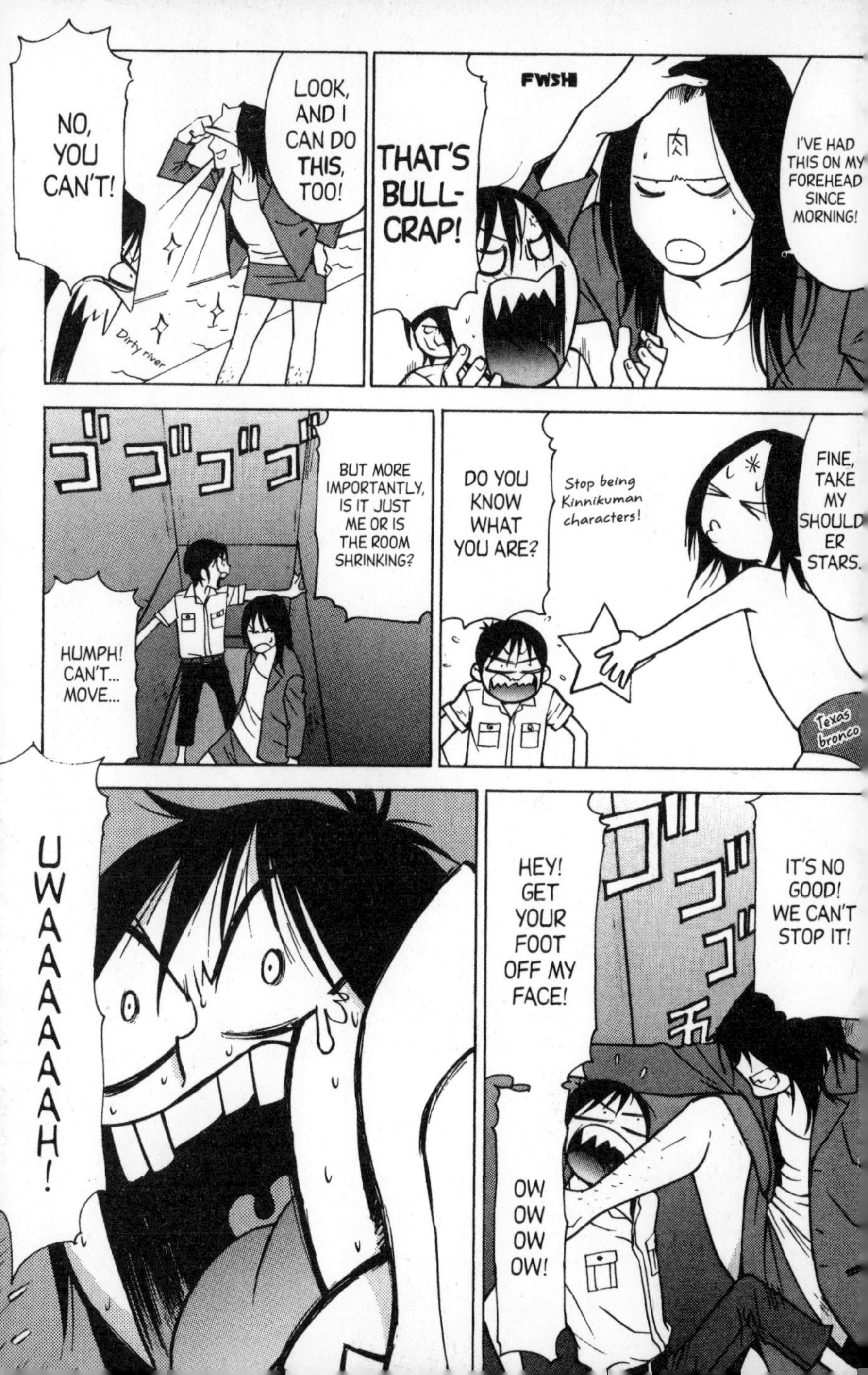
I'VE HAD THIS ON MY FOREHEAD SINCE MORNING!
肉
FWSH
THAT'S BULL-CRAP!
LOOK, AND I CAN DO THIS, TOO!
NO, YOU CAN'T!
Dirty river
FINE, TAKE MY SHOULDER STARS.
Stop being Kinnikuman characters!
DO YOU KNOW WHAT YOU ARE?
Texas bronco
ゴゴゴゴ
BUT MORE IMPORTANTLY, IS IT JUST ME OR IS THE ROOM SHRINKING?
HUMPH! CAN'T... MOVE...
IT'S NO GOOD! WE CAN'T STOP IT!
ゴゴゴ
HEY! GET YOUR FOOT OFF MY FACE!
OW OW OW OW!
UWAAAAAAAAAH!

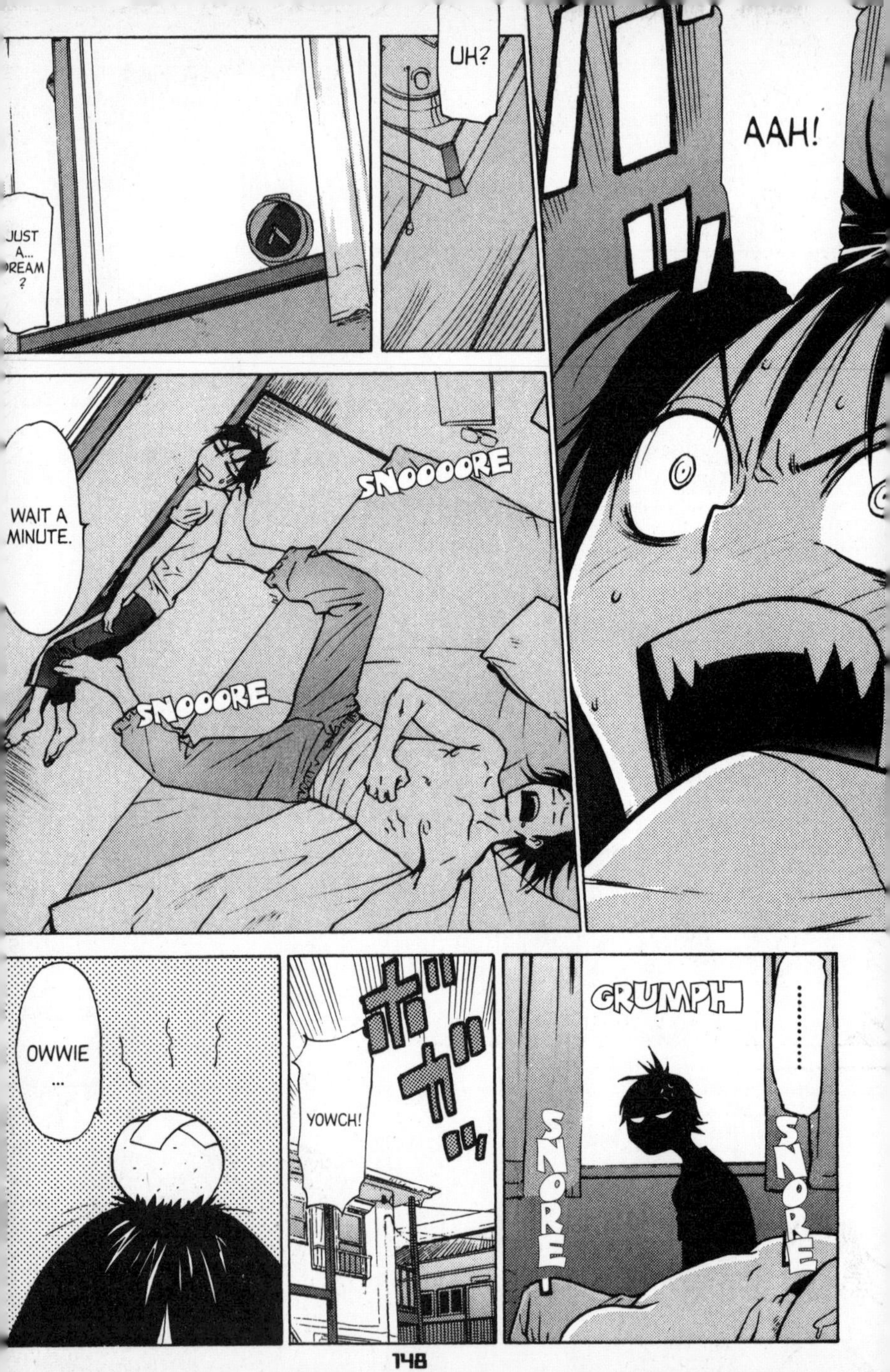
UH?
JUST A... DREAM?
WAIT A MINUTE.
SNOOOORE
SNOOORE
AAH!
GRUMPH
....
SNORE
SNORE
YOWCH!
OWWIE ...

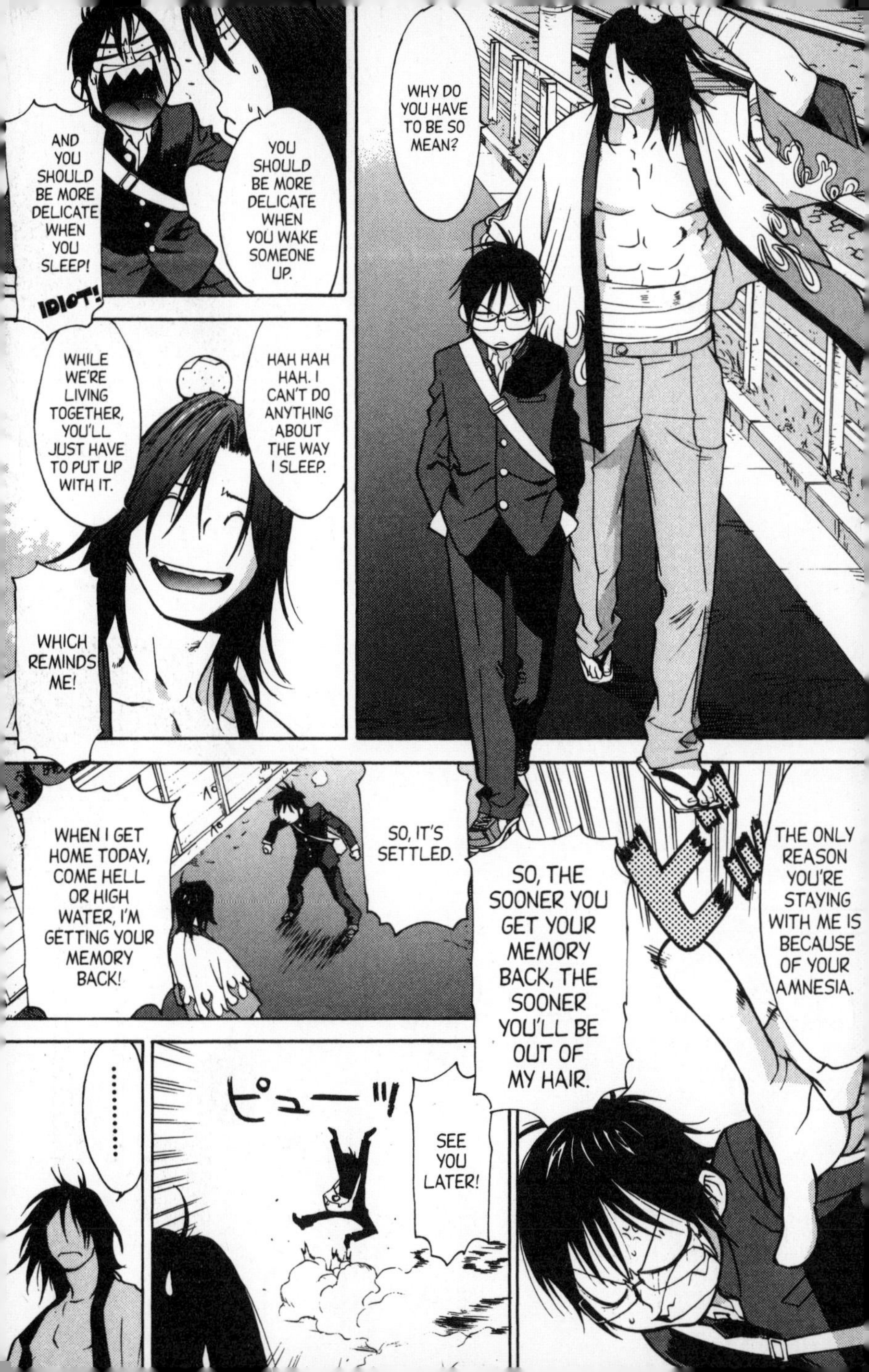
WHY DO YOU HAVE TO BE SO MEAN?
YOU SHOULD BE MORE DELICATE WHEN YOU WAKE SOMEONE UP.
AND YOU SHOULD BE MORE DELICATE WHEN YOU SLEEP!
IDIOT!
HAH HAH HAH. I CAN'T DO ANYTHING ABOUT THE WAY I SLEEP.
WHILE WE'RE LIVING TOGETHER, YOU'LL JUST HAVE TO PUT UP WITH IT.
WHICH REMINDS ME!
THE ONLY REASON YOU'RE STAYING WITH ME IS BECAUSE OF YOUR AMNESIA.
SO, THE SOONER YOU GET YOUR MEMORY BACK, THE SOONER YOU'LL BE OUT OF MY HAIR.
SO, IT'S SETTLED.
WHEN I GET HOME TODAY, COME HELL OR HIGH WATER, I'M GETTING YOUR MEMORY BACK!
SEE YOU LATER!
ピューーッ
………

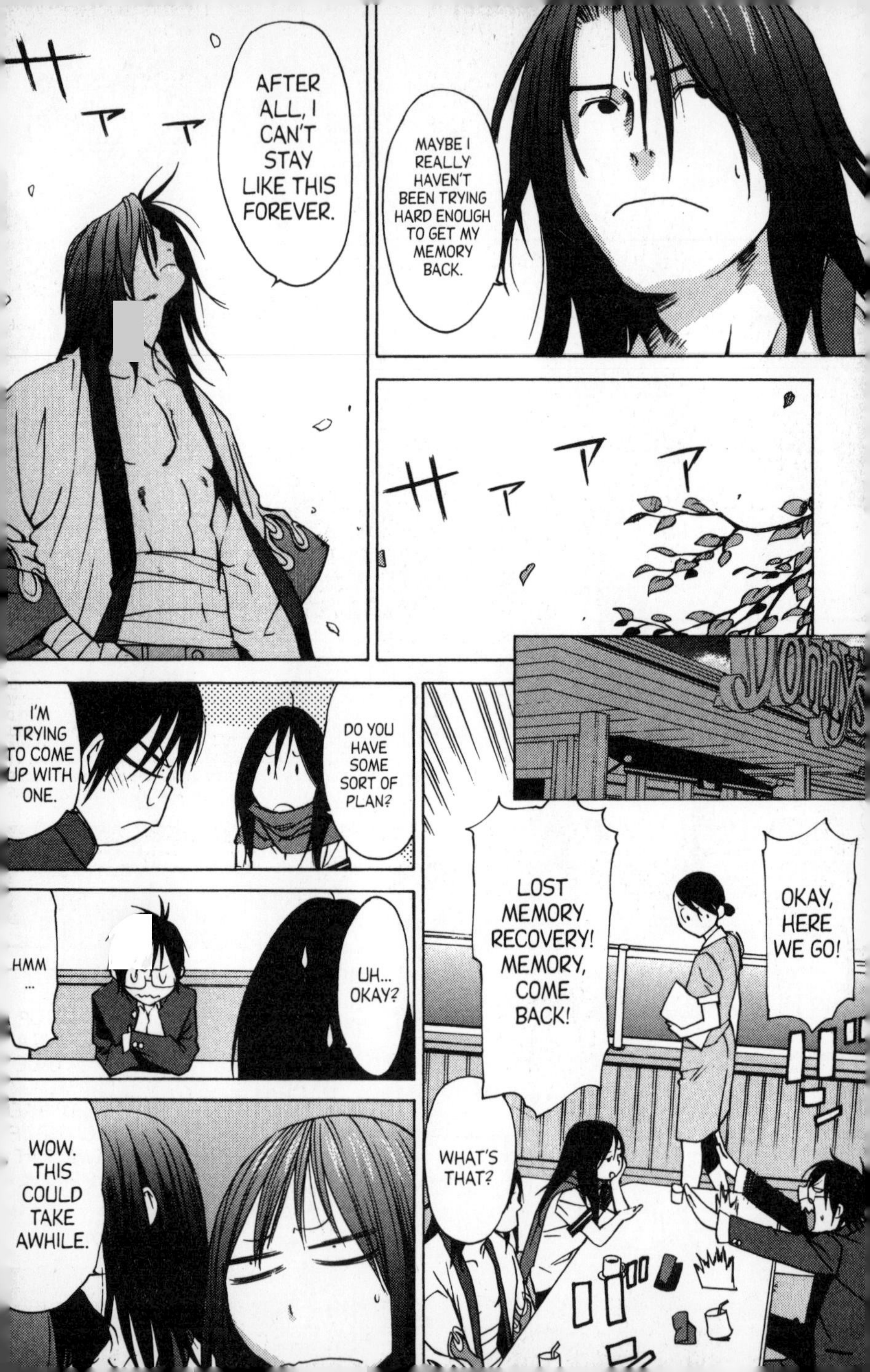
MAYBE I REALLY HAVEN'T BEEN TRYING HARD ENOUGH TO GET MY MEMORY BACK.
サァァ
サァァ
AFTER ALL, I CAN'T STAY LIKE THIS FOREVER.
OKAY, HERE WE GO!
LOST MEMORY RECOVERY! MEMORY, COME BACK!
WHAT'S THAT?
DO YOU HAVE SOME SORT OF PLAN?
I'M TRYING TO COME UP WITH ONE.
UH... OKAY?
HMM...
WOW. THIS COULD TAKE AWHILE.

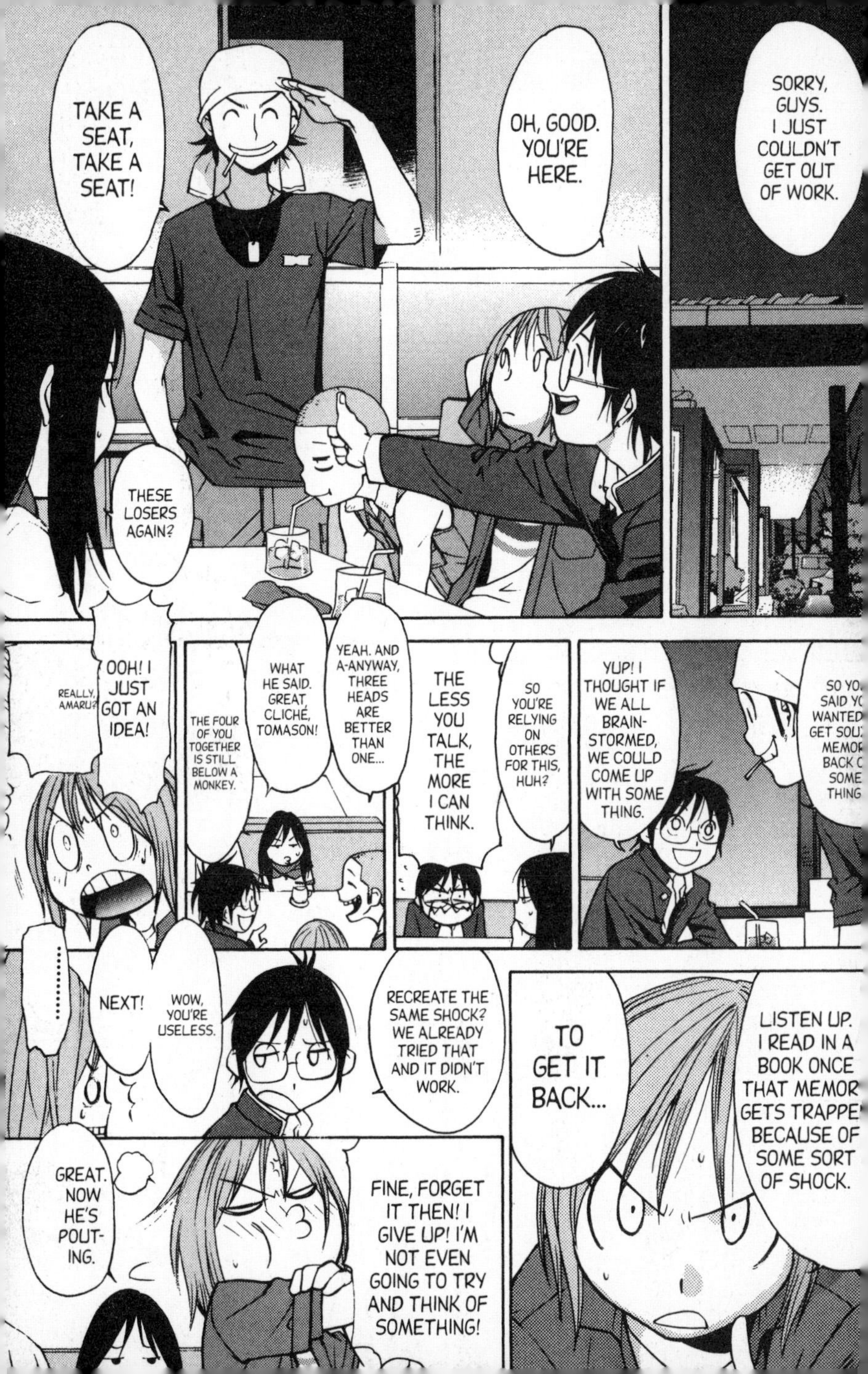
SORRY, GUYS. I JUST COULDN'T GET OUT OF WORK.
OH, GOOD. YOU'RE HERE.
TAKE A SEAT, TAKE A SEAT!
THESE LOSERS AGAIN?
SO YO SAID YO WANTED GET SOU MEMOR BACK O SOME THING
YUP! I THOUGHT IF WE ALL BRAIN-STORMED, WE COULD COME UP WITH SOME THING.
SO YOU'RE RELYING ON OTHERS FOR THIS, HUH?
THE LESS YOU TALK, THE MORE I CAN THINK.
YEAH. AND A-ANYWAY, THREE HEADS ARE BETTER THAN ONE...
WHAT HE SAID. GREAT, CLICHÉ, TOMASON!
THE FOUR OF YOU TOGETHER IS STILL BELOW A MONKEY.
OOH! I JUST GOT AN IDEA!
REALLY, AMARU?
LISTEN UP. I READ IN A BOOK ONCE THAT MEMOR GETS TRAPPE BECAUSE OF SOME SORT OF SHOCK.
TO GET IT BACK...
RECREATE THE SAME SHOCK? WE ALREADY TRIED THAT AND IT DIDN'T WORK.
WOW, YOU'RE USELESS.
NEXT!
......
FINE, FORGET IT THEN! I GIVE UP! I'M NOT EVEN GOING TO TRY AND THINK OF SOMETHING!
GREAT. NOW HE'S POUTING.

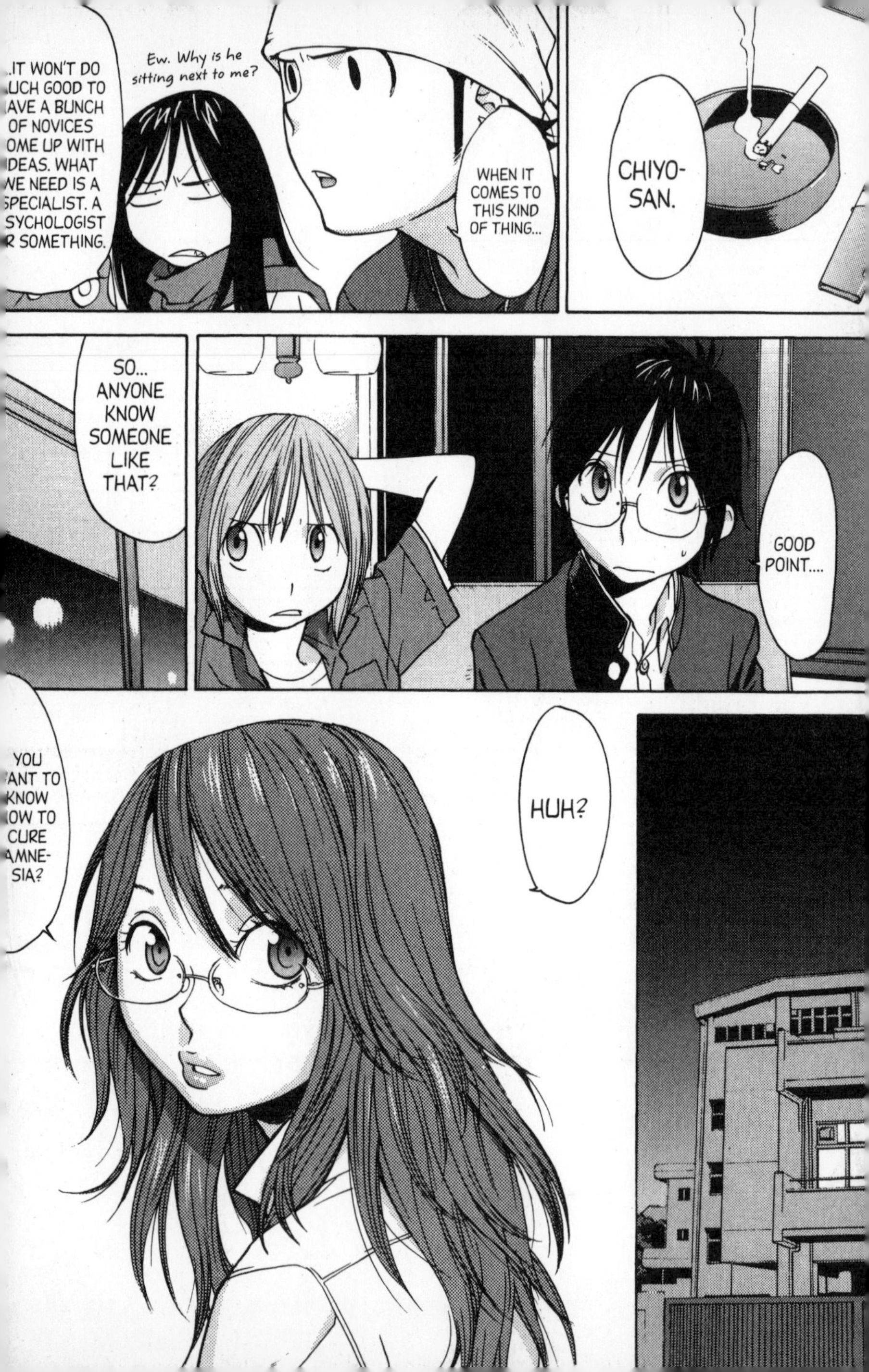
CHIYO-SAN.
WHEN IT COMES TO THIS KIND OF THING...
Ew. Why is he sitting next to me?
.IT WON'T DO UCH GOOD TO AVE A BUNCH OF NOVICES OME UP WITH IDEAS. WHAT WE NEED IS A SPECIALIST. A SYCHOLOGIST R SOMETHING.
GOOD POINT....
SO... ANYONE KNOW SOMEONE LIKE THAT?
HUH?
YOU ANT TO KNOW OW TO CURE AMNE-SIA?

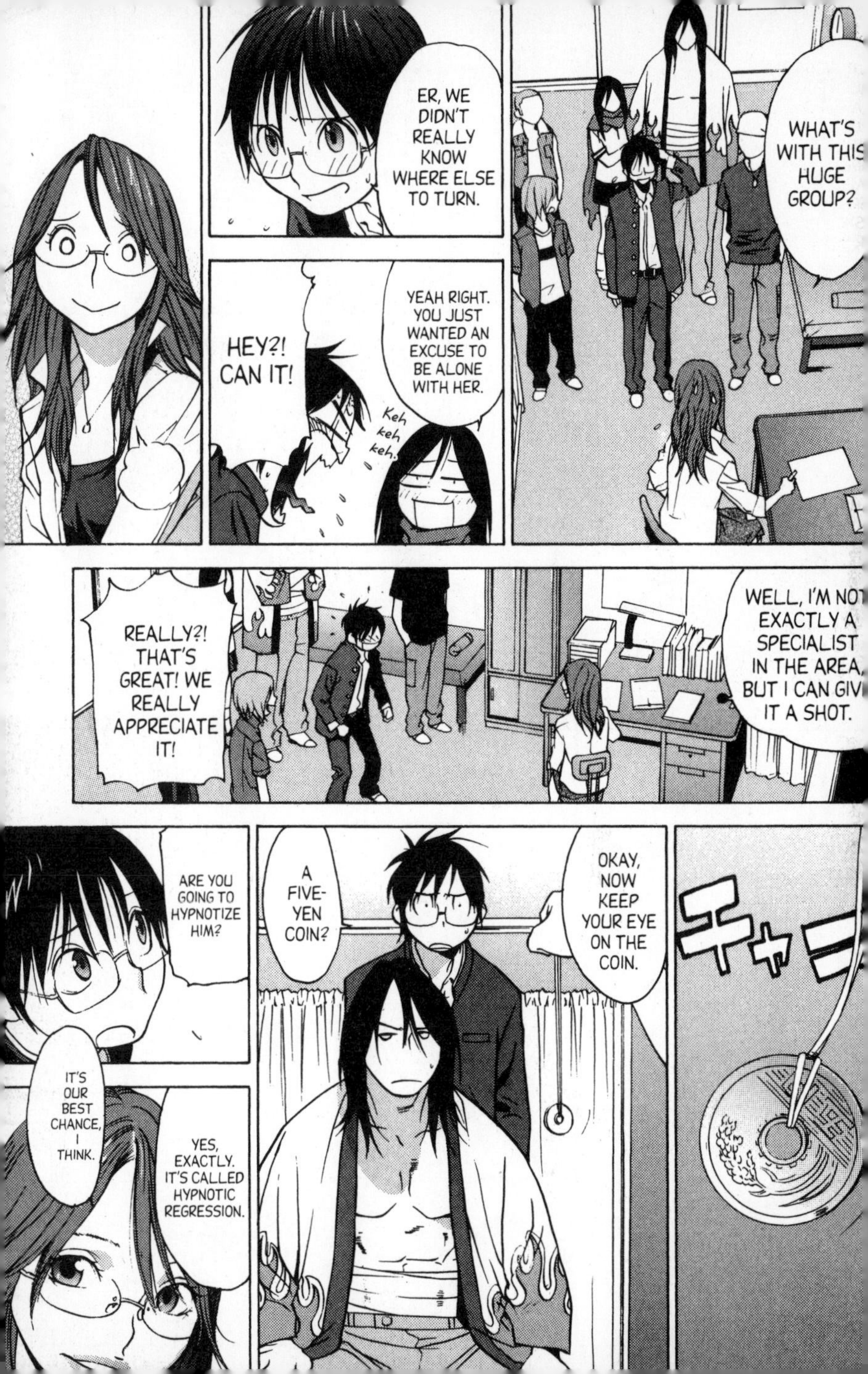
WHAT'S WITH THIS HUGE GROUP?
ER, WE DIDN'T REALLY KNOW WHERE ELSE TO TURN.
YEAH RIGHT. YOU JUST WANTED AN EXCUSE TO BE ALONE WITH HER.
Keh keh keh.
HEY?! CAN IT!
WELL, I'M NO EXACTLY A SPECIALIST IN THE AREA, BUT I CAN GIV IT A SHOT.
REALLY?! THAT'S GREAT! WE REALLY APPRECIATE IT!
OKAY, NOW KEEP YOUR EYE ON THE COIN.
A FIVE-YEN COIN?
ARE YOU GOING TO HYPNOTIZE HIM?
YES, EXACTLY. IT'S CALLED HYPNOTIC REGRESSION.
IT'S OUR BEST CHANCE, I THINK.

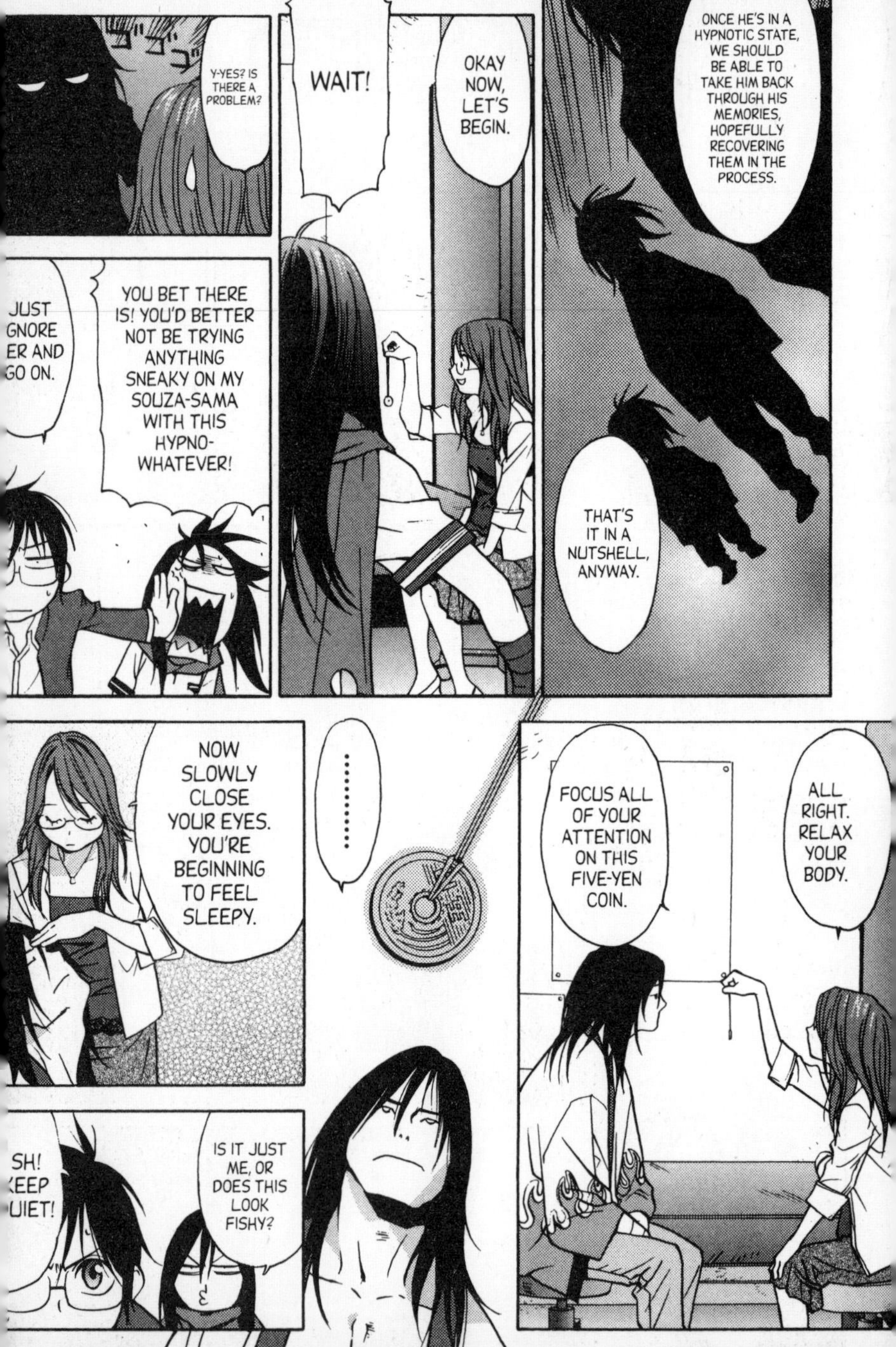

ONCE HE'S IN A HYPNOTIC STATE, WE SHOULD BE ABLE TO TAKE HIM BACK THROUGH HIS MEMORIES, HOPEFULLY RECOVERING THEM IN THE PROCESS.
THAT'S IT IN A NUTSHELL, ANYWAY.
OKAY NOW, LET'S BEGIN.
WAIT!
Y-YES? IS THERE A PROBLEM?
YOU BET THERE IS! YOU'D BETTER NOT BE TRYING ANYTHING SNEAKY ON MY SOUZA-SAMA WITH THIS HYPNO-WHATEVER!
JUST GNORE ER AND GO ON.
ALL RIGHT. RELAX YOUR BODY.
FOCUS ALL OF YOUR ATTENTION ON THIS FIVE-YEN COIN.
....
NOW SLOWLY CLOSE YOUR EYES. YOU'RE BEGINNING TO FEEL SLEEPY.
IS IT JUST ME, OR DOES THIS LOOK FISHY?
SH! EEP UIET!

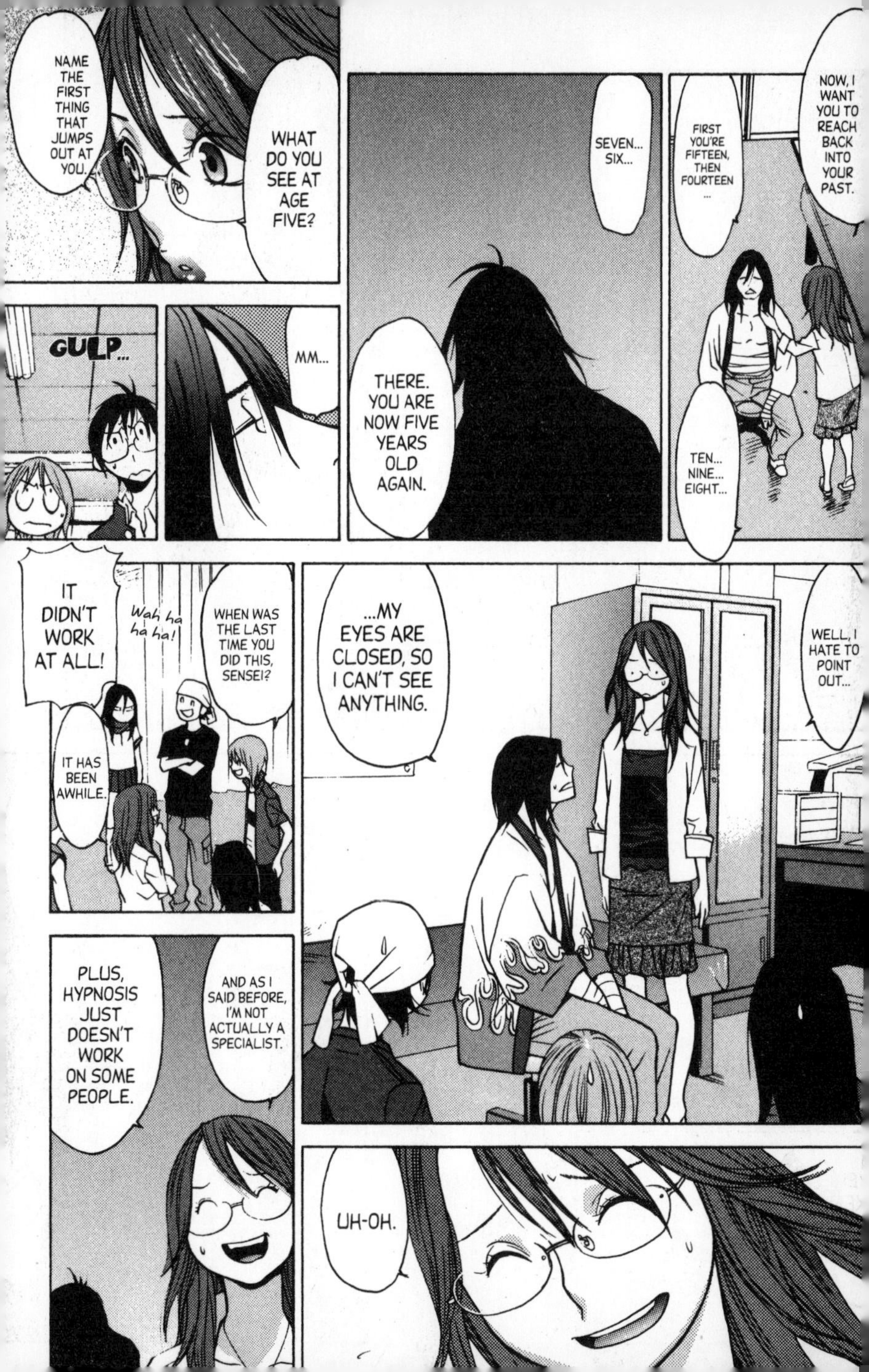
NOW, I WANT YOU TO REACH BACK INTO YOUR PAST.
FIRST YOU'RE FIFTEEN, THEN FOURTEEN ...
TEN... NINE... EIGHT...
SEVEN... SIX...
THERE. YOU ARE NOW FIVE YEARS OLD AGAIN.
WHAT DO YOU SEE AT AGE FIVE?
NAME THE FIRST THING THAT JUMPS OUT AT YOU.
MM...
GULP...
WELL, I HATE TO POINT OUT...
...MY EYES ARE CLOSED, SO I CAN'T SEE ANYTHING.
WHEN WAS THE LAST TIME YOU DID THIS, SENSEI?
Wah ha ha ha!
IT DIDN'T WORK AT ALL!
IT HAS BEEN AWHILE.
UH-OH.
AND AS I SAID BEFORE, I'M NOT ACTUALLY A SPECIALIST.
PLUS, HYPNOSIS JUST DOESN'T WORK ON SOME PEOPLE.

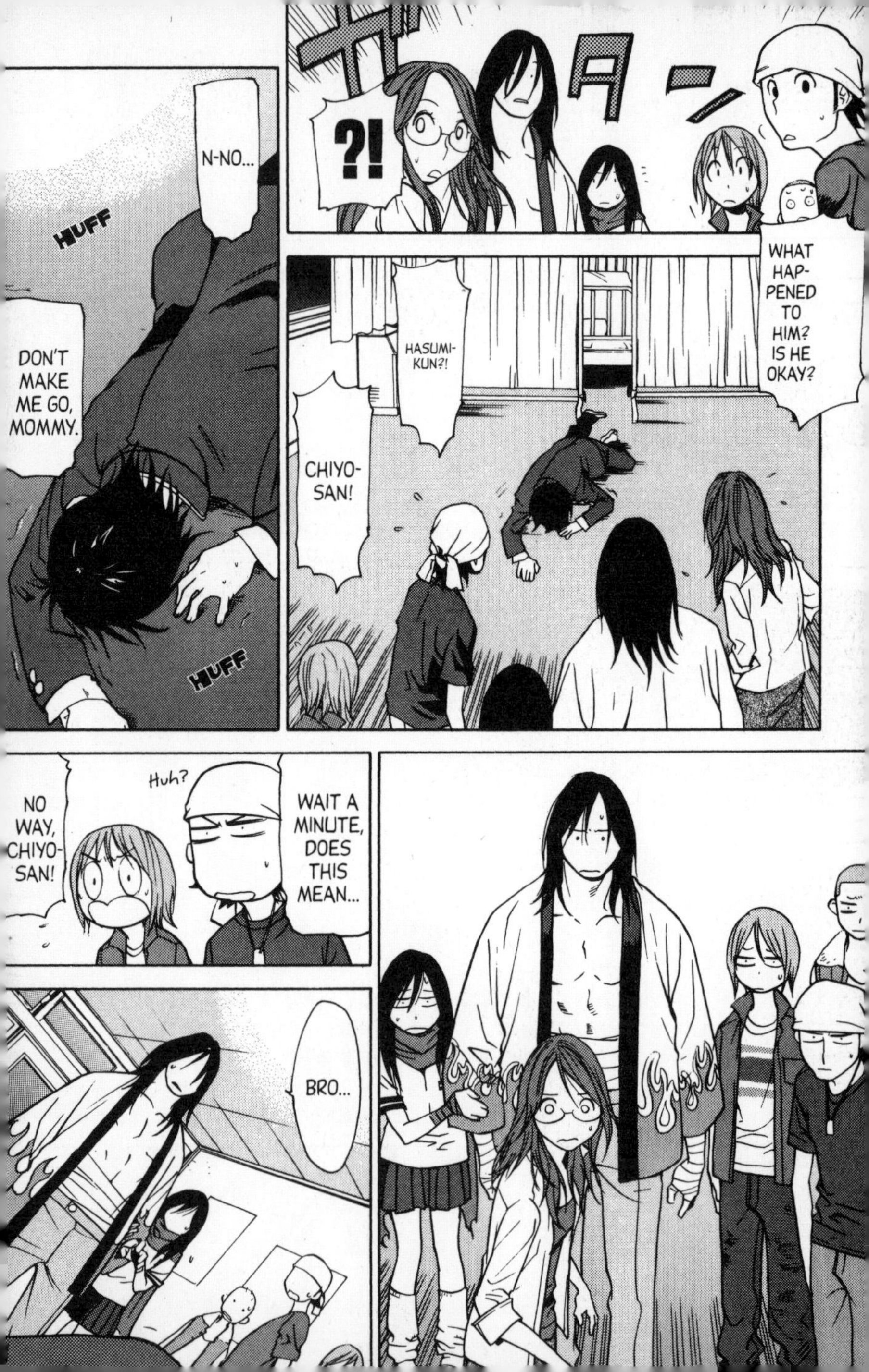
?!
WHAT HAP-PENED TO HIM? IS HE OKAY?
HASUMI-KUN?!
CHIYO-SAN!
N-NO...
HUFF
DON'T MAKE ME GO, MOMMY.
HUFF
WAIT A MINUTE, DOES THIS MEAN...
Huh?
NO WAY, CHIYO-SAN!
BRO...

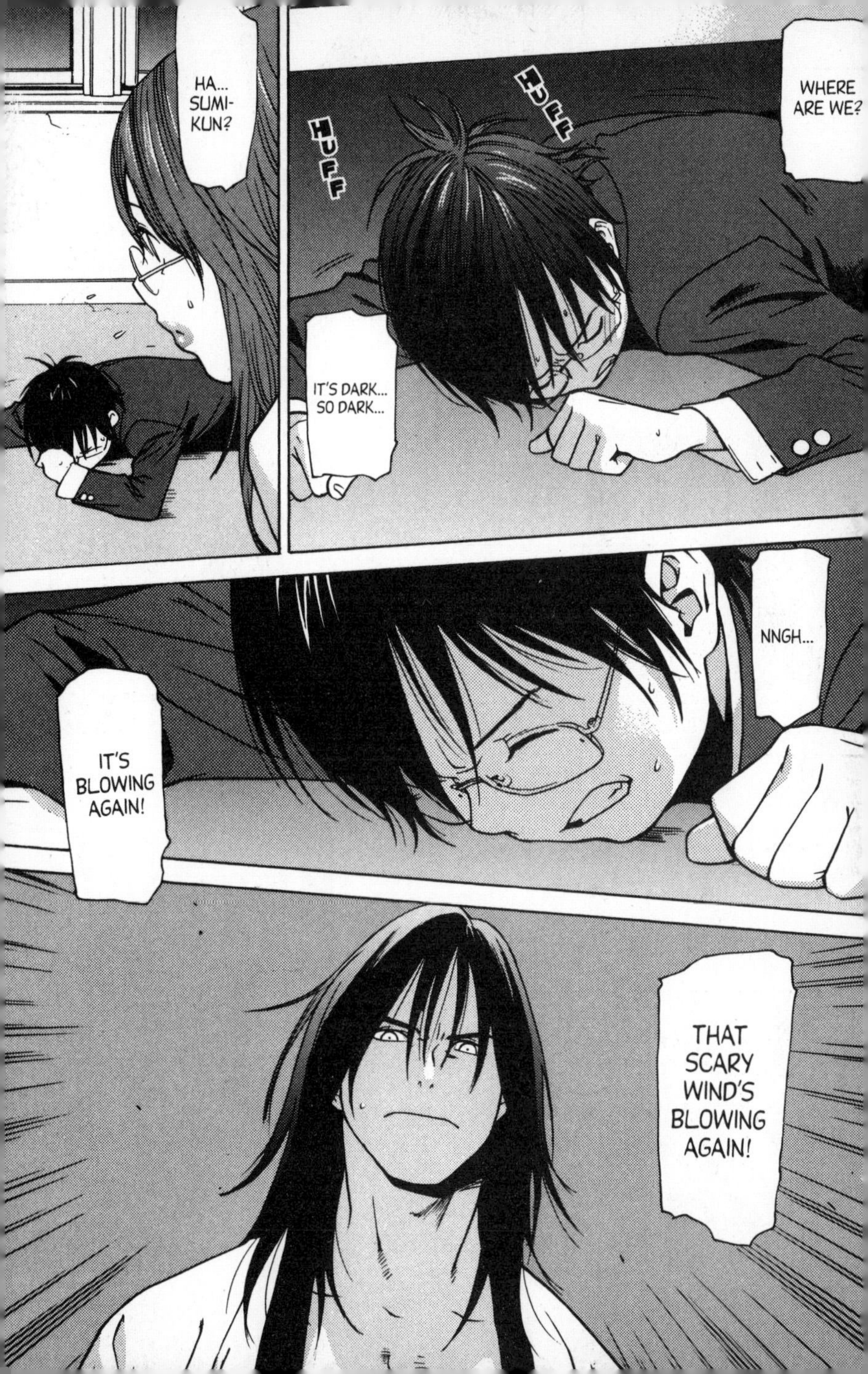
WHERE ARE WE?
HUFF
HUFF
IT'S DARK... SO DARK...
HA... SUMI-KUN?
NNGH...
IT'S BLOWING AGAIN!
THAT SCARY WIND'S BLOWING AGAIN!

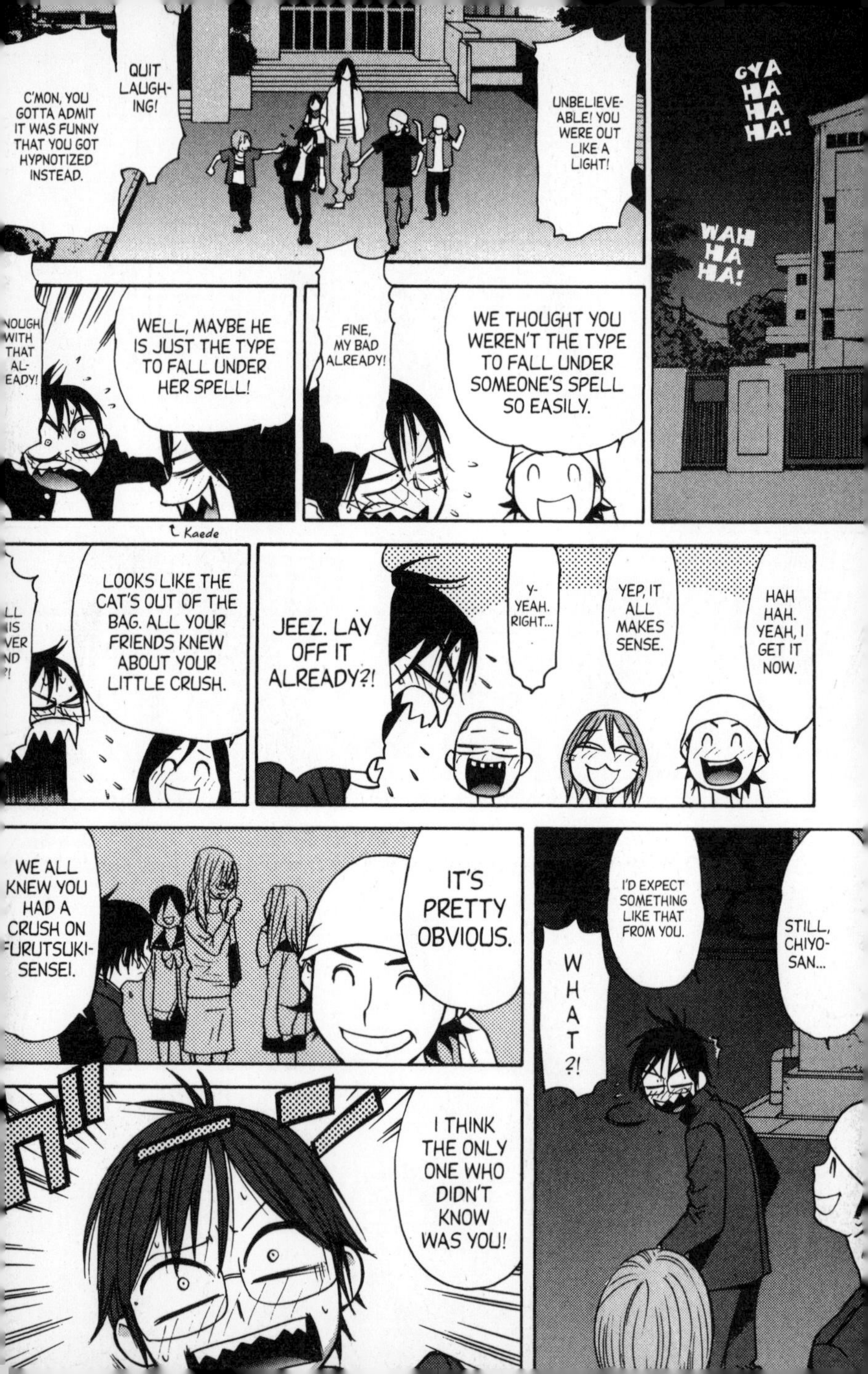
GYA HA HA HA!
WAH HA HA!
UNBELIEVE-ABLE! YOU WERE OUT LIKE A LIGHT!
QUIT LAUGHING!
C'MON, YOU GOTTA ADMIT IT WAS FUNNY THAT YOU GOT HYPNOTIZED INSTEAD.
WE THOUGHT YOU WEREN'T THE TYPE TO FALL UNDER SOMEONE'S SPELL SO EASILY.
FINE, MY BAD ALREADY!
WELL, MAYBE HE IS JUST THE TYPE TO FALL UNDER HER SPELL!
Kaede
NOUGH WITH THAT AL-EADY!
HAH HAH. YEAH, I GET IT NOW.
YEP, IT ALL MAKES SENSE.
Y-YEAH. RIGHT...
JEEZ. LAY OFF IT ALREADY?!
LOOKS LIKE THE CAT'S OUT OF THE BAG. ALL YOUR FRIENDS KNEW ABOUT YOUR LITTLE CRUSH.
STILL, CHIYO-SAN...
I'D EXPECT SOMETHING LIKE THAT FROM YOU.
WHAT?!
IT'S PRETTY OBVIOUS.
WE ALL KNEW YOU HAD A CRUSH ON URUTSUKI-SENSEI.
I THINK THE ONLY ONE WHO DIDN'T KNOW WAS YOU!

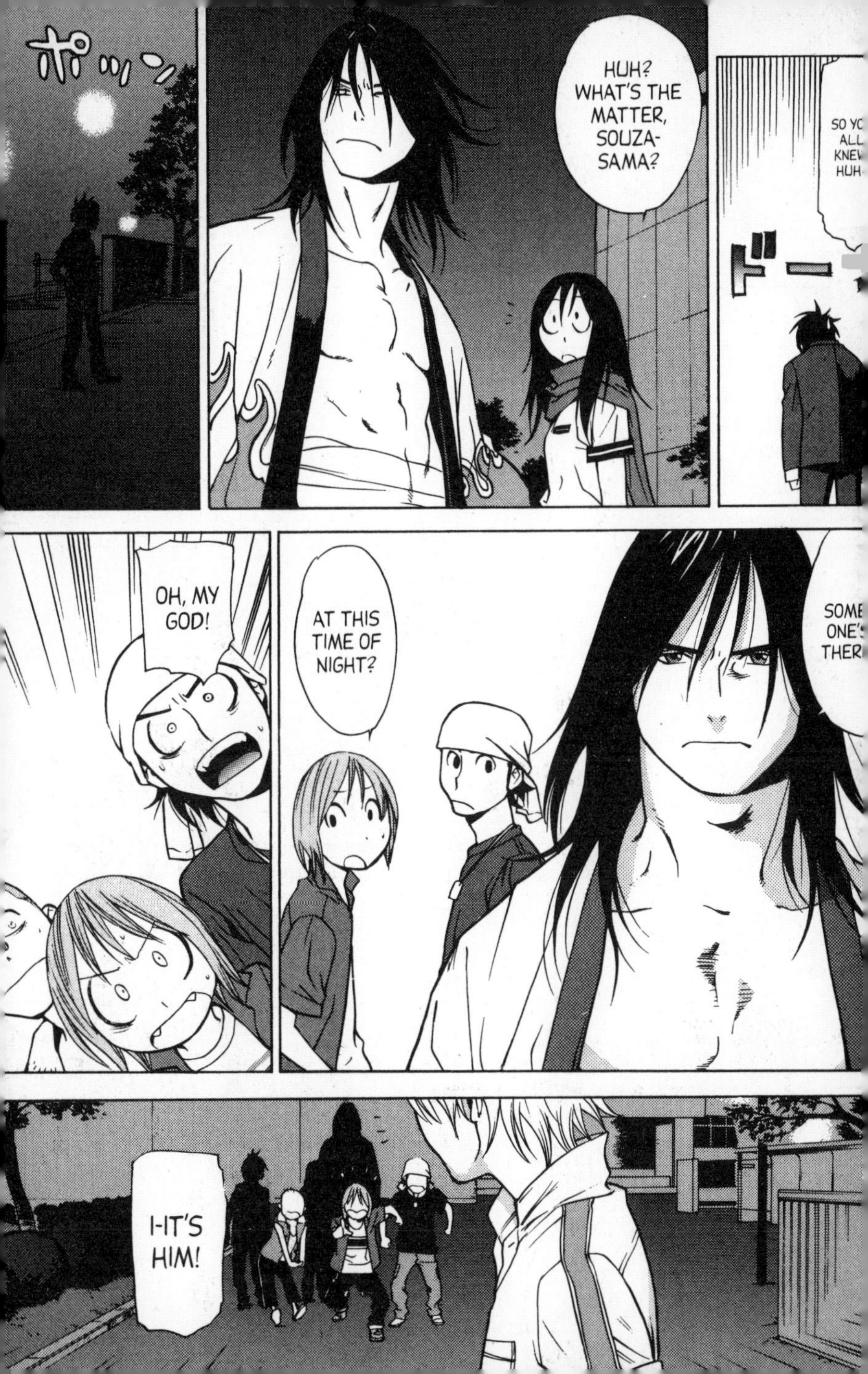
SO YO ALL KNEW HUH
HUH? WHAT'S THE MATTER, SOUZA-SAMA?
SOME ONE'S THER
AT THIS TIME OF NIGHT?
OH, MY GOD!
I-IT'S HIM!

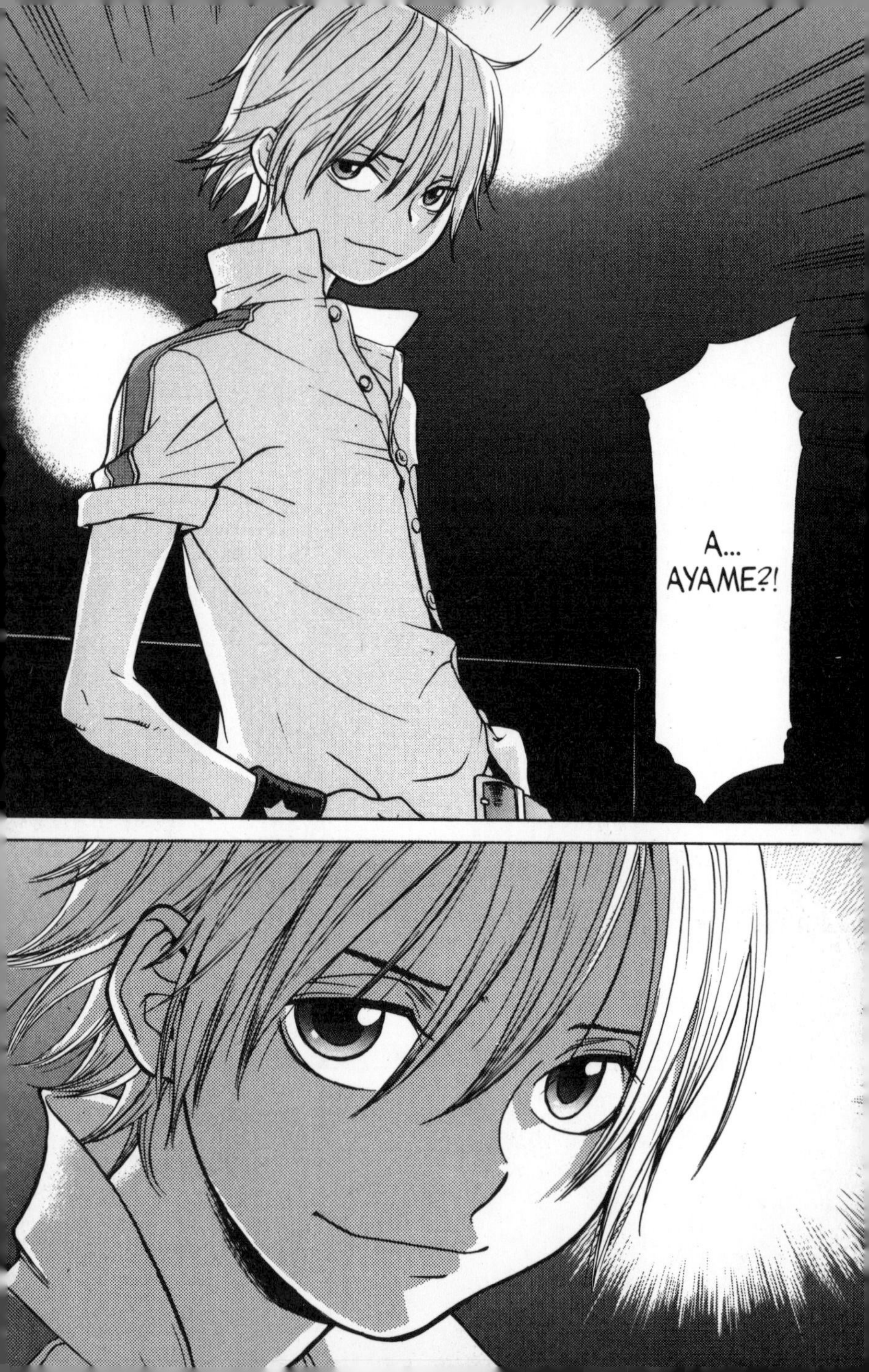
A... AYAME?!

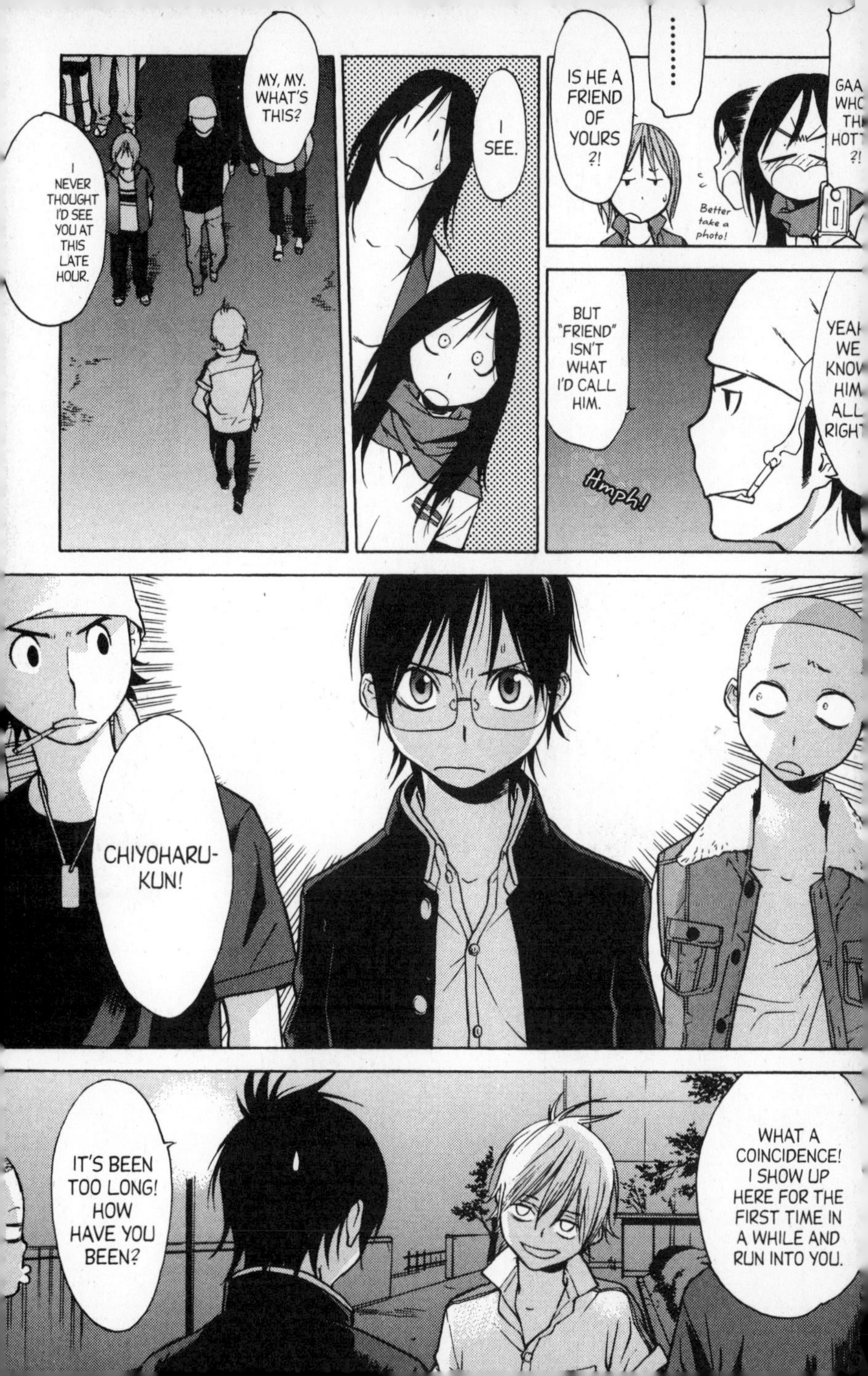
......
GAA WHO THI HOTT ?!
IS HE A FRIEND OF YOURS ?!
Better take a photo!
YEAH WE KNOW HIM ALL RIGHT
BUT "FRIEND" ISN'T WHAT I'D CALL HIM.
Hmph!
I SEE.
MY, MY. WHAT'S THIS?
I NEVER THOUGHT I'D SEE YOU AT THIS LATE HOUR.
CHIYOHARU-KUN!
WHAT A COINCIDENCE! I SHOW UP HERE FOR THE FIRST TIME IN A WHILE AND RUN INTO YOU.
IT'S BEEN TOO LONG! HOW HAVE YOU BEEN?

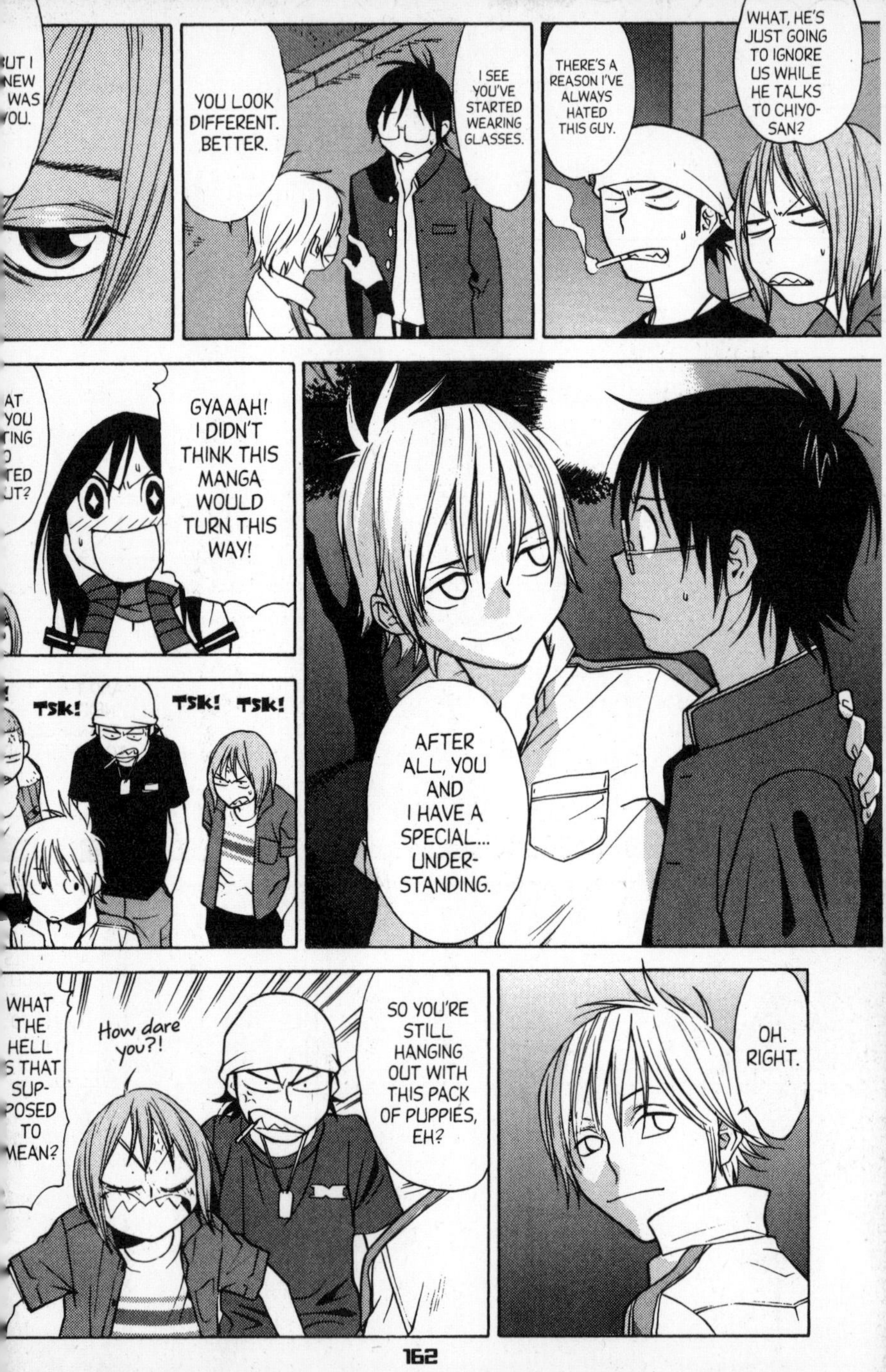
WHAT, HE'S JUST GOING TO IGNORE US WHILE HE TALKS TO CHIYO-SAN?
THERE'S A REASON I'VE ALWAYS HATED THIS GUY.
I SEE YOU'VE STARTED WEARING GLASSES.
YOU LOOK DIFFERENT. BETTER.
AFTER ALL, YOU AND I HAVE A SPECIAL... UNDER-STANDING.
GYAAAH! I DIDN'T THINK THIS MANGA WOULD TURN THIS WAY!
TSK! TSK! TSK!
OH. RIGHT.
SO YOU'RE STILL HANGING OUT WITH THIS PACK OF PUPPIES, EH?
How dare you?!
WHAT THE HELL IS THAT SUP-POSED TO MEAN?

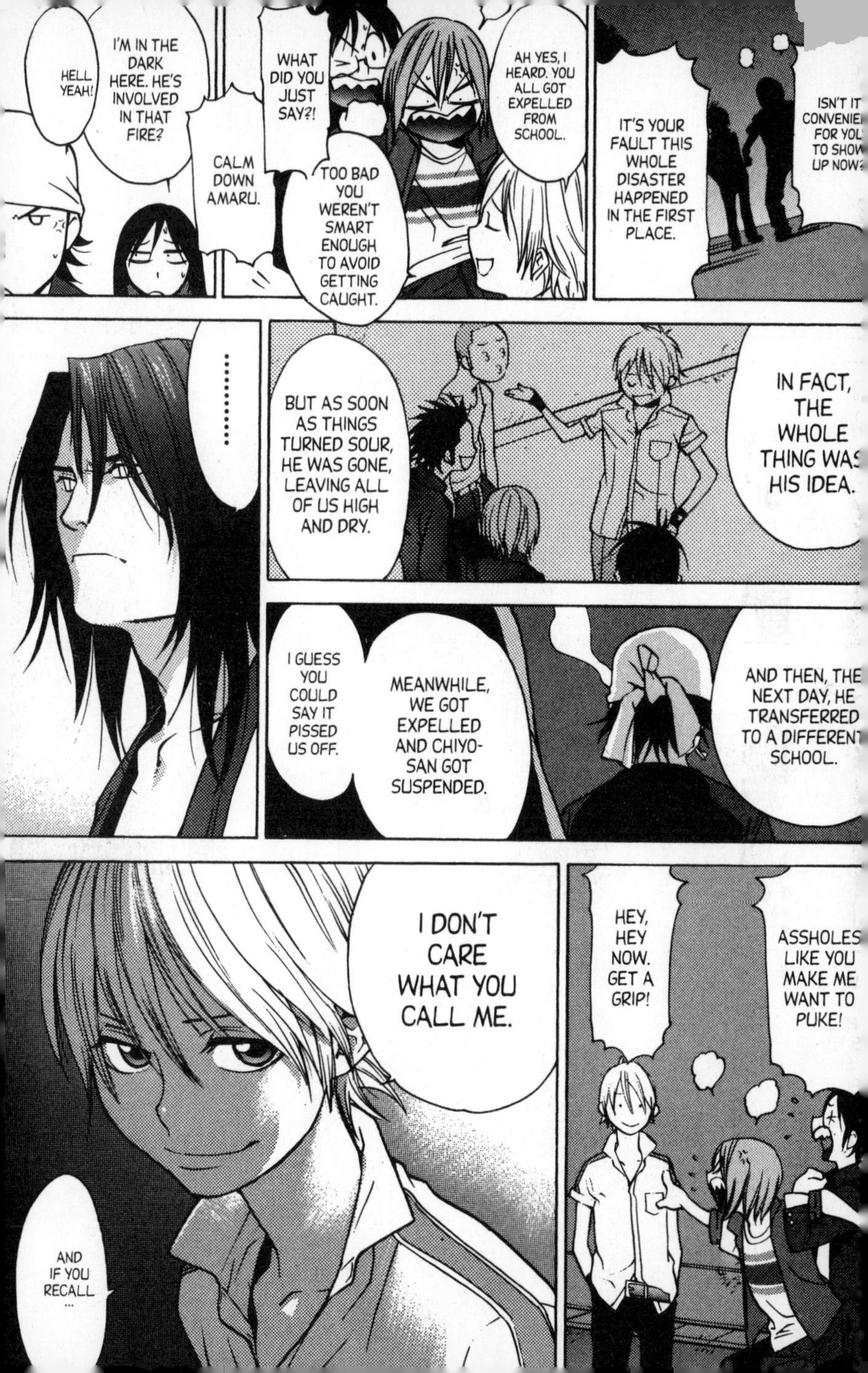
ISN'T IT CONVENIENT FOR YOU TO SHOW UP NOW?
IT'S YOUR FAULT THIS WHOLE DISASTER HAPPENED IN THE FIRST PLACE.
AH YES, I HEARD. YOU ALL GOT EXPELLED FROM SCHOOL.
TOO BAD YOU WEREN'T SMART ENOUGH TO AVOID GETTING CAUGHT.
WHAT DID YOU JUST SAY?!
CALM DOWN AMARU.
I'M IN THE DARK HERE. HE'S INVOLVED IN THAT FIRE?
HELL YEAH!
IN FACT, THE WHOLE THING WAS HIS IDEA.
BUT AS SOON AS THINGS TURNED SOUR, HE WAS GONE, LEAVING ALL OF US HIGH AND DRY.
AND THEN, THE NEXT DAY, HE TRANSFERRED TO A DIFFERENT SCHOOL.
MEANWHILE, WE GOT EXPELLED AND CHIYO-SAN GOT SUSPENDED.
I GUESS YOU COULD SAY IT PISSED US OFF.
....
ASSHOLES LIKE YOU MAKE ME WANT TO PUKE!
HEY, HEY NOW. GET A GRIP!
I DON'T CARE WHAT YOU CALL ME.
AND IF YOU RECALL ...

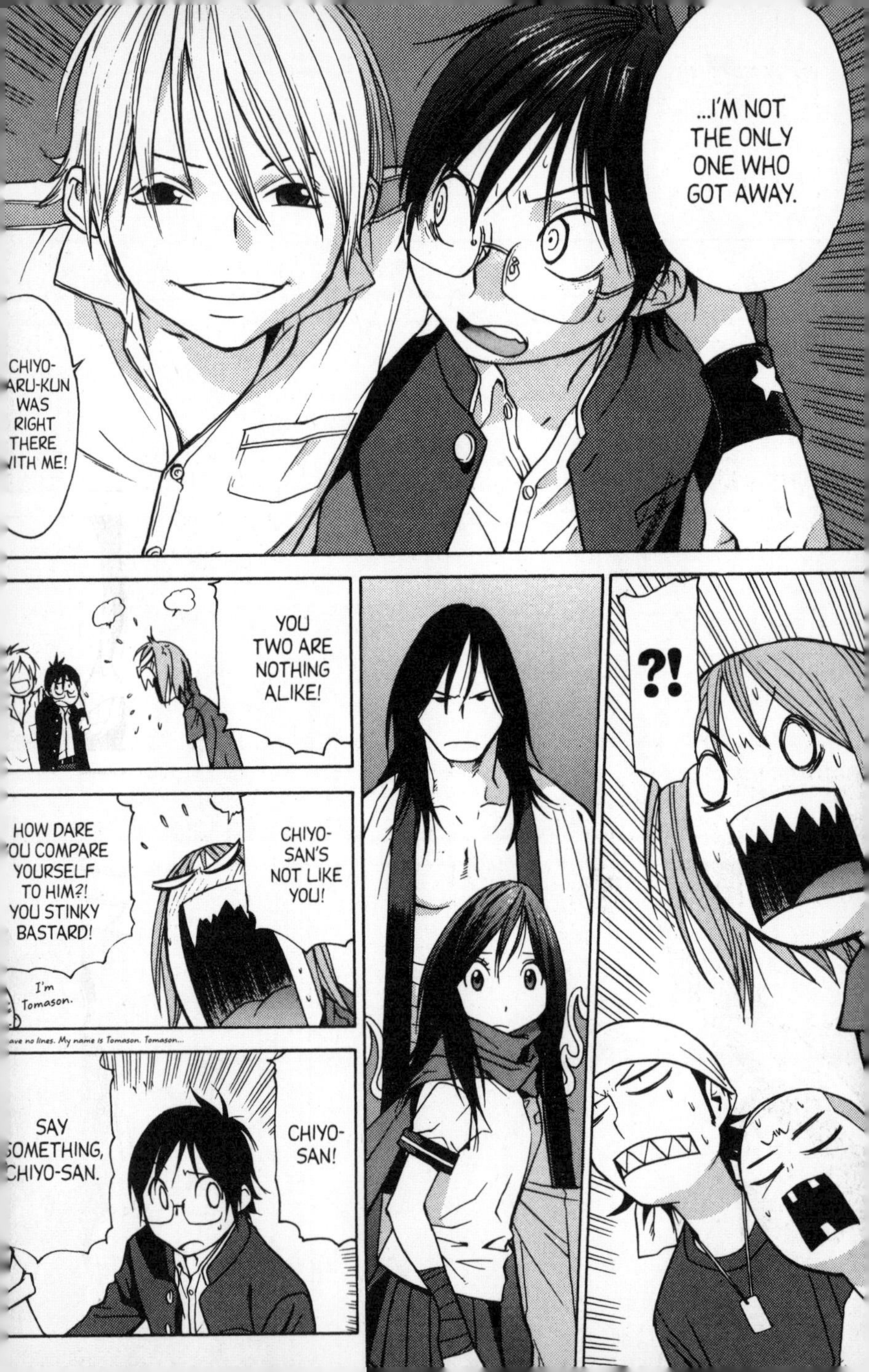
...I'M NOT THE ONLY ONE WHO GOT AWAY.
CHIYO-ARU-KUN WAS RIGHT THERE WITH ME!
?!
YOU TWO ARE NOTHING ALIKE!
CHIYO-SAN'S NOT LIKE YOU!
HOW DARE YOU COMPARE YOURSELF TO HIM?! YOU STINKY BASTARD!
I'm Tomason.
ave no lines. My name is Tomason. Tomason...
CHIYO-SAN!
SAY SOMETHING, CHIYO-SAN.

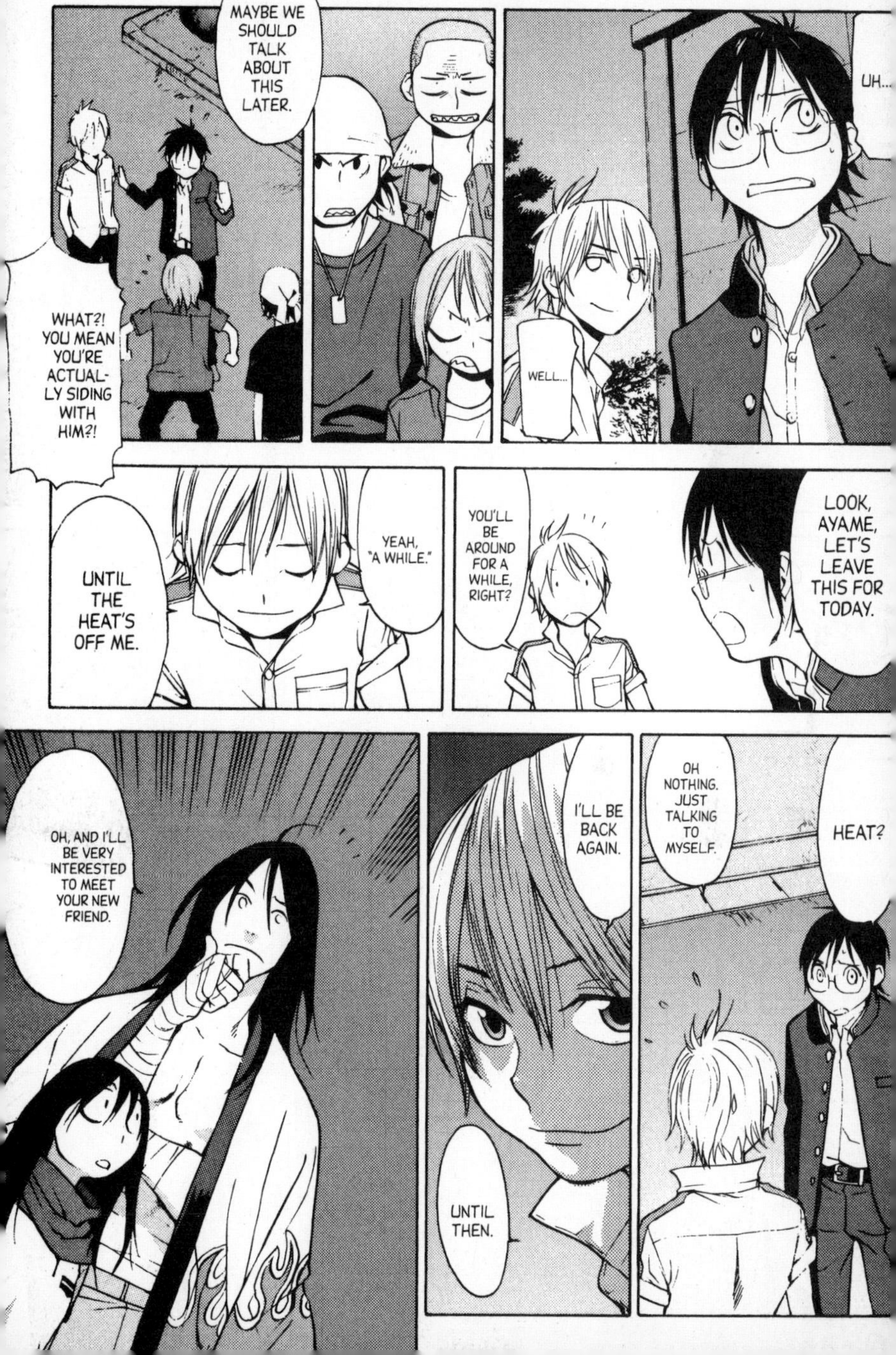
UH...
WELL...
MAYBE WE SHOULD TALK ABOUT THIS LATER.
WHAT?! YOU MEAN YOU'RE ACTUAL-LY SIDING WITH HIM?!
LOOK, AYAME, LET'S LEAVE THIS FOR TODAY.
YOU'LL BE AROUND FOR A WHILE, RIGHT?
YEAH, "A WHILE."
UNTIL THE HEAT'S OFF ME.
HEAT?
OH NOTHING. JUST TALKING TO MYSELF.
I'LL BE BACK AGAIN.
UNTIL THEN.
OH, AND I'LL BE VERY INTERESTED TO MEET YOUR NEW FRIEND.

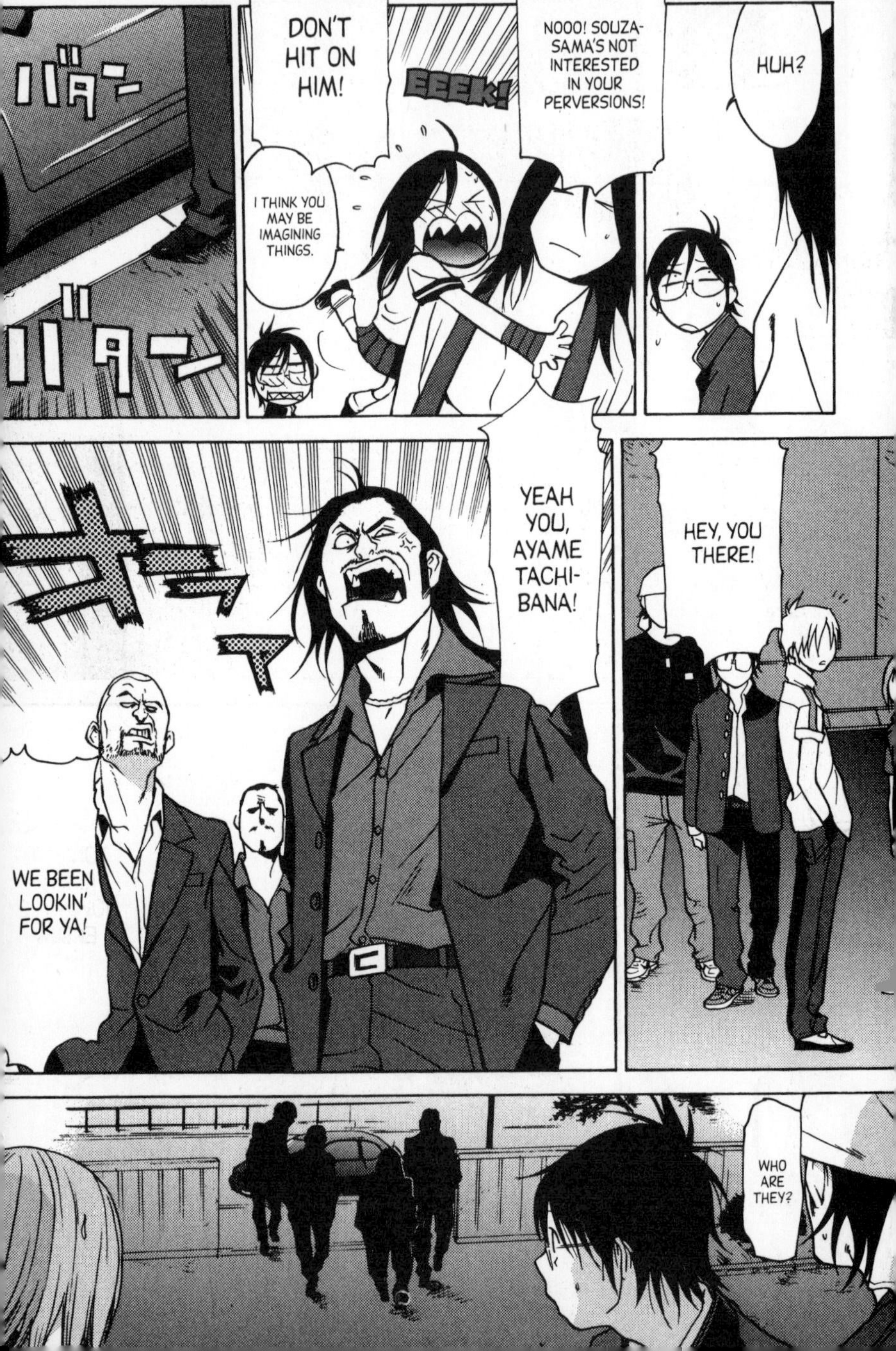
HUH?
NOOO! SOUZA-SAMA'S NOT INTERESTED IN YOUR PERVERSIONS!
EEEK!
DON'T HIT ON HIM!
I THINK YOU MAY BE IMAGINING THINGS.
HEY, YOU THERE!
YEAH YOU, AYAME TACHIBANA!
WE BEEN LOOKIN' FOR YA!
WHO ARE THEY?

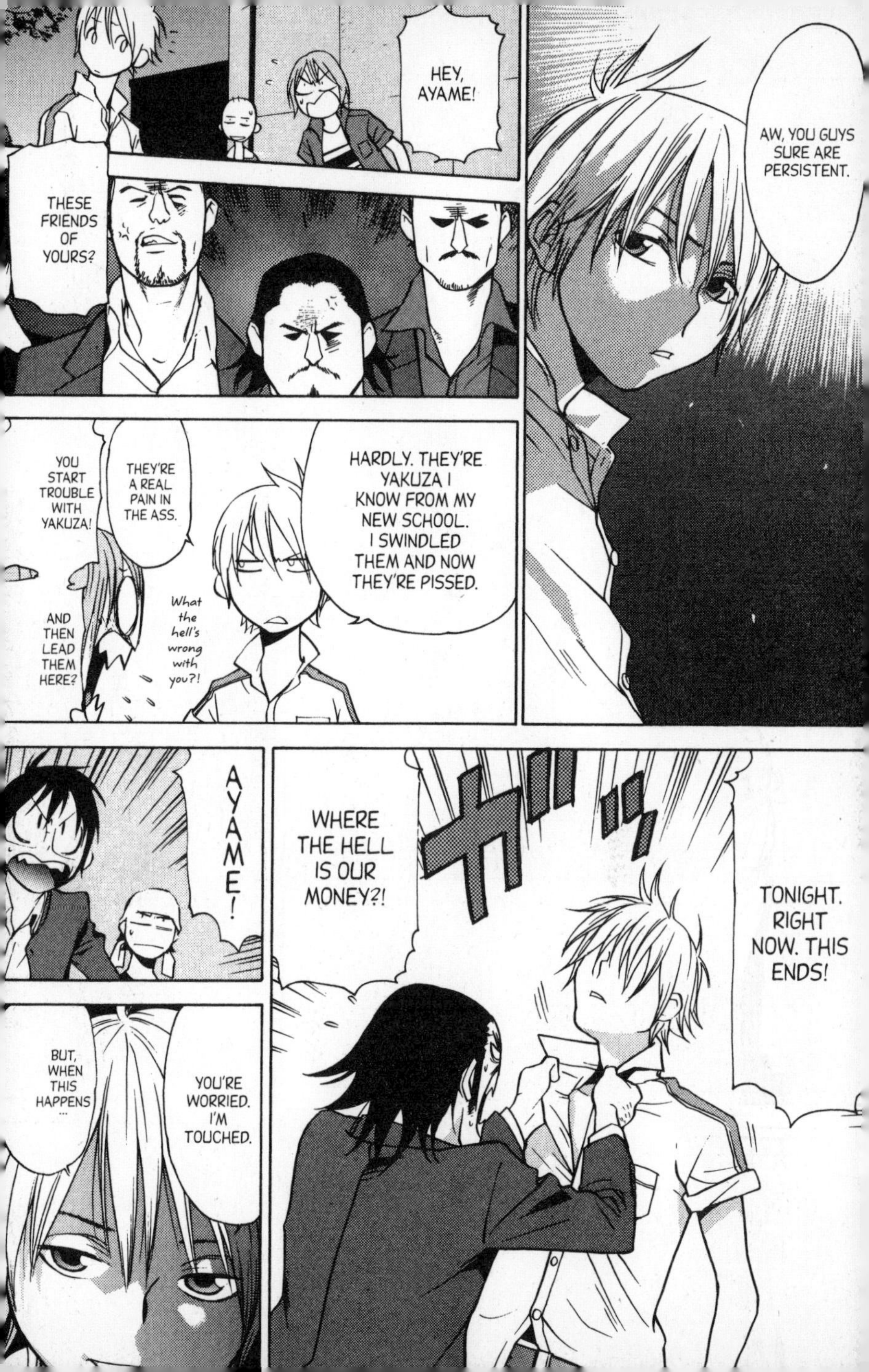
AW, YOU GUYS SURE ARE PERSISTENT.
HEY, AYAME!
THESE FRIENDS OF YOURS?
HARDLY. THEY'RE YAKUZA I KNOW FROM MY NEW SCHOOL. I SWINDLED THEM AND NOW THEY'RE PISSED.
THEY'RE A REAL PAIN IN THE ASS.
YOU START TROUBLE WITH YAKUZA!
What the hell's wrong with you?!
AND THEN LEAD THEM HERE?
TONIGHT. RIGHT NOW. THIS ENDS!
ガッ
WHERE THE HELL IS OUR MONEY?!
AYAME!
YOU'RE WORRIED. I'M TOUCHED.
BUT, WHEN THIS HAPPENS ...

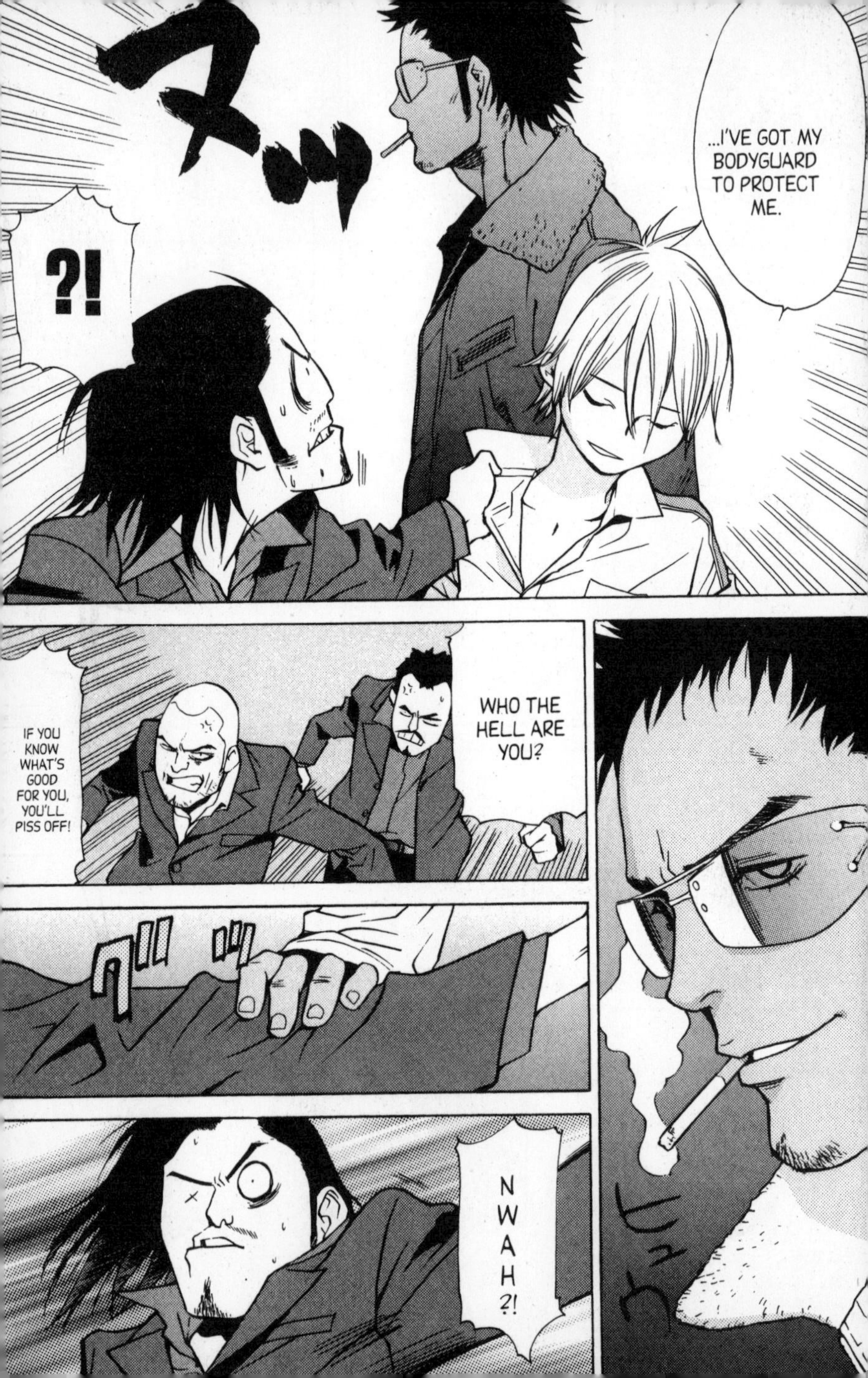
...I'VE GOT MY BODYGUARD TO PROTECT ME.
スッ
?!
WHO THE HELL ARE YOU?
IF YOU KNOW WHAT'S GOOD FOR YOU, YOU'LL PISS OFF!
グッ
NWAH?!

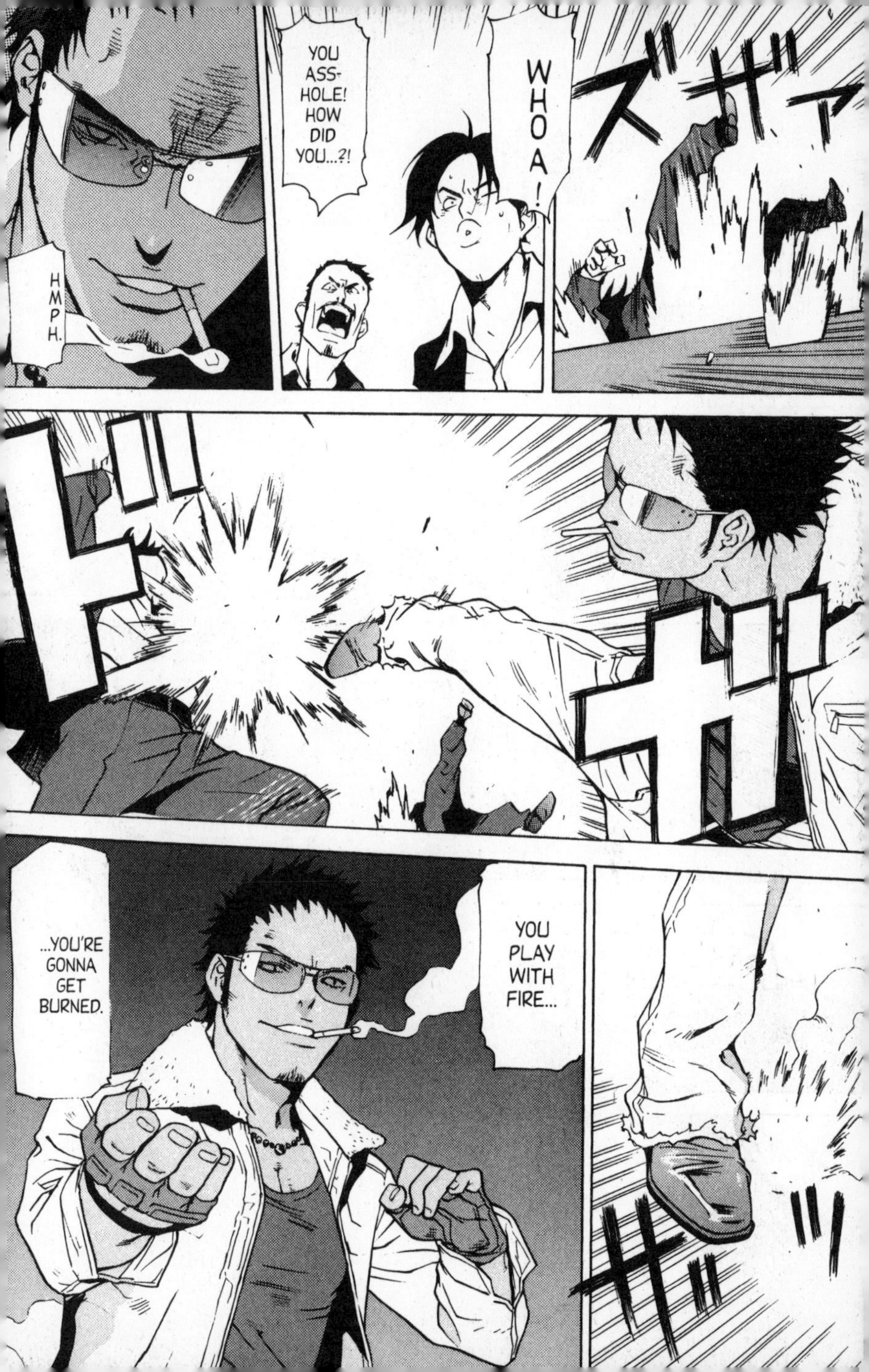
ズザァ
WHOA!
YOU ASS-HOLE! HOW DID YOU...?!
HMPH.
YOU PLAY WITH FIRE...
...YOU'RE GONNA GET BURNED.

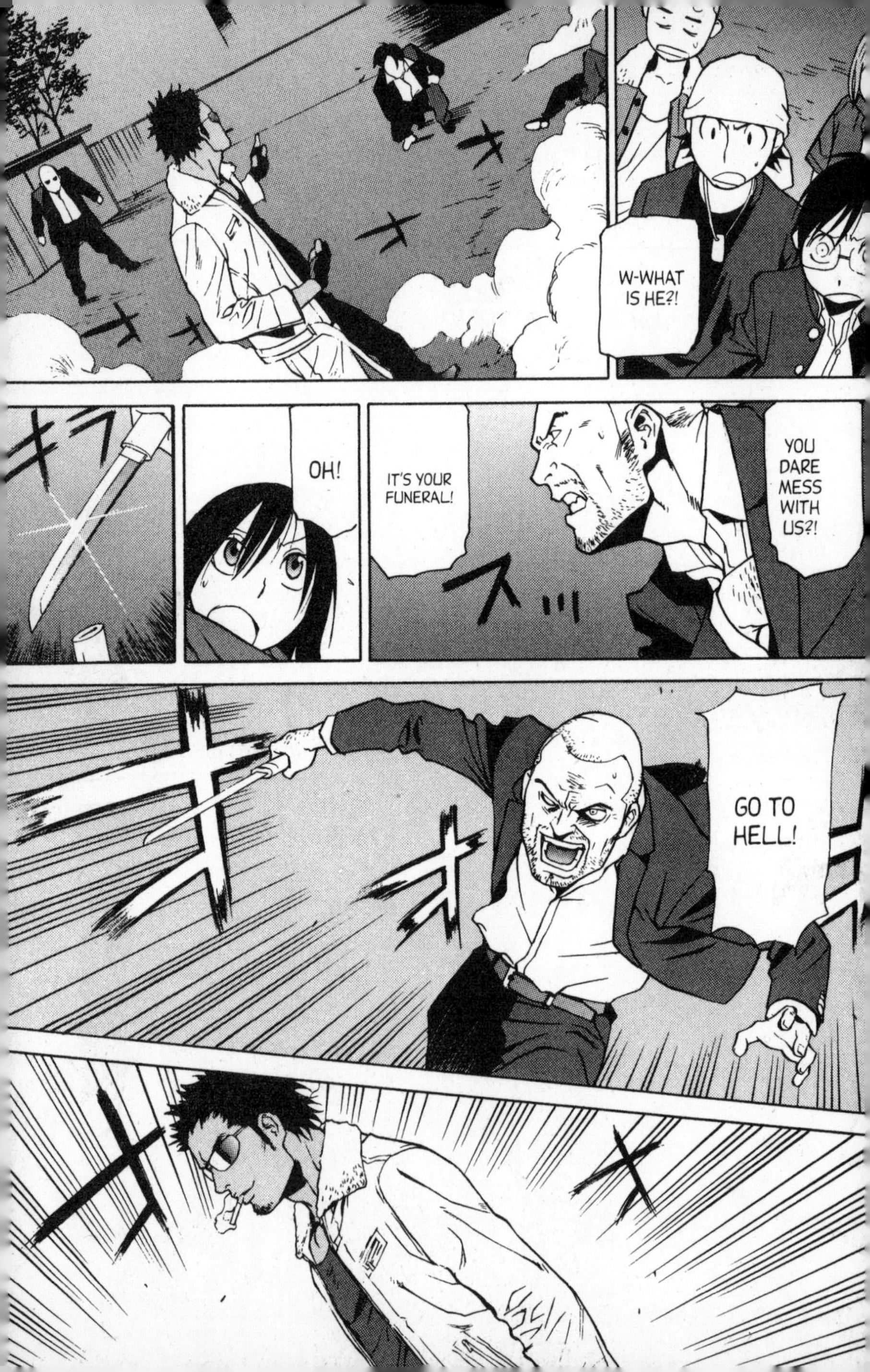
W-WHAT IS HE?!
YOU DARE MESS WITH US?!
IT'S YOUR FUNERAL!
OH!
GO TO HELL!

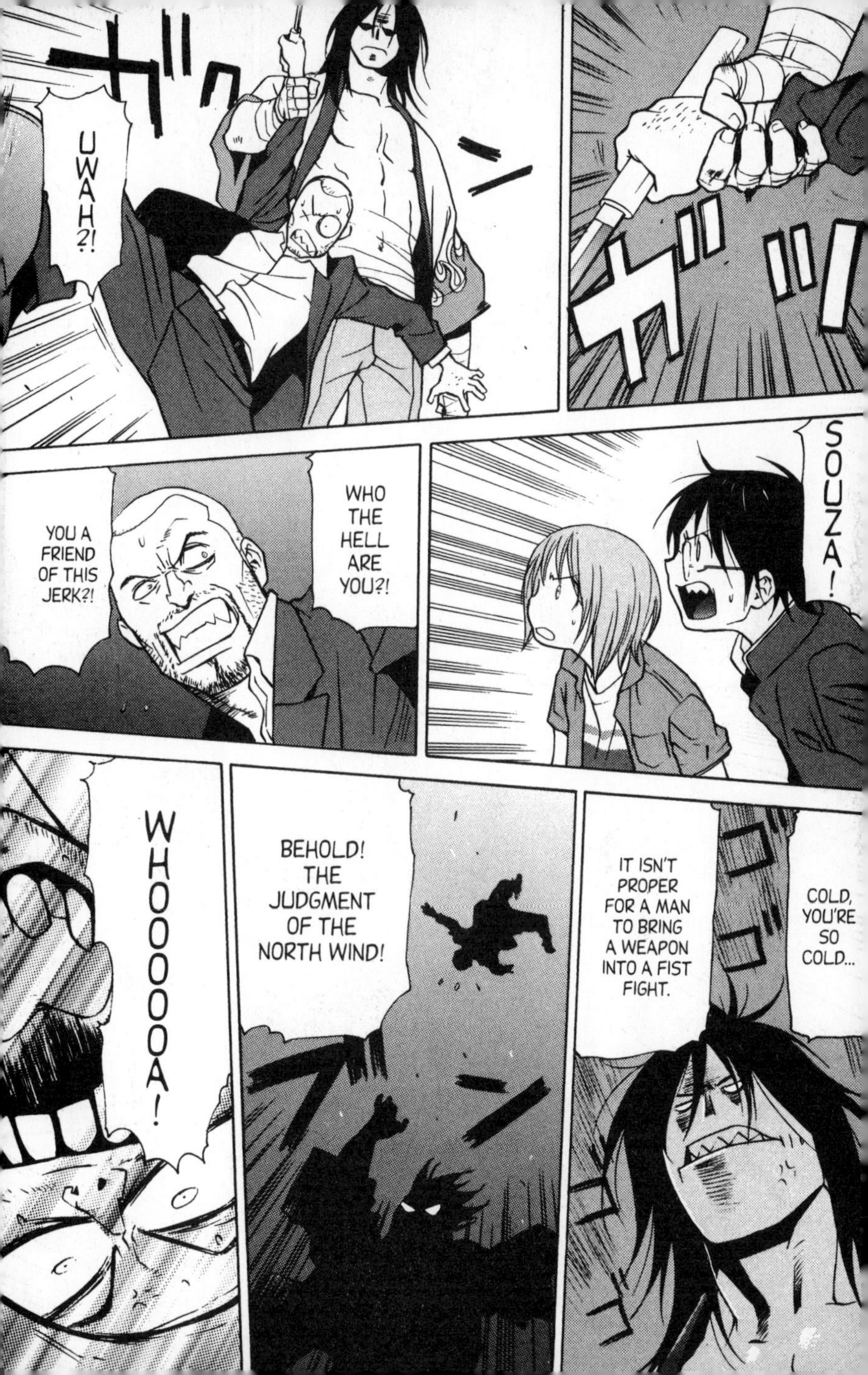
UWAH?!
SOUZA!
WHO THE HELL ARE YOU?!
YOU A FRIEND OF THIS JERK?!
COLD, YOU'RE SO COLD...
IT ISN'T PROPER FOR A MAN TO BRING A WEAPON INTO A FIST FIGHT.
BEHOLD! THE JUDGMENT OF THE NORTH WIND!
WHOOOOOOA!

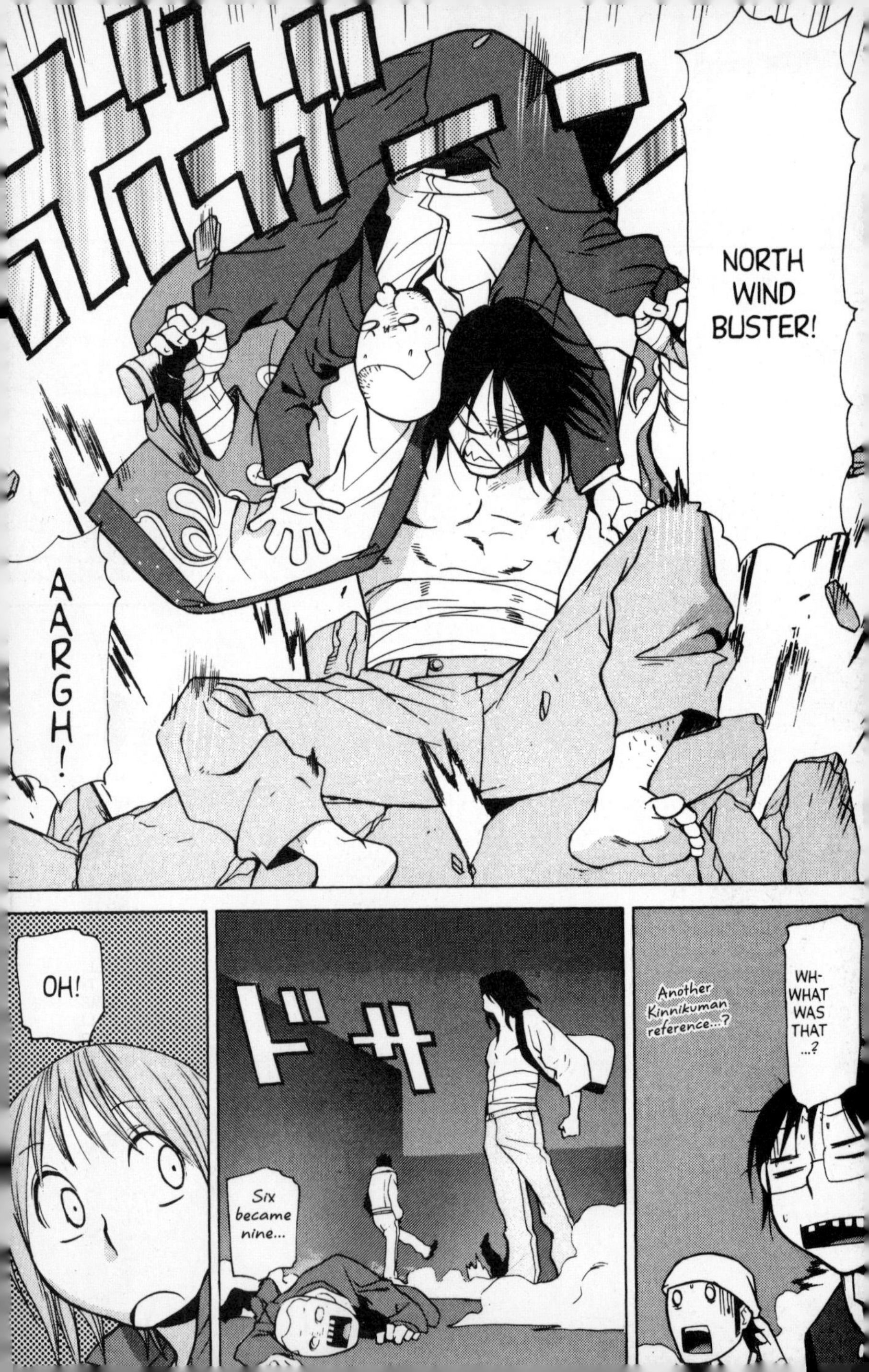
NORTH WIND BUSTER!
AARGH!
WH- WHAT WAS THAT ...?
Another Kinnikuman reference...?
ドサ
Six became nine...
OH!

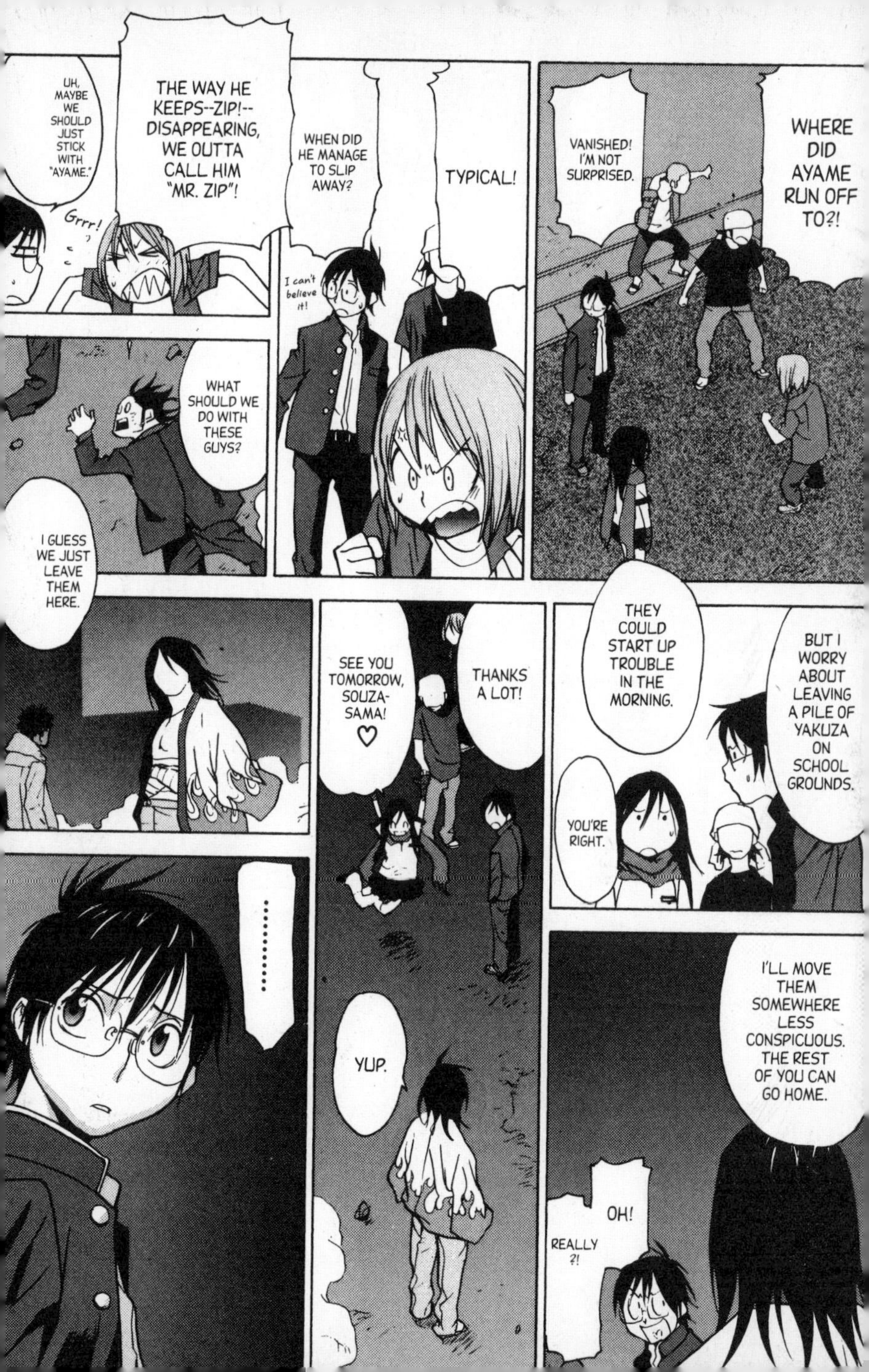
WHERE DID AYAME RUN OFF TO?!
VANISHED! I'M NOT SURPRISED.
TYPICAL!
WHEN DID HE MANAGE TO SLIP AWAY?
I can't believe it!
THE WAY HE KEEPS--ZIP!--DISAPPEARING, WE OUTTA CALL HIM "MR. ZIP"!
UH, MAYBE WE SHOULD JUST STICK WITH "AYAME."
Grrr!
WHAT SHOULD WE DO WITH THESE GUYS?
I GUESS WE JUST LEAVE THEM HERE.
BUT I WORRY ABOUT LEAVING A PILE OF YAKUZA ON SCHOOL GROUNDS.
THEY COULD START UP TROUBLE IN THE MORNING.
YOU'RE RIGHT.
I'LL MOVE THEM SOMEWHERE LESS CONSPICUOUS. THE REST OF YOU CAN GO HOME.
OH!
REALLY?!
THANKS A LOT!
SEE YOU TOMORROW, SOUZA-SAMA! ♡
YUP.
....

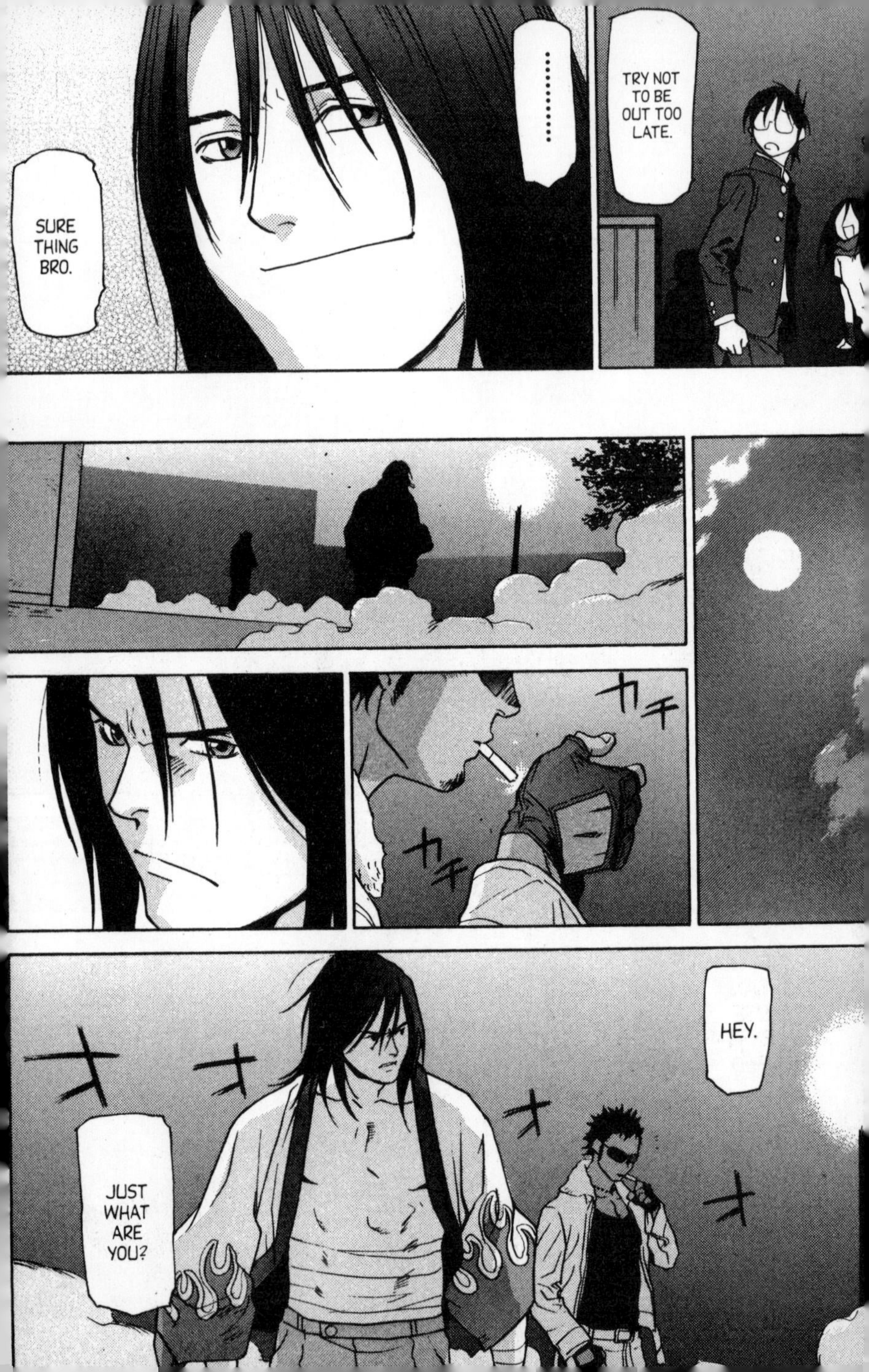
TRY NOT TO BE OUT TOO LATE.
....
SURE THING BRO.
カチ
カチ
HEY.
JUST WHAT ARE YOU?

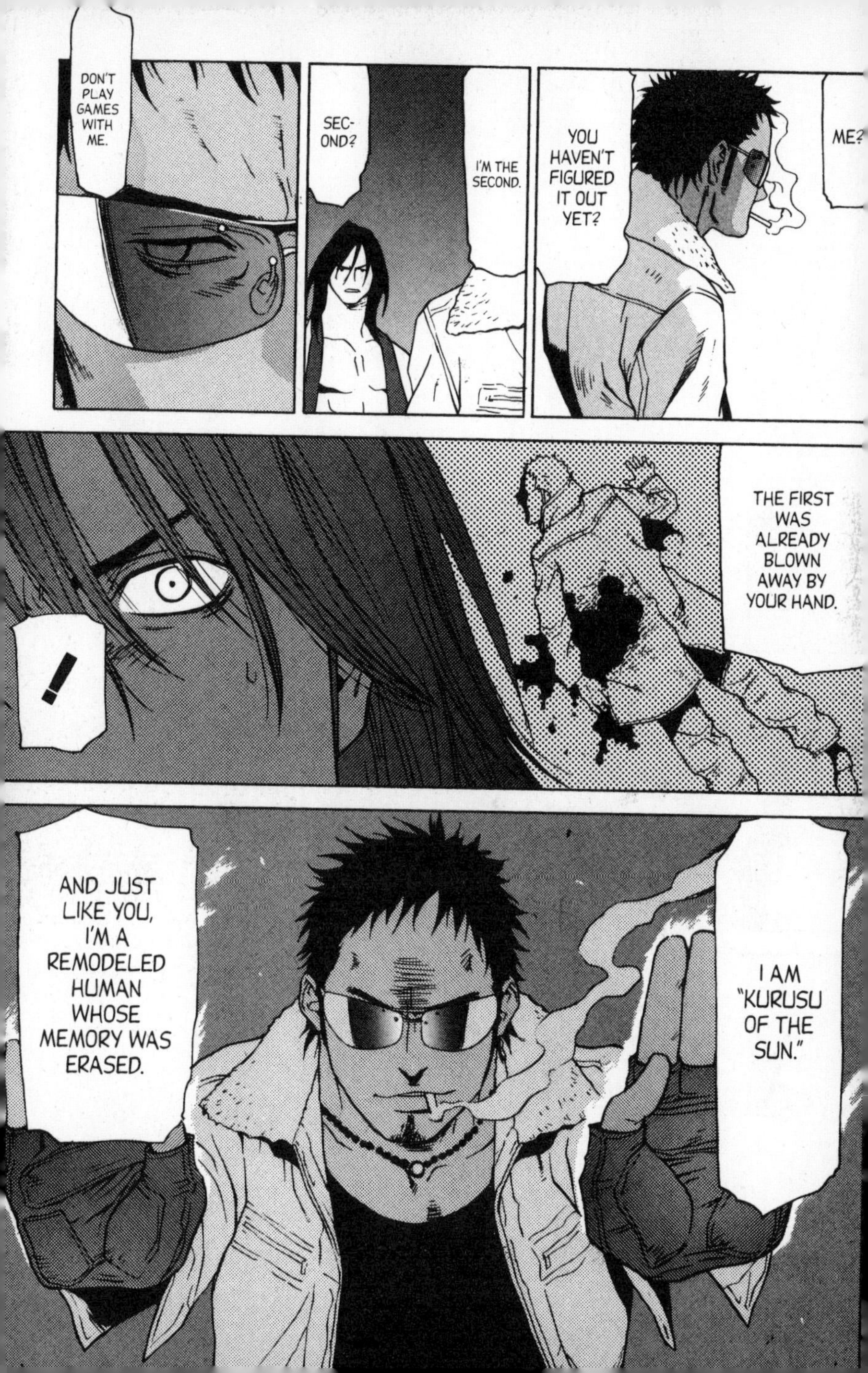
ME?
YOU HAVEN'T FIGURED IT OUT YET?
I'M THE SECOND.
SEC-OND?
DON'T PLAY GAMES WITH ME.
THE FIRST WAS ALREADY BLOWN AWAY BY YOUR HAND.
!
I AM "KURUSU OF THE SUN."
AND JUST LIKE YOU, I'M A REMODELED HUMAN WHOSE MEMORY WAS ERASED.

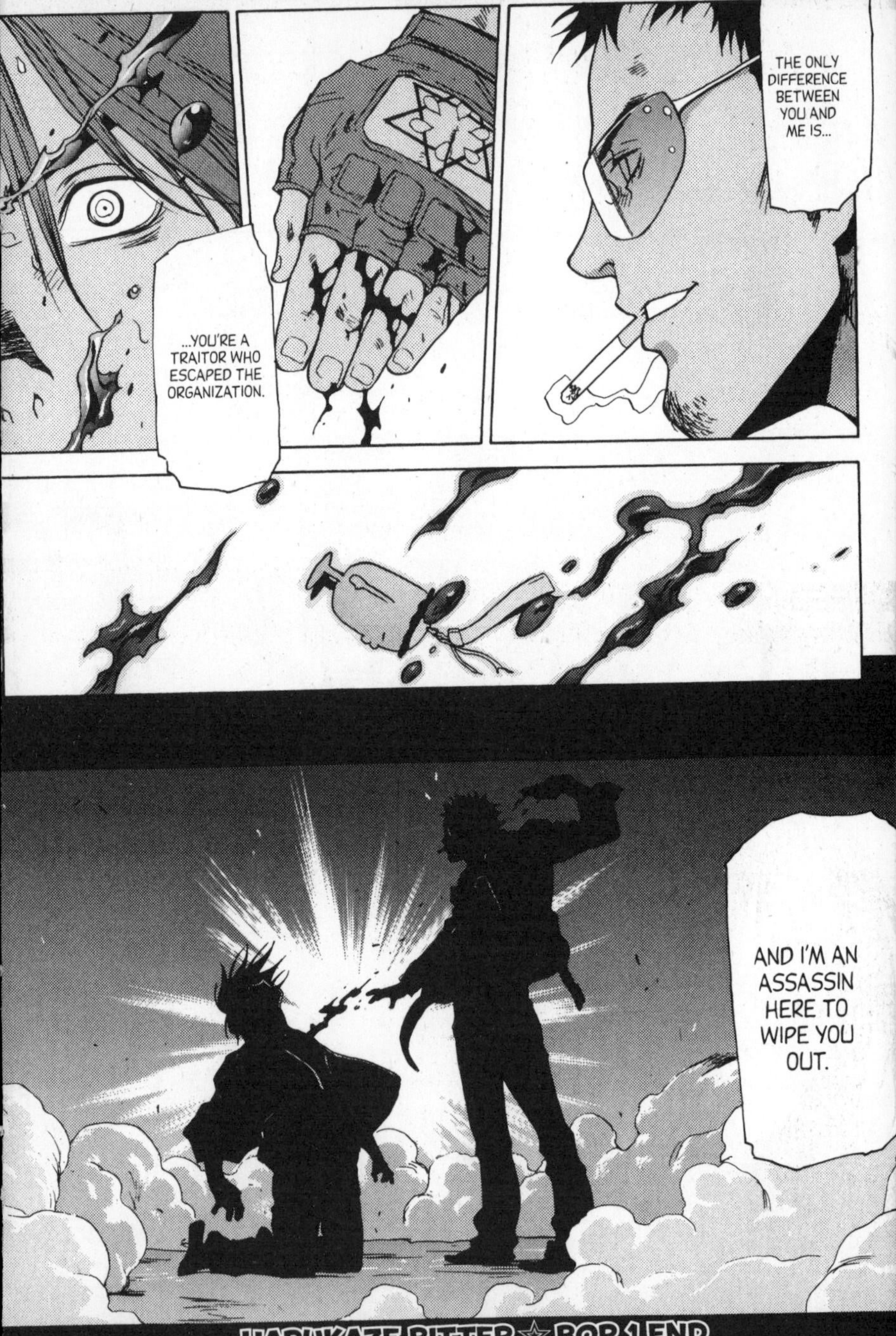
THE ONLY DIFFERENCE BETWEEN YOU AND ME IS...
...YOU'RE A TRAITOR WHO ESCAPED THE ORGANIZATION.
AND I'M AN ASSASSIN HERE TO WIPE YOU OUT.

HARUKAZE BITTER ☆ BOP 1 END

蓮見千代春
ハスミ チヨハル

A HIGH SCHOOL STUDENT, AND THE MAIN CHARACTER OF THIS STORY. HE POSSESSES A FIERY DISPOSITION TO THE POINT THAT HE'S EARNED THE MONIKER "CRAZY CHIYO." HOWEVER, SINCE HE FEELS GUILT OVER WHAT HAPPENED TO HIS BEST FRIENDS (KODAI, TOMASON, AND AMARU) HE'S TONED IT DOWN A BIT IN SCHOOL.
UPON MEETING THE MYSTERIOUS SOUZA AND KAEDE, HE'S RECLAIMED SOME OF HIS OLD FIRE AND IS EVEN HANGING OUT WITH HIS FRIENDS ONCE AGAIN.
HE AND SOUZA LIVE TOGETHER, WHILE SOUZA SEARCHES FOR CLUES TO HIS PAST. THEY GET ALONG ALL RIGHT, BUT CHIYOHARU IS WORRIED BY THE MYSTERIOUS INSIGNIA ON SOUZA'S BACK THAT SEEMS TO HAVE SOME CONNECTION TO HIS OWN PAST. CHIYOHARU MAY HAVE SOMETHING TO DO WITH SOUZA'S MISSING MEMORY. AND IF SO, WHAT IS SOUZA'S TRUE IDENTITY...?

★ CHIYOHARU HASUMI ★

CHARACTER BIOS

CHARACTER INTRODUCTION

★ SOUZA OF NORTH WIND ★

北風の双左
キタカゼノソウザ

A MYSTERIOUS WANDERER WHO HAS NO RECOLLECTION OF HIS PAST EXCEPT HIS NAME. HE DOESN'T SEEM TO FEEL PAIN, EVEN WHEN CRUSHED BY A SPEEDING TRAIN, AND CAN SHOOT A BEAM FROM HIS HANDS THAT SEEMS TO BE A RIP-OFF FROM A CERTAIN MEGA-POPULAR SERIES. IT'S CLEAR HE HAS AN INCREDIBLE AMOUNT OF POWER. HE DOESN'T SEEM LIKE MOST PEOPLE, BUT BECAUSE OF HIS LOST MEMORY, IT'S HARD TO TELL FOR SURE. HE CALLS CHIYOHARU "BROTHER," AND TAKES A LIKING TO HIM.

★ KAEDE TSUBAKI ★

椿カエデ
ツバキ カエデ

A FEMALE HIGH SCHOOL STUDENT, WHOSE ORIGINS ARE A MYSTERY. SHE SAYS SHE IS A SPECIAL DETECTIVE. LITTLE ELSE IS KNOWN. THE WAY SHE SPEAKS WITH KIRIKO IMPLIES SHE HAS SOME CONNECTION TO AN IMPORTANT CASE, BUT FOR SOME REASON SHE'S ALWAYS WITH CHIYOHARU AND HIS FRIENDS. SHE'S BEEN HEAD OVER HEELS FOR SOUZA FROM THE MOMENT SHE FIRST LAID EYES ON HIM, AND IS VERY DEVOTED.

アマル

アマル

CHIYOHARU'S FRIEND, WHO, AFTER THE SCHOOL INCIDENT, HELD A GRUDGE AGAINST CHIYOHARU. HOWEVER, THEY HAVE NOW MADE UP AND ARE FRIENDS AGAIN. IN TRUTH, HE LOOKS UP TO HIM. OF THE THREE FRIENDS, HE SPEAKS THE MOST AND IS VERY CHILDISH AS HE IS THE FIRST TO LOSE HIS TEMPER.

AMARU

TOMASON

トマソン

トマソン

AMONGST THE THREE FRIENDS, TOMASON'S CHARACTER IS THE LEAST KNOWN. HE SEEMS VERY SHY, SPEAKS RARELY, AND IS CLUMSY. WHEN HE DOES SPEAK, HOWEVER, HE'S TO THE POINT, AND DOESN'T MAKE LIGHT OF ANY SITUATION.

KO-DAI

コーダイ

コーダイ

HE ASSUMES THE POSITION OF LEADER AMONGST AMARU AND TOMASON, AND OF THE THREE, IS THE MOST SENSIBLE AND MATURE. HE SEEMS TO BE THE ONLY ONE AMONG THEM THAT WORKS, BECAUSE HE TENDS TO HOOK UP WITH THE OTHERS ON HIS WAY HOME FROM WORK.

古月みちる

フルツキ ミチル

CHIYOHARU'S SOMEWHAT SCATTERBRAINED HOMEROOM TEACHER. SHE IS BEING PURSUED BY YAKUZA FOR OWING MONEY. SHE IS THE SUBJECT OF CHIYOHARU'S FIRST CRUSH, BUT DOES NOT REALIZE IT HERSELF, THOUGH EVERYONE AROUND HER DOES.

MICHIRU HURUTSUKI

桃山霧虎

モモヤマ キリコ

THE LEGENDARY WOMAN FROM THE POLICE HEADQUARTERS, WHO ESTABLISHED THE POSITION OF SPECIAL FEMALE HIGH SCHOOL DETECTIVE, AND KAEDE'S SENPAI. SHE CAN'T RESIST CUTE THINGS, AND IS WILLING TO EXTORT OTHERS WITH HER POWER IN ORDER TO GAIN WHAT SHE WANTS ONCE SHE'S TAKEN AN INTEREST IN IT. IT'S BECAUSE OF THIS THAT KAEDE DOESN'T GET ALONG WITH HER VERY WELL.

KIRIKO MOMOYAMA

AYAME TACHIBANA

橘アヤメ

タチバナ アヤメ

A MYSTERIOUS HIGH SCHOOL BOY WHO HAS AN INTEREST IN CHIYOHARU. HE'S GOOD AT FOOLING OTHERS, AND IS VERY RESOURCEFUL. HE IS ALSO A CALCULATING KID WHO IS ACCOMPANIED BY HIS BODYGUARD, "KURUSU OF THE SUN," A MAN WITH ALMOST THE SAME AMOUNT OF POWER AS SOUZA. HE SEEMS TO KNOW SOMETHING ABOUT SOUZA, AND IS A CHARACTER YOU SHOULD WATCH OUT FOR, FOR HE WILL SURELY MOLD THE CORE OF THE STORY.

HARUKAZE BITTER★BOP

To be continued...

UNTIL NEXT TIME!

Court Betten

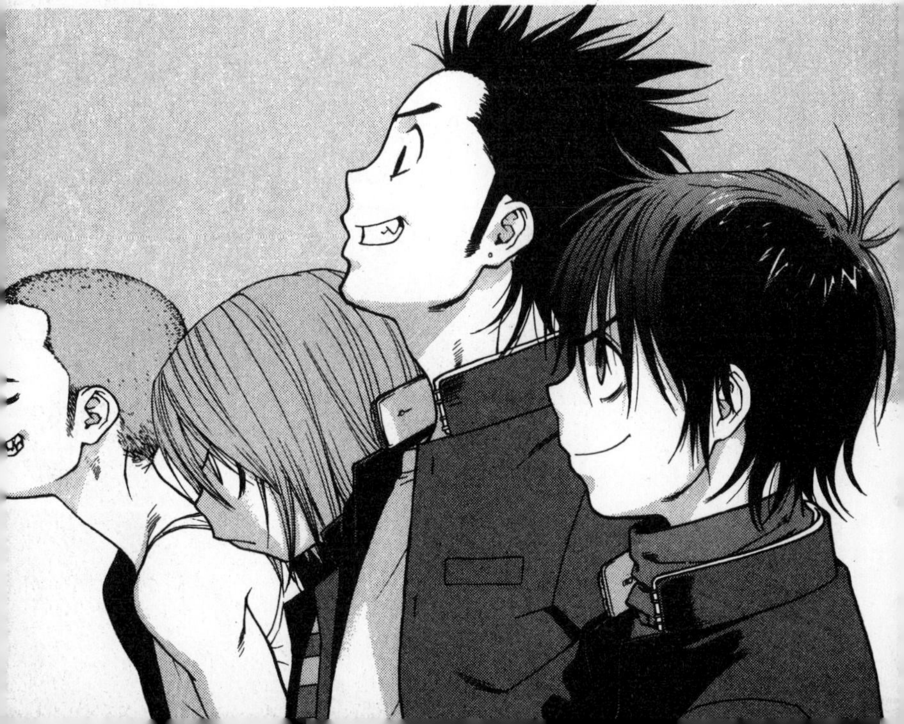

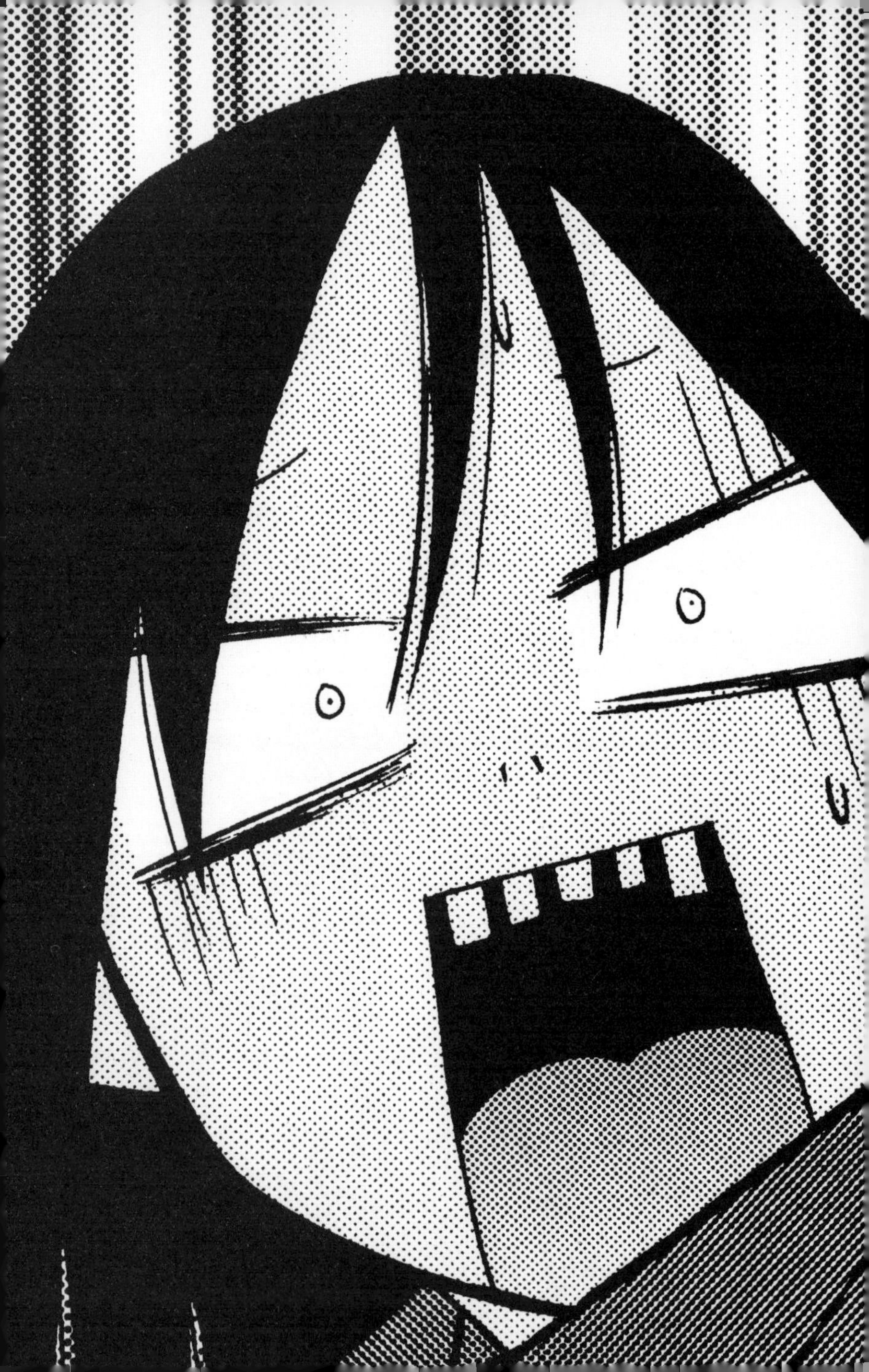

IN THE NEXT

HARUKAZE BITTER★BOP

When Souza suddenly disappears, will Chiyoharu find himself missing the big lug? Kaede, of course, wants to rush out and save the missing Souza, but convincing Chiyoharu to help her may be a tough task. And what is the relationship between the mysterious Ayame and Souza's origins? The action heats up in volume two of Harukaze Bitter Bop when Chiyoharu faces off against a love-struck and insane female detective, a gang of yakuza, a guy wearing a raccoon helmet and what's this, Souza himself?!

AN INSIDE LOOK AT

HARUKAZE BITTER★BOP

KINNIKUMAN

HARUKAZE BITTER BOP IS A SERIES OF MANY FUNNY PARODIES. MOST FANS HAVE PROBABLY EASILY SPOTTED THE *DRAGON BALL* JOKES BUT OTHERS ARE MORE OBSCURE. IN THIS SECTION, I HOPE TO POINT OUT SOME OF THESE HILARIOUS MOMENTS TO THE FANS WOULD WOULDN'T IMMEDIATELY CATCH THEM. AS ONE OF THE FEW HUGE *KINNIKUMAN* FANS IN NORTH AMERICA, I'M VERY HAPPY TO EDIT THIS BOOK AND BE ABLE TO BOTH RECOGNIZE AND EXPLAIN THE REFERENCES/ PARODIES PRESENT IN VOLUME ONE OF *HARUKAZE BITTER BOP. KINNIKUMAN* WAS A HUGELY POPULAR MANGA AND ANIME THAT DOMINATED JAPAN IN THE LATE 80S. IT EVEN SPAWNED AN INDUSTRY OF LITTLE RUBBER FIGURES THAT WERE POPULAR IN THE U.S. UNDER THE NAME M.U.S.C.L.E. THE SEQUEL SERIES WAS RELEASED IN THE U.S. AS BOTH A MANGA AND ANIME UNDER THE TITLE *ULTIMATE MUSCLE.*

NOW TO THE ACTUAL REFERENCES FOUND IN THE BOOK. MOST TAKE PLACE ON PAGE 147, WHERE COURT BETTEN DEDICATES THREE PANELS IN A ROW TO *KINNIKUMAN* WACKINESS! IN THE FIRST PANEL, SOUZA REVEALS KINNIKUMAN'S TRADEMARK "NIKU(MEAT)" MARK ON THE FOREHEAD. IN THE FOLLOWING PANEL, SOUZA IS ACTUALLY LIFTING UP HIS MASK AND RELEASING A MAGICAL LIGHT BEAM FROM HIS FACE THAT TURNS A POLLUTED RIVER INTO A BEAUTIFUL ONE. THIS IS IDENTICAL TO A SCENE IN THE LATER HALF OF THE *KINNIKUMAN* SERIES. IN THE THIRD PANEL, SOUZA HAS NOW TURNED INTO TERRYMAN, A FRIEND/RIVAL TO KINNIKUMAN WHO GOES BY THE NICKNAME OF "THE TEXAS BRONCO." TERRYMAN HAS A STAR ADORNING EACH OF HIS SHOULDERS AND AT ONE MOMENT DURING THE SERIES, REMOVES THEM AND GIVES THEM TO SOMEONE ELSE.(JUST LIKE SOUZA IS DOING HERE.)

ON PAGE 172, SOUZA IS SEEN DOING THE NORTH WIND BUSTER, A PARODY OF THE KINNIKU BUSTER. WHAT'S FUNNY HERE IS THE COMMENT FROM THE VICTIM AT THE BOTTOM OF THE PAGE: "6 BECAME 9..." DURING ONE INTENSE FIGHT IN THE *KINNIKUMAN* SERIES, ONE FOE IS ABLE TO FLIP THE BUSTER IN MIDAIR AND USE IT AGAINST KINNIKUMAN. THE FOE AFTERWARDS EXPLAINS THAT HE MERELY TURNED "6 INTO 9."

-ALEXIS KIRSCH

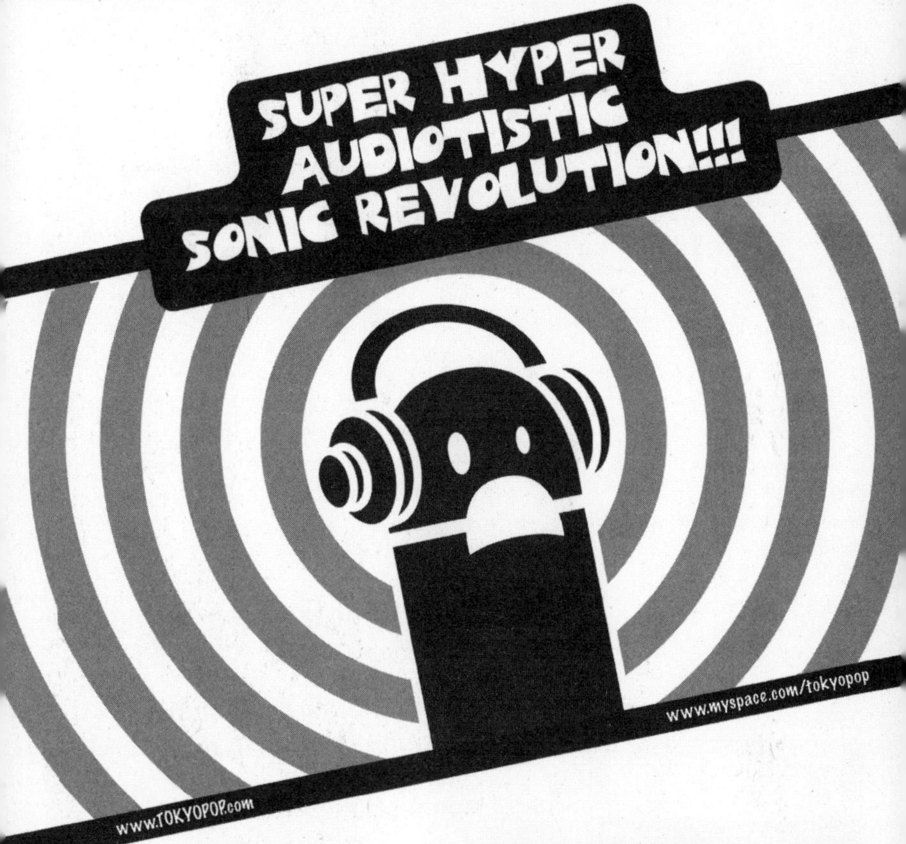
SUPER HYPER
AUDIOTISTIC
SONIC REVOLUTION!!!
www.myspace.com/tokyopop
www.TOKYOPOP.com

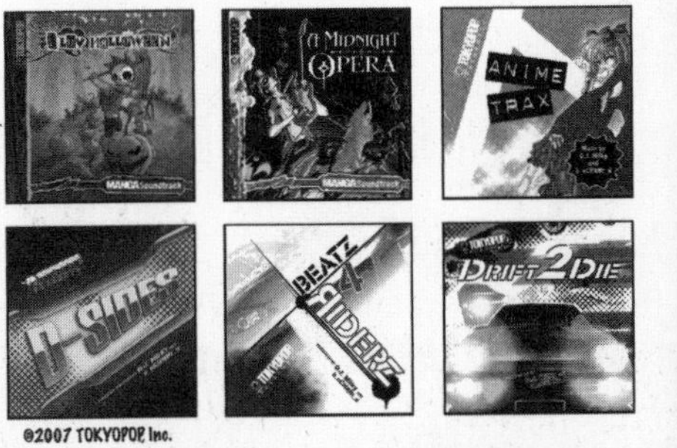

STOP!

This is the back of the book.
You wouldn't want to spoil a great ending!

This book is printed "manga-style," in the authentic Japanese right-to-left format. Since none of the artwork has been flipped or altered, readers get to experience the story just as the creator intended. You've been asking for it, so TOKYOPOP® delivered: authentic, hot-off-the-press, and far more fun!

DIRECTIONS

If this is your first time reading manga-style, here's a quick guide to help you understand how it works.

It's easy... just start in the top right panel and follow the numbers. Have fun, and look for more 100% authentic manga from TOKYOPOP®!